Working-Class Culture

Working-Class Culture

Studies in history and theory

Edited by
J. Clarke, C. Critcher and
R. Johnson

St. Martin's Press   New York

Library of Congress Cataloging in Publication Data

Main entry under title:

Working-class culture.

Includes bibliographical references and index.

1. Labor and laboring classes—Great Britain—
Addresses, essays, lectures. 2. Great Britain—Social
conditions—Addresses, essays, lectures. I. Clarke,
John. II. Critcher, C. III. Johnson, Richard.
HD8390.W67 1980 301.44'42'0941 79–22874
ISBN 0–312–88978–X

Contents

Preface

This book has an unusual form. It has many authors but aims at a somewhat greater unity than is usual in collections of this kind. It is best to begin by explaining how this comes about.

The book was first planned, in collaboration with the Hutchinson Publishing Group, as a collection of essays on working-class culture by members of the Centre for Contemporary Cultural Studies. It was to consist of work already produced or currently in progress, with, perhaps, an initial 'overview' of the field. In planning the volume, however, two facts became obvious. First, the Centre had produced relatively little work that directly followed up one of its 'founding' texts — Richard Hoggart's *Uses of Literacy*; second, 'working-class culture' had itself become very much more difficult to define both because of social changes since 1957 and because of intense theoretical debate around the terms 'culture', 'consciousness' and 'ideology'. There *were* relevant studies, however: some historical in manner, some the product of a qualitative, observational sociology. Moreover, the importance of the project remained, not least because for the period of the modern working class (in Britain from, say, 1850 or 1880) neither historical nor sociological work was very developed. One consequence, then, is that most of the pieces published here have been specially written for the collection. This is wholly the case with the critical or 'theoretical' essays in Parts 1 and 3. Most of the case studies in Part 2 existed in an earlier form, but all have been extensively rewritten. All but one of the authors have worked at this Centre; and the work of Michael Blanch, the exception, was already well known to the editors. It was possible, then, to plan a volume that was more than just a collection of essays, more than a set of individual contributions.

The resulting unity, however, remains much looser than in a single-authored, consecutively written text. For reasons that are explored in the book, it would be difficult to produce an adequate or definitive account of post-war working-class culture, let alone a history of a longer duration. We emphasize, then, the 'studies' of our title. These are a set of related explorations of a common field - some predominantly critical and theoretical, some more substantive. In particular we have not attempted to *start from* a common theoretical framework to be consistently elaborated in each essay. We start, rather, from *problems* and seek to work through them in different ways and on different materials. Thus the more theoretical essays are largely critical and clarifactory, not, until later in the book, prescriptive.

The first part of the book reviews some of the existing literature. It focuses on two main traditions of writing about the working class: a tradition of empirical sociology and a tradition of history. We have sought to understand these traditions in their own historical time, as an expression, importantly, of the dilemmas of certain groups of intellectuals faced with differing political possibilities and expectations. The first essay examines a cluster of works which belong to the same 'moment', the post-war debate about 'affluence' and its immediate aftermath. It ends, deliberately short of some newer sociologies, with the revival of Marxist analyses and the publication, in 1965, of *Towards Socialism*. The second essay looks at a different but related tradition of the historiography of the working class and of popular histories more generally. It deals with the origins of social and labour history from the 1880s onwards and with the new histories, distinctively cultural in emphasis, of the late 1950s and early 1960s. It ends with some attempt to define the dilemmas of history writing in the 1970s, noting the relative weakness of studies of working-class culture for the post-1850 period, and the complexity of the contemporary theoretical debate. Certain ways of working through these difficulties are suggested, to be returned to later in the book.

Part 2 consists of a set of case studies. Though they do not share a common theoretical position, they represent attempts to work through difficulties in the process of research. In selecting or commissioning these pieces, we had two main considerations in mind. First we wanted to span the whole period of the existence of a working class in any identifiable sense, partly to correct the ahistorical character of many of the sociological accounts. This long working-class history is a unique feature of the British experience. We have, however, placed the emphasis on more recent times: two of the studies deal with the period before World War I, two with the period between the wars and two with post-World War II developments. Similarly, we have tried to cover the most important spheres of working-class life. Thus Richard Johnson's essay deals centrally with politics, political ideologies and education, Michael Blanch's and Pam Taylor's with aspects of 'youth', Paul Wild's and Chas Critcher's with recreational forms and their relation to capitalist business, Pam Taylor's and Paul Willis's with waged and with domestic labour. It has not been possible to be comprehensive — we would have liked to have said more, for instance, about forms of the family and the cultural forms of sexuality. though Pam Taylor's and Paul Willis's essays more than touch on these questions. We would also have liked to include a major study of trade unionism as a cultural and political form in some attempt to rethink the central topics of a labour history. In general, however, we have deliberately sought a broad scope and wide coverage rather than the more usual concentration on a particular theme or period.

In Part 3 we return to some of the dilemmas sketched in Part 1. The first essay of this part considers three main ways in which working-class culture may be conceptualized: through the problematics of 'consciousness', 'culture' and 'ideology'. Arguing that each of these paradigms bears the stamp of the moment of their formation, we examine the strengths and weaknesses of each. We point to some elements for a more developed way of thinking about working-class culture, appropriate to present conditions. In the concluding essay of the book, we provide some pointers, based upon a theoretical reading of aspects of current research, towards a history of the post-war working class.

We expect that the book will be used in different ways by different kinds of readers. But we have sought, in general, to break with or to reform a number of separations of this kind' between 'past' and 'present', between 'history' and 'sociology', between the empirical and the theoretical, between the study of the cultural and the not-cultural-at-all. In particular we have sought to make theoretical discussion more aware of its own history and make historical (or 'concrete') studies more aware of theoretical debts and dependencies. Hence our subtitle - 'history' *and* 'theory'.

We wish to thank Claire L'Enfant of Hutchinson for her sustained encouragement of the project and her patience in the face of repeated delays; Linda Zuck, her assistant, for help, among other things, with the cover, and Priscilla O'Reilly for typing a very long manuscript with an accuracy that delighted the (inaccurate) authors. We are grateful to Dave Batchelor, Mike O'Shaugnessey and Roger Shannon for compiling the index with great speed and efficiency. We thank all our contributors for putting up with unending suggestions for revisions. Particular debts are acknowledged in particular studies, but we all owe a larger debt to the Centre, and especially to its teaching and secretarial staff.

Acknowledgement

Although the editorial writing and work for this book has been a co-operative venture, we would like to acknowledge the fact that an unequal burden has fallen on Richard Johnson and to express our thanks for his efficiency and tolerance.

John Clarke
Chas Critcher

Part 1
Traditions and approaches

1 Sociology, cultural studies and the post-war working class

Chas Critcher

Introduction

There is no self-consciously interrelated tradition of sociological writing on working-class culture. In a sense, we have to construct a genre of working-class cultural studies. The following selective list, in which bracketed works are relevant but not 'sociological', indicates the possibility of this, and the types of work with which this essay will deal. It is presented, for reasons that will become obvious, in chronological order.

1956 Dennis *et al., Coal is Our Life*
1957 Bott, *Family and Social Network*
      Young and Wilmott, *Family and Kinship in East London*
      Hoggart, *The Uses of Literacy*
(1958 Williams, *Culture and Society*)
      Titmuss, *Essays on the Welfare State*
1960 Abrams and Rose, *Must Labour Lose?*
      Stacey, *Tradition and Change*
1961 Williams, *The Long Revolution*
      Zweig, *The British Worker in An Affluent Society*
1962 Jackson and Marsden, *Education and the Working Class*
      Titmuss, *Income Distribution and Social Change*
(1963 Thompson, *The Making of the English Working Class*)
1965 Klein, *Samples From English Cultures*
      (New Left Review, *Towards Socialism*)
1966 Frankenberg, *Communities in Britain*
      Runciman, *Relative Deprivation and Social Justice*
1967 Douglas, *The Home and the School*
1968 Goldthorpe and Lockwood, *The Affluent Worker in the Class Structure*
      Jackson, *Working Class Community*
      McKenzie and Silver, *Angels in Marble*
1970 Coates and Silburn, *Poverty: The Forgotten Englishmen*
1971 (Roberts, *The Classic Slum*)
      Parkin, *Class Inequality and Political Order*

Most of these studies have in common a concern with the effects of social change
on the working class. The passivity of the class is a key feature: the sociologies
present people to whom things happen. There is little sense of the working class
an agent of change or even as a conservative force. The approach is through policy or
through the social problems with which policy should deal. One associated tendency
is to fragment a broader social pattern, to present a thin, abstracted element of
working-class life, often dissociated from what determines it. These concerns are
not merely the conclusions of such studies; they also form the initial impetus. An
example may illustrate. Young and Wilmott's study of Bethnal Green is often taken
to be the classic study of a working-class community. In fact, it is nothing of the
sort. It is *par excellence* an example of how to appropriate working-class culture in
terms of a discrete sociological variable: in this case, the family. Jackson and
Marsden are later to adopt this 'variable' approach for education, and Titmuss's
concern throughout the 1950s and 1960s is with the twin variables of income and
welfare. The immediate project of these texts, then, reflects the empirical problem-
oriented and atheoretical stance of British sociology, and its increasing post-war
connection with public policy and it is only within this perspective that the situation
of the working class is examined. Thus Young and Wilmott manage just twelve
pages on the local economy of Bethnal Green: it is for them only important in so
far as it 'affects' the nature of the family. The whole problem of redevelopment is
not interpreted in terms of housing and job markets, much less the complex inter-
relationships between them which shape the changing face of Britain's cities. We
are thus presented with a conclusion which, for all its liberal humaneness, is accepting a doubly limited definition, both of the nature of a working-class neighbourhood
(seen through the family) and of the process of redevelopment (ignoring the structural determinants of redevelopment policies). The planners are blamed for their
destruction of 'community spirit', but we have no sense of the reasons for this
real transformation, save the 'physical size of reconstruction' and the planners'
oversights.[1] *

One feature of this orientation is to divert political and theoretical questions
into policy recommendations, through defining a particular aspect of working-
class life as problematic. Hoggart, untypical in other ways, is concerned to identify
the undermining of traditional working-class values by the influence of the mass
media; Titmuss with the persistence of structural inequality; Jackson with the
tendency for education to act as a channel of improvement for individuals rather
than the class as a whole; Runciman with the quietism of the deprived; Abrams and
Rose with the erosion of Labour support. Thompson and Williams are the
exceptions which prove the rule: it may be significant that they are most outside
the British sociological tradition. Generally we can identify a whole list of 'problems' about the working class; its vulnerability to cultural penetration; the failure
of the welfare state to alter its position of economic and educational disadvantage;
its apparent political and cultural identification with the status quo.

Attention to these problems always operates on two levels: the writers argue

* Notes to each chapter appear in a section beginning on page 254.

with dominant definitions of post-war change and make prescriptions in relation to the programme of the Labour Party. The crisis to which these texts belong is essentially that of a group of social-democratic intellectuals faced with the contention that capitalism works. We need to look more closely at the context of these arguments.

The notion of capitalist success was based on a limited but powerful reading of post-war capitalist societies, especially of America and Britain. The era of 'high mass consumption' was held to have produced the 'affluent society'; the existence and the very idea of a working class was held to have become dated in a society of an overwhelmingly middle-class character. As Goldthorpe and Lockwood have argued, three kinds of propositions underwrote the twin theses of the affluent society and the working class rendered bourgeois. Firstly, the economic propositions emphasized the convergence of incomes and the spread of the ownership of consumer durables throughout the society. Secondly, technological and managerial changes were alleged to have inverted the traditional working-class situation of heavy manual work and low wages: the trend was towards white or blue collar jobs. Thirdly, changes in the structure of urban ecology were leading to the decline of the traditional 'urban village' with its restricted geographical mobility and limited cultural horizons. The authors go on to note that these propositions were not challenged in themselves. Their existence was conceded, but their significance debated:

The argument between the two camps in some part concerns the rate and extent of such changes. But, essentially, it is about the ways in which the changes in question are being experienced and given meaning by the individuals and groups upon whom they impinge and, consequently, about the nature of the latter's responses. The debate is one that *centres* not on questions of income standards of living, conditions of work or patterns of residence but on questions of social value, social relationships and social consciousness.[2]

This may stand as something of an epitaph for working-class cultural studies (and it makes all the more remarkable Goldthorpe and Lockwood's insistence on compounding the error). It is part of the purpose of this book to restore to the centre of the debate the relation between such changes in material life and the forms of working-class consciousness and culture.

The whole affluence-embourgeoisement thesis seems wilfully misconceived when viewed from the 1970s with its manifest conflicts. But the debate had a contemporary rationality: there *were* important changes in the nature of British society in the post-war period, the proper significance of which has never been adequately assessed. Mr Gaitskell's list - 'the changing character of labour, full employment, new housing, the way of life based on the telly, the fridge and the motor-car and the glossy magazines - have all affected our strength'[3] - did point to something real. Changes were often misrepresented, but they were real enough, especially in comparison with the immediate past. The comparison with society before the war not only gave empirical verification for the apostles of progress;

it was also a lived experience of improvement for a whole generation of working people. A situation of full employment, whatever inequalities persisted, was eminently preferable to mass unemployment; the extension of 'welfare', however skeletal, promised some right to security compared with the degradations of pre-war poor relief (even if the means test remained at the heart of the system); the pulling-down of slums and the substitution of houses with decent living space and bathrooms was a measure of improvement even if rents began to spiral and new estates seemed 'unfriendly'; the ownership of a car, a fridge and vacuum cleaner provided partial relief from domestic drudgery and access to new enjoyments, even though each one would need replacing almost before it was paid for.

The sense of change had a real material basis. Later in this book we shall attempt to sketch some of the transformations involved. The elements of improvement were partial and uneven and always affected sections of the class (split by age and sex as well as region) somewhat differently. But social democratic politicians and intellectuals were often paralysed by the apparent transformation of the capitalist demon. As Patrick Gordon-Walker put it 'the Tories identified themselves with the new working classes rather better than we did'.[4] The response was often to abandon socialist terminology and join the chorus pronouncing the end of capitalism, referring, like Crosland, to 'present-day, as opposed to capitalist society'.[5] Underlying this dilemma, however, was the inability to conceptualize class or capitalism except in terms provided by the experience of inter-war life. If capitalism was synonymous with rampant profiteering, mass unemployment, international crises, and a world of war, fear and fascism, had not capitalism disappeared when the state controlled the economy, the economy was expanding, there was a shortage of labour and the main 'threat to world peace' came from a 'communist' power? The political theory of social democracy could not break through these ideas; nor could the students of working-class culture conceive of a working class without the extended family, back-to-backs, or mild beer. Both kinds of thought were profoundly empiricist and oblivious to their own historical specificity: they sought to explain only that which was immediately observable against some stereotypical past.

It is only an apparent paradox that the serious study of working-class culture should emerge just at the moment when it was being loudly proclaimed that the working class had ceased to exist. The discovery of working class culture was a *response* to this argument. The timing and many of the features of the genre can be explained in these terms. The studies typically took the form of finding out who the working classes were, where they lived, and what was happening to them and their way of life - an investigation uninformed by any theoretical discussion. They concentrated first on the nature of traditional working-class life (Dennis *et al.,* Hoggart and Wilmott): then on changes in life-style and attitudes (Abrams, Zweig, Jackson and Marsden); returned hesitantly to problems of inequality (Runciman, Titmuss, Douglas); and commenced, somewhat gingerly, an encounter with theory (most evident in Goldthorpe and, in a different vein altogether, in Williams). There are of course other ways of reading this pattern. It has partly to do with the emergence of a whole generation of scholarship boys and girls whose relationship to the working class and the Labour Party was crucial to their own identity. These books could also be read as a logical outcome of the development of social science. Though it is true that all these works were produced from within higher education, this explanation does not account for the form of social inquiry, very different from that on the continent or in the U S A. Neither would it explain the fact that these works are, sometimes quite self-consciously, related to a tradition of social investigation going back to Edwardian and Victorian times, which predated departments of sociology. Indeed the kinds of connections which can be made with this tradition are revealing in themselves, most obviously that in both cases the examination of the lives of the working class depends for its impetus on defining them as a problem. If the problem is no longer that of the deviant urban dangerous classes, but that of conventionalized suburban quietist citizens, that alters the nature of the problem, but does not diminish the distortion such a perspective may imply.

We have argued at length, then, that the 'genre' of working-class studies does not exist of itself; indeed, these books are frequently written without reference to each other. Nevertheless, we have sought to identify common elements which bind them together. These precisely do not exist at the levels of theory and methodology; as we shall see, the first is almost universally absent, and the second only present in an implicit form. Rather the common focus is the crisis in British social democratic thought in the post-war period, occasioned by changes at the level of appearance in working-class cultural formations. Our next step is to examine critically the genre through some of its main texts. This involves us in an assessment of their relative significance. In selecting texts for closer study, we have chosen works that come nearest to representing working-class culture as a whole.

'The Uses of Literacy'

The Uses of Literacy was published in 1957. In the following year it went into paperback and was reprinted four times in the next seven years. Widely reviewed, it soon appeared on more 'progressive' syllabuses in institutions of higher education. It seemed to have special resonance among left-wing intellectuals in and around the Labour Party. It offered not only affirmation of their own experience as scholarship boys and girls ambivalent about the class they had left, but also a wholly new kind of critique of capitalism. If 'affluence' had made it more difficult to criticize contemporary capitalism as an economic system, Hoggart's work opened up the question of the quality of cultural life. The price of material progress seemed to be a new kind of cultural exploitation. This analysis, and the political programme inherent in it, becomes most explicit in Hoggart's concluding appeal to the working-class movement. Different in kind and tone from Young and Wilmott's exhortations over redevelopment policy, it nevertheless shares the attempt to rewrite the agenda of the social democratic left: 'If the active minority continue to allow themselves too exclusively to think of immediate political and economic objectives, the past will be sold, culturally, behind their backs.'[6] We can get from Hoggart's opening formulation how such a position evolves from his immediate concerns:

It is often said that there are no working-classes in England now, that a 'bloodless revolution' has taken place, which has so reduced social differences that already most of us inhabit an almost flat plain, the plain of the lower middle- to middle-classes. I can see the truth in such a statement, within its proper contexts, and do not wish to under-estimate the extent or the value of many recent social changes. To appreciate afresh the scope of these changes as they affect working-class people in particular, we need only read again a social survey or a few novels from, say, the turn of the century. We are likely to be struck by the extent to which working-class people have improved their lot, acquired more power and more possessions; we are likely to be even more impressed by the degree to which they no longer feel themselves members of 'the lower orders' with a sense of other classes, each above them and each superior in the way the world judges. Some of this remains, but it has been greatly reduced.

In spite of these changes, attitudes alter more slowly than we always realize, as the first half of this book seeks to show. Attitudes alter slowly, but obviously a great number of complex forces are bringing about changes here too: the second half of the book discusses some ways in which a change towards a culturally 'classless' society, is being brought about.[7]

Such a passage can be analysed in different ways. Hoggart's subjective sense of historical evidence - a few novels, a social survey - is, for example, scarcely rigorous. More relevant, perhaps, is the defensiveness of the statement, anxious to concede the reality of change, not wishing to appear reactionary. It becomes an attempt to invert the optimism of the 'affluence' position from within; the validity of the thesis is not questioned, only the assumption that its outcomes cannot but be good. The response to social change is not to assess it against a specific theoretical framework, but to shift the level of analysis from the quantitative to the qualitative, from the structural to the cultural. The result is Hoggart's essential thesis: 'the replacement of an urban culture "of the people" ' by a 'less healthy' new 'mass culture'.[8] 'Mass culture' here is significant. Hoggart is offering a qualified and detailed version of a debate - mainly but not exclusively American in source - which held that the most significant social change had been the triumph of a new way of life - that of 'mass' society - which produces its own 'mass' culture. Homogeneous, commercialized and institutionalized, the new 'mass' culture was held to supersede the previous cultural differentiations of elites, classes and ethnic groups.[9] Hoggart seeks to identify this cultural 'massification' not as an achieved state, but as a contemporary process, which it is the purpose of the book to reveal.

The argument draws on another influence, closer to home. The school of literary criticism advanced by F.R. Leavis, and in more aristocratic mode the social and cultural writings of T.S. Eliot, had both based a resistance to dominant cultural trends, which they saw as those of vulgarization, simplification and commercialization, on a contrast with a (largely mythical) folk culture which the common people had enjoyed at some undefined time in the past.[10] Hoggart was - yet again - to invert a received wisdom, by insisting, here, that the folk culture was in fact urban, working class and contemporary.

Hoggart's work, then can only be understood within the twin contexts of the wide-sweeping pseudo-sociological generalizations of the mass-culture theorists, and the essentially empirical, elitist and moralistic cultural criticism of the English literati. Two false starts are generally sufficient for a disqualification, so it must be some cause for congratulation that Hoggart ever finished the course at all. For some of the obstacles he had to surmount, these traditions were to prove nothing but a dead weight.

Take, for example, the problem of defining the 'working classes'. This is a theoretical problem; it is not resolvable within Hoggart's method. The nearest we get to a specific definition is a list of the kinds of places where working-class people live. A similar circularity runs through the whole book: the working classes are those who share working-class culture.

It is also early in his first chapter that Hoggart seeks to justify his under-representation of what he calls the 'active minority' of socialist and labour organizers. His argument here is that the mainstream working class remain untouched by their activities and that it is with this majority experience that he wishes to engage. However, as Sparks abrasively points out,[12] the cumulative effect of this standpoint is that we are offered a portrait of the working class which omits, not only the Communist and Labour parties, but any encounter with the experience of work and the collective trade-union forms of organization which still depend on large-scale support amongst the work-force for thier very existence. To have eliminated all that, Sparks argues, is to have done more than omit some perhaps discrete arena of untypical activity: it is to suppress the definite if difficult relationship between experience, ideology and organization which stands at the heart of working-class history. It is hard not to agree with such a trenchant criticism.

These are serious deficiencies, yet there is much to appreciate as well. The central and unique achievement of the book is - to reduce it in the formulation - one of method. Here is his famous statement of how to approach working-class language:

we have to try to see beyond the habits to what the habits stand for, to see through the statements to what the statements really mean (which may be the opposite of the statements themselves), to detect the differing pressures of emotion behind idiomatic phrases and ritualistic observances.[13]

The combination of this kind of understanding with Hoggart's own biography delivers us (in the first third of the book) the unique portrait of working-class culture. More is conveyed here than the mere listing of working-class cultural forms - speech and aphorisms; families and neighbourhoods; clubs and pubs. What is revealed is the network of shared cultural meanings which sustains relationships between different facets of the culture, more complex in its structure than could ever be recognized by any sociologist attempting to penetrate the thickets of working-class life, his path but dimly lit, if not obscured, by the concept of 'value system'.

Yet the ambiguities remain. Assessment is difficult: we cannot accept the detailed portrait yet reject the inadequate sense of social theory or history, because both are inextricably intertwined. Hence, when at his strongest, Hoggart is also at his weakest: in his general typification, for example, of 'the essence of working-class life', a 'dense and concrete life' - stressing 'the intimate, the sensory, the detailed, and the personal', like the conversation of groups of girls in a factory - the product of the urge to make life intensely human, to humanize it in spite of everything.[14] Communicated here is a sense of cultural struggle. The mode of recognition is to observe working-class activities, trace their interconnectedness and frame them within the fixed horizons of everyday life. Yet against this patient and humane and consistent openness, we have to balance the closure of more theoretical and political questions. The resistance to abstraction is noted, but not its implications - the impossibility (presumably?) of ever asking working-class people to base political action on a more general understanding of society. Elsewhere the 'us/them' dichotomy is not explored for its intolerance of cultural deviance. Moreover the historical specificity of this working-class culture is ignored, in favour of universal statements about the working class at any time or place. The historically specific cultural characteristics of the inter-war working class is hypostasized into an eternal working-class *Weltanschauung*.

The fragilities of the method are revealed, especially, in the later sections on more recent developments. 'Juke box boys' do not have their own life-style, nor are the determinants of how they live traced with any care. The easy rhetoric of the mass society perspective tends to take over: 'modernistic knick-knacks', 'glaring showiness', 'aesthetic breakdown', 'thin and pallid form of dissipation', a 'sort of spiritual dry-rot'.[15]

Yet for all this the book is not to be dismissed as a historical hangover or as the debris of a less theoretical age. Hoggart revealed the paucity of what passed - then and now - for sociological method. His extension of analysis into the cultural, portraying class as an external and internal mode of definition, hastened the realization that 'embourgeoisement' was no accurate description of change but an attempt to impose an interpretation on much more ambiguous materials. It was not only the homely television personality who was trying to 'unbend the springs of action'; sociologists and social commentators were performing the same sleight of hand - if before smaller audiences. It may well be that, as Sparks argues, the book tended to steer attention towards some of the more conservative aspects of working-class culture, emphasizing the need for cultural conservation rather than radical change. The book certainly stresses the reproductive and recreational spheres at the expense of the male world of work and the world of politics, partly, perhaps, because it is based on a childhood vision. More positively, it corrected the tendency to reduce the denseness of working-class culture to simple categories - places on attitude scales or unified value systems or, scarcely more complex, forms of 'false consciousness'. In its emphasis on culture as the reception and recreation of shared meanings, the book transcends its own implicit theory by demonstrating the nature of cultural struggle as a specific and dynamic process, rather than an eternally sedimented relationship.

'Coal is Our Life'

It is sometimes alleged that the study of working-class culture has been dominated by the genre of 'community studies', which has provided a detailed if microcosmic portrait of working-class life. This tradition evaporates, however, if one tries to get closer to it than a rather vague bibliography. Frankenberg's analysis, *Communities in Britain*, for example, published in 1966, convincingly argues that the common element amongst most of these studies is their involvement with self-contained communities of less than 50,000 people. Though most pay considerable attention to 'class', there is little interest in conceptions of national class cultures, which are precluded from the analysis. If, alternatively, one looks at the work of the Institute of Community Studies, it becomes apparent how different the pieces of research are. Though loosely held together by an empirical focus on the working class, any sense of an overall totality is soon fragmented into the consideration of variables: old age, education, the family. This is not to dismiss such work out of hand; it is merely to suggest that it is better understood as a genre by stressing its (Fabian) commitment to issues of social policy, rather than its concern with working-class culture. If this were not so, then Jackson's rather eclectic and inpressionistic study, *Working Class Community*, would not seem so unique a contribution from this stable. This brief attempt to dismantle the myth about the existence of a 'working-class community studies' genre enables us to concentrate on one of the few examples of work which does attempt to approach the problem of working-class culture through the examination of a community. *Coal is Our Life*, a study of a Yorkshire mining community, was published in 1956. The more immediate focus of the work is on an early version of the embourgeoisement theses as applied to miners:

In his everyday work the miner has seen great improvement in the physical conditions of labour; the reward for his labour has been comparatively great since 1939; mining offers complete security of employment in the West Yorkshire and most other coalfields. Nationalisation, a long standing aim of the miners, has been achieved. The prestige of the miner in the working class is higher than it has ever been, and the miner knows this. Does all this mean that the miner has experienced a basic change in his status and role in society, a change which goes with a transformation of the relation between the miner and his work? In fact no such basic change has occurred. In the first place the actual changes have been absorbed into the miners' traditional ideology rather than transformed it. Secondly, changes within the mining industry, and the quantitative improvement of the miners' position in relation to other workers, have been unaccompanied by any profound modifications in the general economic framework of which mining is part, or of the social structure within which miners exist.[16]

The level at which this problem is to be assessed is very different from any we have previously encountered. It is not the nature of family life or the decline in the quality of leisure activity which is to the fore. Rather, the insistence is on the structural context, and the ideology which explains the group's situation within it. The simultaneous management of the analysis at these two levels enables the authors to achieve what Hoggart could not: the immediate and concrete expressions of the class may be seen as *representations* of the structural situation. The miner may not think of wage labour or class consciousness as abstract categories, but he knows who pays his wages and what they get out of it, and hence sees that they are not on his side: 'he sees and remarks in the main the outward signs of the fundamental relations'.[17] *Coal is Our Life* is firmly distinguished by these two characteristics: that the answers to naively empirical questions are sought at a theoretical level, and that the intimate details of the mining community's life are explained as reactions to, and interactions with, a specific form of wage labour. It should be understood that these considerations are not substituted for empirical data, but provide the framework for its collection and interpretation.

Unfortunately the book is very unselfconscious in its approach to methodology. References scattered throughout the text stress the attempt to emulate the approach of social anthropology, but there is no systematic explanation of how the authors were introduced into the community, whom they met and where, what questions they asked and why, or how they came to select and structure their data. It is obvious from the text that their four main points of focus - work, trade unions, leisure and family life - must have been penetrated to a considerable degree to have yielded such a richness of data: the details of contract, team, day-wages and piece-work; the ambiguous role of local union officials in a nationalized industry; the commitments to gambling, rugby and sex (not necessarily in that order); the complicated pattern of finances within the family. We may trust the data because of its richness, but qualitative sociology of this kind requires a self-consciousness of method if it is to be properly assessed.

Two examples must suffice to illustrate the practical merits of the approach. The first concerns the attitudes of miners towards the spending of money in their leisure time:

Having had his standard of living fixed in the low-wage days of his youth the highly-paid contract-worker therefore regards much of his wages as 'free income' in the sense that nothing has a very firm claim on it. He therefore feels free to spend it on the traditional pleasures of Ashton, in the clubs, in the pubs, and in the bookie's office. And he feels free to refrain from earning it at all - in other words, to absent himself from work . . . . [18]

Drinking, gambling and absenteeism are not seen here as evidence of moral irres-ponsibility, as functions of the social system, or diversions from the revolutionary goal. The analysis traces instead the attitude towards extra money determined by previous use of it, the possibility that at any moment it may disappear, and the choice sometimes made for time off rather than labour for extra money. This is situated firstly in the special case of the mining industry, and secondly within the experience of the working class as a whole. While this may not indeed explain different forms of gambling across various social groups, the particular cultural activities of the Ashton miner are recognized as having an internal logic within the illogicality of external forces.

The second example concerns the other side of this male-dominated world of leisure. Home is the woman's sphere, and nowhere more rigidly than in such mining communities.

Here in the Ashton family is a system of relationships torn by a major contradiction at its heart; husband and wife live separate, and in a sense, secret lives.

It is not merely a question, however, of a peaceful co-existence of roles and spheres:

Not only this but the nature of the alloted spheres places women in a position which although they accept it, is more demanding and smacks of inferiority . . . . the tensions always exist as a social fact by virtue of the social structures of which all husbands and wives are part . . . . The row is the conventional way of expressing the conflict . . . .[19]

This passage is not only remarkable for having been written over ten years before the advent of the modern feminist movement. It is also an implicit demonstration of the impossibility of analysing any one facet of working-class culture - any sociological 'variable' - without a knowledge of the economic and social context. The observation is made that husband/wife relationships in Ashton are characterized by conflict. This is attributed to the miner's attempt to overdevelop a sense of masculinity encouraged by his working situation. The woman is powerless: bereft of psychological support, and economically dependent, she faces disapproval and destitution if she leaves. The rows in Ashton families are not symptoms of social pathology, but evidence of the inflexibility of the basic social institution of the family, exacerbated by the particular structural conditions and ideology of the mining community. The situation is at one and the same time individual, communal and societal, both psychological and economic. Working-class culture is seen as generating values and behaviour within a larger context it only marginally affects.

Such an analysis brings us up against important theoretical questions: the origins of chauvinist ideology and its role in the labour movement; the relationship between family structure and economic system; the problems and possibilities of bringing about change. *Coal is Our Life* was not designed to answer these questions and is limited, in this respect, by its focus on a community. It is significant that Fernando Henriques, in his introduction to the second edition (1969), should be at pains to emphasize the limitations of community studies. Using the example of strikes and family relationships he shows the need for an analysis at 'higher levels of social interaction than that of community'. The relevant institutions and ideologies in the communities themselves actually partake of a broader, national, set of apparatuses or ideological fields.

In practice, however, the community studies genre, even its 'good side', has been, as Henriques pointed out, little developed. Part of the reason here lies in academic specialisms: the growth of urban and regional studies as an academic sub-discipline, hived off in separate institutions, often with a very close relation to bureaucratic pay-masters. The main context for the mobilization of the concept of 'community' has paradoxically been areas where 'community' can least be said to exist but where 'social problems' are seen to be most concentrated: especially inner city areas of high immigration and the evident absence of a coherent class culture. The politically absorbed Community Development Projects and Rex and Moore's famous study of Sparkbrook, *Race, Community and Conflict* (Oxford University Press, 1967), are examples of this very paradoxical form.

More generally, it could be said that the growth of home ownership, of commuting to work and of geographical mobility have made the concept of community everywhere more problematic, even supposing it could be detached from its clearly ideological uses. The communities, it could be said, have actually been destroyed as geographical and cultural entities. While not doubting that there have been real transformations, we remain unconvinced. Such areas exist, even in such an unlikely city as Birmingham; here a settlement of owner-occupiers around a car factory, there a massive post-war housing estate. And even if we abandon the notion of 'community', the kind of study represented by *Coal is Our Life*, broadened and contextualized on the lines of Henriques's auto-critique, is absolutely indispensable for tracing the relation between national (and inter-national) movements of capital and the lived experiences of the effects of these and other processes in the localities.

'Poverty: The Forgotten Englishmen'

The strongest single influence that undercut the affluence thesis was the 'rediscovery of poverty'. A cluster of studies in the mid sixties emanated from welfare researchers aiming to restore the question of poverty to the social democratic agenda. The poor, it was demonstrated, had not vanished; inequality had not diminished. Indeed, if a general rise in living standards was taken into account, the 'affluent' society had relatively more poor members and was characterized by greater differences of income and wealth between particular social groups. Titmuss, in *Income and Social Change* (1962), prepared the ground by revealing the dubiousness of the statistical basis on which some proponents of affluence had built their arguments. With revised data and methods, Abel-Smith and Townsend estimated that as many as one-sixth of the inhabitants of booming Britain were living in poverty. If some had never had it so good, some had never had it at all. The importance of such texts should not be underestimated, and were we concerned more directly with social policy they would occupy a central place in our discussion. Our brief, however, is to concentrate on the relationship between structural inequalities and working-class consciousness. Though the texts mentioned performed an invaluable task in redrawing attention to the former, they were interested only minimally, if at all, in the latter.

For a text which reveals these connections we have chosen Coates and Silburn's study of the St Ann's area of Nottingham, published in 1970 under the title *Poverty: The Forgotten Englishmen*. They begin - as do with remarkable regularity most of the texts cited in this section - by discussing how the 'affluence myth' had reduced 'the age-old malaise of poverty' to 'a slight social hang-over'.[20] They lay the failure to challenge this myth at the door of two particular groups: social investigators in the tradition represented by Seebohm Rowntree and G.R. Lavers, who, in the 1951 study of York, confirmed the belief in the virtual disappearance of the poor; and social workers who, instead of being lobbyists for the poor, retreated into their own mythical world of case-work.

These evasions contributed to official interpretations of the poverty problem as a series of unconnected deficiencies in public provision. The arbitrarily exclusive concerns of particular government departments were allowed to determine the programmes of research and action. Entirely separate strategies were evolved for housing, education and welfare benefits. Hence there were both political and intellectual reasons for embarking on the study of a neighbourhood in which the interconnectedness of the various forms of poverty could be examined, especially an area like St Ann's - 'a typical late Victorian, working-class, city centre neighbourhood in acute decline', where it could be shown 'how all the different types of deprivation mesh one into another'.

The objectives of the study are clear, as is the political and intellectual argument into which it is to be inserted. Perhaps these are some of the advantages of *Poverty* having been written later than most of the other texts, under less direct pressure from the affluence thesis. The book is also clearer at the level of method. Though it does depend, like *Coal is Our Life*, on an intimate knowledge of the area and an empathy with its inhabitants, there is also some more structured data. Two samples of 200 inhabitants were interviewed by members of a local WEA class and undergraduates from Nottingham University, using a lengthy questionnaire (not reproduced in the text) designed to elicit statistical data (family size, income, housing conditions) and more subjective feelings about the neighbourhood and society outside it. Equally important is a descriptive sensitivity which, importantly, allows us to grasp both the uniqueness of the neighbourhood and its similarity to areas in any large industrial city. Physically, St Ann's is threatened with 'comprehensive demolition'. General amenities are 'at the most rudimentary level'. Children endanger themselves playing in derelict sites. The buildings are dingy, the schools old, the second-hand shops full of shabby goods.

Greater familiarity with the district prompts other judgements, more difficult to sustain by physical evidence: to those of us who have come to know it and to feel involved in its life, St. Ann's is an area dominated by a certain hopelessness, in which the sense that things are inexorably running down weighs constantly on every decision, and inhibits many positive responses to make or mend. And yet its people have, somehow, shaped out of this unpromising environment a way of living full of wit and humanity.[21]

Such an approach is vulnerable to criticism, especially from the hard-headed. It may be dismissed as typical of those community studies which Ruth Glass has described as 'the poor sociologist's substitute for a novel'. Yet if one accepts Coates and Silburn's initial premise that 'the moral consequences of poverty in an advanced society are far more dire than its physical results',[22] an open and honest exposure to the perceptions and experiences of others may be more useful than attitude scales.

   A continuing theme of the book is the tracing of the relationship between structural deprivation and neighbourhood culture. The book's middle section treats in
turn income, housing, education and culture. The analysis of the first three reminds
us that for not insubstantial sectors of the working class the new houses, consumer
goods and high incomes supposed to have been bequeathed them by the economic
miracle of post-war British capitalism remained unfulfilled aspirations: 91 per cent
of the St Ann's sample had an outside lavatory, 85 per cent no bathroom and 54.5
per cent no hot water system. Using a similar method to that of Abel-Smith and
Townsend, the researchers found 37 per cent of households or 40 per cent of the
sample population to be in poverty, respectively over twice and nearly three times
the national averages.

   It is a frequent response to see the poor as a category outside the working class,
divorced from the productive process and consequently thought of as the 'lumpen
proletariat', part of the 'reserve army of labour'. Though such concepts may have
some validity, they need to be used with caution. Coates and Silburn relate the
category of the poor to that of the working class as a whole in two ways. Firstly,
they demonstrate that, while 15 per cent of the poor in St Ann's are pensioners
and a similar proportion unemployed, one-half have at least one breadwinner.
Though partly attributable to the sex composition of Nottingham, where unusually
high numbers of working women have tended to depress wages, there still exists
the possibility of generalizing their conclusion: 'it suffices to say that the most
important single cause of poverty is not indolence, nor fecundity, nor sickness, nor
villainy of any kind, but is, quite simply, low wages'.[23]

   The second way in which the experience of the poor can be related to the class
as a whole is touched upon in their review of previous work. The poor are not a
fixed category: poverty is often a transient state, individuals and families moving in
and out as responsibilities increase or circumstances change.[24] The implication of
this - a substantial one for any analysis of working-class culture - is that the experience of poverty has not been eliminated as a common feature of the class. If we add
to this the vulnerability of the old on inadequate pensions and, as the 1970s
have shown, the return to large-scale unemployment, in this case especially of the
young, the persistent insecurities of working-class life, now, can be properly grasped.

   Poverty has also to be recognized as an impediment to the development of
adequate forms of cultural resistance. The daily experience of poverty can be
thoroughly debilitating, tending to atomize and intimidate rather than produce
collective action. The established picture of 'working-class community' is not
relevant to St Ann's. Even networks of informal social relationships were relatively
weakly developed there.[25]

   Chapter 7 on 'A culture of poverty' poses a series of questions about the
ideological significance of neighbourhood culture:

To what extent do St Ann's residents accept the value-system which has grown up as
a function of the received economic structure? How do they regard working as
employees, as wage-slaves, as inevitable? How far do they see the given distribution

of income within society as 'natural'? How far do they see the power structure under which they live as 'normal'?[26]

The questions are certainly directly put; whether they are correctly put is another matter. In attempting to answer them Coates and Silburn draw on quite orthodox Marxist-Leninist categories, especially on Marx's 'commodity fetishism' and on the notion of 'false consciousness'. They have little sense of the reciprocity of ideological and cultural processes, a ground we will explore later in this book. Perhaps because the question is so crudely put, the manner of answering it can be equally mechanical: through individualized questionnaires to elicit, for example, the percentage of respondents advocating equality of incomes or a minimum wage. Perhaps they are also driven to this method by the absence of any institutionalized cultural forms, symbolically expressing and carrying values and ideals. Evidence of key elements of a culture may indeed be difficult to find where deprivation is common but responses fragmented. Economic and political powerlessness extends to cultural resources.

In their final section Coates and Silburn move on to questions of welfare policy and strategy beyond our brief. Two points seem in order to conclude, both related to the relevance of St Ann's for more contemporary analysis. The first is that the fragmentation of neighbourhood culture - its internal tensions and hostility to outsiders, its appropriation of public issues as private troubles - does not represent the absence of culture, the random expressions of individual temperaments. Rather, what we have is evidence of a working-class culture stripped of its formal institutions and informal networks, reliant on its reflexes, directing its hostility against those of its own members who do not conform to values imposed from the outside: blacks, the work-shy, problem families. It is not a negation of the latent radicalism of working-class culture; it is a revelation of those tendencies that hold it back, and even threaten to invert it. Fragmentation is the hidden face of working-class culture, which can don the mask of fascism, as tacit support for the National Front in the 1970s showed.

And since it is a strain in working-class culture, it will survive the demolition or renewal of St Ann's and areas like it. The forms of deprivation may change - a back-to-back exchanged for a high-rise flat or house on a council estate - but the lack of power and money remain. There may cease to be areas exactly like St Ann's, at least in those cities where the juggernaut of redevelopment is rolling, but the kinds of relationships it reveals between the experience of deprivation and cultural response may find new forms and expressions.

'The Affluent Worker'

In the early 1960s John Goldthorpe and David Lockwood, lecturers in the Department of Applied Economics at Cambridge University, initiated a research project into the 'sociology of the affluent worker'. Funded by the forerunner of the Social Science Research Council, the project produced various articles and papers throughout the decade, culminating in a three-volume report. The first two volumes, on industrial and political attitudes, were published in 1968; the extension and conclusion of the argument appeared in the following year under the title of *The Affluent Worker in the Class Structure*.

By any criteria, this research represents a substantial contribution to the debate about working-class culture. The texts - heavily referenced, methodologically meticulous and theoretically sophisticated - cannot be lightly dismissed. The danger that our critique may reduce the complexity and depth of the work is especially severe in this case.

The primary objective was to undertake an empirical test of the embourgeoise-ment thesis. The first chapter of the third volume offers a reconstruction of the emergence of the thesis. The work of especially Abrams and Rose (1960), Zweig (1961) and Klein (1965) is dissected and recomposed to produce a cumulative theory of embourgeoisement, considerably more coherent than that achieved in any individual text. Goldthorpe, Lockwood and their fellow researchers identify in particular three developments which are alleged to be crucial to the embourgeoise-ment of the British working class. These are changes in economic circumstances (increased incomes and access to consumer goods with consequent changes in life-styles); changes in the technology and management of work (the decline of manual labour, the new 'technician' roles involving greater teamwork and integration into the goals of management); changes in the ecology of cities (increased owner-occupation, suburbanization and the redevelopment of the inner city). It is not the objective of the authors to assess the evidence for these changes. Rather, they are concerned to discover whether, in those situations where most of these 'new' factors are most apparent, they have the effects attributed to them.

Goldthorpe and Lockwood were not unaware that the thesis had its critics, especially on the left. They declare themselves unconvinced by the fragmentary and abstract character of the counter-arguments, noting, especially, the irony that many of these arguments - the notion of the 'alienated' consumer for instance - fit ill with a traditional Marxist stress on relations of production. Embourgeoisement theories stress the material character of capitalism; Marxist opponents identify cultural or psychological exploitation as the new ground of conflict.

Goldthorpe and Lockwood also situate their study within the directly political argu-ments which provide the impetus for the debate. They note that the victory of the Tories in 1959 provoked practising politicians, especially within the Labour Party, to assume that the traditional class basis of party politics was being eroded, a conclusion underwritten by more than one psephological study. They are also conscious that the dimensions of this argument change even as their study progresses, since the Labour Party do return to power, but commit themselves to a policy of pragmatic moderniza-tion which quickly embroils them in confrontation with the trade unions.

These, then, were the contexts, more self-consciously recognized than in most other works, for the *Affluent Worker* project. The basic approach was quite straightforward: to find a prototypically affluent working-class population and discover how middle-class it had, or was about to, become. The justification for their eventual choice of three groups of car workers in Luton is outlined in Chapter 2 of volume 3, as is their exclusive use of the interviewing method to collect data.

Six years and several hundred interviews later, the researchers are in a position to formulate their conclusions. They uncovered a portrait of the 'affluent worker' which is unlike either 'traditional' working-class consciousness or what they had inferred from the embourgeoisement theorists to be the attitudes characteristic of the worker-made-middle-class. Thus they find that the car workers do not adopt a 'traditional' men-versus-the-bosses mentality; nor do they see their trade unions as part of a wider labour movement. But they do not identify with the firm for which they work either; nor see themselves as part of a team with the same objectives. They find little intrinsic interest in their jobs at all. They do not see the Labour Party as a working-class organization automatically worthy of their support; nor do they identify with the Conservative Party. The life-style of the affluent worker is most evidently not of a traditional kind, involving neither the networks of kinship nor those of the neighbourhood; yet he does not participate in the mutual entertaining or club membership which might be expected of those aspiring to middle-class habits. Finally, in their conception of society, the affluent workers adhere neither to the dichotomies of class power essential to 'traditional' working-class consciousness, nor to the hierarchies of status and prestige perceived by the middle class.

In each case, then, the 'affluent worker' assumes a set of attitudes related to, but qualitatively different from, each of the two possible models. His attitudes to his employers is that there is a contract between them: he agrees to undertake arduous and boring work in return for which he expects an exceptionally high wage. The contract is subject to continuous negotiation and here, though he may rarely attend a branch meeting, the worker looks to his union to represent him, relying especially on the shop steward to remedy immediate grievances. His attitude to the Labour Party is similarly conditional: he has come to expect it to favour the interests of the working man, and as long as that remains broadly - or relatively - true, he will continue to support it. In his leisure time he has withdrawn from group activity, preferring instead to spend all his time, money and energy within the confines of the nuclear family, to an extent which justifies the use of 'privatized' to describe his outlook. His perception of the wider society depends mainly on a relative assessment of income, so that, while he knows he is better off than some, he is equally conscious that he has less than others. On the basis of these findings the embourgeoisement thesis is rejected.

The findings are not, however, wholly negative. Goldthorpe and Lockwood identify a process 'normative convergence' between what were previously the mutually exclusive value systems of the middle and working classes. The middle class moves towards collective means of self-advancement, particularly in the form of trade-union organization, while the working class accepts the nuclear family as the essential focus of non-work life. In such a situation, they argue, the future pattern of working-class consciousness is especially fluid, since 'social consciousness

is not delimited by the fixed horizons of either deferential or proletarian traditionalism and in which there are indeed few established cultural prescriptions serving
to define the nature of the social order'.

Hence the policies adopted by the Labour Party are themselves a crucial variable
in predicting the future shape of working-class consciousness; how it defines the
'nature of the social order' will powerfully affect the self-perception of the working
class. To stress some 'middle ground' of 'technological progressivism' may well
prove to be counter-productive, since it will serve to undermine that identification
of the Labour Party with the interests of the working man which is a key basis of
its popular support. What needs to be developed, according to the (significantly)
final section of the conclusion to volume 3, is a programme of policies in welfare,
education, leisure provision and environmental planning which seeks to extend and
redefine the interests of working people. The alternative is that an affluent 'classlessness' will become a self-fulfulling prophecy, a future actually chosen and
worked for by labour's political leaders. [27]

The *Affluent Worker* volumes constitute the most formidable example of the
approach of mainstream sociology to the working class and to working-class
consciousness. We have, however, four main criticisms which raise reservations not
just about this project but about sociological approaches more generally. Our
criticisms concern (*a*) the concept of traditional working-class consciousness;
(*b*) the methodology of the study; (*c*) the concept of instrumental orientation; and
(*d*) the definition of class.

Our first cricitism involves one of the two models against which the affluent
workers' attitudes were judged: the model of traditional working-class consciousness. Within volume 3 this 'ideal type', for such we take it to be, is scarcely substan-
tiated. While the authors are rightly critical of embourgeoisement theorists' portrait
of the new affluent worker, their portrait of traditional working-class life is
accepted as unproblematic. This is particularly so with the work of Zweig, whose
later (1960) study is harshly criticized, but whose earlier (1952) study of the
British worker is taken, along with several others, as a valid portrait of traditional
working-class consciousness.

In volume 2 'the traditional worker' is introduced as 'a sociological rather than
an historical concept', referring to workers in particular trades or communities,
not to the whole class at some point in time. So not all the pre-war working class
was 'traditional' and 'traditionalism' persists post-war. It includes both radical and
conservative forms of consciousness. It survives most in single-industry and 'solidary'
communities like those associated with mining, dockwork, fishing and shipbuilding.

The abandonment of 'historical' in favour of 'sociological' categories seems
extraordinary when the whole project is set up as an explanation of empirical
changes. More important still is the abandonment or neglect of historical research
and the absence of a real historical dimension in the study itself; a fuller sense of
the specificity, in time and space, of this section of the working class. Such problems require categories capable of handling problems of change, regardless of
disciplinary repertoires. The uncertainty of the concept itself and in its historical

scope of reference is revealed by the way it is qualified and extended in foot-notes.[28] The point is not a minor one. What is at stake here is the whole concep-tion of working-class culture in relation to which the case of the affluent worker is actually and theoretically situated. If 'traditionalism' is not characteristic of the working class as a whole but only of certain communities - here defined occupa-tionally, there defined ecologically - how valid is the comparison (on which the whole project depends) of the affluent worker with this figure of the traditionalist? Have we really learnt anything bout past, present and future? Or just about co-existing differences? Employing 'sociological' categories in an ahistorical way, Goldthorpe and Lockwood actually disqualify themselves from telling us anything useful on these questions. One suspects that the whole construction of the 'traditional worker' is a clumsy, post-hoc generalization that fails to grasp the variety of past (and present) cultural forms and tends to essentialism - that is, the reduction of a complex and contradictory lived culture to a few simple prin-ciples of action.

Our second criticism concerns the narrowness of the range of methods used in the *Affluent Worker* study. In Chapter 2 of volume 3 there is a vigorous defence of the wholesale reliance on interviews. First, such methods are themselves, with careful interpretation, adequate to the study of social behaviour, social relation-ships and attitudes. Second, the highly privatized life-style of the workers them-selves excluded methods other than self-reporting, in particular observational material. If not studied through interviews, such subjects are difficult to study at all.[29]

This argument may appear convincing, but we must be clear about its implica-tions. Methodological problems require that working-class culture be identified with what can be gauged from considered answers to questions asked in interview. Leaving aside the well-known problems of the external structuring of elicited responses, we have lost here any strong sense of culture as shared symbols and meanings created and reproduced in shared experiences and interactions and sedimented in practices and institutions. If these are really carried, mostly, in the family, then some penetration of the fabric of family life becomes imperative.

But, further, we cannot see why the necessity to observe - to match recorded attitudes to practices - could not be carried into the work-place. Since the *Affluent Worker* study was completed, there have been several ethnographies of the work-place, one of which is represented in this volume (see Chapter 8). Such observations might have tested avowed attitudes, expressed to a researcher in a non-work context, to employers and unions. In all these ways, the study suffers by compari-son with previous texts, including Hoggart's haphazard blend of remembrance and 'criticism'. If, as we shall argue later, a disjunction between attitudes expressed in practical (class) activity and more generalized statements about the public world is a continuing feature of working-class culture, the failure to observe will be especially limiting. In general the study ignores Hoggart's fundamental exhortation to 'see through the statements to what the statements really mean, which may be the opposite of what they say'.

The mode of interpretation used on much of the material produced by the interviewers is yet again our old friend, the ideal type. The concept of 'instrumental orientation' contrasted with those of a 'bureaucratic' or 'solidaristic' kind is intended to explain the affluent worker's attitude to his job. It is our third point of argument. The concept is mobilized initially as an explanation of the fact that affluent workers' evident discontent with the monotony, fragmentation and speed of their work was not accompanied by any desire to look elsewhere. Nor did they show the industrial militancy (ah, happy days) which might be expected from such a severely 'alienated' work-force.

Goldthorpe and Lockwood argue that there is a problem of theory here: the solution is to distinguish between *'satisfaction from* work' on the one hand and *'orientation towards* work' on the other. Assessments of 'satisfaction' must be subordinate to questions of orientation, for it is only when we know what meaning work has, within a whole range of personal expectations, that 'satisfaction' can be assessed.[30] The apparent lack of resolve to change the work experience can then be explained by the inherent meaninglessness of work and the search for extrinsic satisfactions outside the work-place itself.[31] This is the essence of 'instrumental orientation': take the money and run.

One response to this concept is to ask whether such an orientation has not always been a way of surviving kinds of manual work which are not only perceived to be, but actually are, bereft of meaning, especially where conception and execution within the labour process itself are socially separated, the worker being a mere 'hand'.[32] Another, accepting the argument in its own terms, is to question the source of 'instrumental orientation'. We do not think it unfair to suggest that answers to this question, in the study itself, are very unclear.[33] Is a commitment made to privatized family life from which follows the decision to accept highly paid but boring work to benefit the family, or is a decision made to seek a better standard of living which involves both unpleasant work and isolating the family, through migration, from previous social contexts? If that seems to be too naive an insistence on a chain of cause and effect, we might put the matter more completely; which sets of relations have the dominant place in affecting this outcome? It is possible to detect, in the study, a leaning towards the family as the 'overriding commitment' at the cultural (or orientational) level,[34] but no case is made for this preference, empirically or theoretically. The only exception is a tantalizingly brief section on the affluent worker's stress on consumption.[35]

The concept of 'instrumental orientation' may have some descriptive power, but its essentially ahistorical nature and theoretical obtuseness leave us doubtful of its overall usefulness. And, again, we must insist, this is not a mere quibble. 'Instrumental orientation' is used variously to analyse attitudes to work, unions and the Labour Party; it is intended to encompass a major part of working-class consciousness. It is also subsequently used as part of an argument against the Marxist position that the experience of wage labour and alienation at the point of production are the driving force of working-class consciousness.[36]

Indeed, much of the conclusion to volume 3 is taken up by a debate with various Marxist positions on working-class consciousness. We understand this to be an attempt to develop a recognizably radical theory which avoids the 'excesses' or 'inflexibility' of a full-blown Marxist position. The result is a resistance to any (of the many possible) coherent neo-Marxist theories, yet a retention when it comes to major conceptual definitions, of a skeletal Marxism. This constitutes our fourth objection to the book. It is not a question of whether the authors should or should not be Marxists, but of how satisfactory, in terms of its own internal consistency, their theory becomes. If, to abbreviate and point the argument, we take a passage on the definition of class, the dimensions of the debate may become clearer:

But, as we understand it, social stratification is ultimately a matter of sanctioned social relationships; and while major changes in the respects above mentioned will obviously exert an influence on such relationships, this is not necessarily one which transforms class and status structures or the positions of individuals and groups within these structures. A factory worker can double his living standards and still remain a man who sells his labour to an employer in return for wages; he can work at a control panel rather than on an assembly line without changing his subordinate position in the organisation of production: he can live in his own house in a 'middle-class' estate or suburb and still remain little involved in white-collar social worlds. In short, class and status relationships do not change entirely *pari passu* with changes in the economic, technological and ecological infrastructure of social life: they have rather an important degree of autonomy, and can thus accommodate considerable change in this infrastructure without themselves changing in any fundamental way.

Perhaps too much can be read into so short a passage torn from its context. Nevertheless we want to insist that what is represented here is an uneasy and internally destructive fusion of Marxism and conventional sociology. Thus class becomes in the language of formal sociology 'social stratification': it is described as 'socially sanctioned relationships', with little regard for the peculiar inflection by which economic and political factors are subsumed under the term 'social'. Yet at the same time we find an insistence on the worker as a wage labourer without power at the work-place, as somehow basic to any definition of class. We have the recognizably neo-Marxist language of 'relative autonomy' and 'infrastructure' used here to deny any essential relationship between the economic and the 'social'. It may make sense to those who occupy this theoretically schizophrenic terrain to be able to dip into a rag-bag of concepts when confronted by empirical material requiring explanation, but for others, as for us, the results may be confused and confusing. This failure of theoretical nerve appears to us to underly the whole structure of the argument. The total effect is that of an inverse pyramid: a wealth of empirical material resting on a barely perceptible theoretical axis.

In sum, then, we have offered four major criticisms of the *Affluent Worker* study: an ill-considered and ahistorical conception of 'traditional' working-class consciousness; an inflexibility of method; the resort to a concept of 'instrumental orientation', the dimensions and sources of which remain unclear; and a prevarication between the language of straight sociology and that of Marxism, when faced with the problem of defining class. Individually, such criticisms may be countered

or conceded. Our objective here is to suggest that cumulatively these criticisms
reveal the inadequacy of the most sophisticated forms of conventional sociology
when confronted with the problem of working-class culture. This is not to say that
the book does not, given its theoretical and methodological limitations, reveal some
worthwhile information: we do not reject out of hand the thesis that the matrix
of working-class culture, or at least some segments of it, may be formed by the
interacting definitions and experiences of wage labour, family life, and consumerism.
Indeed, it is precisely to the relationship between the generation of these definitions
and the changing infrastructure of capitalism that we believe the study of working-
class culture should be addressed. In our view, the ultimate failure of the *Affluent
Worker* study to pursue these questions confirms the need for a radical break from
the self-enclosed discipline of sociology. That break - into Marxism - is partially
reconstructed in the following section.

'Towards Socialism'

We have argued that the studies of working-class culture so far reviewed were pursued in the shadow cast by an apparently endless series of election victories by the
Conservative Party. The affluence thesis offered a threatening explanation of this
trend, by portraying it as the inevitable decline of working-class solidarity consequent
upon rising prosperity. Few studies accepted this wholesale, though they varied in
the kinds and extent of their reservations about it. Our analysis has aimed to
demonstrate that theoretical, methodological and historical deficiencies limited
their ability to challenge the affluence thesis. They were trapped by the terms of
the debate: its concepts, notions of acceptable evidence, and immutable indices of
significant social change. When occasionally an attempt was made to break through
this intellectual force field, the effect was one of painful disorientation, sufficient
to discourage others from straying from their designated area.

The breakthrough, however, does seem to us to have been made from a Marxist
position, first evident with any clarity in a collection of essays published in 1965
entitled *Towards Socialism.* The intellectual heritage and political experience
whch lay behind such work was qualitatively distinct from that of the sociologies.
Intellectuals of a Marxist persuasion found the political events of the 1950s (Suez,
Hungary, defeats in and of the Labour Party) demanded a new kind of intellectual
response, more in keeping with the mass and youthful protest evident in the
Campaign for Nuclear Disarmament. The organizational loyalties, political strategies
and intellectual analyses tenable within the Labour or Communist parties collapsed
with the credibility of their leaderships. It was back to first principles for the committed Marxists; less a question of how to practise what they preached, than
whether what they preached was correct.

It was in response to this set of problems that in 1957 a group of Oxford students
and lecturers founded a socialist magazine called *Universities and Left Review*. The
immediate aim was to secure a modest forum for the exploration of Marxist ideas,
but the extent of the response provoked the formation of an associated club which

formed branches and held (evidently well-attended) discussion meetings up and down the country. In 1959, after seven editions, the magazine merged with the *New Reasoner*, a similar publication edited by disillusioned ex-Communist Party members, and became the *New Left Review*. It was the editorial board of this by now much more heavily theoretical journal which provided the impetus and many of the articles for the *Towards Socialism* collection.

The debate is present well before this publication, which we take as a convenient and crystallized form of a Marxist approach to working-class culture. In *ULR* numbers 5, 6 and 7, for example, Stuart Hall, Raphael Samuel and Edward Thompson engaged in a fierce debate, the substantive issues of which were summarized thus by the first contributor:

The central problem concerns the different objective factors which shaped and were in turn shaped and humanised by an industrial working class; and the subjective ways in which these factors grew to consciousness within the minds and lives of working people: and the degree to which these shaping factors have changed or are in the process of changing.[38]

These questions persist as the essential ones for the contributors to *Towards Socialism*. As the introduction to the collection stresses, they represent 'a variety of standpoints and idioms' which cannot be subject to 'an artificial unity' but which share 'certain common themes'. We have chosen here to concentrate on three of the eleven essays which we take to deal most directly with the problem of understanding the nature and forms of working-class consciousness. A brief resumé of each piece may enable us to draw general conclusions about the nature of the 'break' with previous formulations of the problem.

John Westergaard's essay - 'The withering away of class: a contemporary myth' - is an attempt to dismantle the affluence thesis. The constituent arguments of the thesis are first assembled: the marked decrease in inequalities; the displacement of manual labour by white collar work; the devolution of economic power to the managers; the erosion of a traditional working-class culture. From these structural changes it was adduced that class as the - or even a - form of social consciousness had been displaced. Rising incomes, educational and occupational mobility and a family-centred consumerist life-style made distinctions between individuals more significant than those between groups. Westergaard sought to discredit each of these (by now familiar) arguments in turn.

The allegedly increasing equality of wealth he perceives to be supported only by a selective use of data: emphasizing change over a longer period than is actually the case; measuring only taxable income and not ownership of wealth; ignoring the dramatic decline in income experienced by both working- and middle-class people as they move into retirement. A few statistics on the minute and static possibility of working-class children getting into university reveals the limits on educational opportunity, while occupational mobility is argued to be limited in scope and kind. The supposed devolution of economic power is countered by emphasizing the common membership, by both managers and owners, of a homogeneous ruling elite, defined by its educational background, political and social assumptions, and ultimate economic interests.

All this amounts to a full-scale counter-attack (rather than sniping from isolated positions). Yet more important as a break from the orthodoxies are the points where Westergaard questions the relation between material changes and cultural configurations. The affluence theorists tended to assume that structural changes had self-evident implications for consciousness. In fact, 'our knowledge of the . . . interplay of socio-psychological attitudes involved is virtually nil'.[39] Hence Westergaard acknowledges the structural shift to white collar work, but questions its political meaning. White collar workers may not be status-ridden conservatives in politics. Changes in the organization of clerical work may place them in a position similar to that of semi-skilled manual workers. It is a possibility that such groups of workers will come to identify with the manual working class.

The argument is careful. It is really about prising open some old assumptions, held both by affluence theorists and inherited from an older Marxism by some of their critics. One orthodoxy here is that radical class consciousness can only be engendered out of the experience of manual labour. Behind this is the further assumption that white collar work is by definition 'middle class'. The implication of Westergaard's argument is that both positions must be questioned - that affluence theories are an over-simplified response (in favourable conditions) to an already over-simplified leftish orthodoxy.

A further implicit assumption of all parties to the debate is held by Westergaard to be fallacious. It is that a radical working-class consciousness can only come from within the values of traditional working-class culture. Hence it disturbs him not at all to concede that the base of this culture - described as 'low absolute levels of living, extreme insecurity and marked local or social isolation'[40] - have been slowly eroded. He attacks 'conservative nostalgia' for the passing away of this life-style and disputes its theoretical underpinnings: the notion that a capacity for national class organizations and perspectives is rooted in 'the simpler and more intimate loyalties of neighbourhood and kin'. Against this he argues that such local loyalties have, in practice, to be transcended; that 'particularistic' ties of neighbourhood, kin and regional culture' are insufficient to maintain or create ' "universalistic" loyalties'.[41]

The terms of this argument are as much those of a radical sociology (the first of many such) as of Marxism. There are points of continuity with older arguments - the retention of the undifferentiated category 'traditional' itself, for example - as well as breaks. But the essay undoubtedly helped to open the way to new thinking about the working class: there may be other routes to socialism than the development of traditional working-class attitudes. Working-class culture is dead: long live socialism!

This negative assessment of the political potential of the traditional working class is shared - to excess - by Perry Anderson, though as the title - 'The origins of the present crisis' - indicates, the essay has a wider purpose. The crisis of the middle 1960s, appropriated as a managerial/technical one in a whole series of Penguin

Specials, cannot, Anderson argues, be properly understood except historically. By taking this stand in 'history', Anderson differentiated himself from the liberal and social democratic sociologies and also from the literary-critical traditions. (He also, as we shall see, remained some distance away from the historians.) One of the most interesting comparisons is with Raymond Williams.

Williams is an elusive figure in the debate: his patient working through of the *Culture and Society* tradition, his overtly political analysis in the *May Day Manifesto,* his attempt to merge the two concerns of culture and politics in *The Long Revolution* and separate contributions to the analysis of mass media: all still seem limited by the overriding concern with the problematic relationship between literature and society. His most recent work very characteristically carries the title *Marxism and Literature.* Of course, Williams is a major literary critic; there is no reason why he should become a sociologist. The question is more whether his ultimate interest in the problem of cultural creativity does not, on occasion, forestall considerations of a structural or historical kind. Here, for instance, is his main major incursion into the debate about working-class culture from the conclusion to *Culture and Society*:

The primary distinction between bourgeois and working class culture is to be sought in the whole way of life, and here, again, we must not confine ourselves to such evidence as housing, dress and modes of leisure. Industrial production tends to create uniformity in such matters, but the vital distinction lies at a different level. The crucial distinguishing element in English life since the Industrial Revolution is not language, not dress, not leisure . . . . The crucial distinction is between alternative ideas of the nature of social relationship.[42]

Working-class culture, then, is not a sum of incidentals but 'the basic collective idea and the institutions, manners, habits of thought and intentions which proceed from this'. It is distinguished from 'bourgeois culture', the 'basic individualist idea' and what follows from that.[43]

Williams's formulations will provide a frequent point of reference throughout this book and we will also assess the impact of his and Hoggart's early work on the historians, and on the study of culture more generally.[44] Anderson, however, has two main criticisms of these formulations and the work that lay behind them. First, he argues that they fall short of a properly historical perspective, constituting 'a purely imminent ideological critique, consciously abstracted from the effective movement of history'.[45] What he means by this movement the rest of the essay is to show. Secondly, and very characteristically for this second phase of the *New Left Review*, the formulations are criticized for the way a sensitive 'reading' of cultural values stands in for the employment of clear categories. Thus Anderson argues, in the crucial criticism, that Williams only partly understands working-class culture.

The truth seems to be that the nature of working-class culture is as he describes it, but that the *will to universalize it, to make it the general model of society,* which he tacitly assumes to be a concomitant, has only rarely existed.[46]

This deficiency of what Anderson calls 'ethical' criticism is coupled with failings of (mainly Marxist) historians to break the boundaries of 'periods'. The result is the 'stupefying absence' (the first of many which Anderson is to identify) of any 'single structural study of our society today'. Such a serious and 'global' history - 'some vision of its full effective past' - is absolutely necessary to grasp present-day movements.[46]

In an attempt to sketch this 'global history', Anderson offers a series of admirably clear, if terrifyingly generalized, propositions about the specific formative moments of the present crisis. Here we are less concerned with the specifics of the argument than with the radical break of perspective which it implies. What is being said here is that the problem of understanding contemporary working-class consciousness in Leeds, Featherstone, or Luton is not one simply for sociological or phenomenological inquiry; it is equally, if not primarily, one of historical interpretation. Yet this history cannot simply be the internal history of the working class. Since class consciousness is created by the relations between classes, the necessary history is one of class relationships, and needs to encompass those between the bourgeoisie and the aristocracy, as well as those in which the working class is directly involved. It is in the history of such struggles between classes that we can identify those ideas, forces, groups and moments which limit or promote the development of particular kinds of class consciousness. It is the insistence on this 'globally' historical perspective which distinguishes Anderson's approach from all those we have previously examined. History is not to be tagged on to contemporary analysis, but must essentially inform it.

The information provided by history, however, is inadequate if that history is itself empiricist. There has to be further reference to a theoretical framework, one moreover which can allow for the cultural complexity Anderson alleges to typify the history of the English. The concern of the new *New Left Review* to examine European Marxist thought bears first fruit in the shape of concepts taken from the work of Antonio Gramsci, the theorist and a leader of Italian communism in the 1920s. The crucial distinction, derived from Gramsci but appropriated in a particular way,[47] is that between a 'hegemonic' and 'corporate' class consciousness.

If a hegemonic class can be defined as one *which imposes its own ends and its own vision on society as a whole,* a corporate class is conversely one *which pursues its own ends within a social totality whose global determination lies outside it.*

Hegemonic classes perform a transformative work over the whole range of society; corporate classes defend and seek to improve a position within a given social order.[48]

The application of a somewhat idealist form of Gramsci's notions yields a kind of typology of classes in England: a dominant 'aristocracy' or patriciate; an unheroic bourgeoisie and a supine working class. The English working class, since the mid nineteenth century, has combined a dense and specific internal cultural identity with 'a permanent failure to set and impose goals for society as a whole'. The intensity of a 'corporate class consciousness' has blocked the emergence of universalistic, socialist ideology of the working class.

The present crisis now becomes identifiable as that of the inertia of both this corporate working class and of a ruling class in which anachronistic values immobilize the technical reform in economic and political policies necessary to sustain the modern form of capitalism. It is this, rather than the spectre of affluence, which presents the left with a distinctive political challenge. And it is to the obstacles to the socialist cause inherent in the traditional political institutions of a corporate working class that Tom Nairn turns his attention in the last of the three essays we wish to consider.

We have previously seen how, almost without exception, studies of working-class culture came to rest with an appeal to Labour Party leaders to recognize the nature of working-class interests and use them as a basis for rethinking socialist policies. Instead of this rather hopeless and naive dependence on the intellectual acumen and worthy motives of Labour politicians, Nairn offers an analysis of why they are likely to ignore such appeals.

In his introduction to 'The Nature of the Labour Party', Nairn stresses the uniqueness of that political organization in the European context: its habitual and massive working-class vote; the indissoluble nature of that power base; its appearance as a working-class form of government. Yet, at the same time, it appears unable or unwilling to instigate fundamental change, organizes itself through a cumbersome and basically undemocratic administrative machinery, and actively seeks to stifle, rather than express, radical thought. It is this set of contradictions Nairn sets out to explore.

The method is clear - 'Any adequate account of the Labour movement must, naturally, be historical.'[49] We cannot here reproduce the argument in its entirety, but only give some indications as to its nature. The Labour Party's origins, in the skilled, pro-Liberal and avowedly unpolitical unionism of the mid nineteenth century sets the tone. The failure of Marxist analysis to obtain any purchase in English culture leaves the more militant unskilled 'New Unionism' of the 1880s without an adequate ideology: a vacuum filled by the prescriptions of middle-class Fabianism. The consequent commitment to an evolutionary and parliamentary path to socialism produces a constitution vague in its statement of socialist strategy, as well as biased in its distribution of power towards the 'responsible' trade union leadership.

These factors which account for the early development of the Labour Party help to explain not only its conciliatory conduct throughout the 1920s and 1930s, but also the rapid exhaustion of the first 'real' Labour government after 1945. That it ran out of ideas and confidence after a few modest reforms was simply a reflection of its historical development. What went wrong after 1945 was in essence what had always been wrong with Labourist socialism in itself.[50] The solution of the dominant Fabian bloc to this lack of a programme was to abandon any commitment to socialism as previously understood and to try to identify the party with a politically neutral kind of technical reformism: the 'white heat of technology'.

There remains the problem of how to change this situation, and the second half of *Towards Socialism* concerns itself with 'problems of socialist strategy'. For our purposes, the importance of Nairn's piece is that it breaks the relationship of working-class cultural studies to the Labour Party in two ways. Firstly, it sees the Labour Party not as a court of appeal where the problem of working-class culture is to be heard; it identifies the party as a distinct and major part of the problem. Secondly, the significant question ceases to be why working-class people do or do not vote Labour, but why the party does not attempt to implement the socialist ideas to which it remains nominally committed. The problem of working-class politics has been radically reconceptualized; no longer one of voting intention or attitudinizing, it is one of historically evolved forms of ideology and organization.

Conclusions

The importance of the *Towards Socialism* collection was that it made three kinds of break with the work we have already described and criticized. First, meeting the sociologists on their own ground, it helped to establish the enduringly class character of post-war British society, while raising substantial questions about the relationship between structural change and consciousness (Westergaard). Second, the whole problem of working-class culture was rethought as a historical one. This involved a stress upon class relationships and the way they changed over time. It also involved a much more explicitly theoretical enterprise than characterized the work of most contemporary historians (Anderson). Third, the Labour Party emerged less as a potential solution and more as part of the problem itself, one means by which the corporate character of the English working-class had been reproduced (Nairn). In each of these respects, the studies represented an advance on the post-war sociologies.

But, it is also important to see *Towards Socialism* as a locus of problems for future analyses and, if taken with its surrounding debates, as an anticipation of important differences within a revived Marxist tradition. The debate between Anderson and Nairn on the one side and Edward Thompson on the other over the 'origins' essay, is especially important here. Many of the most important future issues are crystallized in this debate: a communist or socialist 'populism' (or faith in the creative power of the people) as against a trust in 'Marxism' and Marxist intellectuals; a tension between a somewhat formalist appropriation of 'theory' and an almost invisible ingestion of it in the process of writing detailed histories; a conflict between an older indigenous Marxism (itself undergoing transformations in the 1950s and early 1960s) and the 'newer' continental importations. If *Towards Socialism* represents an attempt to develop forms of Marxist analysis adequate to post-war conditions, it also prefigures, often in rather curious and displaced forms, the debates of the 1970s. But to take this argument further we need first to relocate ourselves in another tradition of writing about the working class - the historical - and then take the story forwards, into the 1970s.

2 Culture and the historians

Richard Johnson

Introduction

It is arguable that much of the writing on the British working class has not been 'sociological' at all. It has taken the form of 'histories', especially histories of popular and working-class movements. The title accorded to much of this writing - 'labour history' - is itself suitably and richly ambiguous, for 'labour' may denote the party, or 'the labour movement' or 'labouring men'. It has, a point to which we shall return, strongly masculine connotations. Yet two unifying features of this tradition can be stressed at the outset. First, 'labour' and associated historiographies have been produced, overwhelmingly, by intellectuals within or to the left of the Labour Party; secondly, they have, despite appearances to the contrary, been continuously shaped by Marxist and communist orthodoxies, whether by attraction or repulsion. This need only surprise if we continue to regard Marxism as an absence on the English intellectual scene.[1] Nowhere is the continuous influence of Marx's work clearer than in British historical traditions. Certainly the association is more long-standing than that recently identified by warriors for a deformed liberalism - the 'Marxist penetration' of sociology.[2]

An essay about the historians and working-class culture has therefore to concern itself with theoretical and political developments. It has especially to deal with the presuppositions which have informed this kind of history. For though abstract discussions about theoretical premises have a limited value, it matters very much, in history as in other social sciences, what starting points are chosen. Some are better - more powerful, more revealing, more fertile of further questioning - than others. This becomes clear as soon as we look at significant *changes* in any intellectual tradition. There are times in the study of any object when a particular set of organizing premises and theories actually becomes a fetter on better understanding. This has happened more than once in the historical study of the working class: it certainly happened to labour history in the 1930s and 1940s. One purpose of this essay is to ask whether we have reached another such turning point, in the later 1970s.

More specifically, we want to map some of the main tendencies in historical writing on the working class, taking the account back to the foundations of the tradition. But we also want to review the main current problems in the field, especially those concerning the relations of history and theory. It is worth being a bit less cryptic about both these aims.

Mapping the field of the relevant histories is not an easy task. Since historians remain somewhat unreflective beings, concerned to 'get on with the work', we lack even the most descriptive starting points for such a study. Existing essays in historiography tend to be of three kinds: strictly practical reviews as a guide to further research; reaffirmations of the character of the discipline, the staple topic of inaugural lectures; iconoclastic attacks on the historians (and sometimes on 'History'), focusing on theoretical problems or 'absences'.[3] Though the last of these genres has a value as a provocation, there is very little explanatory history of history in Britain on which to draw.

Whenever such an account comes to be written, it is likely to identify two periods of great creativity. The first of these occupies the years from the 1860s to the early 1920s. These were the founding decades of economic and social history. It was within this matrix, and from the politics of the time, that the first historical approaches to working-class life and institutions were formed. Some of the achievements of these years were not to be matched until thirty or forty years later. The second moment conforms, quite exactly, to the chronology of the sociologies: it was, indeed, an aspect of the same story - the discovery of working-class culture (or its historical antecedents) in the post-war period. If there had been 'labour history' for several decades, for the historians too the later 1950s and early 1960s saw the salience of 'culture'. This second formative period, most familiar from Edward Thompson's *Making of the English Working Class* (1963) but by no means confined to it, is the immediate context of our own concerns. It provided the most powerful paradigms for the historical study of culture. The first objective is to say something about both these phases, especially the second.

But we want to extend the time-span forward from the 1960s and the argument beyond the formation of English studies of culture. Books like Thompson's *Making*, Richard Hoggart's *Uses of Literacy* (1957) and Raymond Williams's *Culture and Society* (1958) were, and remain, of immense importance. Yet Thompson's and Williams's positions have changed considerably and the traditions to which they belong have been assailed. Criticism has coincided with an internationalization of debate and especially with the growth in Britain of kinds of Marxism strongly influenced by the work of Louis Althusser, the French communist philosopher, and by other 'structuralist' theories.[4] There has also been a revival of interest in the theoretical and historical writings of Antonio Gramsci. The debates that have followed have questioned many of the guiding assumptions of the 1960s. In this essay we do no more than sketch the problems, leaving an attempt at solutions till later in the book.

Economic and social history: the first phase

Histories of the working class only get written when the larger part of the population is held to matter enough to be an object of inquiry. In one sense, of course, anxiety about the working class is very old: more or less systematic social investigation dates from the early nineteenth century, if not earlier. The sociologists of the late

1950s were preceded by the Statistical Societies of the 1830s, the National Association for the Promotion of Social Science, the late-nineteenth-century poverty studies and the social-problem literature of the 1930s. In a not dissimilar way, the modern boom in oral history and popular autobiography has precursors in Henry Mayhew's intelligent listening and the formidable and still underestimated achievement of Mass Observation in the 1930s and 1940s. It was undoubtedly the 1880s, however, that saw the beginnings of the popular histories.

This democratization was part of a broader movement that affected adjacent areas too, especially empirical social investigation and political economy. The general context was the late-Victorian and Edwardian dissolution of the mid-Victorian system, and the crises of hegemony of the 1880s, 1890s and years before the war. These were by no means a simple product of economic developments, the Great Depression or the pre-war inflation. They were quite as much to do with political and ideological relations, both between classes and within them and between classes on the one side and intellectual groups and parties on the other. One problem was who (or what party with what ideological repertoire) was to represent dominant or propertied interests. Another was how a growing working-class insurgency, threatening to break the bonds of a Liberal or a Tory political attachment, was to be managed. Yet another was to do with the appropriate forms of the state, given the long concessionary slide into something like male adult suffrage and the demand for the enfranchisement of women. The history of this period (which was in many ways similar to our own) may be understood as a progressive dissolution of some older solutions to these and other problems, and as the search for some new settlement. The search was only very partially successful, right up until the 1930s, if not the 1950s. One general symptom of this was the revival of political violence, including the use or threat of violence by the state well beyond the usual run of social-controlling measures. This was a marked feature of the late 1880s, 1911-14, 1919 and 1926, to mention only the best-known and inward-turning mobilizations. Resort to force signalled the breakdown, or the fragility, of consent. The period was dominated by an extended crisis of authority. It could have been said of Britain in this period, as of Italy under fascism, that 'the crisis consists precisely in the fact that the old is dying and the new cannot be born'. 'In this interregnum,' as Gramsci remarked, 'a great variety of morbid symptoms appear.'[6]

In this context debates among intellectuals assumed a great importance - they were actually a part of the public search for solutions. They were debates about the whole course of the society, about its past, present and future. They crystallized around certain key issues, especially the past and future functions of the state. Some intellectuals, seeking security in a return to mid-Victorian certitudes, advocated a return to a (mythical) state of *'laissez-faire'*, organized and 'discriminating' charity and the truths of political economy, with or without a dash of Social Darwinism. If 'individualists' like Thomas Mackay or Herbert Spencer were peripheral to policy, the Fabian socialists and radical social-reforming Liberals occupied a more central position, looking to a more interventionist state policy, either as some portentous break into 'collectivism' or as an extension of 'freedoms' into a social sphere. In the meantime, there was a revival of popular conservatism and a move towards the representation of property as a whole, rather than just its landed fraction, within the Tory party itself.[7]

Apart from the long-term fall in the rate of profit, the main 'intruding event', to use Helen Lynd's phrase, was the transformation and growth of working-class industrial and political organization. At first this took the form of a tougher negotiation within the parameters of the mid-Victorian settlement, but from the late 1880s onwards these (essentially Liberal) limits began to burst with the growth of socialism, the New Unionism and the industrial militancy of the pre-war period. The Labour Party was the main political beneficiary of this widespread mobilization; and its growth marked a real transformation of the whole political pattern. It became meaningful to talk of the 'labour movement' and, indeed, to start to write its history.

The new histories were very much a creation of these times, one of the ways, in fact, in which the general debate was carried. More exactly, they were the creation of certain groups of political intellectuals of a Fabian or Radical-Liberal persuasion, and of a slightly younger generation who distanced themselves from Fabianism but remained close to the Labour Party or to trade unionism. Sidney and Beatrice Webb and John and Barbara Hammond were outstanding in the first group; R.H. Tawney and G.D.H. Cole in the second. More complexly, there were perhaps four main tendencies in the historiography of the time.

First, there was the tendency to render economics a historical discipline.[8] This fairly unsuccessful enterprise had more permanent effects on history than on economics. Most of the early economic historians - Thorold Rogers, Arnold Toynbee, William Cunningham and W.J. Ashley - were critical of what Toynbee called 'the old political economy', especially of its abstract and deductive methods and its failure to grasp the broader contexts of economic life. By 1929, Sir John Clapham could declare this period of warfare over and, indeed, by this time, much of the iconoclasm of the discipline had disappeared.[9] Unlike the more 'social' historiographies that accompanied its birth, it was becoming entrenched in the universities as an academic historical sub-discipline. Yet, as has often been noted, the early economic historians had a much broader conception of their subject than later, more specialist practitioners. Their work centred on questions of economic policy and the organization and structures of economic production. Even when arguing against Marx, they often used Marxian categories and sometimes acknowledged the debt.[10] From the 1930s, and still more the 1940s and 1950s, this breadth of interest was lost, partly because of an absorption with questions of 'growth' and partly because of an explicitly Cold War opposition to Marxism. The gulf between 'social' and 'economic' historiographies, artifical though these divisions are, became very wide indeed. One has only to compare the *Economic History Review* (edited by Tawney and Lipson) in its founding moment of 1927 with the modern publication of the same name, to gauge the difference.

The second tendency might be described as histories of social policy, or of 'social institutions'. This was the archetypal Fabian genre of history writing, corresponding to the favoured form of politics. The Webbs were undoubtedly its first and most important proponents, and at the London School of Economics and in their private researches, they trained several successors.[11] In their case, the historical studies were an almost accidental by-product of immediate political campaigns; the close association between 'history' and the Fabian political enterprise was extemely close. *The History of Trade Unionism* (1894), for instance, was intended as 'an historical introduction' to the main work, *Industrial Democracy* (1920): a study of contemporary trade union structure and function designed as 'a criticism of trade unions (for the good of the unionists)' and 'an apology for, or defence of trade unions (for the enlightenment of the middle-class and the economists)'.[12] The multi-volumed history of *English Local Government* was originally intended to deal with the present state and immediate history of these institutions with a mere introductory chapter on 'antiquities', but determinations from the past were found to be so powerful that much of 'six years of strenuous investigation' was spent on the period 1688 to 1832, the heyday of the gentry justices of the peace and of local autonomies.[13] Only in the case of the Poor Law, under the stimulus of the Royal Commission of 1905-9, was the original project completed.[14]

This combination of historical research and political activism was altogether typical of the tradition we are describing. One symptom of this is the fact that 'histories' constitute only a small proportion of the work of leading figures. They were not just historians; they were also journalists, social investigators, writers of texts for adult education, authors of political programmes, political philosophers - in short, political intellectuals. Considering his reputation, for example, Tawney's strictly historical output was tiny, and though Cole and the Hammonds wrote a great deal of history, they wrote continuously on contemporary themes too. Indeed, they came near to breaking down these categories altogether, in so far as much of what they wrote had a historical form and a political purpose.

The third main tendency was a further concomitant of political involvement. Their main political contexts were the Labour Party, the trade unions, the various socialist fractions and educational organizations of different kinds including the Workers' Educational Association. One obvious historical object was, then, the history and the precursors of these institutions. In its more Fabian form, 'labour history' was often an extension into the realm of 'voluntary associations', of the interest in 'social institutions'. This is certainly the case of the Webbs' studies of trade unionism. There were quite clear about it themselves:

That history of the general movement . . . will be found to be part of the political history of England. In spite of all the pleas of modern historians for less history of the actions of government, and more descriptions of the manners and customs of the governed, it remains true that history, however it may relieve and enliven itself with descriptions of the manner and morals of the people, must, if it is to be history at all, follow the course of continuous organisations.[15]

This passage sums up most of the features of Webbian history: the stress on institutions, the adoption of the narrative form, the concern with political determinations, the huge absence of any serious consideration of culture, especially
popular culture (the study of 'morals' and 'manners' being a matter for occasional
refreshment) and the neglect of the informal, lived dimensions of working-class
life. Many of these features were to characterize inter-war 'labour history' too.
What mainly distinguished the Webbs' work from what was to follow was its
sustained *analytical* character and a particularly formidable combination of meticulous reasearch and precise argumentation. A good example of this is their
discussion of the origins of trade unions on which there was considerable controversy among the early economic historians. The Webbs' solution remains extremely
convincing: that trade unions owed little to any pre-existing institution (including
the favourite candidate, the guilds); that the main condition for their existence was
the separation of the labourer from the means of production; but that further,
mainly political, determinations were required for the actual formation of unions in
particular trades. The degree of immiseration of the workers was (rightly) ruled out
as a major determination.[16] We have here a form of explanation that employs
Marxist categories, but avoid, in practice, both an evolutionism and a vulgar economism. We can understand trade unionism as a characteristic organizational form
of the worker under the capitalist mode of production, yet see that the actual
history of trade unions and even their origin are subject to all kinds of contingencies.

It is arguable that none of the tendencies described so far really breaks into a
popular history, and it is certainly the case that Fabian histories remain quite
external to their object. If they adopt a viewpoint close to that of the historical
actors, they tend to espouse the 'prudent administrator', whether sober trade
union leader, or cautious public servant.[17] The Webbs had no feeling at all (except
distrust) for rank-and-file tendencies or for working-class culture outside of the
'educative' institutions which they described. Their viewpoint on the culture as a
whole was that of the late Victorian philanthropist transposed, as it were, to a
Labour Party mode. They never made the transition to a less superior or normative
view of working-class behaviour, never substituted 'culture' for 'morality' or
'manners'. Reading passages like this, with an ear to the implied negatives, the
nature of the relation is clear. The topic is the leadership of mid-nineteenth-
century trade unionism:

The possesion of good manners, though it may seem a trivial detail, was not the
least of their advantages. To perfect self-respect and integrety they added correct-
ness of expression, habits of personal propriety, and remarkable freedom from all
that savoured of the tap-room. In Allan, Applegarth, Guile, Coulson and Odger,
the traducers of Trade Unionism found themselves confronted with a combination
of high personal character, exceptional business capacity, and a large share of
official decorum which the English middle class find so impressive.[18]

No doubt this is a fair description of how a particular *working-class* form of 'respectability' appeared to the mid-Victorian middle class, but it says a good deal about Webbian notions of 'propriety' too.

We have to remember the general character of the lived relations between classes in this period from which the professional middle class was by no means exempt. We have to remember, for instance, that all these intellectuals won time and freedom from menial chores and for intellectual work through the employment of domestic servants. For the most part they took this relation, and the large social distance it expressed, quite for granted: the Webbs were very dependent on their two servants (including 'the devoted Emily'), while in the 1930s, the Coles combined conscience and convenience by hiring an unemployed Barnsley miner and his wife.[19] We have to remember too, again as late as the 1930s, Orwell's agonized attempts to bridge the cultural differences he experienced with such a sharp guilt.[20] It is not at all surprising that the normal way of writing about the working class in this period was through political organization, since this was the only ground of a more or less equal encounter. What remained hidden were precisely all those hinterlands most characteristic of the class's culture. And anyway, was it *really* worth the while writing of *those* things? Even when inhibitions were broached, as, for instance, in Fabian histories of aspects of women's position or of the working-class family, the approach tended to remain inveterately moralistic. Thus Ivy Pinchbeck, whose femaleness should not be identified with a feminism, tended to accept *tout court* male middle-class description of family morality in the nineteenth century and also, by implication, many of the 'solutions' of the Blue Books, especially public education and improvement in environment.[21] She also tended to portray a heroically optimistic picture of the relations between women's position and industrial capitalism, arguing that industry liberated women by drawing them into production and also allowed them, through the separation of home and work, to 'devote their energies to the business of home-making and the care of children'.[22] At root, then, the 'institutional' character of labour history had much to do with the form of the contemporary relationship between the writers and those of whom they wrote.

There were, however, a number of exceptions in this period that anticipated the historiography of the 1960s. The most radically democratic historians of the period were undoubtedly the Hammonds.[23] Paradoxically their virtues grew from their extremely moralistic approach to the writing of history, a moralism applied, however, not to populace, but to the dominant morality of the day. As radical Hobsonian liberals they opposed the dominant jingoism of the 1890s, and as historians they criticized an early industrial 'civilization'. So critical were they of the culture of their own class, or of what they called 'the mind of the rich', that they were able to stand quite outside it and see the rationality of popular responses. Though they are commonly paired with the Webbs in accounts of the origins of social or labour history, they were almost mirror-image opposites. While the Webbs insisted on history's institutional spine, the Hammonds explored what it was like to be governed by a peculiarly oppressive state in a period of extended crisis. Where the Webbs were 'scientific' (or scientistic), the Hammonds drew on a more literary inheritance. In matters of cultural analysis, the Hammonds were more curious and more sophisticated than the Webbs. Working people were credited with 'rational' opinions even under the direst economic pressures. Popular sources were heavily quoted, including petitions and threatening letters. Much attention was paid to the 'politics' of the recreational domain, to the attack on popular amusements. Particular cultural forms - methodism as popular religion, for instance - were closely observed. They even had a kind of practical cultural theory: societies have a dominant culture of 'civilization'; this offers more or less in terms of 'spiritual' and other satisfactions to the mass of the population; where less, the governed improvise cultural forms of their own that make a desolate life inhabitable; so it happens that enormous differences of outlook arise between classes. Of the 1830s they wrote, 'By the end of this period scarcely any aspect of life or politics or economics looked the same to the two worlds', and proceeded, typically, to give instances of great vivacity:

A working-class Reformer, thrown into prison in 1812, asked for a newspaper and was given the Bible instead. He read it with great interest, and wrote to say that after making a careful study of the books of Proverbs, Job, Psalms, Ecclesiastes, Isaiah, Jeremiah and Ezekiel, he had noted that all these writers appeared to represent the rich as oppressing the poor, whereas in England it was the poor who were considered as a burden to the rich.[24]

This is a superb little cameo of how class cultural relations actually work when 'the defences of the poor' are well developed.

The Hammonds are the best example of the cultural content of early social history. It is not surprising that of all historians they are the most praised in the historiographical assessments of Thompson's *Making*. But they were not unique in this phase. There were a number of one-off atypical works of history produced in this period which in different ways anticipated or surpassed later work: Tawney's *Religion and the Rise of Capitalism* (1922): A.E. Dobbs, *Education and Social Movements* (1919; rich in ideas about the relations of material and cultural changes); Alice Clarke, *Working Women in the Seventeenth Century* (1917; a text recently rediscovered, with enthusiasm, by Marxist-feminist historians).

The routinization of labour history

In August 1974, the Society for the Study of Labour History held a conference on early working-class movements. The speakers were Edward Thompson and J.F.C. Harrison. Harrison had published *Learning and Living*, a study of adult education in the West Riding, in 1961, two years before the publication of the *Making*, and was working on a major study of Owenism.[25] Thompson was working back into the nineteenth century, developing the notions of 'paternalism' and popular 'moral economy' which have informed his later work. Both had critical things to say about 'labour history'. Thompson:

The notion of labour history may entail certain dangers - the confinement of our study within boundary walls of our own making. Too narrow a concern with the institutions of the labour movement may exclude from our view larger problems of social context and cultural climate.

Harrison criticized 'certain basic assumptions about the working class . . . which need to be bypassed if further researches into nineteenth-century studies are to be fruitful':

In the narrower meaning of culture, the Owenite contribution through education, propaganda and the dissemination of ideas has already been documented; but Owenism in relation to the broader, anthropological sense of culture (its role in the new industrial civilisation) has yet to be explored.[26]

A few issues later, the society's *Bulletin* mentioned the polemic currently being conducted between Thompson and new *New Left Review*ers over Perry Anderson's 'Origins of the present crisis'. The editors noted that the *New Left Review* had referred to the society's 'narrowly economistic Marxism'.[27] This was shrugged off with too easy a joke about Anderson's 'strange prose', but if we place these two incidents together, they do raise some interesting questions. What happened to 'labour history' (apart from the fact that it acquired a name) between the 1920s and the 1960s? What *was* the relation between the nature of labour history on the one hand and contemporary Marxist theory on the other?

A large part of the answer must lie in G.D.H. Cole's history, for, by common consent, he 'practically invented labour history, as a subject' or, at least 'showed us all the way'.[28] A kind of one-man historical school, he covered the whole scope of the subject, producing biographies of leaders and pioneers,[29] an account of the movement as a whole from Jacobinism to the General Strike,[30] histories of labour representation, the Labour Party and Co-operation,[31] a five-volume history of socialist thought,[32] two closer studies of Chartism and general unionism, and Cole's nearest approach to social history, *The Common People*, large parts of which, however, were written by his brother-in-law, Raymond Postgate.[33]

One key to Cole is undoubtedly his attitude to Marx and to contemporary Marxism. He described himself, as late as 1948, as ' "Marx-influenced" to a high degree', and wrote several works directly on these problems.[34] Despite all the theoretical developments that have occurred since Cole wrote, his *Meaning of Marxism* remains an extremely interesting account of 'what remains alive and capable of . . . growth and adaptation' in Marx's thought. He was sharply critical of Marxism 'as a system'. He made very accurate criticisms of those elements in Marx's work (even in the later texts) that resemble a classical 'philosophy of history', including the tendency to evolutionary or teleological thinking, the assumption of the inevitability of socialist revolution, the essentialism involved in reducing the movement of history to that of 'the powers of production', the retention as a metaphysic, of elements of Hegel's dialectics, and the simplification of all relations down to those of class.

The notion of a simple, unified history of all mankind, proceeding in accordance with some inner necessity from lower to higher forms, is really a metaphysical assumption, for which there is no warrant in the known facts.[35]

It is less easy to define what Cole took from Marx. His theoretical texts are somewhat indecisive and his histories very secretive about their assumptions. Rejecting historical materialism as a description of 'a single world process', he accepted its explanatory power for 'modern times': 'it comes, in its general outline, much nearer to adequacy than any alternative formulation of which I am aware'.[36] Under capitalism, at least, Cole gave a Marx-like priority to economic relations as determinants of general social processes, but insisted on the force of others. His account of what he takes to be Marx's 'best' position, seems also to be a description of his own:

There are many causes at work in history, even if it be true that one set of causes has dominated the rest and shaped the general course of social development within a particular civilisation. Moreover, as Marx and Engels again and again insisted, what is originally derivative has the power of becoming an independent cause . . . . These legal and political powers are . . . in the first instance derivative of the powers of production . . .; but, once established, they become independent factors with a power of their own to influence history and to react upon the course of economic development.[37]

As important for the histories was Cole's understanding of 'class'. In some ways, his reading of Marx was quite orthodox: classes arise out of the 'requirements of the objective situation of the powers of production'. They rest on an 'ordering of the relationships between men and things and between men and men, on a basis consistent with the development of the available productive resources'.[38] The economic relations on which classes were based were very complex and existed independently of a consciousness of them. The development of such a consciousness, indeed, was the other, indispensable aspect of the conception of class, the means by which class and class struggle became 'real', that is an actual force in the making of history.[39]

According to Cole, classes are real 'in and through their capacity for organised collective action'. This builds on 'instinctive' class loyalties and solidarities and is a matter of 'propaganda and organisation' - a 'deliberately organised co-operation'. The creation of trade unions, co-operatives and 'rudimentary' political organizations is a 'first step' towards 'the collective self-expression of the working class'. By stressing these elements of class as practical collective activity, we can escape that tendency in Marxism that endows 'classes' with metaphysical properties, makes them more real than the actual individuals who compose them, and leads to 'much of the ruthlessness and lack of humanism that has characterised the application of the Marxian doctrine'.[40]

At first sight it is hard to establish any relation at all between Cole's particular histories and his understanding of Marxism. They have a form which minimizes

their overt theoretical or explanatory content: a thin unilinear narrative of the development of some set of institutions or practices. The narrative form is very consistently adopted for each of Cole's major objects with very little pause for analysis and only occasional ones for the explanatory supplying of contexts. Biographical works stick rigidly to the form of narrative life histories; the 'story' of the 'labour movement' is 'told' in a number of ways; and even the *History of Socialist Thought* resembles a parade of thinkers who rather breathlessly deliver the essentials of their thought before departing, in strict chronology, in favour of the next performer. Even after the attacks by the Annalistes and the Althusserians on histories with a unified time, there is still need for historians to consider the very real effects - the *un*naturalness - of narrative form in the writing of history.[41]
In Cole's work, it tends to construct ancestries rather than supply explanations, and to abstract some quite thin stream of 'events' from the fuller context in which it was actually placed. The more successful of the histories are those in which the story is thickest and most concentrated in a particular period: the autobiographies of Owen and Cobbett, and *Chartist Portraits*, perhaps the best of all Cole's historical works. But nowhere is Cole's history as dense and 'close-in' yet as broadly contextualized as, for instance, the Hammonds' *The Skilled Labourer*. Nor is it ever so intelligently analytical as the Webbs' *History of Trade Unionism*. It is tempting to relate these features to Cole's pursuit of a popular readership and the fact that many of his books were written for adult education courses or, like *The Common People*, to 'sell in very large quantities and, by its Socialist message, change the opinions of readers'.[42] Much the same could be said, however, of most of the major texts of labour or working-class history from the Hammonds to *Making*: nor is Cole's style of story-telling particularly inspirational, anyway to the modern reader. As his most recent biographer puts it, 'Cole had a tremendous capacity for facts.'[43]

But 'labour history' does have its own organizing presuppositions. These are a good deal nearer to an orthodox, inter-war Marxism-Leninism than Cole's theoretical distancing and the assessments of some commentators would suggest.[44] Cole could not have written a passage as lively but, in his terms, as 'metaphysical' as this:

The result was not frustration and despair but a realisation of the need for a political movement on a higher level, taking into account all the experiences of the past decades and making use of all the forms of struggle which had gone before. So Chartism, the highest stage which any working class movement had reached anywhere in the world at this time, was the product of everything that the workers had done and suffered during the epoch of the industrial revolution.[45]

But Cole's object and his method were not so very different from Morton's. *His* object was the class struggle, viewed from the side of 'labour' or 'the workers': 'the successive efforts of the "lower orders" to achieve representation in parliament', or 'the successive waves of working-class revolt against the new economic and social conditions', or 'the new working-class movements which based themselves on an acceptance of Industrialism'.[46] *The History of Socialist Thought* understands its subject as developing in a dependent relation to 'class-struggle'. *The Common People* ends with an invocation of Disraeli's two nations, its inter-war continuities and the continued salience of class divisions in post-war Britain. Moreover these struggles, whose vicissitudes Cole charted, were understood in a particular way - as essentially political and organizational struggles underpinned by certain economic determinations. In the rather special sense explored below, Cole's history was informed by economism.

As a socialist of a generally 'humanist' kind, he was concerned with the explicitly moral content of socialism.[47] He had a very sharp sense too of the necessity of agitational-educational activity. The absence of any such enterprise was one of his main continuing criticisms of the Labour Party.[48] Yet, in his historical work he was extremely incurious about popular beliefs, even when they might be held to have fuelled major shifts in the history of labour. 'Socialist thought' was the thought of the writers, the leaders and the propagandists, not of 'the masses'. Another symptom of the near-absence of culture was the almost exclusive concentration on formal politics at the expense both of less formal movements and of the whole reproductive sphere. Since this is the sphere of much of women's labour, orthodox labour history structured women firmly out of its concerns. It wrote, in effect, about a single-sexed class. For Cole, indeed, references to women or women's sphere are often synonymous with triviality: in one compressed contemporary image his hostility to orthodox Marxism, yet his staying in some ways within its bounds, are all expressed:

There are some Marxists who cannot see a flapper use her lipstick without producing pat an explanation of her conduct in terms of the powers of production and the class struggle.[49]

If we look at Cole's explanatory moments rather than the normal scope of his narrative, supplementary points can be made. His most important explanatory resource was changes in the economic situation. Economic descriptions provide the main pauses for refreshment in the headlong development of the narrative. But economic explanation actually stands in for any adequate account of popular belief and behaviour. Early nineteenth-century radicalism, as a mass movement, is understood as a reflex of the force of economic relations. Chartism was a form of 'hunger politics'; even as complicated a cultural-political phenomenon as the Chartist Land Plan is understood in these terms. The extension of the notion of instinctual needs or elemental passions to cover the whole realm of the cultural becomes, in the end, absurd:

The land-*hungry* factory operative who was belly-*hungry* as well and in *mortal fear* of the new Poor Law 'Bastille' . . . .

Hunger and *hatred* - these were the forces that made Chartism a mass movement of the British working class. HUNGER GNAWED at the HEARTS of the people.[50]

Images of savagery, of raw unmediated impulses, of 'starving masses', inform all of

Cole's writing on Chartism and this is matched by an overdrawn picture of the 'rationality' and 'idealism' of Lovettite elements in the movement, in this case - in a typical Victorian dichotomy - all head and no belly.[51] Anything as formalized or intellectual as self-education or 'socialist thought' counted as 'culture' in Cole's historical record: he remained completely oblivious of culture as the common sense of classes and social groups - the medium in which economic needs are actually evaluated and popular political conceptions formed.

This feature characterizes Cole's work as a whole; it has, therefore to be explained via Cole's *general* theoretical position, not as an incidental feature of his treatment of Chartism, produced by the phenomenon itself. Chartism declined and the mid-nineteenth-century conformities emerged because, once more, of economic changes of a quite straightforward kind:

The reasons for this are simple. The main body of workers was coming to be rather less hungry, and a good deal less desperate. What the employers and the political economists had been telling the workers about the results of machinery was beginning to come true. Talk about the blessings of capitalist enterprise came to be less a mockery to working-class ears . . . . So Chartism gradually died away.[52]

Late-nineteenth-century mobilizations were understood in a similar way, as products of the Great Depression.[53] As a general principle of explanation, too, changes in working-class politics could be understood in these terms:

The same forces were at work, both in the successive extensions of the franchise and in the struggles of the workers to secure means of political emancipation. These forces were basically economic; they arise out of the changing forms of industrial life, and the changing class-structure in which the successive phases of economic organization worked themselves out.[54]

Cole's recurrent explanatory move, then, was to seek a unity between the movement of economic tendencies and the development of the labour movement. Usually the 'economic' was itself understood very narrowly - very often in terms of the real income of the working class. Cole has little to say, except very derivatively, about changes in economic relations and organization. At its least reductive and on the most friendly reading the typical form of explanation is this: where capitalism succeeds in the most obvious material respects, class politics will not disappear but will take a gradualist or reformist shape. Failure and success is reflected especially in working-class consumption and popular margins of surplus. Relative prosperity breeds a confidence in the capitalist order and a willingness to work within it; economic failure may lead to widespread revolt. The theses about particular movements were very similar to those advanced, from the 1920s onwards, by the economic historians from Clapham to Rostow.[55] The relations which such accounts describe certainly do exist. The problem is that all consideration of the cultural conditions of their operation is omitted: hence the reduction to a mechanical response to economic stimuli characteristic of the accounts of economic historians.[56] We should note, however, that this kind of reduction was characteristic of 'labour history' too. In practice, Cole's problematic (if we can speak of anything so coherent in his work) was a kind of half-hearted or guilty economism. In his emphasis on class struggle, on leadership and on the determining force of 'the economy', he was quite an orthodox inter-war Marxist. Since he tended to reduce Marx's rich conception of economic social relations to something very near the economist's 'standard of living', and could never adequately theorize his concern with 'the individual', his Marxism was, in Hobsbawn's phrase, 'vulgar Marxist'.[57] The different unresolved elements in his thought made it difficult for him to produce a history that would, in practice, surpass current orthodoxies.

Communist historians

Though Cole's work was influential, his labour history was not yet that of the 1960s and 1970s. In the later history of the tradition, up to the present, three main features seem to be important. The first of these has been the sponsorship of official 'labour' and especially trade union studies with an ambivalent relation to the academic study of 'industrial relations'. A second important shift, especially latterly, has been increasing emphasis on teaching and research in higher education and a weakening of the adult education connection. This is seen in anxious debates in the Society for the Study of Labour History's *Bulletin*[58] and in the increasing number of young academics and post-graduate students who contribute to it, and in the lack of the previous close connection with social democratic politics. But by far the most important intellectual-political influence on labour history in the 1950s and 1960s was that of a group of Marxist historians most of whom, up to 1956, were members of the Communist Party.

The achievements of this generation of historians of the left is well known. On their testimony, they owed a huge debt to two older Communist intellectuals, Maurice Dobb and Dona Torr. It was from this grouping that the first editorial board of *Past and Present*, founded in 1952 as a 'journal of scientific history', was drawn.[59] The Society for the Study of Labour History, started in 1960, represents a later moment in the personal histories of some members of the same grouping.[60]

It is important to consider the nature of the Dobb-Torr influence, though without a knowledge of personal intellectual relations, we can only try to assess this through the originality of their work. One important feature was their very close familiarity with the works of Marx and Engels - not always characteristic of defenders of Marxism! Dona Torr was an important translator, editor and explicator of Marx-Engels texts, witness her important edition of the *Selected Correspondence*. Dobb was a major interpreter of classical Marxist theory, as important as many more quarrelled-over figures in 'Western Marxism'. His most influential book, *Studies in the Development of Capitalism* (1945), contained a major restatement of the power and distinctiveness of some of Marx's key categories, especially 'mode of production', 'forces' and 'relations of production', and the capitalist and the feudal modes of production'. Dobb also conducted a critique of sociological (Weberian or Sombartian) categories, on such grounds as their lack of historical specificity, their tendency to an idealism or essentialism, and their lack of power for historical analysis. This explicitly theoretical project, conducted in an abstract manner,[61] was united to a second - the use of Marxist categories to produce a substantive account of the transition from feudalism to capitalism in Britain, drawing on the early economic historians. Dobb's originality, like Marx's, lay in the combination of these aims, a combination usually dissevered in the work of his pupils and comrades. They became mainly 'historians', but Dobb combined a concern with theory or 'abstraction' with a commitment to producing concrete histories. It sometimes seems that, in this way, he supplied a great stock of notions which have fuelled the work of a second generation ever since. Perhaps this is one of the reasons why it may be necessary to get back to a more theoretical discussion over thirty years after *Studies* was published.

One product of this historical and theoretical work was a tentative overall periodization of British history. This provided a framework within which historical specialists might work, together, on different problems and periods. Dobb's main contribution was to supply a periodization at the level, mainly, of the mode of economic production. In the long transition presented by Dobb, there were four main moments: the growth of petty commodity production within a social formation still dominated by the feudal mode of production; the development of capitalist social relations on the basis of petty commodity production, either through differentiation among the producers ('the really revolutionary way') or by the articulation of production to merchant capitalist enterprises; the Puritan revolution of the seventeenth century which created important political conditions for the full development of the capitalist mode of production; and the 'industrial revolution', understood as a phase in which capitalism acquired its own characteristic processes of production. The communist historians were possessed, then, of an account of medieval and modern history which research based on Marxist or 'scientific' principles might go on to elaborate.

Something of Dona Torr's characteristic contribution can be inferred too. She seems to have been particularly interested in the political and ideological aspects of the long transition, especially as they affected the inheritance of nineteenth- and twentieth-century labour movements. These concerns, characteristically linking 'past and present', inform the plan of volume 1 of her study of Tom Mann, the early-twentieth-century syndicalist, Communist and leader of New Unionism. *Tom Mann and His Times*, completed from her own notes after her death by Christopher Hill and A.L. Morton, is an extraordinary book; it combines a biography conveying a real sense of Mann's own times, with a kind of total setting-in-place of the experience of this 'new-fangled man', which ranges back and forth over the whole history of popular struggles in England. One of Torr's most important insights, developed in different ways by Hill and Thompson in their own work, concerned the long history of popular democracy in England, and particularly the importance of the period in which small commodity producers were loosing control of the means of production and consumption from the sixteenth to the early nineteenth centuries. This 'longest chapter in the history of democracy' produced its own characteristic ideologies, based upon an experience of dispossession, and focused around the 'deep-rooted tradition of lost freedom and rights'. Recognition of small-producer democracy and the illumination by Hill and others of the democratic and egalitarian sub-themes of the Puritan revolution, permitted Torr to construct a long tradition of popular democratic struggles of which modern socialists were inheritors. Most of the themes of this communist 'populism' (*not* used here as a term of denigration) are caught in the concluding sections of Hill's essay on the 'Norman yoke':

> Marxism has subsumed what is valuable in the Norman Yoke theory - its recognition of the class basis of politics, its deep sense of the *Englishness* of the common people, of the proud continuity of their lives, institutions and struggles with those of their forefathers, its insistence that a propertied ruling class is from the nature of its position fundamentally alien to the interests of the mass of the people . . . . The working class must stand forth as 'the defender of England'.[62]

Much of *Democracy and the Labour Movement* (1954), the nearest thing to a historical manifesto of this group in the period before 1956, is informed by a similar thesis. The closing item, an essay on Wordsworth by Kiernan, ends with the following quotation from the *Prelude*: 'My heart was all given to the people, and my love theirs.'[63]

We can already see some of the richness of these founding insights. Dobb and Torr were already far removed from a 'vulgar Marxism'. Dobb certainly took mode of production as his central category and worked with a quite classic variant of the base and superstructure metaphor, but he grasped the base itself as an extremely complex formation. At a general abstract level, he clearly distanced himself from technicism and other kinds of essentialism. Social relations of production were given a priority within the general concept of mode of production. In concrete analysis, he stressed the importance of the co-existence and articulation of different modes or of elements of different modes, the continuous real existence of unevenness, the complexity and variance of forms of production, distribution, exchange and surplus extraction, and the fact that most tendencies of development would breed their own forces of counter-action. 'An economic revolution,' he wrote, 'results from a whole set of historical forces in a certain combination: it is not a simple product of one of them alone.'[64] Thus Dobb's understanding of 'the economic' was immeasurably richer (and more true to Marx) than Cole's or that of most non-Marxist economic historians.

In the end, however, Dobb's *Studies* represent a complex non-essentialist economism, the 'limit case of economism' as Schwarz has called it.[65] It is not that political determinations are absent from Dobb's accounts (though it is arguable that ideological determinants *are*). At some points, in explaining national differences, for example, they are crucial.[66] But there is no developed theory in *Studies* of political or ideological relations or of such problems as that of 'representation'. The absences mirror those in Dobb's main theoretical source, Marx's *Capital*. Classes or fractions of classes comprehend their own real interests in a fairly unproblematic manner: political revolutions, even the English, are a fighting out of the manifest issues. Thus the real complexity of Dobb's account of the Puritan revolution, more complex than the better-known early essay by Hill, is the product of his very 'structural' analysis of economic relations, not of any real complexity in thinking politics or ideology. In Hill's *English Revolution* (1940) and in Dobb's *Studies* the specific effects of religion are, for instance, little discussed. Religiously defined parties or issues are quite swiftly reduced to their 'real' contents in the interests of economic classes.[67] This move remains characteristic, indeed, of work which anticipates the late 1950s and early 1960s break: Hill's 'Norman yoke' for instance and Torr's *Tom Mann*. A form of class reductionism was to remain one of the main problems with this kind of Marxism even after 1960.[68]

In general, however, in the case of Dona Torr, we move still further from a simple or mechanical Marxism. We have noted her interest in ideologies. This was different in kind from Cole's concern with 'thought' - it embraced popular conceptions, especially those of slow growth and long duration. It pointed to, even if it did not quite deliver, a form of *cultural* analysis. Torr's work and influence also contained one key feature of the Marxist culturalism of the 1960s - an emphasis on the experiential, 'lived' quality of history, a concern to recreate the past as it felt to contemporaries. Those parts of *Tom Mann* which Torr wrote herself have precisely this quality. Her whole mode of approach to history was not one which could easily coexist with the mechanical scientism and practical fatalism associated with Stalinist orthodoxies. She portrayed historical struggles with immediacy, energy and relevance to the present. 'She made us feel history on our pulses.'[69]

The influence of Torr and Dobb on their younger comrades was evidently immense. In some ways it was the *substance* of the Torr-Dobb account that was most important: the problems with which Dobb dealt have clearly informed the work of Hilton right through to his most recent books; the themes of the long transition and of lost rights have shaped the work of both Hill and Thompson. The influence was greatest on work in the period up to the mid nineteenth century; Thompson's *Morris* and Torr's *Mann* have been nothing like so seminal for the social history of their periods as Hill's work for the seventeenth century or Thompson's for the early nineteenth. Where the work of this generation has been important for later periods it has tended to take a rather different form, best represented by Hobsbawn's early essays on late-nineteenth-century labour movements. The distinctive focus of these studies, mostly completed before the publication of *Primitive Rebels* in 1959, is a concern with 'the economic and technical conditions which allowed labour movements to be effective, or which prevented them from being effective'.[70]

These essays extended the concerns of a Cole-like labour history, but placed phases of the movement within an economic context grasped much more surely than in Cole's brief and derivative sketches. The need to combat the one-sided progressivism of some economic historians on something like their own ground must have pressed in the same direction.[71] As heavily influenced by Lenin as by Marx, these essays tend to return to an economism in which economic tendencies act, relatively unproblematically, as triggers for labour militancy, or provide the context of defeat.[72] Or, as in the important essays on labour aristocracy, fragmentations within the working class in terms of differential wages are assumed to have some rather automatic effects on labour's politics.[73] This union of labour and economic history under Marxist auspices became a standard form of history; another concentrated on the politics of the leadership of labour movements, pragmatic everyday judgements being held to be of more importance than 'ideas'.[74] This, as Edward Thompson argued in 1960, was the characteristic 'double-vision' of labour history: 'elemental forces' directed by 'juntas and parliamentarians'. The casualty was any sense of a movement that 'grew from the bottom up' in the intense and committed activity of provincial militants.[75]

In general, however, the early work of the 'communist historians' was very varied, developing different elements in the Dobb-Torr emphases. We shall argue that the late 1950s and early 1960s saw significant breaks from these roots as well; but in many ways, especially in the substantive concerns, the most important 'breaks' came with Dobb and Torr themselves.

A new kind of history

We have already argued that the period after the mid 1950s was an exceptionally creative one. Like all attempts to define objects very close to the point of vision, what follows can only be a first approximation with which others will quarrel.[76] We might first try to describe, very generally, some of the main shifts that constituted the revolution in historiography in these years.

The most important over-arching change was that historians began to write seriously and with sympathy about the beliefs and behaviour of the mass of historical populations: they actually did, in an important sense, 'give their hearts' to the people.

In case this sounds a very easy thing to do, we need to recall that the study of 'culture' remained firmly within an elitist mould while, on the other hand, 'labour history' was usually cultureless. Two sets of new departures were therefore involved in the new history: a new rendering of the notion of culture which rescued it from elitist or narrowly literary and artistic usages; and a break with the restricted categories of labour history and, what was often the same, with mechanical or triumphalist assumptions about the proper historical destiny and ultimate state of consciousness of the proletariat. Those shifts must have rested (if our earlier argument was correct) on some profound change of relationship between intellectuals and contemporary working people.

Richard Hoggart's *Uses of Literacy* (1957) and Raymond Williams's *Culture and Society* (1958) and *The Long Revolution* (1961) belong, centrally, to the first of these shifts. Writing the history of the idea of culture itself, Williams sought to extend its usage beyond the connoisseurship of cultivated bourgeois fractions, the judgements of the guardians of high culture and even those activities conventionally regarded as 'creative': 'I would then define the theory of culture as the study of relationships between elements in a whole way of life.'[77] As we argued earlier, Williams's concerns have none the less often remained too literary to deliver the full implications of such a profound reordering; his 'cultural materialism' remains, centrally, a form of literary criticism. But it was Hoggart who really supplied an exemplification of Williams's argument, showing how, under certain fragile conditions, 'working-class people' could create and share a way of life with its own strengths and moral and aesthetic values. Both men had personal roots within the working class and were acutely aware both of the novelty and of the dangers of this. Hoggart's introduction to *The Uses of Literacy* maps the range of middle-class perceptions (including those of 'Marxists' and labour historians) with great percipience, but also warns of the difficulties of someone who is 'from the working classes' It was surely the fact that working-class culture was described intimately, from within, that made the book so powerful. For the middle-class reader, it was a solvent of assumed cultural superiorities or a lesson, at the very least, in cultural relativities.[78] The emergence of writers and intellectuals of the working class was, of course, one aspect of the erosion of cultural class differences that marked the 1950s. It was especially important, perhaps, in helping to produce a less agonized pattern of relationships between intellectuals of the left and working people. There is also one further aspect whose history should be written: the continuing importance of adult and working-class education as an arena in which these relations were worked out.

It would require an intimate knowledge of personal and political relations (to which this essay does not pretend) to unravel the influence of Williams and Hoggart on the historians. But the coalescence between their contributions and the populism of the Communist historians is very striking. Hoggart considered that 'historians of the working-class movement' produced histories of the activities of 'significant minorities', not histories of the working classes at all. To the historian-reader of Hoggart, that might have seemed an over-generous judgement, since even these activities were viewed through a severely narrowed frame of politics-and-work, while 'the class' was often present, but in very stereotypical forms. Certainly the richness of the activities of Hoggart's minorities - 'purposive', 'political', 'pious' and 'self-improving' - had hardly begun to be charted in 1957. The state of working-class culture was more often inferred than actually described. Hoggart's work must have constituted a real reproach.

The historians' own innovations, however, took a very particular form. The typical object of the new history was certainly popular behaviour and belief, but overwhelmingly in periods before the growth of stable or routinized labour organization - for Britain, the period before, say, 1850. Moreover the culture of the popular classes was still usually seen within a quite severely political frame: the object was defined as early, primitive, archaic or 'transitional' forms of social protest, the proto-politics of the people. Much of the really creative work of the period - history's points of growth - fits this description with surprising accuracy: Hobsbawn's work on 'primitive rebels', 'bandits' and the Swing Rioters, significantly different, in many ways from early essays; Hill's work on Puritans, Levellers

and millenarians; Hilton's studies of peasant movements; Genovese's examination
of slave culture; Rudé's studies of 'pre-industrial crowds' and the many derivatives,
in France and England, from this work; Thompson's recreation of the characteristic
politics and political culture of the early English working class and his work, with
many others, on eighteenth-century forms of popular protest and communal
discipline; the studies of J.F.C. Harrison, Harold Silver, Brian Simon and others
of Owenism and of early working-class educational traditions; the interest first,
in close local studies of Chartism and other working-class movements and, latterly,
in their characteristic theory, language and rituals.

The titles and authors involved here and the timing of the new history is best
summarized in a chart of dates of publication of some of the more important texts.
Works in brackets may be taken as prefiguring the break in important ways.

(1954   Saville (ed.), *Democracy and the Labour Movement*)
(1955   Thompson, *William Morris*)
(1956   Torr, *Tom Mann and His Times*)
 1957   Hoggart, *The Uses of Literacy*
 1958   Williams, *Culture and Society*
         Hill, *Puritanism and Revolution*
 1959   Hobsbawn, *Primitive Rebels*
         Rudé, *The Crowd in the French Revolution*
 1960   Simon, *Studies in the History of Education*
         Briggs and Saville, *Essays in Labour History 1*
 1961   J.F.C. Harrison, *Learning and Living*
         Genovese, *The Political Economy of Slavery*
 1962   Hobsbawn, *Age of Revolutions*
 1963   Thompson, *The Making of the English Working Class*
 1964   Hobsbawn, *Labouring Men* (*some* essays)
 1965   Hill, *Intellectual Origins of the English Revolution*
         Briggs (ed.), *Chartist Studies*
 1967   Thompson, 'Time, work discipline and industrial capitalism'
 1968   G.H. Williams, *Artisans and Sans Culottes*
 1970   Hollis, *The Pauper Press*
 1971   Thompson, 'The moral economy of the English crowd in the eighteenth
             century'
         Thomas, *Religion and the Decline of Magic*
         Thompson (D), *The Early Chartists*
 1972   Hill, *The World Turned Upside Down*
 1973   Rowbotham, *Hidden from History*
         Hilton, *Bondmen Made Free*
 1974   Thompson, 'Patrician society: plebian culture'

'The people' much more commonly assumed the shape of peasants, small
producers, artisans or *sans culottes* than proletarians. Labour history, strictly
speaking, remained relatively immune to the newer influences. The main exception

was the early nineteenth century, the veritable seedbed of the newer social histories. All this is very clear in the three volumes of *Essays in Labour History*, whose common editorship and title disguise some major differences. Volume 1 (1960) is recognizably a 'culturalist' text. It contained Brigg's influential essay in 'The language of class', a work citing *Culture and Society* and much concerned, Williams-like, with the history of conception and a word; Thompson's 'Homage to Tom Macguire'; and Hobsbawm's study of cultural aspects of wage determination, an interesting and characteristic insertion of culture or custom into a classic concern of the labour and economic historians. Volumes 2 (1971) and 3 (1977) mark a return to much more conventional fare, coinciding with the move forward in terms of historical period. Indeed, nearly twenty years after its publication, 'Homage to Tom Macguire' (like parts of *Morris* and of *The Life and Times of Tom Mann*) remains a strangely isolated work in a sea of labour history, and is correspondingly invigorating on first encounter.

In the 1970s some of the newer emphases have been applied to later periods. The massive development of oral history and the use of autobiographical materials promise (though have hardly yet delivered) an experimentally based history of more recent times as rich yet as systematic as Thompson's *Making*.[79] But the breaks have happened in nothing like so consolidated a way as for the early nineteenth century. One feature has been a return to heavily Leninist interpretations based upon the theory of labour aristocracy. Thus, though John Foster's work has huge virtues, notably the concern with the working class *and* the state *and* the bourgeoisie, it might accurately be read as a kind of throwback to the pre-war period, an indication of where communist history might have gone without Dobb, Torr and 1956. It has therefore been necessary for a new cohort of labour-aristocratic historians to retrace that path, too, for themselves, out of early Hobsbawm and into an encounter with Gramsci.[80] More typically, a similar ground is being covered but in a much more segmented way; interesting histories are being written about working-class leisure culture or provision, about popular religion, about imperialist, nationalist and militarist sentiment, and about the family, the position of women and a popular 'feminism'. Certainly there has been a real discovery of late Victorian and Edwardian popular culture. Yet these themes have only been fleetingly brought together, especially the political and recreational. And these additional kinds of history have tended to grow up alongside the old, without transforming them.[81]

Perhaps the most important inhibition to the transformation of labour history initially was a feeling that much of importance on more modern periods was already 'known' and that, if not, concepts and methods were ready to hand. Cole and others had rendered familiar the story of British social democracy. Miliband was soon to write the same story from a perspective further to the left: Anderson and Nairn were to provide a kind of *coup de grâce* by arguing that English leftism had been utterly futile. Even without these accounts, the concepts themselves, those of a classic Marxism-Leninism, were readily available. Reconceptualization was simply not necessary. There is some substantiation of this argument to be

found in the introduction to *Primitive Rebels,* one of the first of the new histories
to appear. Hobsbawn noted how the movements to be discussed, from banditry
through to labour rituals, had been rendered marginal or regarded as 'forerunners'
of modern social movements. 'Modern' movements, on the other hand, had
'normally been treated according to a well-established and reasonably sound
scheme'.

For obvious [?] reasons the historians have concentrated on labour and socialist
movements, and such other movements as have fitted into the socialist framework.
These are commonly regarded as having their primitive stages - journeyman's
societies, and Luddism, Radicalism, Jacobinism and Utopian Socialisms - and
essentially as developing towards a modern pattern which varies from one country
to the next but has considerable general application . . . .[82]

Primitive rebels, by contrast, posed real problems of interpretation and imaginative
understanding; up till now urban and literate historians had 'too rarely made the
effort to understand people who are unlike themselves'.

The same point could and *should* be made of the Edwardian working class or
of late-nineteenth-century socialists. Indeed, the effort to understand, which
involves the suspension of the belief that we already have the answers, is *always*
necessary, even in social and political interactions in the contemporary world, even
in the same society. It is the sense that 'reasonably sound schemes' already exist
in a kind of Marxist-Leninist common sense about modern labour movements
that has hindered the reconstruction of labour history. It may be that forms of
study of post-1850 British popular history will only shift when that common
sense is explicitly challenged, as indeed, in theoretical debate, it is being challenged
now. In the late 1950s, however, 'archaic' social movements offered a weak point
in orthodox categories: it was easier to make breaks on this ground than on the
'classic' ground of the proletariat.

Further difficulties for more modern studies derive from the object of study
itself. Fragmentations in the historiography express real fragmentation in the
experiences of men and women within a capitalist social order. One feature of the
older Marxist convictions about 'working-class consciousness' was the assumption
of a degree of homogeneity, or at least a real or potential essence or core around
which a whole culture was organized. Even more recent accounts of working-
class culture tend to continue this search for some simple unity. This may
take somewhat dismissive forms, or revert to some romantic variant.[83] One
of our own recurrent recurrent arguments on the other hand, will be to stress
the heterogeneity or complexity of 'working-class culture', fragmented not
only by geographical unevenness and parochialisms, but also by the social and
sexual divisions of labour and by a whole series of divisions into spheres or
sites of existence. The most important of these latter divisions is that which
mainly distinguishes the social worlds of men and women: the division
between the sphere of social production or 'work' on the one hand, and
that of biological reproduction, private consumption and recreation (which

is also the sphere of much of women's work) on the other.[84] Another such
division, the defining division of labour history, is that constructed in the course
of the development of social democratic institutions between a sphere of legitimate
politics and a 'non-political' realm. The distinction between the formal education
system (where people learn) and everywhere else (where learning is absent) is
another such distinction.[85] Thus are created a series of real social separations
whose historical origins are forgotten and which are usually accepted by everyone,
including historians, as 'natural'. These distinctions, once founded and given an
institutional force, are real, and really 'lived', but they are also constructed and
maintained by particular ideologies (of the education system, of domesticity, of
the protestant ethic and so on). It really is the case that it is easier to break with
such fragmentations in studying an eighteenth-century food riot than in studying
an official twentieth-century 'stoppage', for the forms themselves are less differentiated. Hence, too, the privileged status, historically and politically, of those
(revolutionary) moments when political practice and ideological struggle fuse the
spheres by uniting action across them.

A second distinguishing feature of the new histories was their 'social' character.
'Social history' is a category too loaded with contradictory significances to be a
very useful aid to analysis, but as a banner or rallying point it expressed much that
was typical of the period. Younger historians, dissatisfied with a conventional
training in 'economic history' or the history of administration, often found an
identity as 'social' historians. The backwash of Cold War allegiances in economic
history and the increasing narrowness of the foci of economic research pushed in
the same direction. Sociologies of different kinds had an influence; so too, though
much more in America than in Britain, did the French *Annales* tradition. The
development of interests in a very wide range of different empirical areas with no
obvious home in the orthodoxies also contributed their (different) social histories.
Once again, however, shifts within the Marxist tradition were paradigmatic for the
discipline as a whole. The most important change of emphasis between the 1940s/
early 1950s and the 1960s was from a concern with modes of production and the
transition from feudalism and capitalism at that level, to the political and cultural
relations between classes as the primary object of study. Similarly while Dobb's
project had been explicitly theoretical and raised, centrally, epistemological
questions, the new history tended to a quite militant distrust of 'theory' or was,
at best, quite uninterested in the more formal, deductive aspects of Marxism.
The priority, it seems, was to test and develop the Dobb-Torr insights through
detailed research. In other words, though the new history drew on a periodization
of Dobb's *Studies* - his results - it had a different object and a different method. It
undoubtedly broke with his complex economism and the 'rationalist', concept-
building elements in his procedure. An account of this change could be written
around Dobb's *Studies* and Thompson's *Making* or around the earliest and latest
work of Christopher Hill, say, *The English Revolution* and *Economic Problems
of the Church* (1956) on the one side and *The World Turned Upside Down* (1972)
on the other. These aspects of characterization of 'culturalist' Marxism will be

taken further in part 3, especially the implications for views of class and class consciousness.

The third main feature was the centrality of 'experience'. This emphasis is best understood as an opposition, often rooted in political experiences, to all externalizing, mechanical or functionalist accounts of the social world and an insistence on getting inside the minds, perceptions and the feelings of the historical agents themselves. But perhaps, like good ethnographers, we should let the historians speak for themselves:

Hobsbawm in the appendix to *Primitive Rebels* entitled 'In their own voices':

to help readers . . . to think and feel themselves into the skins of such 'primitive rebels' as have been discussed in this book.[86]

Edward Thompson's famous preface to *The Making of the English Working Class*:

I am seeking to rescue the poor stockinger, the Luddite cropper, the 'obsolete' handloom weaver, the 'utopian' artisan, and even the deluded follower of Joanna Southcott, from the enormous condescension of posterity. Their crafts and traditions may have been dying. Their hostility to the new industrialism may have been backward-looking. Their communitarian ideals may have been fantasies. Their insurrectionary conspiracies may have been foolhardy. But they lived through these time of acute social disturbance, and we did not. Their aspirations were valid in terms of their own experience . . . .[87]

Christopher Hill on the writings of seventeenth-century radicals:

Historians may trace sources in Italian Neo-Platonists and German Anabaptists, but what gives life and vigour to these ideas is the relevance which men felt that they had to the affairs of England in the revolutionary decades. The ideas may (or may not) be second-hand; the passion behind them is not. Many radicals claimed to have received their truths not from books or from men but from God, from the spirit within. No doubt they deceived themselves: they gave form and shape to vague ideas that were in the air. But the form and shape were their own, drawn from the experience of their daily life in England during the years when John Warr's 'teeming freedom' exerted itself.[88]

Eugene Genovese on the culture of the slaves in the American south:

But knowing that the ambiguity of the Black experience as a national question lends the evidence to different readings, I have chosen to stay close to my primary responsibility: to tell the story of slave life as carefully and accurately as possible. Many years of studying the astonishing effort of black people to live decently as human beings even in slavery has convinced me that no theoretical advance suggested in their experience could ever deserve as much attention as that demanded by their demonstration of the beauty and power of the human spirit under conditions of extreme oppression.[89]

These themes and tones - the validating ground of 'experience', the suspicion of formal theory, the concern for oppressed peoples and with historically recovering them, and the appeal to an ethical humanism - represent much of what is best in these histories. But they are, as we shall see, symptoms of some limitations and difficulties too.

Before leaving the emphasis on 'experience', we should stress how general this phenomenon has been. The cultural stress of British history, of Marxism and of New Left politics, was by no means unique. Accompanying movements in other countries and other disciplines were enormously diverse and it would be absurd to regard them as identical. Yet, from the point of view of this essay, they did have features in common. They shared a stress upon the inward apprehension of the world, upon 'consciousness' in the most general usage of the term. This rediscovery was especially revelatory within a Marxist tradition scarred by theoretical economism and a Stalinist politics, but it was not limited to it. Similar problems were posed elsewhere.

When English empirical sociology rediscovered 'class', it often did so in the shape of cultural differences. In continental Europe, the period saw a revival of phenomenological philosophies, including Jean-Paul Sartre's blend of existentialism and Marxism. These were characteristically concerned with the individual's inner world. Though Althusserian structuralism was a response to the 'humanisms' of the 1950s, it shared with them a concern with 'consciousness', greatly developing the notion of ideology. Within Marxism generally, structuralism aside, there was a revival of interest in Marx's early work, especially the *1844 Manuscripts*, and in the more experiential categories like 'alienation'. The cross-Atlantic development of Frankfurt-school Marxism, the attempted synthesis with Freudian psychoanalysis, and the concern with the new cultural phenomena of the media, were other similar developments. In the heartland of conventional sociology itself, there was a not-dissimilar revolt. Sociologies with, as in the case of radical ethnomethodology, an almost exclusive concern with the processes of 'making sense', developed in conscious reaction to the dominant functionalism of the theoretical systems. A similar tendency can be seen in sectoral or sub-sociologies: the concern with symbolic and cultural interactions, for instance, in the development of the sociologies of deviancy and education. The parallels between these intellectual systems and the newer forms of politics of the 1960s has often and correctly been noted. All these systems and movements focused in different ways on the inwardness of experience in reaction to sociologies (or to a world) that was seen as mechanical, reductive or deterministic. We might say that the discovery of 'the cultural' was the key shift in the social sciences generally in this period.

'Lions in the path' - and the trouble with ostriches

If the history of history presented here is anything like correct, it should be possible to draw some prescriptions from it. There is one route, indeed, that does appear to be extremely clear. Is it not the responsibility of historians, especially socialist historians, to extend the emphases of the new history forward in time, to complete the reconstruction of labour history, to realize the promise of oral history, to reconstruct, once more, the real connection between historians of the left and a socialist movement? This is, perhaps, the commonest orientation among left historians now, represented in the coalition around the journal *History Workshop*, in sections of the oral history 'movement' and among many feminist historians. The editorials of the first edition of *History Workshop*, with their calls for a history 'relevant to ordinary people' and for an end to 'the scholastic fragmentation of the subject', are a most energetic signalling of this path.[90]

Despite its political rectitude, this solution is not without its difficulties. There is a danger that the extension of some 1960s innovations, without the political experiences that informed them, will lead to an empty, descriptive and passively romantic historiography, popular only in the object which it records. If, as we have argued, the problem of developing a more adequate history of recent times is conceptual in character, a matter of breaking with deeply held assumptions, an unrepentantly empiricist history may not help us very much. Moreover, the popular historians tend also to ignore many of the significant developments of the late 1960s and 1970s, especially encounters of a theoretical kind. There is, in fact, barely an aspect of the historical practices of the 1960s that has not been questioned or potentially enriched by subsequent debates. At this point we are not concerned to argue any of these difficulties through, but we do want to argue against evasions.

New Left history was followed by a quite different kind of intellectual explosion. The main features of this phase were the priority of 'theory', the internationalization of debate and, in common with the histories, a concern especially with ideology or aspects of 'consciousness'. The established concerns of histories and of earlier cultural theorists were worked over in new ways. Much of the impetus for this shift came from the newer editors of the *New Left Review*. Having demonstrated (to their own satisfaction) that the English were parochial, the working class inert and a Marxist culture absent, they set about to repair these deficiencies through the importation of books.[91] This priority, directed at the intellectuals, was pursued at the expense of any real connection with popular politics and was thus completely at odds with the dominant tendency among the historians and the 'older' New Left in the earlier period. The debates between Perry Anderson, Tom Nairn and Edward Thompson in the mid 1960s were centrally about these matters: the relation of the intellectuals to popular and indigenous traditions - not just the 'peculiarities' but actually the *'potentialities'* of the English.[92] These early debates have often been reproduced in the years that have followed: different voices but the same themes. Yet, however we evaluate it, there is no doubt that the *New Left* project has worked: it has helped to transform the character of intellectual Marxism in Britain, shifting the whole centre of gravity of the tradition. Unfortunately there is no time to look at the conditions of this success.

Not all the importations were equally incompatible with the existing Marxisms.

In history and often in politics, Gramsci has been assimilated with relative ease, often at the expense of his originality.[93] The least digestible elements have derived from Marxist structuralism, especially from the work of Louis Althusser. Yet Althusser's work has been enormously influential and has been followed by successive waves of influence, many of them out of the same Parisian milieu. 'Structuralism' has thus developed vigorous roots in Britain too. Two well-known examples are the strong neo-or post-Althusserian tendency among critical social theorists and the use of a heady mix of semiology, Marxism and psychoanalysis by some analysts of film.[94] The reception has been given a particular cast through the contemporaneous growth of the women's movement, as in the case of psycho-analysis for example. Because of the experiential stress of the women's movement itself, the political and other problems of the engagement with theory have often been felt especially acutely there.[95] One effect of all this - to risk a mild chauvi-nism - is that the British have become somewhat less parochial than the French and Germans - at least in what they read! Certainly it no longer makes sense to see 'structuralism' as peculiarly French or Gramsci's legacy as limited to Italy.

We wish to stress two main consequences of this theoretical immersion. So expansive has been the development of Marxist cultural theory that many of the most important questions in the theory and sociology of culture are now posed not between Marxist and other accounts, but *within Marxism itself*. One key element in this very odd state of affairs is the absence of an emergent rival system capable of thinking about culture as a whole (rather than some special, class-bound and form-bound part of it). In Britain, the most important rivals have been based in the study of literature or other aspects of 'high culture', or, in cultural histories with close affinities to political biography, concerned with 'the conversation of the people who counted'.[96] The most crippling defect of all these forms of cultural study is simply the restriction of range: the failure to take seriously the lived culture of the mass of historical populations. Thus, the more one considers the break made by Hoggart and Williams from Leavis, the more significant that departure becomes. It provided a basis for an adequate 'cultural studies'. Only a rival that takes a somewhat similar departure from high-cultural traditions is likely to make serious inroads on the tendency to a Marxist monopoly.

The second consequence of the 1970s developments is to set up a particular opposition within the Marxist debates. It is important to describe this opposition rather carefully, since much of our discussion later in the book will hang upon it.

On the one hand, there is the older British tradition of cultural analysis, formed in the breaks from Leavisite literary criticism and an economistic Marxism. There have been two contributory streams here: the 'literacy' and the 'historical', though they have shared common roots in the 'culture and society' tradition and in non-Fabian forms of British socialism. They have also shared a common mode, very different from that of the other camp: a mode of the dominance of the particular, concerned primarily with the analysis of concrete class experience or specific cultural forms, usually in a 'historical' way. Thus though Edward Thompson describes himself as an historian within the Marxist tradition and Raymond

Williams describes his latest position as a 'cultural materialism', these two key
representatives of the first tradition are very close together, especially in their
opposition to structuralism. For ease of reference, not to invent a 'position', we
term this tradition 'cultural Marxism'.

On the other hand, there is a set of tendencies, still more diverse than the
first, in which, however, Althusserian structuralism is central. The contributory
streams have included the linguistics of Saussure, the structural anthropology of
Levi-Strauss, the epistemological concerns of traditional French philosophy and a
particular, 'philosophical' reading of the Marx of *Capital*. More hidden debts are
owed to Lacan's adaption of Freudian psychoanalysis and to Gramsci's writing
on state and civil society. The central substantive concern might be described as the
structuring of thought and consciousness through ideological processes, though
these are variously described as structures of 'signification', 'representation' or
'discourse'. The typical empirical moment is the analysis of the 'text', literary or
in some other form. But what distinguishes this tradition more clearly than any
other facet is its unrelenting concern with theoretical and epistemological questions
pitched at a higher level of abstraction. We will refer to this tradition as 'structuralism',
following a long-established usage.

The opposition of these tendencies is clear enough from a range of polemics.
There are many structuralist attacks on 'culturalism'.[97] They tend to share a
common mode of critique. The object is to show that a particular text is organized
around definite presuppositions (a 'problematic'). Certain problematics are held to
be inherently flawed, or 'not Marxist'. Chief among these are a trio of tendencies
to which, over and again, structuralist critiques return: 'historicism', 'humanism'
and 'empiricism'. If such a tendency is present, the text as a whole is held to fail,
flawed at its centre. Both the mode of critique and its key terms are derived quite
directly from the work of Althusser, especially from *For Marx* and *Reading
Capital*. The procedural force of the critique rests on a particular epistemological
basis, though this is not always acknowledged. Especially important is the sharp
and definitive distinction between science and ideology which is critical in
Althusser's earlier formulations. In *Reading Capital*, Althusser and his colleagues
attempted to define precisely what it was in *Capital* that distinguished it from
ideology, having already argued in earlier work for a sharp 'epistemological break'
between Marx's earlier and later texts. In his later work, Althusser himself has
questioned the hardness of the science-ideology divide, while in England some of
those most deeply influenced by his work have rejected what they see as the
'rationalism' of this position. Yet it is still sometimes argued, or implied, that the
relation between culturalism and structuralism is one of the total replacement
of one problematic by another more 'scientific' one. As we shall argue later, we do
not accept the mode of total critique nor the view of how 'scientific' advances are
made which informs it.

Fully developed culturalist attacks on structuralist positions are rarer. But
structuralism is certainly seen as an opposed position within (or outside) Marxism.
Here, for example, is Edward Thompson on the subject of Althusser:

But this is a quite distinct question from Althusser's writing, which I see as a mutation, or as a fully exposed development of idealism which uses certain Marxist concepts but which is attempting to wall up, totally, the empirical dialogue and the empirical criticism of those concepts. It ranks as a theology, and as between a theology and what I regard as the major tradition of Marx there can be very little common ground. Then what is at issue is reason itself: whether Marxism is a rational theory available to dialogue with evidence and open rational criticism. If it ceases to be such, then it is disreputable. It is not only disreputable, it is actively injurious. It will mislead all the time. Hence it is a question of principle to oppose this . . . .[98]

Thompson is resolutely anti-Althusserian: hardly a piece passes from his prolific pen without a pot shot or two at 'some structuralist philosophers'[99] A more extended critique is threatened (and eagerly awaited). In the meantime the most sustained riposte is contained in Raymond Williams's *Marxism and Literature*, an important theoretical text, not least for its familiarity and engagement with texts out of other traditions.

The culturalist-structuralist opposition is a very real one, but we wish to end this essay by noting our own somewhat different general orientation. The argument, at this stage, will have to take the form of rather dogmatic assertions, a kind of dogmatic defence of un-dogmatism. Neither of the two traditions which together constitute our field is adequate, taken on its own. *Neither culturalism nor structuralism will do!* It is not possible to develop an adequate theory of culture-ideology from Althusserian (or neo- or post-) positions. There has not been, nor can there be, any simple supercession of a culturalist problematic by positions derived from an Althusserian theory of ideology. Nor is it fruitful to attempt to develop in more and more sophisticated and ethereal ways the most 'advanced' structuralist, semiological, linguistic or psychoanalytic theories. What presents itself as the structuralist critique of culturalism is, very often, merely an exploration of differences between the two positions. It clarifies - but since it too seldom has reference to the analysis of particular situations - it does little more. The typical mode of critique, which we have described, often resembles a kind of intellectual lumberjacking, with all the excitement of the art, especially when the timber is some great classic tree that has stood in the forest for many decades. Down goes Weber! Down go Marxist historians! Down goes Marx! Very intoxicating! But the problem is that this mode of critique is rarely accumulative: one 'problematic' demonstrates its power against another, but we rarely have a second substantive account, still less one incorporating, like Marx's critique of classical political economy, what was 'rational' in the first. This may explain a great deal about contemporary intellectual practice among those considering themselves Marxists: the proliferation of positions, the ephemerality of much debate, and the relative paucity of synthesizing or substantive works that do not merely criticize orthodoxies (Marxist or otherwise) but actually *stand in their place.*

On the other hand 'culturalist' accounts are often extremely vulnerable to aspects of the structuralist critique. As we shall see, this includes some famous

histories of working-class culture and experience. There are definite limitations,
for concrete analysis, in the 'humanist' presuppositions. There is a failure adequately
to theorize the results of concrete studies and to make the theoretical starting
points of further work quite plain. There is a tendency not to write about determinations that are external to, or do not easily show up in, 'culture' or 'experience'.
There is a tendency to trust the 'authentic' experiential text as the exclusive source
of accounts. Marxist culturalism tends to reject two key aspects of Marx's original
contribution to a developed historical method: the process of systematic, self-
conscious abstraction; and the notion of social relations that are structured, have a
logic or tendency or force of their own and operate, in part, 'behind men's backs'.
It is precisely because Althusserianism recovers these genuinely 'structuralist'
elements in classical Marxism that it provides a powerful critique of culturalist
Marxism. That world cannot be (wholly) understood in terms of the recorded
experiences of individuals or classes. Sometimes these lie at the very heart of
inadequate explanations of the world. The object of an adequate history must,
then, not merely be 'people' but the whole complex set of relations in which they
stand, within which, indeed, they are made as social beings.

This point - the unwisdom of neglecting the difficulties raised by structuralist
theory - may be illustrated in another way. Theoretical debates of the last ten years
have raised serious questions against each of the terms that, together, constitute
the title of this book and, indeed, against their juxtaposition. Is 'culture' too loose
to constitute a useful term of analysis? If we expand it to cover 'way of life' does
not its specifity disappear? How do we distinguish between 'culture' and 'non-
culture'? What is the working class anyway? Can we speak of relatively homogenous
cultures that belong to particular classes? Are cultures really generated within
classes, from 'experience'? Is the notion of 'experience' a coherent one? Does it
not confuse the world as it appears to human beings and the stock of notions with
which they make sense of it? Is it not a gross simplification to understand societies
(or cultural formations) in terms of class relations alone? Are not gender, or ethnic
or age-rank relations also of great importance? May not a politically genuine concern
with popular experiences come to stand in for an attempt to understand, in a
harder, more analytical way, the place of culture in a broader process of change or
transformation?

If we do not wish to ignore these problems, there are perhaps two ways past the
Althusserian lion in the path. We can continue to study historical and contemporary
situations (which are in principle the same) with the best means that are to hand.
We may continue to work within paradigms whose vulnerability we acknowledge
but respond to weaknesses and limitations in the actual practice. This way through
is one of the routes adopted here, in part 2.

But there is another way, too, round by a more theoretical detour. What seems
to be needed here is to slow the pace of speculation a little, be less destructively
critical and consider more carefully the strengths and weaknesses of the two traditions by comparing some exemplary texts. What precisely are the differences between
structuralist and culturalist accounts? Are they opposed or just different? Do they

share similar origins, premises, problems? Is it possible to pass the practice of writing the history of culture through a 'structuralist' critique and prescribe a more adequate method? This is the route adopted in part 3 of this book, always under the imperative that we need ways of thinking for the primary task of political and empirical analysis. In this sense the theoretical project is subordinate, limited, clarificatory, but has its uses.

Part 2
Studies

3 'Really useful knowledge': radical education and working-class culture, 1790-1848

Richard Johnson

Introduction

One of the most interesting developments in working-class history has been the rediscovery of popular educational traditions, the springs of action of which owed little to philanthropic, ecclesiastical or state provision. For a long time these traditions remained hidden, though they appear in some early social histories, especially those written in one period of radical education (1890s to 1920s) about another (1790s to 1840s).[1] But it was not until the 1960s that more fully researched accounts appeared, forming part of the general recovery of early working-class radicalism. In 1960 Brian Simon's *Studies in the History of Education* drew attention to the continuity and the liveliness of independent popular education from Jacobinism to Chartism. In 1961, J.F.C. Harrison's *Learning and Living* examined traditions of adult self-education in one locality. Harold Silver's important book, *The Concept of Popular Education* (1965), looked at 'developments in attitudes to the education of the people' more generally, but focused especially on Owen and Owenism, Thompson's *The Making of the English Working Class* (1963) permitted a fuller contextualization of others' findings, but also stressed the intellectual character of early-nineteenth-century radicalism and the role of 'the articulate consciousness of the self-taught'.[2] These themes have become more explicit in later studies of Owenism and Chartism and of the radical press, the main 'educational' medium.[3] Related to radical traditions, but not yet connected in the historiography, were other educational resources which have been receiving increasing attention from historians - especially the extent and uses of private schools.[4] Some recent studies of Sunday schools have shown the co-existence of schools under popular control with more clearly philanthropic institutions.[5] There is, however, no adequate study of the other important popular educational resource: the working-class family itself.

The radical press remains the obvious route of entry into popular educational practices and dilemmas. It was extremely articulate, indeed talkative, providing a weekly set of commentaries on everyday life and politics. Although it is the main source for what follows, this use is in itself problematic, posing additional questions which must be answered *en route*. For we cannot assume that the attitudes of radical leaders and writers were those of 'the workers' (any more than we can assume that radicalism was 'unrepresentative' or the downwards extension of middle-class 'ideas').[6] For one thing, radicals differed a lot on some essential matters. For another, popular opinion itself was not homogeneous. Moreover, radical leaders were clearly involved in a process that was part mediation or expression of some popular feelings, and part a forming or 'education' of them, an attempt to achieve, from very diverse materials, some unity of will and direction. This necessarily involved fostering some tendencies and opposing others. The image of the educator or 'schoolmaster' is itself interesting here. It was one of the commonest guises adopted by radical journalists.[7] Though it was an identity often adopted jokingly and as a conscious play upon Henry Brougham's populist 'schoolmaster abroad' speeches of the 1820s, it was an image that constructed some distance between 'teachers' and 'pupils', despite the involvement in a common enterprise. It is important, then, to understand the particular position of leaders and journalists within radical movements and, more generally, within the popular classes as a whole. It is necessary, in other words, to face squarely the problem of the 'popularity' of radicalism. This is an especially important question for the concerns of this essay, which puzzles around the relation between various kinds of radicalism, understood as 'educative' or transformative ideologies, and the conditions of existence and lived culture of some of the groups which radicalism addressed. But first it is necessary to describe some salient features of radical education over this period, concentrating, at first, on some common elements. Later we shall look, more discriminatingly, at some internal differences and changes over time.

The radical dilemma

There were four main aspects to 'radical education'. First, radicals conducted a running critique of all forms of 'provided' education. This covered the whole gamut of schooling enterprises from clerically dominated Anglican Sunday schools, through Cobbett's 'Bell and Lancaster work', to the state-aided (and usually Anglican) public day schools of the mid century. It also embraced all the institutes, clubs and media designed to influence the older pupil - everything from tracts to mechanics institutes. Plans for a more centralized state system of schooling were also opposed, a feature to which we will return. This tradition, then, was sharply oppositional: it revolved around a contestation of orthodoxies (and some unorthodoxies too) both in theory and practice. Nor was this critique limited to formally 'educational' institutions. In its later phases radicalism developed a practical grasp and a theoretical understanding of cultural and ideological struggle in a more general sense.

The second main feature was the development of alternative educational goals. At one level these embraced a vision of a whole alternative future - a future in which educational utopias, among other needs, could actually be achieved. At another, radicalism developed its own curricula and pedagogies, its own definition of 'really useful knowledge', a characteristically radical *content*, a sense of what it was really important to know.

Thirdly, radicalism conducted an important internal debate about education as a political strategy or as a means of changing the world. Like most aspects of counter-education, this debate was also directed at dominant middle-class conceptions of the relation between education and politics, especially the argument that 'national education' was a necessary condition for the granting of universal suffrage. But it expressed real radical dilemmas too.

Finally, radical movements developed a vigorous and varied educational practice. The distinctive feature was, at first sight, an emphasis upon informing mature understandings and upon the education of men and women as adult citizens of a more just social order. But radicals were also concerned with men and women as educators of their own children and they improvised forms for this task too. It might, however, be truer to say that the child-adult distinction was itself less stressed in this tradition, or in parts of it, than in the contemporary middle-class culture of childhood. This is one reason why, in what follows, no large distinction is made between the education of 'children' and 'adults'. Such a distinction is not found in nature by educators, but has actually, in large part, been constructed.

We can move beyond a rather descriptive listing like this by seeing these elements as aspects of a particular, lived, dilemma. This dilemma was not unique to early nineteenth-century radicals. It is arguable that it represents the *typical* popular educational dilemma under capitalist social conditions. Nineteenth-century radicals, however, certainly experienced it with a particular sharpness. On the one hand, they valued the acquisition of knowledge very highly indeed, often with a quite abstract passion. Knowledge or 'enlightenment' was *generally* sought: it was a good in itself, a use value. This passion can be traced in many working-class autobiographies in which the fervent 'pursuit of knowledge' always looms large, in the language and educational stance of the unstamped press, in the popular reception of quite abstract texts, and in an educational rhetoric as exalted and sometimes as high-flown as the more familiar Broughamite language of middle-class liberals:

Self-reformation is the only reform that will establish the happiness of mankind. Man must be taught to know what are, as well as what are not his rights; he must learn the dependence of his happiness on the happiness of his fellow-creatures; his mind must be cleansed of all the many and pernicious prejudices, which, when it was too weak to resist their influence, even at the time of its birth, took root around it, and have hitherto choked up its real nature and hidden from it the lights of truth; he must be made to love, instead of fearing - to pity, instead of blaming - to reason, instead of listening - to be convinced, instead of believing - and, above all, he must know his weakness as an individual, and his strength in proportion only as he UNITES and co-operates with others.[8]

At the same time, however, radicals were aware of the poverty of educational resources to hand - a recognition often enforced by personal experience. This was partly a quantitative scarcity - lack of schools, lack of books, lack of energy, lack of time. But there was also a qualitative question involved. In the course of the period some of the quantitative deficiencies were supplied: certainly from the 1830s there was a growth, in real terms, of educational facilities of the provided kind, if not of opportunities for their use. Yet as 'facilities' grew, the dilemma actually deepened. The quality of what was on offer never matched the aspirations. Far indeed from promising liberation, provided education threatened subjection. It seemed at best a laughable and irrelevant divergence (*useless* knowledge in fact); or, at worst, a species of tyranny, an outward extension of the power of factory master, or priest, or corrupt state apparatus. There is a continuity of comment of this kind from Paine's initial warnings on the educational tendencies of hereditary monarchies and established religions to the caveats of the *Northern Star* on government education schemes. Paine taught radicals that monarchy, being based on so irrational a device as inheritance, tended to 'buy reason up' and that priests were employed to keep the people ignorant.[9] Cobbett, the original de-schooler, extended this to cover schools and schoolmasters. Note the industrial and political analogies:

He is their over-looker; he is a spy upon them; his authority is maintained by his absolute power of punishment; the parent commits them to that power; to be taught is to be held in restraint; and, as the sparks fly upwards, the teaching and restraint will not be divided in the estimation of the boy.[10]

Early radical journalists put each new educational innovation into a place already prepared for it in Painite theory. Schooling was not about 'political education' at all, not about 'rights' and 'liberties'; it was about 'servility', 'slavery' and 'surveillance', about government spies in every parish, about the tyranny of the schoolroom. This theme was elaborated in a hundred ingenious ways: reporting injustice in individual schools, parodying hymns, catechisms and teaching methods, exposing Dr Bell's sinecure, stressing the ideological rationale of schooling by which all evils were ascribed to 'popular ignorance'.[11] By the 1830s new forms of provided education had appeared, especially mechanics institutes, infant schools and the Society for the Diffusion of Useful Knowledge (SDUK), some of which were less obviously 'knowledge-denying' than tracts or monitorial schools. Yet radicals maintained a critical opposition. The SDUK was universally ridiculed: infant schools were attacked by Owenites (as a corruption of Owen's ideals) and parodied in the Chartist press;[12] and mechanics institutes, the most popular of the innovations, were very cautiously evaluated and, on the ground, openly opposed or instrumentally used.[13] *The English Chartist Circular*'s comment on the SDUK was typical:

Their determination is to stifle inquiry respecting the great principles which question their right to larger shares of the national produce than those which the physical producers of the wealth themselves enjoy.[14]

There was also a host of jokes on all possible variants of the epithet 'useful knowledge'.

In conformity with the advice of Lord Brougham and the Useful Knowledge Society, the Milton fishermen, finding their occupation gone, have resolved to become capitalists forthwith.[15]

'Why', it was asked, 'did not the lass Victoria learn *really* useful knowledge by being apprenticed to a milliner?'[16] 'What' asked the *Poor Man's Guardian*, 'is useful *ignorance*? - ignorance useful to constitutional tyrants.'[17] One editor of the Unstamped even produced a one-off issue of a little thing called 'The Penny Comic Magazine of an Amorous, Clamorous, Uproarious and Glorious Society for the Diffusion of Broad Grins'.[18]

It was '*really* useful knowledge', then, that was important. But 'education-mongers' offered the opposite. They didn't offer 'education' at all; only, in Cobbett's coinage, 'Heddekashun', a very different thing.[19] So how was really useful knowledge to be got? How were radicals to educate themselves, their children and their class within cramping limits of time, and income? The main answer for the whole of this period was by their own collective enterprise. The preferred strategy was substitutional. They were to do it themselves. A series of solutions of this kind were improvised, all resourceful, though none wholly adequate. Radical education may be understood as the history of these attempts.

Forms

The key feature was *in*formality. Certainly, Owenites and Chartists did found their own educational institutions and even planned a whole alternative system. Secular Sunday schools and Owenite Halls of Science, for instance, represent the most visible, formalized (and best documented) aspects of activity. They remain extremely interesting. Yet to concentrate on counter-institutions would be seriously to misread the character of the radical response and the nature of the transition in the practices of cultural reproduction through which working people were living. There is a danger, too, of separating out 'the educational' and constructing a story parallel to but different from the usual tales of schools and colleges.[20] Radical education was not just different in content from orthodox schooling: its formal principles were different. It was constructed in a wholly different way. There is also a temptation to exaggerate the extent and, especially, the permanence of such institutions in collusion with the invariably euphoric reporting of their activities.

Typically, then, educational pursuits were not separated out and labelled 'school' or 'institute' or even 'rational recreation'. They did not typically occur in purpose-built premises or places appropriated for one purpose. The typical forms were improvised, haphazard and therefore ephemeral, having little permanent existence beyond the more immediate needs of individuals and groups. Educational forms were closely related to other activities or inserted within them, temporally and spatially. Men and women learned as they acted and were encouraged to teach their children, too, out of an accumulated experience. The distinction between 'education' (i.e. school) and not-education-at-all (everything outside school) was certainly in the process of construction in this period, but radicals breached it all the time. As George Jacob Holyoake put it, 'knowledge lies everywhere to hand for those who observe and think'.[21] It lay in nature, in a few much-prized books, but above all in the social circumstances of everyday life.

Radical education cannot be understood aside from inherited educational resources. It rested on this basis but also developed and enriched it. We mean the whole range of indigenous educational resources, indigenous in the sense that they were under popular control or within the reach of some popular contestation. Struggle of some kind was possible, of course, in every type of school or institute but there were also whole areas that were relatively immune from direct intervention or compulsion by capital or capital's agencies. We include, then, the educational resources of family, neighbourhood and even place of work, whether within the household or outside it, the acquisition of literacy from mothers or fathers, the use of the knowledgeable friend or neighbour, or the 'scholar' in neighbouring town or village, the work-place discussion and formal and informal apprenticeships, the extensive networks of private schools and, in many cases, the local Sunday schools, most un-school-like of the new devices, excellently adapted to working-class needs.

On top of this legacy, which in nineteenth-century conditions was very fragile, radicals made their own cultural inventions. These included the various kinds of communal reading and discussion groups, the facilities for newspapers in pub, coffee house or reading room, the broader cultural politics of Chartist or Owenite branch-life, the institution of the travelling lecturer who, often indistinguishable from 'missionary' or demagogue, toured the radical centres, and, above all, the radical press, the most successful radical invention and an extremely flexible (and therefore ubiquitous) educational form.

The product of these two levels of activity may best be thought of as a series of educational networks. 'Network' is a better word than 'system', suggesting a limited availability, fragile existence and a highly contingent use. The ability to use them, even at high points of radical activity, was always heavily dependent on chance individual combinations of more structural features. Accordingly, the working-class intellectual was (and is) a rare creation. The fully educated working man and, still more, working woman was, in Thomas Wright's phrase, 'an accidental being'.[22]

We have, however, many accounts of such people, for they often wrote about their lives. It is worth tracing through a few individual histories, not to present them as representative, but to illustrate the place of the various elements as we have mentioned in a kind of educational progression. It is in autobiographies, besides, that we have the clearest evidence of networks and their use.

Biographies

Parents, relations and friends were a crucial initial influence. Samuel Bamford's parents bestowed on their children 'a sort of daily fireside education'.[23] It was his father - a 'superior man', a weaver, a Painite, once a private schoolmaster - who implanted in the future radical a predisposition towards politics. Bamford, typically, was sure he had learned more at home than at school, regretting only his father's refusal to let him learn Latin.[24] William Lovett's educational experiences commenced with a disciplinarian Methodist mother and a great-grandmother of eighty who taught him to read.[25] Joseph Gutteridge, silk-weaver and amateur scientist, owed much to a schoolmaster uncle, a father who 'always carefully helped me' and the freedom to botanize in the fields and lanes around Coventry.[26] Roland Detroisier, the radical lecturer, was brought up by a Swedenborgian tailor who established his fertile contact with the Sunday schools of that sect.[27] 'My father', wrote John Wood, son of a West Riding weaver, 'being able to read and write a little taught me all he knew.'[28] But, like other lads, John also took lessons, *gratis*, from friends who, for instance, knew more arithmetic than he. We might note, in passing, that something more is suggested in these cases than the generalization that parental influence is enormously important in forming the interests and character of children. More interesting are the historical (and historically changing) conditions in which, say, fathers could quite commonly teach their sons to read, a practice which requires both an inherited literacy and time for its reproduction.

The educational resources of home and neighbours were invariably supplemented by some form of schooling. Schooling was common but took different forms, differently used. Dame schools and private schools, for instance, were quite casually used. When public or charity schools were also included they were used in much the same way, were changed often and were left early. Tutelage under any one schoolteacher in any one school was, in the total sum of educational experiences, usually quite marginal. The major exception here, in some cases, was Sunday schooling, which seems to have been more likely to create an abiding loyalty than any other form of contemporary schooling. Thus, George Jacob Holyoake, after attending dame schools in fits and starts, went to a Methodist Sunday school for five years, later joining John Collins, another Birmingham Chartist and Co-operator, teaching Sunday school at Harborne.[29] Bamford attended several Sunday schools and two different free grammar schools; J. Passmore Edwards, later a radical journalist, learned the three Rs at 3d. a week in a school kept by an injured ex-tin miner.[30] Julian Harney, the revolutionary Chartist, was, exceptionally, educated at the Boys' Naval School at Greenwich in the expectation that he would become a merchant sailor.[31] Gutteridge remembered with affection a Quaker dame who helped him to read newspapers by the age of seven, but suffered under a savage schoolmaster at a local charity school.[32] Lovett's mother sent him off to school after school, strictly enforcing attendance. He went to 'all the dame schools in the town', two private schools with severe, even sadistic masters, and ended up at a local Anglican school.[33] This somewhat experimental approach to schooling was, according to later official reports, a not uncommon one: some respectable working-class parents certainly sought a better school by a process of trial and error.

One of the most interesting aspects of the relation of radicalism and the education of children is the quite pervasive figure of the radical schoolmaster or mistress. The common philanthropic distrust of the intelligent but unsupervised teacher of working-class loyalties undoubtedly had a basis in fact.[34] Schoolmaster was quite a common occupation among prominent radicals.[35] Teaching was indeed an obvious resource for an intelligent, self-educated man or woman especially if he or she had already fallen foul of employers or other authorities. Two examples must suffice to illustrate the way in which such people actually became schoolteachers, either full-time or as a bye-employment.

Mary Smith, radical schoolmistress of Carlisle, was the daughter of a rural artisan, a shoemaker, in a Gloucester village. She could not remember a time when she could not read and her father took pains to provide her with books from second-hand sales.[36] Even so, she went to a string of schools, ending with one of 'higher grade' run by Methodist ladies who stressed deportment and polite accomplishments. Unmarried and with characteristic independence, she left home and, in the 1840s, set up school in Carlisle. Supporting herself by teaching farmers' daughters, she soon developed an alliance with some local workers, sharing many of their political enthusiasms. She attended lectures by James Silk Buckingham and by Henry Vincent, of whom she became an enthusiastic supporter.[37] She rejoiced 'with the best when unkingly kings were uncrowned' in 1848, and later took to freelance, crusading journalism and became involved in the campaign against the Contagious Diseases Act. Violently anti-Tory and not afraid to offend the orthodox religions, she gave secular lectures to working women on Sundays and helped in evening schools.[38] One imagines she had something useful to teach.

Roger Langdon's father was a parish clerk and Sunday school teacher but sent the boy off to work under a brutal ploughman at the age of eight.[39] He ran away and after many wanderings, became a railwayman and eventually, in 1867, a stationmaster. He was a self-taught amateur astronomer, making his own telescopes. He never went to school himself, but 'somehow or other' learnt to write. For most of their married life, he and his wife ran a private school, a practice begun for the education of their own children. His wife taught reading, writing, arithmetic, geography and sewing, while Roger taught scripture, provided scientific apparatus and made the benches for the schoolroom.

His teaching [recorded his daughter] was unorthodox and advanced, and he always gave us plenty to think about. When later on we went to school at Taunton we found ourselves in most subjects in advance of children who attended schools in the town.[40]

Two main factors seem to have been important in maintaining an educational progression once the influence of parents or schoolteachers came to an end. The passion for reading was sometimes expressed in a catholic appetite for print (as in the famous case of Thomas Cooper) or in the desire to devour, and preferably to possess, a very particular book.[41] But the reading habit itself needed to be supported by some kind of fellowship in the effort to understand. This might be associated with religious questioning, a very common feature in youth, or with accounting for ordinary conditions of life, or might happen in a less self-conscious way in the course of ordinary sociality. For George Howell, for example, who learned his later liberalism within a radical culture, it was discussion with his mates in a shoemaker's workshop which provided the stimulus. The radical press, in this case as very often, furnished texts of debate, bridging a more private educational experience and the more public world of a movement.[42] (Mayhew's typification of London trades by 'intelligence' suggests that an education at the work-place was, where conditions still allowed, quite common). From this point on 'the educational' becomes indistinguishable from more general currents in radical culture and the approach via individuals distorts a more collective pattern, in which 'living' and 'learning' are hard to disentangle. The most important experiences were those that have been examined by students of the cultural life of 'infidelity', the more heterodox forms of religion and especially Sunday school teaching, the local life of radicalism, Owenism and Chartism. Thus Holyoake, under the influence of the Birmingham Owenites and Unitarians, became a social missionary, while Lovett, Cooper and Harney brought very different attributes to Chartism. Gutteridge, still pondering on nature, read Voltaire, Volney, Paine and Owen and joined a group of free-thinkers. A later generation, following Bamford in many ways, brought a characteristically educational orientation to popular liberalism.

Press

It was, perhaps, the press, in each distinctive phase, that epitomized the forms of radical education. Its general historical importance is now well established. In the first phase it was the main source of unity: '1816-1820 were, above all, years in which popular Radicalism took its style from the hand-press and the weekly periodical.'[43] The unstamped press from 1830 to 1836 was both an educative force, developing much later Chartist theory, and a practical example of the struggle against unjust laws and oppressive government.[44] More recently, it has been established that the press was important within the dynamics of Chartism itself and that 'the establishment of a national newspaper [the *Northern Star*] was a vital prerequisite to the emergence of the Chartist party'.[45]

The political importance of the press was closely linked to its versatility as an educational form. It was a resource that could be used with great flexibility. It could be carefully studied and pondered over, as the more expository parts of, say, the *Poor Man's Guardian* must have been. It could be read aloud in declamatory style in pub or public place as Cobbett's or O'Connor's addresses were.[46] It reached its 'pupils' at different levels of literacy and preparedness for study. The conjunction, it is true, sounds somewhat paradoxical: because of our experience of the modern popular press, we are not used to thinking of a newspaper as an educative medium. An example may convince. We can take the *Northern Star* as the hardest case, the most newspaperly of the radical media and that with the strongest reputation for sheer demagoguery.

The *Star* was certainly a newspaper. It 'could complete with any adversary for coverage', using paid journalists and local correspondents.[47] It remains, as a result, the best source for the study of Chartism everywhere. Yet the *Star* was also saturated with an educational content, even if we interpret 'education' in the most conventional sense. It contained regular advertisements and reviews of radical literature, drew attention to travelling lecturers likely to appeal to popular audiences, noted prosecutions of flogging schoolmasters (presumably to warn readers off such offenders) and published Charles Dickens's exposé of boarding schools from *Nicholas Nickleby*.[48] It gave special attention to Sunday schools, noting the opening of new ones, reporting on meetings of Sunday school teachers and covering the doings of Sunday school unions in Chartist localities. It supported the fund-raising efforts of schools belonging to the more adventurous chapels and sects.[49] It carried reports of Sunday school festivals and outings. In June 1838, for instance, it printed an account of the festival at Keighley, noting a Radical presence in the usual procession through the town: 'the most conspicuous was the Providence, or as it has been charitably denominated by its pious neighbours, the Infidel Sunday School'. The children were preceded by an 'excellent band' and a banner carrying the words 'No Sin to Write'.[50] O'Connor, in his strenuous tours of branches of the National Charter Association, often noted and praised their educational efforts, including those for children.[51] In all these ways, quite aside from its 'teaching', we can certainly see the *Star* as an educational medium. The distinction between 'physical' and 'moral' force Chartism and the tendency to identify O'Connor with the latter has distorted understandings of the *Star* as a newspaper and of O'Connor as a leader.[52] A study of the newspaper itself does not support the contention of R.C. Gammage, Chartism's first historian, that O'Connor 'never sought to raise the Chartist body by enlightening its members'.[53]

Content

Perhaps the phrase 'really useful knowledge' is the best starting point. It was more than just a parody of the Society for the Diffusion of Useful Knowledge. It was a way of distancing working-class aims from some immediate (capitalist) conception of utility and from recreational or diversionary notions. It expressed the conviction that real knowledge served practical ends, ends, that is, for the knower. The insistence on this was unanimous:

This knowledge will be of the best kind because it will be practical. [The *Co-operator*, an early Owenite journal]

All useful knowledge consists in the acquirement of ideas concerning our conditions in life. [*The Pioneer*, an Owenite/trade union journal]

It is a wrong use of words to call a man an ignorant man, who well understands the business he has to carry on . . . . [Cobbett]

What we want to be informed about is - *how to get out of our present troubles.* [*Poor Man's Guardian*]

A man may be amused and instructed by scientific literature but the language which describes his wrongs clings to his mind with an unparalleled pertinacity. [*Poor Man's Guardian*][54]

A concern that knowledge should be relevant to the experienced problems of life was reflected in the criticisms of the SDUK and of the fare of mechanics institutes as trivial and childish.[55] A slightly different criticism was sometimes addressed to lecturers and to the more 'philosophical' of fellow radicals: a criticism of wilful abstractness or abstruseness, of the failure to speak plainly. When a reviewer in the *Pioneer* exhorted his readers 'to call on men of talent to instruct you in the highest branches of science', a fine Cobbett-like editorial, probably by James Morrison, put him in his place:

No proud, conceited scholar knows the way - the rugged path that we are forced to travel; they sit them down and sigh, and make a puny wail of human nature; they fill their writings full of quaint allusions, which we can fix no meaning to; they are by far too classical for our poor knowledge-box; they preach up temperance, and build no places for our sober meetings . . . but we will make them bend to suit our circumstances.[56]

There is a lot going on in these few pungent sentences. There is a hostility to the scholar and a recognition that his skills may dominate or mystify. There is a moment of self-deprecation ('Poor knowledge-box'). But there is also a sense of the idealism or triviality of much 'preaching' and of the absence of that really materialist grasp of conditions which 'we' ourselves (for all our lack of learning) actually possess. There is also a determination to work through the problems politically, to make the 'intellectuals' work *for* us. Very similar themes appear in a running debate within radicalism between those who argued that we remain ignorant and need to get knowledge and those who inverted the intellectual pyramid and argued that 'we' were really wiser than 'they'.

Radicals, however, also argued that their conception of knowledge was wide, much more liberal than philanthropic offerings. Education should be comprehensive in *every* meaning of the word: widely available and extensive in content. The language of universal enlightenment occurs again and again in radical propaganda, the contrast being with the confining of knowledge by monopoly or control. In one of its earthier analogies, the *Poor Man's Guardian* compared knowledge with capital and with manure:

If manure be suffered to lie in idle heaps, it breeds stink and vermin. If properly diffused, it vivifies and fertilizes. The same is true of capital and knowledge. A monopoly of either breeds filth and abomination. A proper diffusion of them fills a country with joy and abundance.[57]

A fuller formulation was that given in 1853 by Benjamin Warden, a Marylebone artisan, trade unionist, Co-operator and later Chartist.

Knowledge was very differently understood in its application to the people generally. Brougham and others summed it up as little more than honour and obey the King, and all who are in authority under him. 'You may get practical science', say they, 'but it is only to make you better servants'. Their views expressed a limited range, while our own were founded on all known facts. Mechanics Institutes were not intended to teach the most useful knowledge but to teach only as might be profitable to the unproductive, He trusted, however, we should now get working men to inquire how the produce of their labour was so cunningly and avariciously abstracted from them, and thence go on to the attainment of truth, in order to obtain, before long . . . happiness and community.[58]

The 'practical' and the 'Liberal' were not seen as incompatible as they tend to be in modern education debates. For the practical embraced 'all known facts' and 'the attainment of truth'. Despite the stress on a relation to the knower's experience, there is no narrowly *pragmatic* conception of knowledge here. Knowledge is not just a political instrument; the search for 'truth' matters.

Radicals did distinguish, however, between different kinds of knowledge and the practical priorities between them. While a really full or human education, embracing a knowledge of man and nature, would certainly be achieved once the Charter had been won or the New Moral World ushered in, some substantive understandings had a special priority, here and now. Certain truths had a pressing immediacy. They were indispensable means to emancipation. These truths were several simple insights. Once grasped they provided explanations for whole areas of experience and fact. Once these truths were understood, the old world could indeed be shaken.

Because the radical 'theory' of this period is already well known, it is possible to be very brief. There were three main components in what we might term the 'spearhead knowledge' of early-nineteenth-century radicalism. For the radical mainstream, running from Jacobinism through Cobbett and the unstamped and into the Chartist movement, 'political knowledge' maintained its pre-eminence. As a number of studies have now shown, Paine's popular radical liberalism was the most powerful continuing influence on radical political theory.[59] Yet it is important to stress the historical distance that separates Paine's world of the French and American Revolutions from the Britain of the 1830s. The changes had been very great, not least within the British state. This was not just a question of the Reform Act of 1832, the bringing of industrial interests within 'the constitution' and the exclusion of the propertyless. Under Whig auspices after 1832 the state was increasingly employed in a dynamic and transformative manner both to discipline individual capitals and to secure the conditions of capital accumulation as a whole. This involved attacking the customary defences of the poor and handling the hostility which this itself produced, both by coercive means and by modifying the most aggressively forward policies. Radicals schooled in natural right theory and the 'aristocratic' character of state and church had to come to some understanding of Poor Law, Factory Acts, the professionalization of civilian police, the reform of secondary punishments and important changes in the criminal law. Nor was it altogether convincing to attack the educationalists of the 1830s in the same terms as the conservatives of the 1800s like Dr Bell, John Weyland and Patrick Colquhoun.

Something of these changes was grasped in later radical theory, especially in the *Poor Man's Guardian* and the *Northern Star*. While retaining the theory of natural rights as a kind of moral underpinning of the demand for universal suffrage and, certainly, on occasion, speaking of the evils of taxation, the *Guardian* changed Paine's political sociology and developed a more active, interventionist view of 'government'. From the Reform Act, the *Guardian* learnt to draw relations of power (and exploitation) between property as a whole and the working class, not, as in Paine, between 'aristocracy' and 'people'.[60] The *Guardian* was much more interested too in the law and in the actual operations of government: government was an instrument of great power - hence the absolute priority of changing it and the centrality of political solutions:

From government all good proceeds - and from government - all evils that afflict the human race emanate. There is no power except that of government, that can extensively effect the state of man. How necessary - how important it is - that government should be pure, not alone in its acts but in its constitution - in its construction.[61]

The primary strategic problem was how to secure a 'government of the whole people to protect the whole people'. This once achieved 'the majority' would be in a position to introduce 'Owenism, St. Simonism or any other -ism' that would ensure the well-being of the whole.[62] This was the core of what the *Guardian* called 'knowledge calculated to make you free'.[63]

Like 'political knowledge', the Owenite's 'social science' or 'science of society' incorporated a central ethical notion and a simple principle of social explanation. In advanced versions of 'political knowledge' these were the rights of man and an extreme (political) democracy and the principle of the class nature of the state. Owenism centred on 'community' and a rational altruism and the principle of the educative force of competitive social relationships and institutions. Social co-operation among equals-in-circumstances was the only enduring source of progress and happiness. (It was also 'true Christianity', unlike the priestly kinds.) But why was Society so unlike what Reason prescribed? The explanation hinged on the socializing force of institutions and, in the end, on a fairly mechanical environ-mentalism. To live in this old immoral world was to become irrational, to have one's character misshapen as competitive, disharmonious and violent, and to learn the great untruth that the fault lay with oneself. The competitiveness of the economic system was reinforced by a whole range of social institutions. There was little indeed which did not, in the Owenite analysis, count as an ideological resource. But it was in relation to three key institutions - the family, the church and the school - that Owenite ideas were most forcibly expressed: in Owenite feminism, in Owenite secularism and in Owenite educational theory.[64] Owenism, then, added whole dimensions to the analysis of privations and a much more rounded view of liberation. It also tended to counter the overwhelmingly con-spiratorial view of ruling-class actions promulgated by most of the radical press. The *Crisis*, for instance, spent some time explaining why it was impossible for men like Lords Grey and Brougham or the Duke of Wellington to analyse society rationally. They too were creatures of circumstance:

The circumstances of an hereditary Earl, of one trained in the profession of law, and especially of English law, and now a Lord, and of a successful soldier of fortune, now a Duke, are the most unlikely to form human beings competent to understand the *real cause* of the errors and evils of society . . . .[65]

Or as the *Pioneer* put it, 'Ye are as circumstances made you; nor praise nor blame from us.'[66]

The third main element of spearhead knowledge concerned questions of poverty and exploitation. How was it, in the midst of the production of wealth, that the labourers remained so poor? Economic justice prescribed that the labourer should have the full fruits of his toil; 'labour economics' or 'moral' or 'co-operative political economy' showed how capitalists stole a proportion in the shape of a 'tax' called profit. Though such theories gave a central place to capital, unlike the older notions of poverty through taxation or land theft, the capitalist still tended to be understood in his role as factor, merchant or external organizer of production, and exploitation was still understood as something that happened in exchange. The characteristic solution was to attempt to cut out the middle man from the process altogether and subject production and distribution to communal control.[67]

When radicals spoke of 'really useful knowledge' they usually meant one or other or all of these understandings of existing circumstances. As Patricia Hollis has argued the radical repertoire was built accumulatively not in some simple developmental sequence towards the more 'socialist' elements. Newer insights tended to be expressed in the older rhetoric.[68] Yet these understandings were very powerful. They embraced, after all, a theory of economic exploitation, a theory of the class character of the state and a theory of social or cultural domination, understood as the formation of social character.

'How to do as many useful things as possible'

It is not possible to do justice here to all the elements in radical conceptions of knowledge. Chartism, for instance, was possessed of a rich literary culture. There was a widespread popular interest in the natural sciences, important in some forms of radicalism for its iconoclastic relation to 'Superstition' and 'Church Christianity'. Any more complete treatment should also consider the startling modernity of Owenite experiments in the education of children, especially the stress on the child's own activity, the width of the curriculum and the insistence on reasonable adult behaviour towards the young.[69] One more theme must suffice: the relation of knowledge to production, or what is now often summed up (misleadingly) as the question of 'skills'.

Cobbett's approach to this question is particularly interesting.[70] Like all radicals he was concerned with political education. 'I was', he wrote, with typical immodesty and a grain of truth, 'the teacher of the nation: the great source of political knowledge.'[71] But he added a stock of notions about the education of children, attempting to distinguish a real 'education' (a word worth rescuing) from mere 'Heddekashun'. Education meant 'bringing up', 'breeding up' or 'rearing up'. It included the cultivation of 'everything with regard to the *mind* as well as the *body* of the child.[72] It embraced book-learning where this was useful, but much more besides. One central concern was to teach the child to earn a living, to acquire an economic independence - a 'competence' in both sets of meanings of the word. Such an education should occur almost imperceptibly in the course of play or labour. 'Heddekashun' by contrast was artificial, coercive and divorced from real needs. It involved learning irrelevancies from books. It was a thing quite outside the control of parents and children, resting on alien purposes. It meant 'taking boys and girls from their father's and mother's houses, and sending them to what is called a school . . . .'[73]

The two most important constituents of 'rearing up' were an emphasis on practical skills and on the educative context of the home. Since Cobbett almost always had in mind the village labourer or small farmer, his prescriptions often have an old-fashioned or 'Tory' ring. He sometimes used the language of a traditionalist squire or farmer, especially when blaming 'Heddekashun' for encouraging artificial social ambitions.[74] Yet the appropriate education of the labourer or small farmer was not particularly limiting. The first priority was to teach the practical skills of husbandry and of 'cottage economy': gardening, rearing animals, making bread, beer, bacon, butter and cheese, tending trees, and, for boys, ploughing, hedging and ditching. Farmers must know how to ride, hunt, shoot and manage accounts. A healthy body and sober habits were also important. Yet more literary skills, as tools, should also be accessible to all. 'Book-learning is by no means to be despised; and it is a thing that may be laudably sought after by persons in all states of life.'[75] So when Cobbett praised the native wisdom of the untutored person, it was not to justify the withholding of literacy, a common argument among 'Tories'.[76] Cobbett was concerned, rather, to stress the value and rootedness of common sense and customary knowledge and to show the inadequacy of purely literary or abstract study. This was most startlingly expressed in a defence of the illiterate.

Men are not to be called *ignorant* merely because they cannot make upon paper certain marks with a pen, or because they do not know the meaning of such marks when made by others.[77]

By the same rule, those whom the world called wise were often very stupid. Of the editor of the *Morning Chronicle* and of others with a facility for words, he wrote, 'they were extremely enlightened, but they had no knowledge'.[78]

Cobbett's positive evaluation of more literary skills was expressed more fully in his *Advice to Young Men*, and his *Grammar of the English Language*, works which ought to establish his reputation as a conscious educator. These texts were certainly intended for a popular audience, though one that was almost wholly male. *Advice to Young Men* was sub-titled 'and incidentally to Young Women' and addressed to 'every father'; The *Grammar* was intended for 'soldiers, sailors, apprentices and ploughboys'. (Cobbett was indeed the original patriarch, a theme to which we will return.) In the *Grammar* Cobbett sought to democratize the subject and to rescue it from its association with dead languages. He understood the connection between forms of language and social domination and saw the teaching of grammar as a way of protecting the ordinary man 'from being the willing slave of the rich and titled part of the community'.[79] Arithmetic too was a 'thing of everyday utility'.[80] History also was valuable, as a study of 'how these things came'. Cobbett actually wrote his own history book, but he was teaching how these things (tithes, taxes, the National Debt and his whole demonology) came, all the time.[81]

His curriculum, then, had the same feature as other radical versions. Working back from the living situation of adults, he ended with a range of 'competences' that combined the practical and the liberal.

His stress on the educative role of the family was linked to his political suspicion of schools. But we cannot understand this part of his writing without remembering two points made about Cobbett in *The Making of the English Working Class*: his 'personalisation of political issues' and the fact that 'his outlook approximated most closely to the ideology of the small producers'.[82] The central experience in his educational writing is Cobbett the father. Moreover, he actually lived (or envisaged) a situation in which production, domestic labour and the reproduction of skills all remained within the control of the father in the family of the direct producer. In such a situation the natural way for boys or girls to learn was along-side father or mother in the ordinary tasks of the day. All Cobbett's descriptions emphasize such learning situations; learning to make hurdles by helping father at work in a Hampshire copse; learning to manage a farm and read and write letters through the medium of a hamper that passed from family to prison cell; the daring image of the Sandhill, a description of a childhood game to set beside the philan-thropic ban on play.[83] His own children were taught 'indirectly'. Things were made available - ink, pens and paper - 'and everyone scrabbled about as he or she pleased'. So 'the book-learning crept in of its own accord, by imperceptible degrees'. Cobbett's conclusions, then, appear equally inevitable:

What need had we of *schools?* What need of *teachers?* What need of scolding or force, to induce children to read and write and love books.[84]

Cobbett's personalisms were based on rather special circumstances, 'a marvellous concatenation of circumstances such as can hardly befall one man out of a thousand', according to the *Poor Man's Guardian's* critique.[85] As writer and farmer, engaged (between politics, prison and exile) in two unalienated forms of labour, Cobbett spent much time at home in conditions of economic independence. (One is also curious about the relative roles of Mr and Mrs Cobbett in the 'rearing up' of their children.) If he expressed, in ideal form educational practices appropriate to the small producer household, he expressed them at a time when they were becoming less easy to realize.

Cobbett's ideal united mental and manual labour through the father's control of production. Owenites argued that monopoly or distortion of knowledge was a feature of capitalist industry. Capital seized hold of the secrets of the trades (once reproduced within the labourer's culture) and made of their workers 'unthinking slaves'.[86] Although these themes are everywhere present in the theory and practice of co-operation, they were most elaborately expressed by the 'early Socialist', William Thompson.[87]

Thompson argued that capitalist production tended to divorce labour from a knowledge of productive processes, to divide, in Marx's terms, mental and manual labour, conception and execution. He also argued that 'commercial society' had a more general effect on the production of knowledge itself. There was a direct interest in the development and application of the physical sciences which, by multiplying machinery, would enrich the wealthy. Political and moral sciences, however, were neglected or shaped according to the interests of the rich. In the absence of a knowledge of 'the natural laws of distribution', machinery became a means of oppression. In co-operative activity and ultimately in a new world, mental and manual labour would be reunited and knowledge of man and nature develop in harmony. Co-operative activity was often a conscious living out of these themes. It aimed at re-appropriating the capitalist's control of production and exchange. As the *Birmingham Co-operative Herald* put it:

Labourers must become capitalists, and must acquire knowledge to regulate their labour on a large and united scale before they will be able to enjoy the whole product of their labour.[88]

The knowledge part of this was important: the Co-operative equivalent of Cobbett's 'how to do as many useful things as possible' was how to repossess the knowledge and skills appropriated by capital. The activity of the collective organization of 'affairs', including affairs of business, was itself an important education:

They are obliged to exercise their judgement, to weigh and balance probabilities - to count the profit and loss - and to acquire a knowledge of human character . . . . If the mind continues to be occupied in this manner, for a series of years, it will receive a practical education much more improving than the dry lessons of schools, which exercise the memory by rote, without opening and strengthening the understanding. All co-operators will become, to a certain extent, men of business. But they cannot become men of business without becoming men of knowledge.[89]

Popularity

It is difficult, perhaps foolish, to try to weigh the impact of the solutions we have discussed - their 'popularity' - in some simple quantitative sense. We have neither the conceptual means nor the evidence. We do not really know how to 'think' the 'circuit' of such effects: from the conditions from which radical theory arose in the first place, through the educational practices themselves, to success or failure in actually forming people's principles of life and action. The difficulty illustrates the need for an adequate theory of culture/ideology. Empirically, we might begin by establishing what David Jones has called 'the various indices of activity'.[90] We can assess the circulation of the presses, multiplying for collective readership. We can count and place geographically the more formal solutions of schools and halls. We can set this beside the overall geography of the movements themselves and an assessment of the extent to which they moved masses in different places and at different times. Beyond this there are really imponderable questions. How many working men followed Lovett's 'unpopular' advice to economize on drink and spend the surplus on radical journals?[91] How many talked politics with their wives in the spirit of equality advocated by radical women? How common was the practice of Sophia of Birmingham who gave her children a political education by telling them 'all we learn of good' and never shirking difficult questions?[92] How many recipients of tracts conducted this kind of dialogue with the authors?

When a tract is left me (which is the case almost every Sunday) I examine it, and where I find a blank, there I write some very pithy political or philosophical sentence, and so make them subservient to a purpose diametrically opposed to their intent - namely the diffusion of truth.[93]

How significant a contribution did radical education make to basic attainments - literacy for instance? What kind of effect did radical hostility to provided schooling have on popular patterns of school use?

From existing knowledge something can be said on some of these questions. The indices run very high at peak points of radical activity. The largest ever circulation for a radical paper was that achieved by the *Northern Star* in the summer of 1839 - perhaps 50,000 copies.[94] At such moments radicalism acquired a mass character. Radical ideas and organization could also penetrate into the most unpromising environments, under the noses, for example, of conscientious local paternalists.[95] But even Chartism had marked geographical limits. Whole communities, especially in the countryside and in the south and east, lacked organization, though it is impossible to assess sympathies.[96] (The prior defeat of the southern labourer in 1830 is a crucial unevenness in working-class history.) In the north and Midlands, by contrast, many localities had a continuous history of radicalism throughout the period, often punctuated by major mobilizations. In such areas radical education in its various forms had a continuous and lively history, supported by groups of provincial leaders. It is also clear that radical politics and cultural activity secured, for thousands of individuals, some educational progression, providing a motive for learning. Yet it is certain too that radicalism's more formal solutions did not and could not match the provided forms in extent and solidity. The dream of Lovett and others, of a whole alternative system of education, remained a dream. One might guess, however, that the more democratic institutions had a greater effect on their pupil's consciousness of the social world than a more routine schooling.

It is important to do more work on all these questions, but it may be more useful to approach the broader problem somewhat differently.

As our knowledge of popular movements, especially of Chartism and its antecedents, deepens, much of an older anonymity has been dispersed. It is possible now to identify and name levels of leadership well beyond the kind of national figures discussed in Cole's *Chartist Portraits* and subsequent biographies. For some localities a local leadership has been described quite closely. These were the people whom we have termed, with deliberate looseness, 'radicals' throughout this study. They were the journalists, the demagogues, the lecturers, the national and provincial leaders, the organizers, directors and 'educators' of radical movements. We may refer to many of these people as 'intellectuals'. The value of this term is to mark both the coherence of understanding that was developed and the 'educative' functions that were performed. We might even speak of radicals, and especially Chartists and

Owenites, as constituting political parties or proto-parties. In some analyses of party, indeed, the terms party and intellectual are closely connected. For Gramsci, for example, parties were organizations that enabled the production of intellectuals whose experiences and allegiances were, organically, those of the class which they served. Certainly some such distinction - between party and class - between radical 'intellectual' and those whom they addressed - is in this context a useful one. We may then speak of a more or a less 'internal' or 'organic' relation between the two.[97] The question of the 'popularity of radicalism' becomes, then, more qualititive and relational.

There are, of course, great difficulties in answering this question too: it needs to be explored for each movement, each locality and perhaps for each major leader. Edward Thompson's comparison of Owen and Cobbett underlines the importance of individuality:

If Cobbett's writings can be seen as a relationship with his readers Owen's can be seen as ideological raw material diffused among working-people, and worked up by them into different products.[98]

We might none the less risk the generalization that from 1816 to the early 1840s the relationship between radical leadership and working-class people was extra-ordinarily close.

One common, but not decisive, test of the organicism of a leadership is its social class origins. It is a common test because it is 'obvious' that people of working-class origin will have a more intimate knowledge of the problems of their class and a stronger sense of loyalty than others. It is not 'decisive' because there seems to have been very many exceptions to this rule: renegades, 'gentleman agitators', 'intellectuals'. The relationship between some of the radicals who were not working class and their working-class 'constituents' seems often to have been peculiarly close - John Fielden, Feargus O'Connor and Bronterre O'Brien are exemplary cases.[99] It would be wrong, however, to regard Chartism or its pre-decessors as typically led by middle-class people. Perhaps the most important feature of nineteenth-century radicalism was its capacity to produce an indigenous leadership. It is not difficult to understand why this was so, for working people with an inclination towards mental labour *had* to stay within their own class, or occupy positions of great social ambiguity like elementary or private school-mastering or journalism or lecturing. There were few open roads to co-option. At the same time an education and a sort of career were available within radical movements themselves.

The more decisive tests of organicism are those discussed by Gramsci in a 'note' on Italian idealism, though, as usual, the problems of popular communist organization were not far from his mind:

One could only have had . . . an organic quality of thought if there had existed the same unity between the intellectuals and the simple as there should be between theory and practice. That is, if the intellectuals had been organically the intellectuals

of those masses, and if they had worked out and made coherent the principles and
the problems raised by the masses in their practical activity . . . . Is a philosophical
movement properly so called when it is devoted to creating a specialised culture
among restricted intellectual groups, or rather when, or only when, in the process
of elaborating a form of thought superior to 'common sense' and coherent on a
scientific plane, it never forgets to remain in contact with the 'simple' and indeed
finds in this contact the source of the problem it sets out to study and to resolve?
Only by this contact does a philosophy become 'historical', purify itself of
intellectualistic elements of an individual character and become life.[100]

Early nineteenth-century radicalism did indeed find in the everyday life of the
masses 'the source of the problems it set out to study and resolve'. 'Spearhead
knowledge' centred, as we have seen, on the experiences of poverty, political
oppression and social and cultural apartheid. It gave a wider, more 'historical', more
coherent view of everyday life than customary or individual understandings. This
was possible, in part, because the commonest inhibitions to such an internal
relation were weakly developed. There was nowhere else but contemporary
experience from which an appropriate theory could derive: no pre-existing socialist
doctrine to be learnt and therefore no danger of the rigidity or autonomy of
dogmas. Perhaps there was a tendency of Painite theory to crystallize thus, but, in
general, there were simply no historical parallels for the situation of working people
in England from which relevant theory might have been derived. A similar
argument relates to forms of organization. Though radical groups can be considered
parties in a looser Gramscian sense, they were hardly parties on a stricter Leninist
model. But organizational looseness had compensations. There were few organizational orthodoxies either, little growth of bureaucracies, little of the more
extreme kinds of internal division between 'officials' and 'rank and file' which
were to dominate trade union, social democratic and communist politics. The
main inhibition to a notably democratic practice was the *amour propre* and charis-
matic character of some leaders, who, however, could be jettisoned or ignored. In
this sense, radicalism had little except its 'popularity' on which to depend. Many
of the formal characteristics of its education project stem from this: informality
for instance, and the 'practical', 'unintellectualistic' (had we better say un-
academic?) character of its 'theory'.

Shifts and differences

The most important shift, over time, was a heightened awareness of the immense
difficulty of sustaining radical education. We can, with the benefit of hindsight, see
this as the beginning of a longer transformation in working-class educational
strategies. From the 1850s and more surely from the later 1860s, the strategy of
substitution - of an alternative working-class system - was replaced by the demand
for more equal access to facilities that were to be provided by the state. This became
the main feature of popular liberal politics and then of the Labour Party's

educational stance.[101] Thus while radicals, Chartists and Owenites all opposed 'state education' except as the work of a transformed state, later socialists actually fuelled the growth of state schooling by their own agitations. The consequences of this adaptation were immense: it involved, for instance, accepting, in a very sharp form, the child-adult divide, the tendency to equate education with school, the depoliticization of educational content, and the professionalization of teaching. In all these ways the state as educator was by no means a neutral apparatus.

A study of discussions in the radical press from the later 1830s shows very clearly the preference for, but also the limitations of, a more independent route. Independence remained the central feature of the tradition. Most early radicals had accepted the Godwinian case against every authoritative direction of learning. Cobbett opposed 'national education' right up to his death in 1835. The *Black Dwarf* even opposed the setting up of national libraries on the ground that learning should support itself.[102] Owen himself sometimes, and rather rhetorically, called on government to supply (an Owenite) education: most Owenites probably agreed with Shepherd Smith about 'the folly of looking to governments for aid'. [103] The usual Chartist line was an inversion of that of middle-class reformers: 'national education' could and would follow universal suffrage rather than precede it: any education worth the name was unlikely and would probably be very dangerous beforehand. There was even some debate about the wisdom of a state organization of schooling after the Charter was achieved.[104]

As independence was asserted in still more class-conscious forms, difficulties multiplied. Radicals before the 1830s had tended to see the problem mainly in terms of monopoly. Secular and religious authority kept the people ignorant, ignorant even of the laws they were to obey. The task, then, was to spread knowledge where none had existed before - or only that lack of knowledge which Paine had called 'superstitution': hence that unreasonable faith in reason and in their own presses, legacy in part from their own Enlightenment sources.[105] Besides, as Thompson has stressed, enlightenment seemed to work. But radicals of the 1830s and 1840s, faced by defeats, developed a greater sense of the ideological resources of competitive society, the need to 'un-teach' old associations and the significance, as positive sources of 'error', of institutions like the churches. The Owenite analysis of society's immense ideological weight, which in less sanguine times might have bred a deep fatalism, posed at least the problems of where to start.

The second set of difficulties concerned the material conditions for radical education. There was now much more emphasis on such practical limitations as lack of time, income, rest, and peace and quiet. A sense of these problems seems to have fuelled a move towards more collective and formal solutions, especially for children, different in kind from Cobbett's hearth-based remedies.[106] It was those media with readerships rooted in the industrial north and Midlands - the organs of the factory movement, the Birmingham and union-based *Pioneer* and the *Northern Star* - that seem to have responded most sensitively to new needs.

The factory movement itself is the most obvious example of the newer emphases, for it campaigned on matters of time and the reduction of the working day both for children and adults. It was also the first example of a working-class strategy of pressure on the state to secure well-defined reforms. Of course, the educational content of the movement should not be exaggerated: freedom from excessive toil as a human right or a Christian obligation was also stressed and the factory was attacked as a source of many evils. But the agitation over hours can certainly be read as an attempt to reinstate the educational importance of the family. The need for education was often cited as a motor of the movement and factory reformers put forward their own educational schemes. These sometimes had a Tory or Anglican character but the programme of the Society for Promoting National Regeneration, for instance, put forward a working-class alternative, similar to but more modest than later substitutional schemes.[107]

Working-class difficulties were also often explored in debates with 'education-mongers' - those who saw education as a sufficient remedy for social evils. When Thomas Wyse, a leading educational reformer of the 1830s, commenced his own agitation, he had a series of visits from Robert Owen who gently explained the irrationality of his plans.

In fact, while the labouring population are kept constantly immersed in pecuniary difficulties, struggling in a whirlpool of evils arising from intermittent employment, and low wages while in employment, the amelioration hoped for by the mere mental reformer can never be achieved.[108]

Similar arguments were repeatedly put by the *Northern Star*. O'Connor himself often wrote on this theme, stressing the indispensability of leisure, the attacks of authority on popular amusements, the perversion of Sunday, the exhaustion produced by 'debasing and life-destroying drudgery', the destruction of physical health and the removal from nature. Working people had little positive incentive to learn or to educate their children. They were shut out from opportunities for economic and political initiatives. The solution was to secure their comforts and political rights first. Once this was done, the people could be trusted to educate themselves.[109] *The Pioneer* put the same argument in more literary form, but with typical concreteness.

Now mark the toilsome artisan: the bell arouses him from slumber:- soft ease invites him to another nap, but jerk must go to the eyelids, - the half-stretched limbs must spring, - on go the vestments, - up lifts the latch, - and with a hurried steep he hastes to work . . . . To work, toil, toil, till strength requires a breakfast - thanks if the cupboard hold one; - a demi-hour allowed to gulp it down. To work again till hunger calls for dinner, - a scanty meal, - and off again to labour until night. Night comes, and now for peaceful leisure. - A book perchance - A book! - A noisy brat to nurse; a scramble for a loaf's small dividend; a cry of pain; a half-a-dozen little feet held up, petitioning for shoes; fit scene for quiet musing. A cluster round the homely hearth, scrambling for scanty rays of heat. A pretty picture, that - fine opportunity for useful training! The mother half worn out, her temper chafed, too busy far to rear the tender thought, - a rap 'o the head more like, eliciting a charming chorus. O, what a wretched catechism is that between a labourer's child and his poor jaded mother! Their little souls grow full of brambles; their health depends on fickle chance; their wanton playfulness has no room to sport in; and *these are but the sweets of poverty.*

Having portrayed family circumstances in this poem of everyday life, the author turns angrily on the charitable:

Pooh! Cry the rich, it is the lot of poverty - There *must* be rich and poor - the poor are *naturally* ignorant. . . . Wrapped up in vile conceit, and ever ready with the admonition, ye, too, do join the cry, the craft cry of over abundant wages; the hackneyed slang respecting rights of capital; the enormous wrong of scorning our base origin; the wicked partiality of law; the sordid crippling of light amusements; the maw-worm whine of puffed up charity; the tract, the soup, the caps and tippett tippetts, and little leather breeches . . . . .

Were conditions equalized - 'just let our noisy brats enjoy a turn or two in your trim nurseries' - there would be no more charges of ignorance and brutishness.[110]

Most of these arguments were directed at targets outside the movement, but they also bore on internal radical debates. The radical enthusiasm for education was composed of several strands, some of them in potential conflict. We began by stressing the dilemma of the desire for education in straightened circumstances, further complicated by the distrust of philanthropy. Counter-education *was* an attempt to solve this dilemma, but it was not *merely* compensatory. Although all radicals saw education as an aspect of equal rights and a goal to be fought for, education was also part of a strategy or method. For Owenites, education (which always included the power of 'institutions', 'writings' and 'discourses' as well as schooling) was the principle means of agitation, but as J.F.C. Harrison has stressed, Owenism was 'not purely a movement to found schools and literary institutes'.[111] Similarly, in the political-radical mainstream, politics and education went together in a complicated web of means-ends relationships. Education without politics was deemed inadequate: it must be allied to some kind of power, some 'physical' or 'moral' force, some purchase on authority. As the *Poor Man's Guardian* put it:

I may be plundered of my purse by a gang of thieves - I may know *how* they took - *where* they have placed it - *the best way of recovering it;* but, without the means,' will this knowledge restore the purse? Certainly not. In England a gang of thieves legislate for the community, and it is not sufficient that we *know* this to be the case, we must possess the means of protecting ourselves from this depredation.[112]

But politics without education was also inadequate. Certain kinds of knowledge were immediate means to the Charter: all sections of the Chartist movement gave to 'intelligence' a key role in mass agitation. This in turn meant that all activity that led to a general raising of levels of literacy and articulacy was to be fostered. There was no division at all in Chartist ranks on this particular theme.

The unity of the compensatory and political aspects of educational enthusiasm did rest, however, on very particular conditions. The whole substitutional strategy was sustained by the belief that sooner or later the Charter or the New Moral World would be secured. Within the terms of this belief, the individual pursuit of knowledge or the general aim of 'improving' the whole class, or the desire to concentrate on the education of children, could all be held together. The task was to prepare for success and speed it. The larger education objectives, utopian indeed in existing circumstances, could be asked to wait. Soon, all would be achieved.

So when political challenges were blunted and hopes of immediate success began to fail, difficult tactical and strategic questions emerged. The commonest response was to hold the existing combination, limit educational ambitions, hope and work for some resolution at other (i.e. political) levels. But the history here is different within the Owenite and Chartist connections. Owenism was a protean movement that met frustrations by once more changing form, stressing yet another aspect of a very fertile repertoire. Chartism faced the problem of power, and had intermediate goals of great clarity (universal suffrage). Setbacks were correspondingly more traumatic, diversions more contentious and battles about strategy more ferocious and debilitating. None the less, somewhat similar debates can be traced within the two movements.

From the perspective of what remained the dominant tendency, the characteristic 'deviation' was to give to education schemes a priority independent of sensible tactical judgement. Since the commonest form of such schemes focused on the education of children, the threat was that radicals would become *merely* schoolmasters. This was certainly a tendency recurrently feared by the sanest of Owenite theorists: William Thompson up to his death in 1833, James Morrison in the *Pioneer* and Shephard Smith in the *Crisis*. They warned against the expenses, the diversion of effort and the tendency to 'sectarianism'.[113] But the history of Owenism is full of instances of education project-launching. In 1830, John Finch of Liverpool planned a college to provide a 'superior' residential education for hundreds of children of Co-operators.[114] The *Birmingham Co-operative Herald* enlarged this scheme: there should be preparatory schools in every town and country college with model farms and small-scale manufactories.[115] In 1833 this plan was revived by two groups. One scheme, proposed by a Mr Reynolds, was supported by Monsieur Philip Baume, a French philanthropist, who offered to lease fourteen acres for a college and give 'everything I possess'.[116] In the same year a group called 'the Social Reformers', meeting in Lovett's Coffee House, planned a boarding school to be supported by 'the intelligent and well-disposed among all classes'.[117] In 1835, an Owenite lecturer called Henderson described a plan for 'a very superior school' before an audience at the Charlotte Street Institute. Children were to board at from £18 to £28 per annum, to study all subjects and, since it had not been positively proved whether Man was 'herbaceous, gramnivorous or carnivorous', they were not to eat too much meat.[118] In 1838 there was a debate in the *New Moral World* about whether to accept £1000 from William Devonshire Saull, a London wine merchant, for educational purposes. The money was eventually used to start an 'Educational Friendly Society', one object of which was to found an

'Educational Community'. At the same time, plans for a Co-operative College were revived.[119] There was more than a hint of education project-building in the programme of the Association of All Classes of All Nations and in the Rational School Movement of 1839 to 1843. In 1839, 'Socius' in the *New Moral World* advocated converting Halls of Science into schools and the setting up of a 'Model Normal School'.[120] The proposal coincided with the debate between church and state over the Whig government's 'Normal School' plan of February 1839.

It was natural that Owenites should wish to found their own schools to show the world how children really could be educated and to avoid using the schools of Church or Dissent. In its more usual forms - more improvised, combining adults and children, and connecting schooling with other activities - Owenite schooling, especially at the level of the local branch, was a widespread and sensible response. But the education projects often bear the mark of the crankier, more philanthropic aspects of the movement and invariably involved middle-class aid and, perhaps, a loss of independence. One might doubt the value of 'superior' residential education to the children of working-class Co-operators or their ability to raise £1 per month per child (the Social Reformer's scheme) or £18 a year (Henderson's).

The equivalent within Chartism was the Lovett/Collins pamphlet of 1840, the ostracism of the 'new movers' in the battle that followed and the swinging of the main Chartist body behind O'Connor and the *Northern Star*.[121] Lovett's plan was to build a comprehensive system of counter-education eschewing the aid of 'irresponsible government' but allowing a role for middle-class sympathizers. The plan bore the stamp of Owenite influence, not least in its ambition: infant, preparatory and high schools in every place, reading rooms, lectures and libraries for adults in newly built district halls, agricultural and industrial schools for orphans, tracts, schoolbooks, and a system for the training of teachers with at least one 'normal school'.[122]

This was less a middle-class scheme, as the O'Connorite criticism went, than an illustration of the ultimate limitations of the strategy of substitution. While mainstream Chartists continued more modest educational work and indeed increased its intensity, Lovett's association became a progressive but not too successful experiment in middle-class philanthropy. The founding of the first day school was delayed till 1848. By this time Lovett himself had actually become a schoolmaster and, under the influence of William Ellis, had entered 'a new epoch in my life'.[123] Ellis, a founder of the Birkbeck Schools, was a militant teacher of political economy.[124]

But the orthodox Chartist route did not constitute a solution either. By the mid 1840s it had reached its limits. In the decades that followed and in the wake of the political defeats, independent working-class education continued; in the better-off sectors it may even have increased. But it took on more individualized forms ('self-education') or lost its connection with politics ('mutual improvement') or became the cultural preserve of the aristocracies. It certainly lost the ambition of being an alternative system, especially with regard to children. At the same time a new kind of educational agitation began to emerge, linked to popular liberalism and the anti-Anglican alliance. Working-class activists began to demand education through the state, even though initially, like the Chartist rump of 1851, they insisted still on some popular control.

Future questions

Explanations of the whole mid-nineteenth-century shift, of which the story of radical education is a part, have tended to focus on material improvements (economic trends of a largely quantitative kind) or on changes in the mode of 'hegemony' or 'social control' understood mainly as occurring within cultural and political relations. There have also been attempts to rework Lenin's theory of 'the aristocracy of labour'.[125] One common tendency, across very different accounts, has been to treat early-nineteenth-century radicalism rather unproblematically as the politics of a class-conscious working class, made or in the making.[126] We now know a great deal about the culture and forms of organization of this period, yet the position of the different groups of working people within economic relations remains surprisingly obscure. The most important questions concern the relations between labour and capital in the actual production of commodities, in what we might call the direct relations of production. What were the forms and degrees of the dependence of labour within production? How far did capital control through the labour process itself, as opposed to more externally or 'formally' through the ownership of materials or a monopoly or exchange? We badly need more exact categories for describing all the transitional forms between the relatively independent small producer and the fully proletarianized worker. The terms derived from contemporary parlance, like 'artisan', remain too loose for serious analytic use.[127]

These questions have tended to be bypassed by social historians though they are present in Marx and in some of the older economic histories. Yet they are crucial for an understanding of the wider questions which now concern our historiography, especially all the questions around 'control', 'hegemony' or 'reproduction' (in the global sense). For capital's control and labour's subordination were formed first and foremost in production. Certainly the forms of the relations there set the terms of what was struggled over elsewhere. But there are other very important questions too. For our educational themes, it is crucial to establish the effects of a deepening subordination of labour in production on the forms of the reproduction of labour, especially, of course, the production of new generations of labourers. The study of forms of the family and of relations between the sexes then becomes very important. The family was a site of reproduction *and* of production of both capitalist and non-capitalist kinds. These latter questions are only now being properly posed. Answering them requires a different sort of research, one that focuses on structure rather than culture. Even so, it is worth ending with some speculations on what structural changes our materials might suggest.

Initially, the independent tradition appears to have drawn on educational resources that could only have existed had capital's control of production and of the reproduction of labour power been relatively loose. Perhaps the most important of these resources lay in various forms of the small producer household, already partially transformed in its relations to capital, but still possessed of a space or autonomy for activities of an educational kind, including the teaching of skills to children. The educational story we have just described (not by any means the whole story of working-class education) corresponds to the economic experience of the small-producer-becoming-proletarian. The main mechanism here seems to have been the curtailment or interruption of the educative or reproductive autonomies of family and community through, primarily, the more complete subordination of labour (male, female and juvenile) in production. This pressure from the sphere of production and the enforcement of capitalist economic relations was reinforced, of course, by direct intervention into the reproductive sphere, of which the growth of state and provided schooling is the most relevant example. At the same time as indigenous educational resources were squeezed, alternative forms were offered or enforced. The erosion of an indigenous educational capacity seems to have occurred in different ways. It happened in a few trades through the concentration of production in the factory and, eventually, the separation of the household and the sphere of capitalist production. The employment of children, often a concomitant of factory production but occurring on an extended scale outside, had, itself, obvious educative effects. But perhaps the most important form of pressure on the family was through a deepening dependence of domestic outwork on the capitalist merchant, factor or middleman and the reduction of margins of time and income through the prolongation of the working day. Low income not only changed the (necessarily educative) relations within the family but also made the family more and more dependent on the labour of the children. But effects such as these would have to be established for particular trades, times and places.[128]

We may understand radical education as an attempt to expand and develop those areas of autonomy and control over reproduction which remained. If this is accurate, it is important to say that it was not a fully 'working-class' phenomenon: it did not rest on fully proletarian conditions of existence. Indeed, the material spaces which it occupied were actually shrinking. This was accentuated by the changing geographical basis of radicalism which was also a changing social basis. The early radical phases rested upon artisans, trades like weaving with relatively recent histories of some independence, and, perhaps, petit bourgeois and lesser professional groups, more modern analogues of the small producer. The spread of the factories, the deepening subordination of the outworkers, the growth of sweated trades, together with the geographic shift northwards in Chartism, gave to radicalism a more fully proletarian base. To such people some of the earlier solutions must have seemed grossly inapplicable. We might compare Cobbett's fatherly idyll with Morrison's poem of everyday life. Perhaps the whole substitutional strategy was inapplicable too: certainly its ambitious Lovettite forms were. Yet it took time to find another route, appropriate to proletarian conditions, and a much longer haul to socialism. The priority, perhaps, *was* to build barriers to capital's appetite for labour and then to its tendency to intensify it. So far as education is concerned the period from the 1790s to the 1830s did *not* see 'the making of the English working class', did not see, that is, the development of the characteristic class strategies of later periods. *This* story really begins, thinly, with the factory movement and continues with the educational strategies of late Chartism, popular liberalism and the early-twentieth-century labour movement.[129]

4 Imperialism, nationalism and organized youth

Michael Blanch

Introduction

An important area of cultural transactions between classes is that of 'youth', a term with strongly masculine and delinquent connotations. Public concern about 'youth', even the identification of urban sub-cultures, has a long history, as Henry Mayhew's description of London coster-monger culture in the mid nineteenth century testify.[1] But this history is punctuated by peaks and troughs in the 'visibility' of youth. Two such peaks, for instance, separated by almost 200 years, were the widespread anxiety over the juvenile crowd which sparked off the Sunday school movement in the 1780s and the panics over youth sub-cultures in the period since World War II. As a comparison of these instances would show, however, there have also been significant qualitative shifts in the way the problem of 'youth' has been perceived. It is clear that the late nineteenth century saw one such shift.[2]

Prior to this period urban delinquency had mainly been associated with 'the children of the street'. Their removal into the classroom with the beginning of (more or less) effective compulsory attendance, directed attention towards the 'youth' as adolescent. Gillis suggests that this was a period when conceptions of youth, as a particular stage in biological, psychological and social development, came to be fixed. He also argues that the issue of delinquency played a major part in this process.

Working-class youth appeared, typically, in the form of the delinquent. Much of the rise in 'delinquency' in Gillis's study of Oxford is accounted for, however, in a rise of non-indictable offences - playing football in the streets, loitering and public bathing. The increase in prosecutions represents an attempt to use the law for the regulation of leisure pursuits, removing the working-class young from uncontrolled contexts and sweeping them into more 'provided' leisure forms. Those who were involved in bringing prosecutions were often the same groups who were providing alternative leisure pursuits. The whole combined enterprise produced a polarized image of 'youth': on the one side the 'good' - constructive, disciplined, worthwhile and *organized*; on the other the 'bad' - disorderly, delinquent and *out of control*. Gillis's work suggests that what was at stake was an attempt to suppress or divert informal youth sub-cultures of the streets by both coercive means and counter-attractions. One purpose of this essay is to examine some similar processes in a big industrial city.

But the period 1890 to 1918 is a significant one for the study of working-class culture in other ways. As the case of youth suggests, it was marked more generally by a massive attempt to transform popular ways of life and modes of belief, an attempt not dissimilar to that of the classic period of the 'Industrial Revolution'. The characteristic vehicles of this enterprise were imperialism and nationalism, ideologies with reference to both political and economic goals. The period from before the Boer War down to World War I formed the heyday of popular national-ism and imperialism. These features raise interesting questions about the extent and form of the diffusion of imperialist-nationalist ideas and about their 'popularity'. This essay contributes to a discussion of some of these themes by examining the role of certain youth movements in the city environment. The material is mostly drawn from Birmingham, though comparative references are made to Manchester.[3]

Youth, police and clubs

The pattern that Gillis describes is, broadly, visible in Birmingham and Manchester too. The most obvious symptom was the application of both belt and petty law to compel children to conform to adult and middle-class attempts to organize their leisure time.[4] As a reaction to the increasing attentions of the constabulary, a child folklore shows a distinct lack of respect:

I spy this, I spy that
I spy a copper in his shiny hat.[5]

or, in London, 'Gertch y'mucking copper you'.[6] Such ditties probably passed from generation to generation in the communities of the unskilled and semi-skilled workers.[7] There is some evidence to suggest that better-off workers and petty property holders viewed policemen more sympathetically.[8] The conflicts between police and youth were certainly sharpest in the central working-class districts where unskilled and semi-skilled workers mainly lived.

In these areas older boys formed their own gangs. One popular 'style' of the period, known as 'peaky blinder', 'slogger' or 'scuttler',[9] could be distinguished by a uniform of shaven cropped head, long peaked cap, a line of vivid brass buttons, wide leather belt and narrow-kneed fustian bell-bottomed trousers. Weapons ranged from a distinctive argot to buckles, knives and half bricks.[10] Most active in Birmingham in St Lawrence's (Lancaster Street), St Martin's (Rea Street) and in Manchester in Ancoats (Forty Row), and organized around the pubs, they were said to terrorize whole districts.

The chaos of gang fights, police whistles, blood and buckles, screaming women - local newspapers would bring out a special Sunday edition which exacted as much interest as the bells of the fire brigade.[11]

This sub-culture represented a violent and sometimes criminal rejection of 'expected' standards of behaviour. It marked the weak transitional stage in the socialization process between the family and the school and the assumption of adult responsibilities, a time of increasing sexual experience and independence.[12] But the peakies seem also to have been reacting against other attempts to organize them. Their uniform seems a riposte to the uniforms of the paramilitary organizations; on occasions they would attack youth groups on the streets and in clubs.[13] But the sub-culture may also represent a brief moment of release from a repressive discipline at school[14] and the discipline that might shortly or already be experienced at work.[15]

In many skilled-worker families the twin effects of continuing education and family assistance in job-finding may have brought these two stages of life into a closer connection.[16] The children who were most susceptible to the approaches of Organized Youth were those who, by the definition of the organizers, needed the movements least. In general, however, Organized Youth was intended to cover the whole spectrum of social classes and occupational groups as the wide range of organizations testifies.

Nearly all the clubs and movements vied for the custom of working-class children, for they amounted to roughly 80 per cent of the child population. For many of these who ran the clubs, indeed, it was working-class culture which constituted the problem against which their movements were to battle. For all the clubs, of whatever description, a principal evil to which working-class children were susceptible was that of indiscipline. In this, they carried over the ethos of the elementary schools; for some clubs, the discipline which they intended to impose was starkly barren of imagination.

Children required salvation from the vices of their parent culture too; a second set of evils lay in the wiles of gambling, moral laxity, the 'animal excitement' of theatres and cinemas, and the curse of drink. Clubs, then, wished to direct working-class leisure into 'respectable channels', with either a religious or a military bias or both. They also existed to act as a focal point for loyalties. To their organizers, the closed nature of working-class society evidenced a self-centred and selfish perspective upon life. Children needed to receive a sense of group identity, group loyalty and group pride above and beyond the peaky gang, and well above the divisive 'working class' identification. The clubs were to act to promote loyalty from sub-group to local institution, thus to society and to nation; the loyalty they demanded from their members was but one strand in a complicated web of national identity and the connection of the one to the other was achieved in various ways by the different movements. For the purposes of analysis, the movements are grouped as paramilitary, semi-military, and philanthropic/civilian. Paramilitary movements were closely connected to the army: their members wore uniforms, carried weapons, practised drill and were superintended or officered by ex-army officers, officers from the Volunteers or members of the National Service League, the teaching profession and the clergy.[17] In this group were included the Boys' Brigade, the Church Lads' Brigade, the Incorporated Church Scout Patrols (ICSP), the army cadets, the naval cadets and some units of the Jewish Lads' Brigade.[18] Semi-military movements were distinguished in overtly trying to avoid direct military identification; their literature criticized militarism, and they carried no weapons.

Usually, however, they wore uniforms and practised drill, and their organizers were drawn from the same broad group as the paramilitary. Examples were the Boy Scouts, the Boys Life Brigade, and units of the Jewish Lads Brigade. Finally, non-military movements abandoned drill, weapons and uniform; again, however, the personalities within their central organizations were closely connected to the military, and again discipline was the key word. In this category were included the Street Children's Union, the YMCA and miscellaneous youth clubs attached to churches, orphanages, factories and local grammar schools.

For the purpose of analysis, too, we will focus on the recruitment figures for youth movements in six central working-class wards of Birmingham,[19] and particularly in the destitute wards of St Mary and Bartholomew in 1913. Manchester statistics are only available for 1917, by which time numbers were swelled by a more militaristic society. Manchester's figures are given on page 116 for seven central working-class wards.[20]

Paramilitary organization

Paramilitary movement organizers appear to have been violently disciplinarian, seeking strong links between social and military discipline. Such attitudes are well summarized in a quote from a Boys' Brigade lieutenant - himself both a member of the local Volunteer force and a chaplain:

There was a lack of obedience and of discipline in society. Boys of thirteen and fourteen tried to be their own masters at home, and in the world, going out, like young colts, without any restraint being put upon them, heedless of their duties to parents and employers, desirous only of recreation and pleasure, and callous of what their future prospects would be. It meant a growing individualism in society, and this . . . increase of selfishness, this want of cohesion and lack of proper discipline, were unmistakable signs of the times.[21]

The Boys' Brigade, like the Church Lads' Brigade, was a semi-religious organization, being usually attached to Nonconformist churches. It claimed 450 Birmingham boys in 1909 (although by 1913, it seems to have grown to about 900 boys)[22] and some 2378 Manchester boys in 1917,[23] all aged 12 to 17 years. They paid 6d. to join, 6d. for the cap, and subscriptions of between ½d.-2d. per week. Training included drill and discipline, playing brass instruments, first aid and religion. Once a year, the brigade attended a two-week camp (a martinet institution, involving days crammed with parades and drill from 5 a.m. until 8 p.m.), which cost each individual between 12s. and 18s.[24] The Boys' Brigade was at times popular with working-class children, though for the 'wrong' reasons and in the 'wrong' way:

At the same time, in those days, boys in uniform were the object of a considerable amount of ridicule in the street from other boys . . . many other things besides words being thrown at us:

'Ere comes the Boys' Brigade
All covered with marmalade;
A tuppenny-'apenny pill box,
And 'arf a yard of braid.
Keep yer 'air on . . . etc.'[25]

In their Eton collars, officered by King Edward high school boys, and carrying
Martini-Henry carbines, they thus occasioned considerable attention. There were
four companies of the Boys' Brigade in the Birmingham central area in 1913. Two
were attached to Nonconformist churches in St Bartholomew and Mary, one to
Cattell Road Mission and one to the Digbeth Institute. In Manchester, there were
six companies in the central wards in 1917, the largest being attached to Heyrod
Street Boys' Club, itself formed from a Ragged School. Parading resplendent
under its mounted officers,[26] this working-class unit was told not to act like
'Ancoats hooligans' but

we have a reputation for gentlemanly conduct. Stick to it! . . . if any of the older
chaps, however, see any lad . . . acting cruelly in any way, he has our permission
to hurt that lad. Punch his head![27]

These working-class units touched but the fringes of the unskilled worker youth -
some 5½ per cent as a mean figure for the Birmingham and Manchester central
city areas, aged 12 to 17 years.[28] Units were more popular with children of skilled
workers. Some companies were attached to the adult schools and institutes. Nelson
Street Adult School, Birmingham, for instance, had a Boys' Brigade formed in 1902:
within two months it had 120 members. Thus did the children of skilled artisans
march about the streets at 10.30 a.m. on Sunday mornings, blowing bugles ('to get
the laggards out of bed') and sporting rifles . . .

the sole object being to promote cleanliness, discipline and obedience, and to
encourage physical, mental and moral culture.[29]

The Church Lads' Brigade (CLB), although attached to the Established Church,
was in most other respects very similar. It was even more closely connected with
the military; its vice presidents included two field marshals,[30] nine generals, the
chaplain-general of the forces and the chaplain of the fleet. While the Boys' Brigade,
however, rejected in a referendum the opportunity to become a part of the military
army cadet force (attached to the Territorial Force),[31] the CLB amalgamated with
the army cadet scheme in 1911.

   The CLB took boys from 13 to 19 years old; it taught military drill and shooting
and demanded the usual subscription of between ½d. and 2d. per week.[32] Like the
Boys' Brigade, the high point of its activities was an annual camp. In 1909 582
cadets from Birmingham attended this camp, paying 10s. 6d. each:

The camp is necessarily run on strict military lines, and as the War Office inspecting
officers signify in their reports on the inspection, does provide a week's sound

military training for lads who work in our crowded towns, and who will soon be taking their place as men and citizens of the Empire.[33]

In the central city areas in 1913, the CLB had six companies varying from twenty to sixty members each. Three of these were in the two lower-working-class wards, but such ventures tended to be temporary. In 1898, for instance, a 'street arab' detachment was started in the parish of St Lawrence's, but by 1903 nothing more was heard of it.[34] Again, the recruitment from Sunday schools in working-class areas was likely to be fruitful only up to school-leaving age. It is likely, then, that CLB detachments in working-class areas would therefore have a high turnover and be composed of many younger children, and consequently be impermanent groups.

The central city area also boasted one troop of the Incorporated Church Scout Patrols (ICSP), run until 1914 by the CLB. This organization was fiercely militant:

Here at home, if you ever hear a boy crying down his country, or telling lies about the King, tell him to shut up, and if he won't then punch his head.[35]

Of the army cadets outside the grammar schools, Manchester was much better endowed than Birmingham. Its first Cadet Battalion began in 1858; by 1890 it had 258 boys[36] and was attached to the local Volunteer battalion. Until 1909, no public grant was provided, and membership of the corps (including its scarlet coat) involved some expense. Thus the First Cadet Battalion charged 15s. 10d. for camp and 5s. annually. Yet it attracted 600 members - and it was claimed that the number could easily have been doubled with financial support for uniform purchase.[37] Such units catered for the 14 to 17 year-old age group, whose members were too young to join the Volunteers.[38] The membership was drawn from a similar social strata as the Volunteers, many of the Manchester regiment cadets being fitters in boiler works, engine shops, grocer's assistants and general factory labour.[39] Its popularity with the working class might be expected to be higher than for the religious cadet units; it did not demand Sunday school or church attendance, nor did it patronize its members with religious moralizing. It was more closely connected with 'legitimate' soldiering and taught mostly drill, shooting and elementary fieldcraft and tactics.

For employers of labour too it held some attraction, for at least one unit was supported by their kind donations.[40] The change which cadet membership was alleged to have wrought in character and personality was, as was also alleged for Volunteers, thought to be of great benefit to prospective employers:

You have explained the fact of your taking these boys into the cadet battalion has some effect on their character and habits; do you attach very great importance to that?

Yes, I attach very great importance to that, and employers of labour in Manchester attach importance to it; the big merchants will come and ask whether I have got any boys that I can recommend as office boys, and they tell me that my boys are keener and more alert and much more quickly learn their duties than boys who have not been so trained.

I suppose before the boys come to you they have been to Board Schools where they had had some previous physical drill?

Yes.

Do you find that an advantage?

A very great advantage.

Am I right in supposing that . . . you attach the greatest importance from a military point of view to boys being caught young and taught to shoot?

I do.[41]

Indeed it was claimed that in Manchester, the movement had stamped out the incidence of other forms of violence - 'Hooliganism, fighting with belts and knives'.[42]

In Birmingham, the movement was slow to start. The elementary schools themselves never formed cadet corps. There was no need - as the Lord Mayor succinctly explained that:

the youth of Birmingham in the Board Schools had been subject to that system for the past twenty years . . . .[43]

i.e. 'compulsory military training' (*sic*). Since 1886, all public elementary schools had been giving a fifteen- to twenty-minute military drill session every day as physical exercise. Indeed, some schools exceeded this; the local authority inspector reported that one infants' school (Arden Road) was holding forty-five-minutes-a-day marching drill for all classes, 'including the babies' which, he concluded, was too long.[44]

Birmingham, however, had a weak and flagging Volunteer organization down to 1909, whereas Manchester's was much more dynamic. From 1909, when the Volunteers were reorganized into the battalions of Haldane's Territorial Force, (TF), the adult membership soared.[45] At the same time, and more fully from May 1910, cadet battalions were formally affiliated to County Territorial Force Associations and a Treasury grant paid of £5 per annum per company of thirty qualified cadets. Haldane's original proposal in 1907 to provide money for the creation of cadet corps in elementary schools had been defeated by an amendment proposed by the fifty-six Labour MP's, which restricted financial support to those aged over sixteen years old.

Following TF reorganization, the Eighth Battalion of the Royal Warwickshire Regiment in Birmingham began to introduce a cadet scheme; its first success was to capture three troops of Boy Scouts (discussed below), some ninety-three boys.[46] By 1909 the commanding officer, Col. Ludlow, was writing to the newspapers. He required the boys to be teetotalers and non-smokers, and not particularly fond of enjoying themselves:

The boys of working class parents who leave school early have no real opportunities of usefully employing their spare time, and in consequence you will find our cheap music halls crowded every evening with young fellows who would be far better employed learning habits of order, discipline and patriotism and in improving their physique in every way.[47]

The cost was 2d. per week and after the first thirty 'drills' the recruits were given uniforms. Ludlow required 406 boys.[48] The response was in fact very strong but Ludlow was cautious, rejecting 48 per cent of youths who applied on medical grounds.[49] And although it seems from the regimental histories that the force proved popular and soon reached its target, one wonders just how much more support it would have attracted had the medical standards not been so exclusive, nor the moral standards so puritan. It is most probably the case that recruits to the Eighth Battalion's cadet force were drawn from the children of the officers and soldiers; soldiers in Birmingham's TF tended to be drawn from skilled-worker groups. The high standards indicate at least that they were from families of relatively comfortable incomes.

Of the uniformed paramilitary youth, then, the possible total from the Birmingham central wards was unlikely to have exceeded 700 - about 10 per cent of all males aged 12 to 17 years. Manchester's figure of 450 represented a slightly higher proportion - 12.9 per cent.[50]

The cost of being a member of any of these units was not prohibitive to working-class boys in employment, but the expense of annual camp in both time and money might have dissuaded the poorer ones. The attachment of the BB, CLB and ICSP to religious and educational institutions probably tended to make these movements more popular with children of skilled parents. Organizations formed in the casual labourer areas tended to fail for the reasons outlined at the beginning of this chapter - the discontinuity of socialization - and the high removal rates.

Semi-military organization

The semi-military organizations deliberately tried to avoid more extreme military overtones yet dressed in uniforms and performed army marching drill. The Boys' Life Brigade (BLB) and the Girls' Life Brigade (GLB), claiming to be non-military, were 'formed to inculcate principles of discipline, self reliance and humanity'; they taught drill and first aid.[51]

There were nine companies of the BLB in Birmingham in 1913; eighteen BLB and eleven GLB in Manchester in 1917.[52] Five of the Birmingham (but only one of the Manchester) companies were in the central wards outlined above. Two of Birmingham's were in the 'blackest' streets - Floodgate and Fazely Streets - attached to medical missions. Thus about seventy boys, 12 to 18 years old, joined at 1d. per week in these destitute areas. Although no shooting was taught in the Life Brigades, the ethos of patriotic manliness/womanhood and disciplined duty appears no different from the paramilitary.

More attention must be given to the Boy Scouts, for the whole movement originated in Birmingham with the visit of Baden-Powell to Dale End in 1908.

However, although it had been Baden-Powell's intention that the movement should grow among Birmingham working-class boys, Springhall notes by the 1950s that it had become principally localized to the south-east and, again, was predominantly middle class.[53] The initial years were not unencouraging; after Baden-Powell left the city, an advisory committee was set up to implement his scheme. Yet this committee was overlorded and controlled by the paramilitary Boys' Brigade and Church Lads' Brigade, as well as the Police Court Mission, Dr Barnados and the Street Boys' Union. Baden-Powell's speech had denounced militarism:

They were taught the three R's in schools, but they were not taught discipline, manliness, self-sacrifice and patriotism . . . . His object was to make good citizens, not soldiers. One could teach patriotism without encouraging militarism.[54]

Yet the Boy Scouts could not shake off their military birth; by 1910, of the 250 presidents and commissioners, 140 were military officers.[55] The president of the Birmingham Scouts Association was a senior member of the National Service League (NSL) executive (A.M. Chance), the vice-presidents were members of the NSL Council (E. Parkes and R. Cary Gibson) and the honorary secretary was a 5/- member of the NSL (F. Bennet).[56] The role of the membership of this league, together with that of the officers of the Volunteers/Territorial Force was crucial in the organization of youth movements in the pre-war years. The NSL, formed in 1902, advocated military conscription; it was convinced that Germany was shortly to launch an imperialist war offensive. But it was sure, too, that both physically and morally, 'degeneration of one kind or another was rampant among us'.[57] The militarization of the adult and youth civil population, then, was to achieve as well a physical and a spiritual regeneration of the nation.

Thus the regulation drill for Scouts included 'fall in, dressing, eyes front, numbering, form fours, quick march, Arms Drill with Staves'.[58] Baden-Powell always denied military connections:

Our Scouting has nothing to do with soldiering, it is merely the practice of back-woodsmanship. His manliness and sense of patriotism would no doubt cause every Scout to prepare himself to take his share in the defence of his country should this ever be necessary, and incidentally the practice which he gets in camp life, scouting, signalling, despatch riding etc. afford the soundest foundation on which to model a soldier of the best quality. But we do not preach war and bloodshed to the lads, nor do we favour military drill for them.[59]

But the connection is clearly there, not only in drill, but in the cautious mention of home defence and in the eulogy of soldierly characteristics. More than this, the Scout was to be a 'brick' in the national fabric: upright, self reliant, loyal and, of course, patriotic. Baden-Powell despised social welfare, denigrated 'socialistic' strikers and condemned the 'professional agitators' who, he thought, controlled them.[60]

In Birmingham the numbers of Scouts rose rapidly from 500 in November 1909 to 2878 in January 1913.[61] The 'Imperial Scouts Exhibition Rally and Sea Scouts

Display' of 2-8 July 1913, gave a fillip to the movement, which increased by another 1000.[62] World War I interrupted a massive publicity campaign which burst upon local newspapers in July 1914 to raise money for more working-class units. Employers in particular were then told that 'lads so trained in Birmingham were clean, smart, obedient and thoroughly trustworthy'.[63] Certainly, Scout numbers increased and diversified during the war. In 1917 Manchester, the Scouts, Cubs and Girl Guides accounted for over 7 per cent of all boys and girls 10 to 18 years old.[64] In the central wards the membership was proportionately higher, some 13 per cent.[65]

In the central wards of Birmingham there were some eighteen troops of Scouts (*c.* 700)[66] by 1913, seven of these being in St Bartholomew's and St Mary's (*c.* 270). All these seven were attached to churches, including two Catholic churches, possibly recruiting in the Irish and Italian communities. The ages of boys in units in more destitute areas ranged from 11 to 14 years;[67] clearly, leaving school for work meant leaving the Sunday school and the Scouts. The subscription was 1d. to 2d. per week; the uniform cost about 7s. although this could be reduced by a discount scheme and paid for by a savings scheme.[68] The cost was clearly not too large for many working-class parents.

Some units were well versed at a little sleight of hand; the Digbeth Scouts, ('bounding, exuberant boys'[69]) 100-strong in 1908, recruited from a gymnastics class. Council schools were asked to send boys to the class at the Digbeth Institute, 'the intention being to pass them from class into the troop'.[70] And of course this action could be justified by the usual nationalist argument:

Sure I am that no nobler and more Imperialistic work is being done in Birmingham than that which is being done in the gymnasium at Digbeth. And in promoting imperialism at home, Digbeth is doing service to the nation and the Empire, whose policy Birmingham has done so much to mould.[71]

The military connection caused the Scouts considerable division. On 1 April 1909, for instance, a large military parade was to be held before Haldane, to include Territorial, regular and youth organizations. The Birmingham Scout Association declined the Territorial Force's invitation to join in; F.C. Bennet, its honorary secretary, wrote to the *Birmingham Daily Mail* that the Scouts were 'peace Scouts' and could not therefore contemplate participation.[72] This shows considerable duplicity; both Bennet, his president and his vice-presidents belonged to the National Service League. Their refusal must only be seen in terms of the bitter political wrangling then being waged between the NSL and the TF.

Scoutmasters wrote to protest; how could they 'be loyal to God and the King'[73] like this? And at this point the First St Paul's Troop over in Lozells left the BDSA and attached itself to Col. Ludlow's Eighth Battalion. More Scout-masters wrote in:

The Boy Scouts are no more a peace organisation than the Boys Brigade or the Church Lads Brigade.[74]

Even Boy Scouts complained:

the Birmingham Scouts Council says that the boys are being trained in a peace
scouting movement, and not as war scouts. If this is so, it was never understood by
the boys themselves, or at least those whom I have spoken to. We always understood that we were being trained to be of use to our country in the time of need.[75]

And another twenty scouts in Edgbaston, horrified to discover that they were not
'military scouts', hoped 'that steps are taken in the matter'.[76]

The wealth of letters that arose out of this decision demonstrates both the
expectations of ordinary youth in the movement and the attitudes of its leadership.
It was more military and militant than its founder admitted. Springhall notes that
in the rift which developed in 1910 between Sir Francis Vane and the N.S.L.
military 'cabal', and which resulted in the formation of the 'British Boy Scouts' as
'peace scouts', Birmingham and the Midlands were 'converted' to the idea of peace
scouting with the support of George Cadbury.[77] No evidence of this has been
forthcoming from local sources, however, and the indications are that such support
was limited.

The paramilitary and semi-military youth organizations adopted essentially
similar attitudes to working-class youth. The social role of youth work was the
inculcation of discipline and kindred respectable moral values, and the army served
as a model for both its organization and training goals. Loyalty and patriotism
were essential, the individual being taught of his duties within that national fabric
which the youth organizations existed both to preserve and to strengthen.

They attracted the support of about 1550 boys from principally working-class
areas of Birmingham centre, and 1100 boys in the selected Manchester wards.[78]
They tended to draw less support from families of unskilled workers:

. . . they deal with a class of boy who is, as a rule, higher up in the social scale
than the boy in the slum.

For in demanding strict discipline, it was quite impossible to establish a very
intimate relationship with the children:

this may very likely be a wise plan with the better class of boy who comes from
a decent home, and whose individual training is done by the parents, for his main
need is a sense of discipline and obedience. It is a system however, which is not
adapted for this reason, to work among the poorer boys.[74]

Civilian organizations

Leisure time for working-class children of school age was scarce, for over 12 per
cent of boys and 8 per cent of girls were averaging twenty hours per week work as
well.[80] Every year, 13,000 left school in Birmingham to be immediately absorbed
into the grey anonymity of factories and warehouses. For these, seventy local
committees with 1500 workers in 124 schools were set up in 1913, as school care
committees 'to furnish every child with an industrial Godfather or Godmother'.[81]
For such working-class children too, the Birmingham Street Children's Union was

begun in about 1904. In 1906, it boasted eighteen clubs; by 1913/14, forty-three boys' clubs, totalling 2500 members and forty-one girls' clubs.[82] Thirty-six of these boys' clubs, perhaps containing 2000 boys, were located in the six central city parishes.

The Street Children's Union was deliberately aimed at the children of the unskilled working class and the slum labourers; it organized Junior (10 to 14½ yrs) and Senior (14½+) Clubs for both boys and girls. In St Bartholomew's and St Mary's there were seventeen boys' clubs, of which nine were attached to churches or missions, five attached to the Women's Settlements, and one independent.[83] In Manchester, large clubs began to flourish well before the Boer War. Hugh Oldham's Lads' Club began in 1883, and by late 1913 its daily attendance in winter averaged nearly 1000.[84] Hulme Lads' Club, formed in 1893, had a membership exceeding 2000; Ancoats Club, formed in 1895, claimed a similar junior membership.[85] Then there was the famed Heyrod Street Lads' Club with its attached Boys' Brigade, and more besides. In the eleven central wards there were thirty-one lads' and girls' clubs in 1917.

The aims of the Birmingham clubs were to give personal and sympathetic attention to the problem children from the slums and to provide sports and games without uniform and without military drill - except at camp.[86] But disciplines was still the keyword: the work of the council schools in this was fully supported for 'they are the source of all that tends to uplift children from the slum'. The council schools were said then to be succeeding with little or no home support:

in turning wild and reckless youngsters into smart and obedient boys . . . the regular drills, the insistence on punctuality, and the strict maintenance of order have a far reaching effect on character, and it is an encouraging sight to visit a slum school and see the results of such training in older boys.[87]

The focus of training was a two-week summer camp; the Birmingham camp in 1913 was attended by 500 boys and girls. At the camp, three 'prefects', six 'magistrates' and an indeterminate number of 'monitors' were elected from among the children to 'administer discipline'. Smoking, bad language, indiscipline and moral laxity met with strong censure.[88] Miscreants were summoned, tried and sentenced. The respectable and conformist values thought by middle-class society to be so advantageous an acquisition for working-class children were adopted and assimilated into the fabric of these micro-societies. The sympathetic counsellors were often drawn from the middle-class-endowed grammar schools; the Birmingham Old Edwardians were said to be 'putting boys under beneficial discipline', and the ethic of the clubs was 'discipline, honesty, keenness'.[89] The Old Boys of the Manchester Grammar School worked at the Hugh Oldham club:

The mutual confidence between the embryo master and workman may be a potent influence in years to follow . . . . He would find great pleasure in managing a sports team and in 'bossing his men' in their contests with other clubs.[90]

Clearly, then, the clubs were of value too to their organizers - and to their financial backers. Most clubs heavily relied upon donations from local firms; one club, which published the names of eighteen principal subscriber firms, also added that:

Subscribers are requested to notify the Secretary who is usually in a position to recommend suitable lads.[91]

There was certainly a very strong relationship in Birmingham between the conscriptionist National Service League Council and governing bodies of youth organizations. Six National Service League Council members were also members of the twenty-strong Birmingham Street Children's Union Council and, between them, twenty NSL Council members subscribed nearly 10 per cent of the Birmingham Street Children's Union Funds.[92] These NSL Council members included two of the town's MP's, three prominent churchmen (including the bishop), ten aldermen and town councillors and twenty-five JP's.[93]

And so the familiar pattern of attempted resocialization emerges. For each club cultivated its own *esprit de corps*; in its football, its games and even in the behaviour of its members was exerted the demand for a loyalty to uphold its good name. The focus of such loyalty was a deliberate and calculated first step in socialization, in the formation of a local group loyalty, which was to be extended to the wider group of society and nation.[94]

The normal pursuits of working-class children were seen as either selfish or morally perilous. Films were 'dangerously suggestive' and the music halls were 'rotten to the core'; gambling and sexual laxity were allegedly 'widespread'. To become a useful member of society required the destruction of their working-class culture and its replacement with values which were essentially in harmony with the concepts of discipline and respectability.[95] Such ideals of an ordered society were the same ideals pursued by the more militarist youth organizations. With such close contact with the church, the National Service League, the endowed grammar schools and the University, perhaps it is not surprising that the Birmingham Street Children's Union and Manchester Lads' Clubs could not rise measurably above paramilitary youth.

The biggest problem, however, was in 'preventing a club from getting respectable'.[96] One estimate claimed that the Street Children's Union only attracted 400 lower-working-class boys to its eight senior clubs, and another that the boys from the 'higher grades' who joined other clubs also flocked to the Street Children's Union.[97] The clubs might attempt to control the leisure lives of their members, but could not control who became members in the first place.

Membership, gender and social class

Involvement in all these movements was closely related to social class. In one study of seventy-one Birmingham seventeen-year-old working-class boys, the only youth to attend church, a club, evening classes and the TF was from the 'comfortably off artisan classes'.[98] Of thirty-one boys in the general 'middle group' of semi-skilled, ten attended various clubs and went to church regularly. Of twenty-one poorer, unskilled and casual worker families, only one went to church and one to a club regularly. Economic restrictions on leisure time, constant migration in housing, poor clothing but, above all, an independent sub-culture which refused to be disciplined, kept many of these latter groups away from Organized Youth.

A summary of involvement with all movements of boys and girls aged 10 to 18 in pre-war Birmingham and war time Manchester is given in the table below. It provides some interesting comparisons.

		Birmingham (1913)		Manchester (1917)		
		Boys		*Boys*		*Girls*
		Total census	*Centre wards*	*Total census*	*Centre wards*	*Total census*	*Centre wards*
Population 10 to 18 yrs		71,880	10,390	63,000	5250	65,770	5480
Involvement in paramilitary and semi-military movements	no.	6000	1550	14,083	1100	2870	300
	%	8.3	14.9	22.4	21.0	4.4	5.5
Involvement in Lads'/Girls' Street Children's Clubs	no.	5000	1600	6645	1500	6000	1200
	%	7.0	15.4	10.5	28.6	9.1	21.9

Involvement by adolescents aged 10 to 18 years in organized youth in Birmingham (1913) and in Manchester (1917)[99]

First, there was clearly a focus of all forms of youth activity in pre-war Birmingham on the children of the central wards. The children of unskilled and semi-skilled parents were thought to be more in need. In these areas the Street Children's Clubs were more patronized than the uniformed youth. The depressed areas of St Mary's and St Bartholomew's, with 2600 boys, had an estimated involvement of about 1300 (50 per cent).[100] With the onset of war all movements became more catholic in intake.

Second, the Manchester boys' tables show a massive increase in the war in the uniformed youth of the city.[101] This increase was proportionately greater in the non-central wards where the uniformed youth predominate; this pattern is reversed in the central areas.

Third, girls received much less attention. In particular uniformed organizations made little headway, even in wartime. Before the war their non-uniformed organizations lagged well behind the boys. In 1908 there were only twelve girls' clubs to forty-seven boys' clubs in Birmingham.[102] This reflected an overwhelmingly male definition of (delinquent) youth and a key feature of imperialist-nationalist

ideology; its strongly connotatively male character. Its militaristic and leadership
models were essentially patriarchal. It awarded girls a much less visible, subordinate
role in the fabric of the nation - as reproducers. Yet there was an increasing insistence that children be brought up by their mothers correctly to become fit
members of the new Empire.[103] This may be reflected in an increasing attention
to girls after 1908: by 1911 there were twenty-two Birmingham clubs. But these
clubs were smaller than the boys' and the actual number of girls attending Street
Children's Union clubs in Birmingham was only about 700 in 1913 (approximately
1 per cent).[104] If the patterns in Birmingham and Manchester are at all similar, the
war, however, saw considerable growth.

Conclusions

The organization of youth

Before any assessment can be made of the *effects* of all this activity, we have to
place youth organizations in a much wider context. They were only one of the
ideological apparatuses at work in the production of nationalism and imperialism
in this period. So far as youth is concerned we also have to consider the schools
and a host of other more informal agencies. We have also to consider, more closely,
the actual content of those ideologies, under which the diverse agencies were given
a kind of unity.

Certainly schools could be a more pervasive source of imperialist and nationalist
sentiment than the youth organizations. Schools explicitly taught patriotic duties,
loyalty and kindred virtues in moral lessons - a practice which increased with the
formation of the Moral Instruction League in 1897. By 1908, 100 out of 327
Local Education Authorities in England and Wales were providing systematic moral
education, many as a substitute for religious education.[105] Included, too, must
be the whole range of nationalistic and religious values current in the teaching
of history and geography.[106] Inspired by Seeley's *Expansion of England* (1883)
many teachers repeated values which had their origins in the public schools. Others
made an explicit identification between the leadership modes of the youth movements and the prefect systems of their own (elementary) schools:

[The prefect system is] a most potent instrument in producing those fine qualities
of character which we are proud to call English . . . . To play the game in whatever
they do . . . to do their duty at any cost . . . to know the things a 'fellow can't
do' . . . they have all learned at school, young as they are to govern and lead
others . . . and the bearded veteran or hoarse-throated tar eagerly follows to the
sabre's point, or the cannon's mouth, the piping treble of the erst-while school
prefect.[107]

And, of course, once a year, on 24 May, these school activities were supplemented
in Empire Day. Its originator, Lord Meath, claimed this Roman circus promoted

loyalty, patriotism, courage, obedience, endurance, respect for and obedience to lawful authority and . . . self sacrifice for the public good and . . . a determination to do their duty.[108]

If to the formal and informal aspects of schooling and to the youth organizations we add the popularity of the display and spectacle of military and nationalistic events, the daily reproduction of imperialist slogans in the press, the fact that most contemporary elections were fought between imperialist candidates, the early impact of media like film and the fact that popular forms of amusement, like music hall, were saturated with similar sentiments, we obtain some idea of the sheer weight and pervasiveness of the nationalist mood.

Of course, each movement and organization and pressure group felt that the others were too militaristic, or too religious, or too disciplinarian, or not 'committed' enough. Yet what is striking across all these organizations is the degree of ideological unity. There were three strands of nationalistic attitude which link the social roles of the youth organizations, the schools and the Empire Day movement. They link through, too, to the Volunteers/Territorial Force and the National Service League, both powerful pressure groups at local and national levels and both undergoing considerable recruitment in the period 1902-14. First, there is the clear and continuing strand of *national efficiency* in the drive to mental and physical fitness, rooted in drill and discipline. But here the concept of the role of the military as guardian of the state was expanded: the army became a source of spiritual or social values too. The military became a metaphor for national destinies in general. The very illiberality of drill and discipline reflected the attitudes of those concerned with youth to 'freedom' (and therefore chaos). The established values to be defended were inalienable, unchallengeable, ordered metaphorically into serried ranks and directed at the straight-jacketed goal of national efficiency in empire and in production. Patriotism, stimulated by the challenge of the German industrial giant, was linked to perseverance, punctuality and diligence. Boys trained as Scouts or cadets or in the lads' clubs or Street Boys' Union were all said to be that much more hard-working and useful to their employers.

The second pervasive idea was that of a *model authority*. The military structure of organized authority by ranks and by levels was a structure thought to provide a model for social organization. Discipline and authority in the army proceeds from the top downwards. All of the organizations studied eulogized the sovereign's position at the top of the social pyramid, and many adopted deferential attitudes to the 'born' leadership of the aristocracy, and sometimes the 'embryo' leadership of the bourgeois grammar-school boy. Even the non-military Street Boys' Union saw it necessary to order its hierarchy with a whole panoply of prefects, magistrates and monitors. Every movement that advocates national discipline has to invest in someone, or some group, the authority to exercize it, but such authoritarianism does not easily co-exist with liberalism and democracy. Thus the adult military movements advocated compulsion of the civil population into some form of military service. Thus the youth movements would tend to discount as presumptuous the more 'lived' culture of their members, and as dangerous the indiscipline of normal child development. The political authority to exercise national discipline, therefore, needed no democratic ratification; this military view of ordered society could be almost feudal in its hierarchical structure and in its deference to 'leadership'.

The third linking belief was that in the *enemy outside*. Outside Britain there lay a hostile force, bent on mischief. The Empire Day movement especially articulated this belief, as did the officers of the National Service League and the Territorial Forces.

Unity was also given by the complex network of personal interrelations which held the different movements together. We have noted these in passing but should stress the importance of the church, the army and the employer fraternities. The military movements all had their own padres; the Sunday schools often provided membership to the youth movements; priests played a major part in the youth clubs; and, as noted above, the Bishop of Birmingham was a prominent member of the National Service League. Employer involvement should not be underestimated. Many saw a clear link between military and industrial discipline. The importance of drill and discipline for German industrial successes was noted.[109] Employers in Manchester and Birmingham gave massive support to the Volunteers and the Territorials, often forming companies in the factories with foremen NCOs and manager-officers.[110]

The production of nationalism

There are several ways of trying to gauge the effects of this ideological work - none of them, on its own, very satisfactory. Cumulatively, however, they do suggest, in Birmingham at least, that imperialist and nationalist sentiment obtained real roots in working-class opinion.[111] There is, for example, the case of formal politics. The various elements of nationalist ideology and organization were closely linked, in Birmingham, with the dominant Unionist Party. Nationalist arguments were used to attack the socialists as 'un-English' and 'a German-made canker';[112] to promote tariff reform;[113] to attack home rule for Ireland[114] and to isolate and stigmatize 'the alien'.[115] And the people continued to vote Unionist, especially in the most destitute parts of the city.[116] A further possible index of the success of propaganda directed at youth was the substantial and increasing recruitment to the parallel adult organizations. By 1911, one in eleven of all males in Birmingham aged 17 to 25 years was a member of the Territorial Force and a further one in twenty-five was a member of the Army Special Reserve.[117] Army records do not show whether regular army recuits had youth organization experience, but research has shown that 13.4 per cent of all regular recruits in Birmingham, 1910-14, were previously members of the local TF battalions.[118] The patterns of recruitment of these to the regular army is not adequately explained by local employment conditions, and there is some evidence of the responsiveness of recruiting figures to periods of royal and nationalist display - a visit of the king to the city for example.[119] The most responsive groups appear to have been the unskilled. It is reasonable to suggest that a sizable proportion of working-class boys passed from schools where nationalist values were taught, to paramilitary youth, to paramilitary adulthood, and thence into a 'peace-time' army, stimulated by just the sorts of nationalistic appeal we have tried to identify. But these categories of recruits still represent a small proportion of the annual average recruitment of 1000 for the period 1910-14. Perhaps a more significant statistic is that within one month of war being declared on Germany, 21.6 per cent of the entire available male population of Greater Birmingham had gone to war.[120] More directly, numbers were certainly swelled by organized youth crimping their older charges into His Majesty's Forces:

We felt that, if properly handled and without delay . . . a great opportunity had arisen to test the value of the Lads' Club Movement . . . . It was clearly our duty to place the general call before our lads, not as an invitation to volunteer, but as a direct call . . . which each one must consider applying to himself.[121]

Of particular value were those clubs that had installed rifle ranges and could now supply nation and empire in her hour of need, with trained shots.[122] It was then, in the moment of total war, that the work of organized youth was fully realized.

5 Daughters and mothers - maids and mistresses: domestic service between the wars

Pam Taylor

Several recent studies give the impression that domestic service was a Victorian and Edwardian phenomenon that was declining by the 1920s.[1] In so far as it persisted, so the argument goes, attitudes to servants and conditions of work underwent important changes. One of the objects of this essay, and of the larger project on which it is based, is to argue that living-in domestic service for women persisted through the inter-war period to a surprising extent.[2] Numbers of servants remained high and actually increased by 16 per cent between 1920 and 1931, from 1,148,698 to 1,332,224.[3] In 1931, 23 per cent of occupied women were domestic servants. It is true that the proportion of this total that lived in may have declined, but we may estimate that over 800,000 servants continued to live in the households of their employers.[4] Overall servant numbers may even have increased during the 1930s.[5] Domestic service remained a central experience for working-class women and especially for girls. It is contended here that improvement in conditions of work and shifts in employers' attitudes were slight and uneven in an occupation untouched by government regulation. In this aspect, as in others, inter-war Britain, far from showing a gradual and steady movement to more egalitarian social relations, remained extremely conservative. In no area were these persistences so great as in the relation between servant and mistress. Domestic service reproduced in servant and employer alike very conservative attitudes which were being eroded in other areas of social life. The changes after World War II were correspondingly sharp.

Why, then, did domestic service persist? There were, as we shall see, some clear economic imperatives: the demand from certain classes for domestic labour and a desperate need for work among working-class women. But there were also cultural and ideological supports for a system so strong and taken for granted that it seemed 'natural'.[6] These ideological and cultural features are the main focus of this essay, though it is also necessary to say something about the servant's conditions of employment and of work. The central question concern the servant's compliance and the constraints, of an ideological kind, on resistance. This involves looking at a relationship between two cultures, of poorer sections of the working class and of the employing classes. More specifically it involves the relation between two households and the girl's place in each: the household of origin and the household in which the servant was to work. We can learn a good deal of these relationships by tracing the experience of working-class girls from their own families, through the moment of transition to the employer's household and to their adaptation to an alien environment, where the servant was materially indispensable but culturally excluded.

The evidence is drawn mainly from about forty personal accounts by women who were domestic servants over the inter-war period. These include published autobiographies, oral evidence collected by other historians and oral and written evidence collected specially for the study on which this essay is based.[7] But more conventional historical sources are also used to frame the autobiographical material.

Patterns of persistence

It is not the case that World War I dramatically affected domestic service as an institution or as a predominant form of women's employment. The return to normality, after the war, often took the form of a return to domestic service: over one million women were in domestic service by the time of the 1921 census. It is relatively easy, at one level, to see why service continued: persistence was a product of the very marked unevenness of inter-war economic development both in terms of the experiences of different classes and of great variations between regions.[8]

The period saw the rapid decline of heavy engineering industries, mining and textiles and the rise of newer technologically developed industries based on the motor car, building, consumer durables and chemicals. These were located in different areas from the old staples, chiefly in the Midlands, London and the south-east. New incomes and rising prosperity in these areas of growth was accompanied by long-term unemployment in what came to be called the 'depressed areas'. In addition earned incomes were often too low to support a family in key industries like mining, agriculture, the railways and postal services. Rowntree, in his survey of the whole working population of York in 1935-6, found that 31 per cent lived below the poverty line, defined as the minimum income on which a family could live adequately with sufficient food after paying rent. He calculated that 14 per cent lived in abject poverty on an income of less than 33s. 6d. (£1.70) a week.[9] Similar results were found in a Bristol survey. Thus, despite the fall in the cost of living index and the overall rise in the consumption of food per head between 1913 and 1934, there were many working-class areas where the most obvious symptoms of poverty - undernourishment and deficiency diseases - persisted.[10] With no system of family allowances and no free medical service for wives and dependants (for only wage earners were covered by health insurance), families suffered deprivation in food, clothing or medical attention especially when a breadwinner was out of work. As personal accounts reveal, doctors were not called in unless illnesses were very serious. Winifred Foley's childhood experience was not unique:

Life was wonderful except for one constant nagging irritation. HUNGER. We knew the wages Dad brought home from the pit were not enough to keep us out of debt, let alone fill our bellies properly.[10]

It seems clear, then, that in spite of new openings for women in light industry and retailing and clerical work, there were large numbers of girls and women in areas of heavy unemployment or areas with no industrial employment for women. In such cases domestic service, away from home, was an important resource, serving two purposes. It removed the girl from her own home, making more space and relieving the family of the burden of keeping her. It also gave the girl herself a job, a home and some supervision, without which leaving home for a 'respectable' fourteen-year-old would have been unthinkable. Flora Thompson describes the departure from her village of all the young girls for domestic service in an account set in the 1880s:

There was no girl over 12 or 13 living permanently at home. As soon as a girl approached school-leaving age her mother would say 'About time you was earning your own living' or 'I shan't be sorry when young So & So gets her knees under someone else's table.' From that time onward the child was made to feel herself one too many in the overcrowded home while her brothers when they started to bring home a few shillings a week were treated with new consideration and made much of.[11]

Winifred Foley's description differs little from this, except that the child had to be over fourteen before she could leave for work. The similarities between the situation of a girl in rural Oxfordshire in the 1880s and in a mining family in the Forest of Dean in the 1920s are striking:

Like the sword of Damocles my 14th birthday approached - to cut me in half, my spirit to remain with everything familiar that I knew and loved and the reluctant rest of me to go into domestic service. This was the common lot of every girl in our mining village . . . and I had grown up in this knowledge. Now the time had come, I found it hard to bear.[12]

Other evidence points very strongly to the conclusion that living-in servants in more prosperous houses in better-off areas came from the kinds of area just described.[13] The really heavy concentrations of domestic service were in particular kinds of towns: the middle-class residential areas of the big cities; spa towns and holiday resorts; all areas, in fact, with large middle-class populations.[14] The proportions of women in domestic service compared with other occupations were low in cities with a range of industries like Birmingham.

The demand for domestic labour was, in part, institutional: hotels, hospitals, private boarding schools and private nursing homes (more numerous than now) all needed domestic labour to function. As for private families, servant-keeping was a long tradition. Starting with the aristocracy and gentry, it had been extended to the industrial and professional middle classes. It reached its apogee in the mid nineteenth century when middle-class life-styles became more elaborate and servants, as well as being needed for the extra work involved, became also a sign of status and respectability.[15] The employment of servant was linked to a domestic ideal in which wives were expected to be idle, to be well dressed in elaborate surroundings and to entertain. Entertaining was one way in which to display one's house. Leonore Davidoff points out that social and status distinctions, important in a competitive society, were most clearly symbolized in the domestic sphere rather than in the husband's work.[16] The husband earned the money, the wife displayed it and servants helped in this display. This remained true, too, for the 1920s and 1930s but with an additional extension of the servant-keeping practice. Large numbers of lower-middle-class families could afford one maid. The incomes of clerks, elementary schoolteachers or shopkeepers might be no higher than those of skilled manual workers, but their aspirations were towards the middle-class life-styles, particularly in the matters of home, the rearing of children, education and aspirations for their children's futures.[17]

The elaborate domestic rituals of the Edwardian middle class had been simplified by the 1920s, but country-house life and entertaining continued, in lavish styles. Geoffrey Tyack, in a wide-ranging investigation of the domestic running of Cliveden, seat of the Astors, concludes

There were 19 indoor staff in 1928, 4 laundry maids, 52 outdoor staff . . . . The establishment continued to run on a Victorian scale right up to the second World War.[18]

Harold Macmillan writes:

We all lunched and dined a great deal together. Hatfield and Cliveden and many others were the almost weekly gatherings of all kinds of people. Indeed there was nothing so agreeable as the country house party in a large English house. There were no rules except the necessity of appearing at dinner and a certain bias in favour of turning up to lunch.[19]

This living style, although confined to a small section of wealthy 'aristocratic' society, is significant because it accounted for a large proportion of living-in servants. Below the level of Hatfield and Cliveden, where entertaining had political as well as social functions, there were many more households which entertained visitors for Ascot, for shooting or for the 'coming out' of daughters. Families still 'took a house' for the London season, a major upheaval for the indispensable servants.[20] Professional and business families occupied large houses, often with two or more maids, while a huge variety of people employed one maid. The single servant might be cook-general, general domestic or mother's help. According to the sample survey or the 1931 census, 357,000 girls worked under these conditions.

The needs that were satisfied by the employment of servants may be summed up as the performance of domestic labour and the enhancement of social status. The extent and laborious character of the work involved in running a household in the style expected should be stressed. Before the universal use of electricity and in an age of coal fires and even coal-fired cooking, running a house was especially hard work. Widespread use of refrigerators and vacuum cleaners did not come till after World War II. Although many electrical household aids were being manufactured ('Hoovers' from 1921), many houses were not wired for electricity and were lit by gas. Tile floors had to be scrubbed; wood floors polished (the fashionable parquet wooden blocks). Laundry - washing, starching, drying, ironing - took up a whole day a week. Snacks were thought no substitute for proper meals. Detergents - apart from soap and soda - had not been invented.[21]

The burden of this work depended on the number of servants kept and the standard expected. It was a universal experience, reflected in all the autobiographical material, that maids rose early, worked before breakfast and continued to work or be 'on call' for a very long day. Evenings, nominally free, could be interrupted with demands for service and Saturdays and Sundays were normal working days without extra payment. The single servant was often the most hardworked and was, in addition, isolated from family and friends. Since labour was cheap, the impulse to save it was weak: indeed work might actually be created to fill the servant's time. In a sense, the servant was a captive employee, all of whose time was at the employer's disposal. Since housework is, as Anne Oakley has suggested, an infinitely expandable task, [22] jobs could be found to fill time - mending linen, cleaning brass and silver, making jam.

One general function of servant-keeping - in grand houses or small - was to free the wife from some of the burden of domestic work. Wives in turn were bound by dominant conceptions of their role - by the ideal of domesticity and the concept of the 'woman in the home'. Middle- and upper-class women retained this basic responsibility even where many servants were employed. The employment of servants meant that life-styles could become more ambitious and impressive: but more entertaining meant more labour and increased the work of supervision and organization. The middle-class wife, then, was also a victim of this life-style.

Servant-keeping itself, aside from the relief from labour and the support of higher standards, was a mark of status. The presence of servants in uniform signalled the importance of the family to neighbours, visitors and callers.

This [1930] was the era of maids. Everyone seemed to boast or complain of the maids. I remember girls at school judging each other's wealth by the number of maids each had. And sometimes, I suspect, inventing an extra one to impress their friends. We had two.[23]

The fact that uniform (two sets: one for morning and one for afternoon) was insisted upon till 1939 suggests the importance of servants as symbols of status. After all, white aprons were very impractical for dirty housework. Even the single servant, often a teenager, had to provide two sets of uniform for herself - a costly outlay. She might also play many roles - suitably dressed for each:

Mrs. Stratton Brown remembers that when she lived at Chatham in 1936 she had a young girl who 'started the day in a pink linen dress to do all the housework; after lunch she added a stiff white collar and became a Nanny taking my son out for walks with other Nannies; then for tea she changed into a brown dress and coffee-coloured apron and became parlourmaid'.[24]

These elements of status, and also the social subordination of the servant, were symbolized in various rituals: uniform, the uses of bells to summon service (often installed in quite small modern houses), the segregation of the servant's living space from the family's, the use of separate entrances and stairs. The evidence of personal experience suggests that these practices were as strong as ever in the inter-war period. Indeed they may even have become more common as servant-keeping spread to new strata. Certainly the ideology of domestic service was strong and pervasive. It was carried in novels, plays, films, cartoons and gossip.[25] The 'folk knowledge' of how one should treat one's servants was widespread and linked to class attitudes in general. Rules and codes were set not by legislation but by custom and practice, though they were often surprisingly uniform.[26]

Girls and mothers

Most of the women from whom I have evidence came from large families where money was scarce. The overall economic pressure on the family was very tight and this was relayed to the children. They were disciplined to expect very little and girls were expected to take a full part in helping with household chores and taking charge of younger children. Authority relations, too, seem to have been very strict: parents' words were law and their decisions final. This seems to have been especially the case in the relations between mothers and daughters. This is shown very clearly in many recorded experiences.

Margaret Powell had to go home from school at midday and make a meal for the family. She would have been about ten at the time. After afternoon school she would collect her younger sister and brother from a day nursery and do more housework at home before her working mother returned. This hard round was not resented; it was normal.

I never used to feel that I was suffering in any sense from ill usage. It was just the thing. When you were the eldest girl in a working-class family it was expected of you. Of course Mum took over in the evenings. She came back at 6 and got our tea which was the same as breakfast. Bread and margarine. Being a girl I never went out at night and my parents were very strict about this.[27]

Later, when Margaret Powell was fifteen, her mother demanded that she should go into service; she herself was not keen on the idea. Her mother (who had been in service herself) accompanied her to the interview, 'spoke for her' and decided that Margaret should take the job:

My spirits sank lower and lower. I felt I was in jail at the finish. When I got outside I told Mum how I felt but she had decided that the job would do for me. So that was that.[28]

Could it be that hard work and resourcefulness at home, coupled with obedience to a strict parental authority produced, in fact, a very 'good' servant? Parents, who had to be strict to manage at all, inculcated qualities in a girl relevant to domestic service. Once in a new job in new surroundings the girl's ability to speak up and defend herself against excessive demands was handicapped by her own training in the home.

Because this is a rather large claim, I want to explore it through several other examples. Dolly Scannell was at school in East London in the 1920s: she had failed the scholarship examination for secondary school but had been selected for a central school, a higher grade of elementary school, on the strength of a composition:

I was so excited I fell over twice on the way home and arrived with knees bleeding and stockings torn. While Mother was bathing my knees I stammered out my marvellous news. Mother said quite calmly 'Thank Miss Wilkie for her kindness but we don't think a mixed school is suitable for you'. My father had seen the boys and girls larking about on the way home and had conveyed his views to Mother. There was no point in telling Mother I wouldn't lark about. I only wanted to be a teacher. I told Miss Wilkie and she said 'Such a pity, such a pity'.[29]

The title of Dolly Scannell's autobiography sums it all up: *Mother Knew Best*. Would parental decisions for a son have been the same and enforced thus?

In an Open University history programme, Thea Vigne talked to a woman who had been in service. She asked if she ever remembered having rows with her employers or answering back.

Not an awful lot. I used to hold my own, as I thought, now and again, but not an awful lot. You see, we hadn't been allowed cheek at home and it didn't come naturally.[30]

Mrs Sturgeon was fourteen in 1931 and she took her first job in the Suffolk town in which she lived.

There was myself and another girl. We ran the whole house. We worked from morning till night. And I went there as a privilege for doing well at school. I got the prize for domestic science; for being the best pupil. So I was allowed to go and work there for one of the big men. They thought they'd got a valet and staff. Oh! That was awful.

There follows an astonishing account of the work she had to do.

It was terrible. I had the kindest mother; but you see she said, 'This is what it is to work for your living. All the others had to do it. This is just what you have to do'.[31]

As often happens in stories like these the girl defends her mother for her seemingly unkind treatment.

These three incidents relate to young girls on first leaving home, but the cases of two older women show how strong the early tendencies to obedience, acceptance and patience could be. Jean Rennie did not go into service till she was eighteen. She had qualified for university entrance, but could not contemplate this because of poverty at home. She held many menial jobs in service before becoming a cook. Yet she too was aware of her own instinctive obedience. In an altercation with a cook about carrying a heavy side of bacon from the larder, she records, 'I looked at her almost defying her but obedience was deeply rooted in my character.'[32]

Miss Maud Walton had other jobs in a Shropshire village before she went into service in Birmingham in 1929. Used to some freedom in her social life, as a domestic servant she did not have her evenings free and only got home once a month. She felt lonely and, in her own words, 'cut away'. On one visit home, she complained to her mother:

'Mum, I'm not going to stay. I can't stay there'. She'd say 'Try it another month; now you haven't been there long. Now Lily's at Summerfield Crescent [Maud's sister working nearby]. Lily's got you the job - so try again!' So I tried.

> *Question:* How old were you by this time?
> How old would I be? Twenty I suppose.[33]

But it important to stress the elements of practical resourcefulness required in a working-class girl in a large and poor family as well as the elements of obedience. Since most girls helped with housework, shopping and looking after the other children, they were allowed to be out and about. They had to deal with the accidents of smaller children when these happened. Daisy Noakes took her brother out for picnics and was away all day fortified by bottles of cold tea.[34] Such freedom and resourcefulness would have been less common within middle-class families where children were protected and had a longer schooling. They literally had a longer childhood. A girl of fourteen who knew she was staying at school till sixteen or eighteen was still a dependent child. Working-class girls knew well before that age that childhood finished at fourteen and full-time work began. Two of the girls already quoted were aware of the 'loss' of their childhood. They were doing part-time paid work from the age of twelve as well as helping their mothers. Others remember being prevented from working by mothers who needed them at home.

Mother was working at Grays in town [Birmingham] so I spent my time helping out at home. I never had any pocket-money and the lady next door asked me to scrub her kitchen floor and scullery for 3d and I was able to get to the pictures for 2d and a quarter of sweets for 1d. My clothes were what my sister left off - that is how I came to have my name down at a domestic agency . . . . My mother didn't want me to take the job as I was too useful to her at home: but I was fed up of having no money and no clothes.[35]

There is evidence of other cases like this where, rather than be an unpaid servant at home, girls decided to leave home and seek adventure and a job with a wage.

Much of what is recorded in their interviews and autobiographies is clearly specific to the situation of girls. Girls were expected to do more in the house than boys, a situation which some still see as normal. This form of dependency could also be long lasting, while, in fact, any close connection was kept with home. One woman noted how she and all her sisters had household tasks to do even after they started work. Daisy Noakes says:

John and Arthur living at home had time for hobbies and recreation where the girls had no opportunity.[36]

The main findings of this section may be summarized as follows. Girls in a working-class home were 'prepared for' domestic service in several important ways. They received a training in housework, laundry and other chores. They learnt to be resourceful in the care of smaller children. Above all, perhaps, they learnt to expect very little for themselves and to comply with parental decisions, which were re-inforced, ideologically and economically, by the fact of the family's poverty.

These features of the girl's life help to explain why long hours and small financial returns could, so often, be tolerated. It is the nature and use of the servant's wage, indeed, that provides us with the last example of familial relations.

I have elsewhere investigated wages and concluded that while appearing low, they did include keep. When this is allowed for, wages in domestic service do not compare badly with factory or shop work. Yet this does not allow for the elastic quality of the servant's hours of work. Most women's paid work had become regulated by the forty-eight-hour statutory week and the minimum wages set by trade boards.[37] But hours in domestic service were completely unregulated. Time off quoted to me and noted in written accounts differed little throughout the period (or from the pre-war evidence): one half-day a week from 2.30 p.m. till 9.30 or 10 p.m. and one half-day on every other Sunday. These times seem universal despite government recommendations for shorter hours.[38] It is important to remember that by 2.30 p.m. a servant might have performed at least six hours of work, including most of the heavy and physically onerous tasks of the day. On public holidays, of course, servants were especially in demand: Christmas was normally worked, though Boxing Day was usually free.

At my (conservative) estimate, assuming servants 'finished' and were free by 7 p.m., they worked a sixty-one-hour week which included Saturdays and Sundays. By this test, earnings for hours worked were considerably lower than those in ordinary work, though standards of life - food, lodging, etc. - might well be higher.

Even after this calculation, however, we have not reached an assessment of the girl's own spending money. A large number of servants in my evidence 'sent money home' or 'gave my money up'. This is a strong reminder of the desperate poverty at home and of the girl's own sense of duty. They were often acutely aware of the needs of those they had left behind.

Mrs Jennie Owen, one of five sisters from Wales who all went into service in London, explained the situation thus:

We had money in our pockets then; we'd go to London and every month when we had our money, all the sisters would get together and we'd pool so much and we'd send a parcel home every month - either bedding to renew the bedding - a blouse for my mother - or an apron - whatever we thought was needed - every month we girls got together and we sent nearly half our wages - not in money but in things that were needed. And through us all in service, we practically furnished my mother's home and the bedding . . . . Well, my father said more than once he would prefer to have 12 girls again than 2 boys. We'd done so much for them.[39]

Transition to servantdom

The moment of change from family home to employer's household is a privileged moment to look at the social relations of service. This was the point at which the two cultures met. From this moment the girl was taking cues, observing her employers, adjusting her behaviour and attitudes. Once she had begun her new life, she lost the sense of novelty, adapted herself, accommodated to the new regime and, before long, saw it as 'normal'.[40]

If the girl attended in person for an interview, this was her first encounter with the employer and much would be learned about future demeanour from that meeting. Minnie Cowley, thirteen in 1923, sought a job through an agency on her own initiative and attended the interview without telling her parents. Her memories are very vivid:

Feeling as though I was going to my doom I walked up to the house lifted the fancy latch of the front gate, stepped up the tiled pathway and banged twice on the door. The door was opened by a woman with staring blue eyes. 'Yes, what do you want?' she said eyeing me up and down. 'I'm from the agency and have to see this lady at 2 o'clock' I said.[41]

Minnie was told she should have used the servants' entrance, was ushered into a red-carpeted hall, past a huge grandfather clock, and into a room with brown leather armchairs where she was told to wait for the mistress.

The fireplace and over-mantel were white and in the middle of the mantelpiece stood a marble clock which with its pillars looked like the front of a building. At each end was a small statue. How different this was to our mantelpiece at home which was always covered with odds and ends! I was just looking at the clock when Madam came in and right then I felt hungry and scared.

Already Minnie was learning much about her new position and how she was expected to behave. She was engaged at 7s.6d. (37p) but had to pay her employer 16s. at the rate of 2s.6d. a week to cover the cost of her two uniforms. The household consisted of master, mistress, a son of four, a companion, a cook, and Minnie, the general domestic. It was to take her six weeks to repay the 16s. When she reported for duty two days later she was shown to her bedroom. This time her overwhelming memories were of space, loneliness and silence:

I had never had so much space all to myself and certainly nothing as posh as this. 'This must be a mistake' I thought. Perhaps the boy will have to sleep with me. It doesn't seem right that this big room should be just for one person . . . . Sleeping alone was very frightening. I felt very lonely and would have given anything to wake up and find my sisters there with me. The quiet was a bit frightening after the noise and bustle I was used to.

Later she found that 'middle class people certainly had their pound of flesh in those days', requiring of her a fifteen-hour day. She got the sack from this job for taking the four-year old son to her own home in the course of her daily walk. She could be admitted to the employer's home to care for children there; that children should visit the servant's own home was unthinkable.

Winifred Foley has described how she felt 'cut in half' on leaving her Gloucester-shire village at fourteen. She travelled to London by train by herself and found her employer lived on the upper two floors of a house in a London suburb. Again, she remembered the early encounters vividly.

Fancy, I thought, I've got an upside down job in half a house . . . . I had heard too much from my Aunties in service to expect much in the way of sleeping quarters. My room was the home of the family junk . . . . Mrs. Fox told me to put on my black afternoon dress and white apron. I was in mourning for my lost self. I was in a strange new world with entirely new people to adjust to. My childhood was dead: now I was the skivvy. I was near to wishing she was dead too. I was given supper in the tiny kitchen . . . . It was strange to be considered not fit to eat in the same room as other human beings. It was a good supper . . . but loneliness and misery had taken away my appetite. How delicious in comparison seemed the slice of marg-spread toast given me by Mam and eaten as a member of a family.[42]

Mr and Mrs Fox turned out to be kind employers. Having locked herself out of the house, failed to finish reassembling the gas cooker and having damaged a gas mantle, she was scared of their reaction to her early incompetences:

I started to cry again as soon as the Foxes walked up towards me. To my incredible surprise and relief Mrs. Fox seemed more annoyed about my miserable reaction than she did about my misdeeds. If she had not been my mistress I would have loved to hug her in gratitude.[43]

In this, as in other examples, it is the difference between home and household, mother and mistress, that are emphasized. Mrs Fox seems to have been embarrassed by 'Poll's' tears; Poll knew that the mistress-servant relation did not permit her to hug her employer.

When Daisy Noakes approached fourteen in 1922 it was decided by her parents that she would work at Ovingdean Hall Boys' Preparatory School where her sister already worked. Her mother went with her for the interview and she wore someone else's 'too big' costume and her mother's large hat into which all her long hair was pushed. She was briefed by her mother to say 'ma'am' and stand up straight when-ever she was spoken to.

By now I was getting a bit nervous, but I knew I had to face it. We went round to the back door as staff were never allowed to use the front door or front drive. The butler was called and said 'I'll see if Madam will see you': we were shown into the large drawing room. I was bewildered. I did not want to be in all these elaborate surroundings. Madam entered and asked us to sit. Mum was asked if I was hard-working; reliable; an early riser . . . . To all this Mum replied that I was. I was asked to stand up and Madam said 'You will look taller when you have a longer skirt and your hair done up in a bun'.[44]

The similarities with Minnie Cowley's account are striking. Both felt over-awed at 'posh' surroundings and by the rituals - different entrances, having to wait on Madam's convenience, the permission to sit and the order to stand - intended to reinforce their sense of social inferiority. Especially striking in both cases was the role of the senior servant - the woman with blue eyes and the butler - who received them and told them to wait while 'Madam' was consulted, a characteristic distance-building mechanism. In the cases of Daisy Noakes and Margaret Powell (not quoted here) the mother not only attended the interview but answered all the questions for her daughter, questions about, precisely, those qualities of a daughter that were held to be relevant to servantdom. Mother duly promised all such qualities. The girls were, in a sense, vassals, being handed over by the family to the employer for a small sum of money, plus lodging. On this occasion, too, conditions of service were fixed, not just pay and hours, but whether skirts should be lengthened or hair put up. In the middle classes, girls put their long hair into a coil or bun at about seventeen or eighteen to denote adulthood. Daisy, according to a photograph in her autobiography, was made to bundle all her hair into a Dorcas cap so that not a single hair was visible. She was expected to be a trainee adult servant. With the anonymity of uniform and the putting up of the hair under a cap went, to some extent, the disappearance of the individual person. All these exchanges must be reckoned of special significance when the child also witnessed the deference of her mother, the fount of authority so far, to a woman of another class.

Daisy was thus delivered into a particularly oppressive situation. Like the other girls, she comments on her 'private' space, the place where she was to sleep - in this case, however, a bedroom for four servant girls. In bed she

lay there thinking about running home but knew I would only be sent back, and I cried at the thought. Something went BANG under my bed. It was the knocked out dent in the lid of my trunk reverting to shape. From that moment my child-hood ended and I realized I had been launched on the world to earn my own living.[45]

She was called next morning at 5.30 and entered a regime of labour which seems to have amounted to 107 hours a week. For this she was paid a wage of 6s., to which we might add 10s. as the value of her keep. In fact, she was being used as slave labour. For her small pay and her keep her total life and energy were at the disposal of her employer. But she did not complain and knew that she would be sent back if she ran home. Though Daisy's case was perhaps exceptional, similar demands were made on all girl servants, and a similar compliance achieved. This interchange between myself and Mrs Owen shows the pattern clearly, especially the correspondences and and differences between home and work-place:

Question: What did you do on your day off?
Mrs Owen: Oh, we used to go up to London. We all used to meet - friends and
                  sisters - and we'd go and have tea at Lyons Corner House and then
                  we'd go to the pictures and then, of course, we'd have to be in by ten.
Question: Was that a strict rule?
Mrs Owen: Oh, yes! Yes, in London, yes.
Question: What happened if you were late in?
Mrs Owen: The door would be locked.
Question: And then what would you do?
Mrs Owen: We never tried (laughter) because we were always in before ten.
Question: You were never late?
Mrs Owen: No. No. We didn't dare to be late. We were too scared to be late.
Question: So her word was law. You didn't rebel?
Mrs Owen: No, no, no. And we were very happy and we were well fed and we had
                  a comfortable bed and to us that meant a lot.[46]

Employers' attitudes

Employers were not of the same outlook and had varying incomes and life-styles. But servant-keeping, even at it's 'lowest' levels, certainly went along with a social distancing from working-class ways of life and culture. Working-class habits, appearance and especially speech - the whole culture in fact - were 'beyond the pale'. The servant-mistress relation, then, was always a relation between radically unequal individuals in which power and subordination were continually reproduced.

John Burnett, in his introduction to the section on servants in *Useful Toil,* discusses the peculiar qualities of this relationship:

An exact analogy is not easy to draw but in the Victorian attitudes to servants there was much in common with the attitude towards children, dumb animals and the feeble-minded; as God's creatures they all deserved kindness and consideration but above all they required firm authority, discipline and the direction of their natural superiors.[47]

Though Burnett misses some elements of what is specific to 'service' - often a relation between an *older woman* of one class with a *younger woman* of another - the attitude he describes seems hardly to have changed in the inter-war period. The following are extracts from 'Rules for Domestic Staff' at Chipscroft Hall, Cheshire, issued by a Mrs Ernest West and in use in the 1920s and 1930s:

. . . that you will enjoy giving of yourself as much as possible to them [the family] never being afraid to give a little more than you might consider necessary, and then you will find that more than you expect will come back to you: perhaps not always at once but at some time or other and you are the better and happier woman from it and have grown to a fuller extent on this path of your wide road in life . . . . [48]

Other working women and middle-class daughters were gaining more freedom and
independence, and perhaps Mrs West was old or of 'the old school' and felt she
must take a hard line against the spread of ideas of rights or freedom to her servants.
Yet what is really interesting about this quotation is the fact that one woman is
addressing other women and calling on a cultural repertoire of middle-class wife-
liness and femininity to describe the ideal (female) servant. Wifely 'giving' is clearly
the model for servant subordination.

We have seen how girls were introduced to strict rules and rituals in the moment
of transition. Their continuous application - Mrs West's rules about not talking to
the (male) 'outdoor staff' for instance - were an assertion of the employer's superiority over members of a class who were in need of guidance and correction. The most
decisive effect of these rituals was to define the servant as not-family, and it is this
exclusion - the main psychic difference from her own home - that was most often
commented on by my interviewees. As Thea Vigne's witness put it:

You were just a servant: that was it. You didn't have to have any personality or
anything - 'Course, that's where I used to be in trouble didn't I? And they didn't
expect you to chime in with the conversation or smile or let on you were interested
at all. You had to keep sort of strong-faced. I was always getting in a row about
that.[49]

The 1944 government committee on domestic servants reports that girls entering
service after World War I were less docile than pre-war.[50] If the period since 1919
saw the maintenance of a very conservative social order, it was still marked by
challenges to the authority of the dominant classes: the short Labour government
of 1924 and above all the post-war strike waves and the General Strike of 1926. It
is by no means 'obvious', however, that the dominant response to such challenges
was a *loosening* of social disciplines. The reaction might well have been to behave
more strictly and oppressively: to exact vengeance by penalizing trade unions or, in
the domestic sphere, to act more oppressively towards servants. If the old attitudes
of respect were being eroded and questioned by the servants themselves or if this
was feared, employers would have to work harder to maintain their position of
authority. Individual discipline might have to be strengthened to compensate for
the weakening of more general ideological supports. The effectiveness of such
compensation would be very much dependent on local situations - especially the
supply of servants.

Tone of voice and methods of address were some of the means used to maintain
the right relationship. The employer's tone should be kindly but not intimate; the
servant's should be respectful and not familiar. This is a difficult area to explore
because the evidence, available only to the ear, has largely vanished. Robert Roberts,
talking of the period up to the mid 1920s, put it this way:

As a whole, the middle and upper classes, self-confident to arrogance, kept two
modes of address for use among the poor. The first was a kindly form in which each
word was clearly enunciated. The second had a loud self-assured hectoring note.

Both seemed devised to ensure that, though the hearer might be stupid, he would know enough in general to defer at once to breeding and superiority. Hospital staff, doctors, judges, magistrates, officials, and clergy were expert at this sort of social intimidation . . . . The trade unionist facing his well-dressed employer knew it only too well. It was a tactic, conscious or not, that confused or over-faced the simple.[51]

In the following incident one can almost hear the 'kindly' tone adopted by Mrs Clydesdale, just as other servants, adopting the language of the employer in recounting tales of particularly humiliating incidents, sometimes adopt the 'hectoring note'. Margaret had skimped the cleaning of the brass door-knocker.

The parlour maid would come down and say to me 'Madam has sent down a message that she wants to speak to Langley (that was me) in the morning room'. My legs used to feel like rubber at the very thought of going up there because I knew what she was going to say. I knew it was about the front door. She would start off with an ambiguous remark 'Langley, whatever happened to the front door this morning?' I knew perfectly well what she meant. Then she would go on 'Langley, you have a good home here, you have good food and you have comfortable lodgings and you are being taught a trade; in return I expect the work to be done well.' By this time I was in tears what with feeling so inferior.[52]

The Woman's Book, published in 1931 to give advice to middle-class homemakers, had a sizable chapter on servants. It gave some general advice on this question of address:

As we expect civility and courtesy from our maids it is only fair that we should render them the same. A fear of familiarity should never be the excuse for a curt answer nor justify the omission of please, nor a word of thanks for services rendered. Neither should we be reluctant to wish them the common salutations and good morning and good night.[53]

These methods of intimidation are subtle and many servants did not perceive them as such. Some did perceive them at the time and inwardly resented them. Others have come to perceive them much later when a quite new way of thinking about domestic service has 'allowed' them to break with the old ideology. Margaret Powell's book in 1968, and the widespread media interest in service, including 'Upstairs, Downstairs' (1972), were important release mechanisms for some ex-servants. It was now acceptable to talk about having been in service and even to have opinions about it. Much of the material on which this essay draws was, in this way, made available. The final section of this essay, however, concerns the servants' own (contemporary) responses to their experiences.

Servants' responses

There were certainly some servants who accepted class divisions and accorded their masters a 'natural respect'. This response was commonest among servants from rural areas whose aristocratic employers had large households. But this traditional pattern was not enough to secure respect. The employer had to be seen to be kind and considerate as well. Thus two of the women in my study still speak happily of their experience and have few regrets. Resistance was neither contemplated nor thought necessary. Mrs Florence Follet went to work as a parlourmaid/valet for Major and Mrs Evans at the local manor house. She worked there happily until she was married eight years later. There were eight servants caring for two people, so work was not onerous. Mrs Follet looked up to, even 'adored', the major, whose clothes she looked after. Mrs Evans took an interest in Florence's family and lent their house, garden and car for Florence's wedding.[54]

The second type of response was to resent subordination and, to some extent, to show this resentment - though active resistance was rare. The rebels, also in my work a minority, often came from more radical families, though this might not be reflected in their position at home. They had nearly all qualified for higher education but were forced into domestic service through economic hard times. There were seven servants in my sample with this response, including four out of five of the autobiographers and three out of four of the women from Wales. They did not accept the ideology of domestic service and resisted, in minor ways, whenever possible.

Mrs Cross is the most angry ex-servant I have heard from. She is still full of fury at the way she was treated. She actively resisted her employers' attempts to categorize her as inferior. She fiercely resented being treated as an 'illiterate moron' by employers less intelligent than herself. She records here an incident in 1932 when she was nineteen and had had several service jobs in London and Oxfordshire:

I was however beginning to kick back. The young son here was one day in floods of tears because he couldn't manage his Maths homework. We sat down in the diningroom and worked things out; after all he was only 7 years younger than I was. However, Mother arrived and raved 'how dare you sit in the dining room with my son?' I removed myself but my turn came a week later, when Madam asked me to help the boy. I told her 'I am not good enough to sit with your son: he is not good enough for me to help'. I had proved I was not an illiterate moron.[55]

Many girls whose ability and education should have led them to far better jobs found themselves forced to enter domestic service. Educational opportunities for working-class girls, limited though they were, were ahead of job opportunities. Jean Rennie, for instance, had obtained Scottish Higher Leaving Certificate at seventeen which would have gained her university entrance, but her father was only intermittently in work and when in work he drank a good part of his wages. The family of four lived in a one-room tenement. After getting and losing two jobs locally, she answered an advertisement for a third housemaid. This was in 1924; she remained in service until 1940, rising to be head cook.[56]

Winifred Foley's father was a radically minded miner in the Forest of Dean who had once lost a job because of his views. The children, though poor, had been brought up to have a sense of their own identity. We have already seen how Winifred felt at having to eat separately from her employers. She perceived that she was being defined as inferior, but for the time accepted it, until an incident at the Teacher Training College where she worked in 1934. She had been 'caught' talking to one of the 'lady' students on the stairs. She was called before the bursar, Miss Robson, next morning 'for a lecture in proper decorum for kitchen maids'.

Having choked on this bitter pill nearly all night and not being able to swallow it, next morning I asked to be allowed to speak to Miss Robson. Hurt pride had puffed me up on to my very high horse which has no bridle alas and now I was ready to give *her* a lecture and my month's notice to go with it.

So she did not attend compulsory prayers that morning and was duly summoned before Miss Robson once more.

'Come in' called Miss Robson and I stood squarely in front of her, my head held a bit on the high side. She asked me why I had not attended prayers that morning and reminded me once again that I had been seen talking and laughing with one of the lady students. Now, yet more incensed than in the first interview, I told her the young lady had got into conversation with *me*. Secondly, if I was not fit to talk to the students how could I talk to God who, I was under the impression, was considered a good deal superior to any student. 'You do not talk to God. You pray to God that He may listen to you' Miss Robson reprimanded me but her tone was not unkind. 'Well, even if I'm praying to Him, if we're all good enough to do that together in His presence, why aren't we good enough to talk to each other?'
　Miss Robson gave a deep sigh and then a kindly-meant lecture in humility. She herself would have to curtsey to royalty, we all had our place in society, and ducks could never be happy trying to pretend to be swans . . . . I agreed with her that College Hall was a very good place for the servants but she could now offer mine to a more deserving girl as I was giving in my notice . . . . After my previous jobs I thought perhaps I had cut off my nose to spite my face but I felt a kind of glory in my rebellion. I sang 'the Red Flag' as loud as I dared among the clatter of pots and pans and thought of my Dad and all the down-trodden workers of the world and nearly cried.[57]

But defending her principles and her identity cost Winifred Foley a job which she regretted leaving.
　There is a similar awareness of exploitation and unfairness in Margaret Powell's book, *Below Stairs*. One theme running through her account is a recognition of the double standard which the employing class applied to their own or their children's behaviour and to the behaviour of servants. One example was the situation forced on servants by the ban on 'followers' - itself 'a degrading term' - when seen beside the whole paraphernalia of the debutante.

Why should the fact that you are a servant and in love be wrong when the whole deb set-up was manufactured to bring their daughters together with young men.[58]

The commonest response was to express neither pleasure nor resentment in their experience but to accept hard conditions and long hours as part of working-class life. Parents, brothers and sisters all worked hard too for low wages. Why should *they* complain? Although, of course, things happened to make them resentful, slights were borne stoically.

You just did as you were told. As you were often told, 'You're paid to do as you're told, not to think'. So in the end you sort of lost your identity you know.[59]

The necessity of being a servant was accepted, but often grudgingly and with mental reservations. More active resistance was experienced as very difficult. Many women spoke of the inhibitions which they felt on answering back.

I've never exerted myself somehow and said 'I'm not doing that' - I suppose it was going into service and you had to do everything you were told. You couldn't answer back - and I think it grows on you.[60]

Of course, 'answering back' did risk penalties - dismissal and the risk of getting a bad reference. Jean Rennie thinks that the reason she found it so difficult to get a second job was that she was sacked from the first for 'questioning the Divine Right of the Gentry'. It was much easier to leave for another job with the minimum of antagonism and even with apparent regret.

When you gave in your notice you always tried to give the impression you were loath to leave: you just had to make it seem that you were sorry to go. It was because of the reference - you couldn't get another job without a good reference.[61]

Yet people who have been servants very often remember the humiliations to which they were subject through particularly vivid episodes. Mrs Evans gave notice after the following incident, though, for reasons which Margaret Powell has suggested, she did not tell her employer the reasons.

Question: What did she do in the end that made you leave?
Mrs Evans: Well, in the end all the children came home from boarding school and there was extra work, you know, and one day there was two teacloths missing and I said I hadn't had them: but it *was* my habit to hang the day's tea towels on the triplex oven door to dry: and these two tea-cloths were missing and Mrs Kerr said [here Mrs Evans assumed the tone of voice of her employer] 'I expect you've burnt them on the oven door - you haven't got the brains to own up'. I said 'I haven't burned them. I don't know where the teacloths are'. Anyway, two shillings was stopped from my wages that week. And when the laundry came back on Friday - there was the teacloths in the laundry basket. They'd probably been put on top of the laundry basket and got pushed in. But, you got no apology. I got the two shillings back but I got no apology. No.[62]

Mrs Evans was talking to me in 1972, but this incident of the 1930s still rankled.

In conclusion, I will return to the questions posed at the beginning of this study. I have argued that the place and training of the working-class girl in the home contributed not just to her skills but also to her willingness and obedience in service. There is a sense in which mothers were contributing to the exploitation of their daughters. Secondly, girls adapted quite quickly to service, but this was a process of conforming to the employer's expectations about work, behaviour and demeanour, and could create a feeling of the loss of identity. The environment remained alien and not like home. Where there were several other servants there might be compensations in companionship, but the girl often lost her neighbourhood contacts, friends and familiar surroundings. Because of the peculiar limitations of the job, it was difficult to forge a new set of 'familiars'. Finally, most servants perceived that they were being defined as inferior or of a lower status. Most resented this but for both material and ideological reasons, fear of the future and, often, a long habituation to patience and obedience, could not make this feeling a basis for actions that openly challenged authority. Some servants seem to have made this break at some point in their lives. Some also developed an analysis of the economic system that made domestic service possible:

It was the poverty that gave them servants. No pride in appearance, no new clothes. It was us in Wales and in different parts like Northumberland. Our mothers were glad (they weren't glad to see us go) for us to go to a meal of food and for someone to clothe us, 'cause they couldn't . . . . It was heartbreaking . . . and they - what was the word now? They exploited us, more or less.[63]

6 Recreation in Rochdale, 1900-40

Paul Wild

Despite the growth of a historiography of 'leisure', we remain quite uninformed, on a closely observed local level, of the actual changes in recreational forms.[1] Most of the research to date has focused upon the 'classic' periods of social history, especially the early nineteenth century and, increasingly, upon the late-Victorian and Edwardian periods. The inter-war decades in most of their cultural and social aspects remain especially obscure. This essay seeks to help to repair this deficiency by looking at the changing patterns of recreational provision in one smallish northern industrial town in the first half of the twentieth century.[2] Special stress will be laid on the years up to World War II, subsequent changes being only very lightly sketched. The main focus will be the provenance, nature and extent of the organization of non-work time: the main theme will be the penetration of capitalist enterprise into the 'leisure' domain itself and the tendency of this invasion to replace older, uncommercial or less capitalized forms of provision.

In Rochdale this transition occurs in the form of the decline of the pub, the music hall and the chapel relative to the rise of the dance hall and the cinema. At the beginning of the century leisure for the popular classes was already extensively commercialized. It revolved, however, around drink, the music hall and religion, with the pub and the chapel often expressing poles of respectability and roughness within a popular cultural repertoire embracing both the working class and the inter-mediate strata. In the fifty years that followed, the primacy of the pub as the most extensive and popular form was challenged, the churches and chapels were stripped of many of their recreational functions, and the music hall disappeared. The dance hall and the cinema were two of the most important newer rivals, though other leisure industries, capturing mass markets, were also developed in this period. The basis of the excursion and holiday industries, for instance, had already been laid by the railway companies in the later nineteenth century. The speedy develop-ment of motor coach companies aided further provision for a growing demand. There was, of course, no simple, smooth, evolutionary development from one set of forms to another. Changes were very uneven. The stories of different aspects of recreation belong, in a sense, to different 'times': on the one hand, for instance, there are the longer continuities and transformations of Rochdale's 'Rush Week', circuses and fairs; on the other hand there is the extraordinarily compacted, fully twentieth-century history of cinema. Older forms often persisted in more attenuated ways alongside their rivals, though now, demographically, of little significance. In what follows, however, we shall look first at those forms of recreational provision that Rochdale's population inherited from the nineteenth century, then at those forms whose explosive growth was characteristic of twentieth-century capitalist enterprises.

The role of the churches and chapels in Rochdale

The churches and chapels in the decade or so up to World War I were at their zenith as centres for leisure. As local outlets they had rivals only in the pub and had not felt the worst effects of cinema competition before war broke out. Activities fell into two main categories. Firstly, there were irregular celebrations which occurred as part of the religious calendar such as the Whit-Walks, chapel anniversaries, annual trips and outings. Secondly, there were the more regular happenings such as tea parties, bazaars, concerts, indoor games, lectures, coffee evenings, young men's and ladies' classes and debating societies.

As the church or chapel varied so did the provision for leisure. Some would only offer the less regular forms of entertainment and celebration for the congregation, yet put every effort into creating such an event to earn money for church use. For instance St Mary's (C of E) held an elaborate bazaar in Rochdale Town Hall entailing various stalls and entertainments plus a restaurant in 1908 and in 1912.[3] On both occasions the church took over £1000. Others, like St Clement's (C of E), offered a regular and comprehensive programme. Here sport played a particular role: a rugby club had been formed as early as 1878, a cricket club in 1868, but by 1909, mainly due to competition from professional opponents being too strong, the clubs were disbanded.[4] Regular events included the day school scholars' annual concert, the choir concert, the Sunday school annual trip, church institute tea party and institute trip. A surprising total of 928 people had gone on the annual Rushbearing trip with the church in 1890, but trips tended to be less frequent in the new century. A sewing circle with fifty-four members in 1914, men's and ladies' classes, a church institute and reading room, plus various indoor games and pastimes, completed the church's social programme.

Within Rochdale Nonconformity, provision was also varied. Union Street Methodist Church, close to a number of packed areas of housing and the town centre, took advantage of its geographical position and began to show a regular moving-picture show to large audiences in the few years before World War I, a practice that continued into the 1930s, even though the show began with prayer and song.[5] In addition to this, Union Street was the centre for a recreation club, a men's institute, regular concert parties and 'sunshine Bands', Girl Guides, Brownies, Boy Scouts and the Girls League with fifty members in 1924.[6]

St Clement's and Union Street Church were by no means the only churches offering such facilities; the majority of the religious institutions in Rochdale before 1914 offered some kind of regular club or activity. A third category, often those with a highly evangelical view of the world, offered little other than worship. For instance, the Baptist church in the town had been split by a furious debate

centring around the opposition of evangelism to recreation in the fight for
Christianity. In the 150th Anniversary Speech the Rev. S.W. Hughes insisted, 'it
was not the duty of the church to amuse the world, but to bring a knowledge of
Christ to it'.[7]

Finally, after much heated argument, classrooms behind the school gallery were
converted into an institute with billiards room, games and reading room, plus a
canteen. Yet these efforts came too late to alter the degree to which the church
was losing popularity as a centre for religion and leisure:

From a peak of 250 baptisms and a membership of 500 between 1900 and 1908,
West Street Baptist Church declined to a baptism rate of less than five a year in
the early thirties.[8]

The decline at West Street came slightly earlier than at most churches and
chapels; in the five years before the war West Street had experienced what others
were to know in the decade or so following the outbreak of war. This decline,
affecting all sections of the church, appears tangibly and emphatically especially
when viewed alongside the successes and achievements of the period before the war.
The social activities at St Clement's had by 1920 become a shadow of what they
once were;[9] Union Street ceased to exist at all after a long period of decline leading
up to World War II. A contemporary from Dearnley Methodist Church remembers
things as they were:

Time has brought some changes in the social activities which have always been a
prominent feature of church and communal life at Dearnley. In the years preceding
and immediately following the First World War the men's social section flourished
exceedingly. The weekly meetings in the 'Band Room', friendly and informal
with 'tuppenny pies' and coffee to round off a pleasant hour of games and
discussions were greatly enjoyed.[10]

Soon after the war both the men's club and recreation club went out of existence
due to lack of support, following roughly the pattern all church-based recreation
took in these years (i.e. persistent decline), save only the yearly celebrations such as
Whitsun and Easter Sunday.[11]

Regular and mostly free recreation, based around the church and chapel, became
less significant in Rochdale as the cinema and dance hall grew to their maturity
in the 1930s and 1940s.[12] Compared with what was to replace them, the religious
institutions were in one sense highly democratic: the congregation often organized
and ran its own affairs, through committees and clubs. The cinemas and the dance
halls were forms which ran on the basis of the aspirations of an entrepreneur with
very little feedback from his audience except for that approval or disapproval
interpreted through a commercial logic. The main impulses behind the cinema and
dance halls were undoubtedly commercial; the chapels and churches were essentially
social institutions. On the other hand, social hierarchies did exist within the
churches, which were often headed by local families of power and wealth. For
instance, three manufacturing families - the Pillings, Chadwicks and Whitakers - had

been prominent at St Clements during its heyday.[13] In a less tangible way the Unitarian church in Rochdale had strong ties with manufacturing elites like the Petries and Ashworths who were closely linked with the Rochdale Co-operative movement from its early days.[14] As several studies of the mid-Victorian period have now shown, membership of Nonconformist chapels, mutual improvement societies, temperance organizations and a whole range of secular clubs was significant because of the element of exclusion: membership delineated social and cultural boundaries. These boundaries were, moreover, not merely or even mainly *between* classes, but were rather a form of cultural fragmentation *within* the working class. Often a section of workers drawn from particular trades in particular towns seem to have identified more with sections of a local petty bourgoisie than with the rest of their fellow workers, at least in so far as their recreational activities were concerned. Certainly churches and chapels could very often present a narrow and moralizing attitude to those on the outside; some, like Lowerfold Methodist Chapel, had more than the usual emphasis on 'getting on'. In its handbooks and souvenirs great store was placed by the men's and ladies' improvement classes and these, together with anniversary and the usual religious celebrations, were the main events outside worship.[15] The cinema manager, by contrast, imposed few criteria of entry save the ability to pay. Though there was much contemporary moralizing about cinema audiences and some social segregation within and between cinemas, the form itself expressed the egalitarianism of all consumers. In some ways, twentieth-century cultural forms expressed and helped to forge a greater cultural homogeneity within the working class, or at least helped to erode the older forms of divisions.

The churches and chapels in Rochdale could at their worst be censorious and clannish; at their best they could be warm and enterprising, in a way which fed on the backgrounds they most often found themselves in - the socially restricted community of the tightly packed 'urban villages' and neighbourhoods which made up the town. An old Sunday school teacher, remembering his days at Holland Street Chapel, which had to close in 1942, described something of what these institutions could stand for:

My memory was impressed with the famous anniversaries, the Whit-Friday treats, the watchnight services, and I hope your history will give some idea of the real warmth and enthusiasm that existed then . . . .
. . . I have copies of the hymn books that were compiled and well remember the afternoon addresses with the boys on the left hand side and the girls on the right.[16]

By 1914 the church had reached a watershed; it had increasing difficulty holding on to its members as the years progressed and the alternatives grew. By 1922, for instance, five commercially run cinemas were playing to full audiences on most nights,[17] and a proportion of these would probably have otherwise been at chapel or church entertainment twenty years earlier. As early as 1914 the foundations of a mass commercial sector were there; four established and highly competitive cinemas existed; a skating rink had also been opened, and a new theatre which concentrated on melodramas had regular audiences.[18] The municipal library and

swimming baths did more and more business as the century wore on. The quad-
rupling of mainly fictional books issued between 1900 and 1931[19] points to a
probable underlying trend towards home-centred leisure, which was underlined by
the growth in gramophone and record sales, as the dance boom took effect. The
number of beer shops in the town stayed around the 150-mark in the first two
decades of the century, but the number of pubs was halved to 70 in the same
period, a factor which seems to fit both with the underlying trend towards staying
at home in the Edwardian period, and a relative reduction in the significance of
the pub as the first and foremost resort.[20] In his biographical account of Edwardian
Salford, Robert Roberts talks of the way the films affected publicans' trade: men
would often only appear in the pubs after the films were over.[21]

But the pub in Rochdale suffered far less than the churches and chapels from
the onset of new and extending forms of leisure in this period. After World
War I a definite shift towards specialized and commercially based leisure, spear-
headed by the cinema, was clearly taking place in Rochdale. This change appears to
have been contemporaneous with a drastic reduction in the importance of localized
and relatively diverse church and chapel leisure.

The secular societies

The Co-operative societies in the early part of the century were important social
institutions for a small percentage of Rochdalians. As well as the retail and service
aspect, the Co-ops inhabited a very similar social sphere to that of the churches and
chapels. The Equitable Pioneers Society had a library and reading room, run by its
education department which also had responsibility for various children's concerts,
a rambling society and a choir. The Rambling Society had regular trips during the
summer on Saturdays and Sundays when a train or a tram would be caught to places
of interest, with a picnic tea served after the walk.[22] Adult concert parties were
invariably well attended before the war and fell into the usual routine of a singing
troupe with accompaniment and recitations. In March 1914 the local press reported,

. . . a large audience at the Assembly Room, Toad Lane on Saturday evening, when
an excellent concert arranged by the Education Department of the Rochdale
Pioneers Society was given by Mrs Olive Margison's Concert Party.[23]

After the war the Co-op slowly ceased to exist as an all-round social institution
as it had once done. Starting with the three retail boom years that followed 1918,
the emphasis lay increasingly with business.[24]

Since its inception in Rochdale in 1889 the Temperance League had been an
integral part of the Liberal/Nonconformist alignment which had so characterized
Lancashire in the first decade of the twentieth century.[25] As such it shared a similar
political and social location with the chapels and the Co-op, opposing the demon
drink as a form of recreation. Like the Co-op and the church, the Temperance
Society had offered a programme of concerts, musical evenings, and club events
and in the end shared the same decline. Once the fervour set in motion by John

Bright and the other industrialists in the previous century had receded - some time between 1900 and 1914 - things stumbled on and finally collapsed.[26] The Temperance Society had never enjoyed a massive following from the population as a whole but is significant in the sense that its changing fortunes perhaps mirror 'external' happenings. For instance, the demise of the Temperance movement in Rochdale seems to have come within a circular relationship between the lessening problem of drink and the slowly advancing availability of alternatives.

Another society, the Clarion Cycling Club, prominent in Rochdale between 1900 and 1930, owed its origins and early development both to the socialist revival and to the traditions of the chapel, Temperance, and Liberalism. The early gatherings, consisted mostly of skilled workers and the lower middle classes, met weekly; runs to place of interest or beauty were the norm.[27] Social functions of the kind common in the chapels were held during the winter; for instance in 1900 one of the parties at the Labour Hall entailed 'songs and recitations from the Band of Hope as well as temperance dialogues'.[28]

Before and just after World War I the Clarion Club was both an ideological and recreational movement in the mould which seems to have been ubiquitous in that period.[29] But as the inter-war years progressed, an easy-going amateurism and 'brotherhood' began to give way to serious riding and racing. From the mid 1930s onwards the trend was further emphasized by the separation of the club, nationally, into two tiers. The new group, known as the Clarion Cycling and Athletics Club, marked a definite departure from the old logic of the movement and was to have an effect at all levels. As an enthusiast wrote in 1944,

I'm afraid the easy going era of Clarion racing men is over. Some years ago the club decided to give the racers their head .... We set up the Clarion Cycling and Athletics Club.[30]

Here, as in the case of the other peripheral forms like the Co-op and the Temperance movement, the impulses of the pre-1914 era were not to survive. The changing character of the clubs seems to underline a shift away from the diverse forms epitomized by the chapel and church, which was occurring generally in the post-1914 period. It is also notable that the new emphasis within the Clarion movement falls in with a growing specialization in the area of leisure as a whole, and in some way parallels a professionalism and competitiveness to be found increasingly in spectator sports such as football after World War II.[31] Bearing in mind the counter-cultural origins of the Clarion movement itself and its criticism of passive forms of leisure, this outcome was testimony to the force of the underlying tendencies.

The development of commercial forms: holidays

The minority of Rochdalians went away for Rushbearing[32] at the turn of the century, and of that minority, most booked through an intermediate body which, to a varying degree, would organize the day trip or holiday and sometimes offer a cheaper rate than a direct booking with the railway. Bodies like the Co-op, the chapels, working men's clubs and trade associations would often organize excursions on a group basis to places like Morecambe, Blackpool and North Wales, each institution catering for a certain level within a reasonably distinct and exclusive holiday market. In 1900, for instance, the Co-op Holiday Association offered excursions to Glasgow and Edinburgh for one, eight or sixteen days with fares at 6s.6d., 9s.6d. and 13s.[33] The Rochdale Merchants and Traders Association had excursions to the Isle of Wight and South Coast for eight and sixteen days at fares between 24s. and 15s.;[34] The Rochdale Tradesmen's Trip consisted of a day trip to Bournemouth, 'with return railway tickets, two good meals and a long drive for 13/6d.'[35]

On a less demanding financial level the Rochdale and District Federation of Liberal Clubs took a day excursion to Hardcastle Craggs near Halifax for 1s.5d.[36] Provision at this time seems to have centred on the middle classes and the skilled working class, the limits being set by income. The Co-op alone seems to have offered the widest possible access in this early period: for instance, in Rushbearing Week 1900, 10,000 people booked holidays (mostly day excursions) through the Co-op as against 4000 who did so directly with the railway companies.[37] But, still, for many a holiday was too expensive to consider; at a time when the average wage of a weaver at Kelsall and Kemps Woollen Mill was 20s. per week (by no means meagre),[38] the majority of the town stayed at home.

The Co-operative societies' trips, those of Cooks and of the two railway stations, plus the workmen's excursions, totalled 23,000 in 1901 and in 1902, 28,000, barely accounting for one-third of the population.[39] And of the 1901 figure, 11,000 had travelled in special trains organized by the Co-op.[40] In that year two fairs attended Rochdale for Rushbearing Week with their gingerbread stalls, shows of strength, wrestling, shooting galleries, swings and roundabouts, all in abundant supply.[41] For others, who had to forgo a holiday, a short train ride to a local man-made lake would suffice for a day out. The tea rooms there boasted their worth:

'If you want a good tea go to Victoria House. Every accommodation for parties and cyclists; swings, see saws and playground free. Can dine 400 anytime. Hot water supplied.'[42]

or

'Nichols Hall is open for the season. Skating and dancing daily 4d each. Teas supplied on the premises. Catering for schools, picnics, parties or club parties - can dine 800 at any time.'[43]

During the first decade of the new century, a severe depression in the cotton mills of the town began to have its effect on the numbers going away for holidays. Particularly between 1909 and 1911 the reduction was marked; as a correspondent wrote,

. . . those who have watched the crowds of departing holiday makers for the last few years hardly thought that the platforms were as continually thronged as at some former vacations.[44]

These few years were probably the high points for the 'chapel trip' or 'choir trip' in Rochdale. For after World War I they became less and less important as an outlet for a minority of people, as alternative and relatively cheap opportunities began to develop. Someone from the congregation at Castlemere Methodist Church remembers,

whilst Whit Friday was chiefly devoted to the children's enjoyment, Rushbearing was the time for the older ones. A week's holiday was out of the question for the majority, and so the chief holiday of the year was the day trip . . . .[45]

In these same years motor coach tours began to appear regularly in the summer months. Holt Brothers and Greenof and Shaw were the two main pioneers, with trips to Hollingworth Lake and Hardcastle Craggs and later to places like Blackpool and Morecambe. By the early 1920s they shared a growing market with four other coach firms and the LMS which constantly tried to shake off its competitors in a growing rivalry. By now Blackpool, which had been an early favourite, began to be the single most popular resort for the railways and the coach operators; twenty out of the fifty trains which left Rochdale in Rushbearing Week 1922 were bound there.[46] In that same year the local press reported that coach traffic was also heavy.[47] In 1926 Reliance coaches had established a rival service to the railways for those who wanted to go boating or dancing by Hollingworth Lake,[48] and by 1928 coach and rail operators had brought prices down to 5s. (return) on special cheap trips to Blackpool or Morecambe.[49]

But the depression of the early 1930s brought a great set-back to the trend towards cheaper and therefore more accessible holiday provision for the majority of people. On longer runs especially, the railway and coach operators suffered considerably.[50] This situation probably had some part in the state of the business by 1934, for by then three coach companies and the railway were dominant. As the 1930s progressed, business grew better, special trains (a significant number still being organized by the Co-op) topped 100 in number and coach operators were celebrating record traffic.[51] Nationally, the Co-operative Holiday Association continued to organize tours, excursions and hostels, but, post-1945, tended to be less of an operator and more of an agent for other companies, its name being changed to Co-operative Travel Services in these years.[52]

In Rochdale the trend, though fluctuating, was toward a definite increase in the availability of the day trip or holiday for the majority of the population, and this compares to a similar national trend. Pimlott estimates that over thirty million people took holidays away from home in 1960[53] compared with Mowat's figure of around fifteen million for 1937.[54] Happenings, for which the developments in the retail and service sectors in the last quarter of the nineteenth century were perhaps a portent, are revealed in increases in the number of people employed in the service industries, which between 1929 and 1937 outpaced other sectors in this respect.[55] Within this grouping, hotels and restaurants increased their number of employees from 302,00 in 1930 to 379,000 in 1937; those in entertainment and sport from 65,000 to 116,000 in the same period.[56] From the mid 1930s onward the national trend toward more extensive holiday provision continued alongside a regeneration in the consumer and service industries as a whole. But it seems that this wavering yet pronounced extension in commercial provision took on an order in the post-war years, as basic economic horizons began to change and 'almost every employed Briton', received the benefit of a paid holiday.[57]

The dance halls

Rochdale saw its share of dancing in the 1920s but it was the middle of the decade before any regular venue for dancing on a commercial basis was set. The Lakeside Pavilion at Hollingworth offered weekly dances as a regular attraction in the summer. In addition to this there were several less regular dances held by employers, the churches and chapels, the Co-op and the Dance Schools; when combined, these offered a full range of outlets for those who wished to dance in the 1920s. For instance, in the weeks leading up to Rushbearing in 1926 the dance hall at Hollingworth Lake offered dancing to a syncopated band.[58] On the other side of town the Labour Hall offered 'novelty trio dancing for 1s. from 7 till 11 pm'.[59] The Havanna Band (obviously popular) was billed to appear at several dance halls in town in the week before the holidays.[60] Phil Richardson's Rythmeans, 'an up to date six piece combination',[61] were to appear at Balderstone Hall from 7.30 until 11 p.m., but for 2s. On one Saturday before the holidays in 1930 there were at least six well-attended dances.

In the early 1920s, when provision had been sparse, dancing schools had done much to propagate the pastime by holding their own 'evenings'. Lobels's, Turner's, Rafferty's and Bailey's were the pioneers and were later joined by another eight schools in the task of teaching the Charleston, black bottom, fox-trot, tango and waltz to the youths of Rochdale.[63] Turner's and Bailey's from the outset had offered classes in elocution and deportment to equip young ladies in a situation that increasingly revolved around 'getting a man'. At prices ranging between 6d. and 2s., dancing in a local hall or at one of the dancing schools became a real possibility for large numbers of young people. Now, for a reasonable sum, most could gain access to a world where catch phrases and dances were a new and common social currency. In the boom, which seems to have been more pronounced in Roberts's Salford than it was in Rochdale, dancing was the thing for all between sixteen and twenty-five:

The great 'barn' we patronised as apprentices held at least a thousand. Almost every evening except Friday (cleaning night at home) it was jammed with a mass of young men and women, class de-segregated for the first time. At 6d. per head (1s. on Saturdays) youth at every level of the manual working class, from the bound apprentices to the 'scum of the slum', fox trotted through the new bliss in each other's arms.[64]

In Rochdale the dance venues and dance schools continued to cater for an expanding audience of mainly young people throughout the late 1920s and into the 1930s. These events seem to have developed in tandem with the gramophone, which during this period grew in importance as an aid to home-centred leisure. Regular advertisement appeared in the local press for gramophones at 'cut prices' and for the latest record releases of dance band music. Columbia records claimed to have sold over two million of their 'new process' records from their London factory in one month in 1928[65] - records, for instance, of the Piccadilly Revels Band playing tow fox-trots entitled 'Persian Rosebud', 'Is she my Girl friend' and various other tunes like 'Deep River Blues', and 'Variety Yale Blues'. These, and records like them found their way into countless homes, where they were probably used for quiet practice, and into the many dance schools where they would help mass tuition. In a mood informed by some of the films being shown then, record and dance band jostled to reveal the latest step or routine before an audience increasingly tuned in to a world of novelty and the appearance of glamour.

By 1934 the first permanent, purpose-built dance hall was opened in Rochdale.[66] The Carlton, as it was called, was owned by Embassy Amusements Ltd and offered standards similar to those of the new super-cinemas which had recently opened in the town. It was, from the start, a far more glamorous establishment than the Drill Hall or Ambulance Hall, which were both used regularly for dances. The Carlton even had its own resident band and a restaurant to entice the dancers,[67] but by no means did it have the market to itself even in 1938. For instance, on one Saturday in that year there was a dance at the Ambulance Drill Hall (price: 1s. 3d.), the Dunlop Mill Companies Social Club held a dance (1s.6d.)[68] and, at the Fire Station, 'Johnny Rosen and his famous Broadcasting Band'[69] played from 7 p.m. till midnight for 1s.6d.

Dancing in Rochdale seems to have been dominated from the commercial level but within this there were different interests: from the Carlton, which was part of a larger circuit, to the smaller, though basically commercial dances, and the affairs run by firms for their employees. The development of the dance-hall industry roughly paralleled that of the cinema: a peak in the 1930s and a post-war decline broken, in this case, by a short rebirth in the 1950s. There was a similar pattern of closures and takeovers. The Carlton in Rochdale became, inevitably, a part of the Mecca empire, turning its attention first to the teenage market and then to bingo. In general, the post-war pop music industry largely replaced the hall and the live band. Dancing itself, in the older styles, took on the character of a professionally performed competitive television spectacle, assuming a quite remarkable formality.

The cinema: origins

More spectacular and perhaps more significant than the growth of the dance halls was the development of the cinema. Between the earliest days when films were the domain of the artisan, producer and distributor, and the years when a highly complex international industry was reaching its peak, there stood barely fifty years. Out of a mass of technical developments which led to the cinema, two of the earliest stand out as milestones. By 1891 the Edison Laboratories in America had patented the first real rapid-take camera to use the new roll-film marketed by Eastman Kodak in 1888.[70] But they did not perfect any medium of projection beyond the coin-operated peep-show device known as the kinetoscope, which only allowed one viewer at a time. Nevertheless a kinetoscope company was founded in 1894 by Raff and Gammon to exploit the new wonder machine; in that year several penny arcades and parlours followed the first one opened in April on Broadway. However, it was the Lumiere Brothers who were first to produce a machine that projected as well as recorded pictures. They (like Edison) had the benefit of a factory and a laboratory with plenty of money to back research and experiments, unlike the many amateur inventors spread around Europe and America at this time. In 1895 they began to market the cinematographe, a machine which allowed its owner to make a as well as exhibit films: this must have had a major effect on the European film industry, which right up to World War I, had not really shaken off its artisan heritage. The very first audiences set a pattern which was only just beginning to change by 1905; they were interested in the fact that the pictures moved and little else:

. . . they were fairly unconcerned with what they saw. Any familiar scene or action was exciting in itself: 'High Seas at Brighton', 'Arrival of a Train', 'Workers leaving a Factory', 'Man Playing Cards' or, for the big thrills, 'Demolition of a Wall', or 'The Turn-out of the Leeds Fire Brigade'.

Many of the neighbourhood and itinerant picture pioneers took shots of events in the town where they were due to exhibit and cashed in on local pride with pictures of a town hall or civic event. Most commonly the men who showed these pictures in the towns around Britain were a part of travelling fairs and circuses. In October 1896 Randall Williams caused a sensation with his bioscope show at Hull Fair, using the first 'double entry' bioscope in the country. He started with a tent, a gas generator and an organ, plus horse and dray for transport, and begun a list of several showmen and their families to turn to films: Marshall, Buttershaw, Hollands, Pat Collins, President Kemp, Captain Payne, Wadbrook and Scard, Studt Seager and Scott, Doover Relph and Pedley, Barker and Thurston, Biddal, Bliss, Proctor, Haggar, Crecraft and Marshall Hill.[71] As David Robinson says in *World Cinema*,

For the showmen it was no great leap to transform their puppet shows, fit up theatres, wax works exhibitions into electric theatres and bioscopes. For several years the fairground cinemas prospered without competition.[72]

In 1889, Chipperfields Circus became one of the first to incorporate a bioscope into its performances.

In the same year that Randall Williams delighted audiences in Hull, Mo Trewey embarked upon a tour of England as agent for the recently developed Lumiere Cinematographe. But instead of showing to audiences in tents and improvised huts, he hired major halls and meeting places. So it was that Manchester saw its first real moving pictures in 1896 at the Free Trade Hall.[73] This tour set a precedent for touring 'animated picture' companies such as the New Century, Pringle's North American and Golden Rays - concerns which hired public halls, or shared the bill in music halls. Yet by 1912 both the travelling fair and picture company entrepreneurs had largely disappeared or become incorporated into established halls or theatres. Under the influence of the Cinematograph Act of 1910, the scene was set for the emergence of the specialist, purpose-built cinema. How were these more general developments worked through in Rochdale?

Cinema in Rochdale: circuses and showmen

At the turn of the century in Rochdale, Messrs Smith, Lee and Hargreaves were showing film sequences on an experimental basis as part of their 'Circus of Varieties' programme. For instance, an advertisement appeared in the *Rochdale Observer* on Saturday, 29 September 1900, offering 'the American Bio Montograph with latest war pictures' as part of a bill of mainly novelty and burlesque acts. During that year films were shown as part of the attractions at the Rochdale Trades and Domestic Exhibition at the Drill Hall;[74] and also at a 'Saturday Pop' concert in the Provident (Co-op) Hall organized by Mr Charles Parker. Singing to banjo, mandolin and guitar accompaniment, piano solos and Whit Cuncliffe, a humorist and mimic, offered most of the entertainment, while:

An attractive feature of this accompaniment was the exhibition of 'living' picture by Messrs Inman Holt and Woolfendens bioscope. The views included: Rochdale Cycle Parade, return of the C.I.V's, pantomime of Cinderella. Portraits of military and political figures were also shown; the portrait of Lord Roberts - an exceedingly fine one - was enthusiastically cheered; Mr Chamberlain's likeness met with an unfavourable reception.[75]

In the town in 1900 only one established music hall existed - Smith, Lee and Hargreaves's 'old wooden circus'; in addition the Theatre Royal presented drama and musical comedy. It was the Circus and the pop concerts, rather than the theatre, which popularized film in these early days. During 1901 Parker's pop concerts continued with 'Milnrowgraph No Flicker Animated Pictures', which included the Rochdale Volunteers Camp at Conway:

'Admission, 6d. and 1s., reserved seats 1s.6d. Secure your seats at Wrigleys Music Depot, Drake St., and support your Saturday popular concerts. Fun without vulgarity.'[76]

As before, with the pop concerts, films were shown by three local men, Inman, Holt and Woolfenden, who offered their services for rent. The programme often included the showing of films shot by them at local newsworthy events or ten-minute dramas shot in the Milnrow studios.[77]

Further pop concerts occurred in February and March of that year, the latter containing variety and the

. . . latest animated pictures by the cinematographs of the funeral of Queen Victoria,

Edward the Seventh opening Parliament and 'Joan of Arc' - a spectacular production in twelve scenes.[78]

But Parker and his associates were not the only ones to be taking advantage of the preoccupation with Queen Victoria's death (the Town Hall, Town Hall Square, Public Hall, Baillie Street Chapel and Baillie Street as well as the parish church were packed to capacity for memorial services on Saturday, 2 February). Smith, Lee and Hargreaves also showed film of the event:

The Circus - This week a capital company of skilled entertainers is attracting large audiences to the Circus of Varieties, Newgate, and on Monday night the performances given were enthusiatically received. The principal item on the programme is the exhibition of a series of excellent 'living' pictures, shown by means of Tweedale and Hargreaves American Bio Motograph, and making up what is probably the finest cinematographic display yet seen in Rochdale. Its views are remarkably clear, steady and effective. Among them are pictures relating to the death of Queen Victoria. And the Royal funeral procession of Saturday. Artists engaged for the week include, Mons. De Lil, Magician; Ballad Vocalist; Rutland Allen, Tenor Vocalist; Chirgo, Japanese rope equilibrist; Meg Rehan, Commedienne and dancer; Princess Moto, with the nine swords; Arthur Prior, Comedian; Professor Hulbert, 'Ten minutes with the merry folk'; and Jenny Lynne Commedienne.[79]

However, no more films were offered at the Circus for the rest of February and March; indeed, no more film shows were advertised in the *Observer* until December, when it reported pictures at the Circus:

Every part of the spacious building was literally packed to overflowing. The programme was almost certainly filled by Edison's animated pictures which have for many weeks been attracting great audiences to the Great Street James's Hall, Manchester. Mondays viewing included the illustrations of a large number of military, naval and historic incidents and several local scenes. One of the last names group - a turn out of the Rochdale Fire Brigade - was especially realistic and it caused much enthusiasm in the audience. All the pictures shown are remarkably life-like and steady.[80]

A few months earlier, in October, Parker had shown his fourth and final pop concert to 'large and appreciative audiences' at the Provident Hall, but did not include films. The Circus opened its new season on 1 September 1902 with a mixture of variety and films, but omitted the latter in the following week. The third week of September saw:

J.Johnson-Wood's Edisonscope series of animated pictures, reproducing many fine scenes including the coronation ceremony and the King's visit to the Isle of Man.[81]

Johnson-Wood filled the Circus again with pictures of Preston Guild in the week after that.[82] No pictures were offered there from October till December 1902.

In November 1905 New Century Pictures came to the town and offered seats at 1s. 6d., 1s., 3d., and half-price for all seats except threepennies, in the Provident Hall. The concern was run by Sydney Carter, who owned St George's Hall, Bradford, and F.D. Sunderland (an ex-fishmonger), who imported films together with Walter Jeffs, a Birmingham showman, who helped form the group in 1902.[83] The second major travelling picture show to visit was Pringle's North American Pictures, who were at the Circus for a fortnight in January 1906 and showed films including 'The Sailor's Wedding' and 'The Old Chorister'.[84] Pringle's firm started when the former Huddersfield variety artist and northern representative for Edison's Electric Pictures hired the Victoria Hall in Buxton, Derbyshire, to show latest Boer War film and the Corbett v. Fitzsimmons fight on film. In Easter 1902 he took the title of North American Animated Picture Co. and bought a hall in Newcastle-on-Tyne. Pringle later established himself at Edinburgh, Nottingham and Rochdale where in 1908 he took over an ex-music hall called the Empire, built only four years previously.

By 1908 pictures had become a regular feature and the Empire and Circus and three travelling picture shows (New Century, Pringle's and Golden Rays) visited regularly; the Theatre Royal continued to offer drama or musical comedy. During January 1908 New Century Pictures arrived for a two-week stay and was described by the *Observer:*

The popularity of Mr. Carter's New Century Pictures which are being shown at the Provident Hall, Rochdale is attested by crowded audiences. On Monday the last of the series was commenced and an entirely new set of pictures was shown on the screen. Steadiness, clearness and variety are the outstanding features. There is not a dull moment. The chief set in this week's programme is a beautiful pantomime story, 'The Talisman', in which some exceedingly rich colouring is introduced. The roaring torrent of Niagra, life and scenes in West Africa and a night in dreamland are among the most charming of the other films. Amusing scenes depicted include 'The Heavenly Twins', 'The Milliner's Dream' and 'Housebreaking for Love', and there are others in which a strong dramatic element is present.[85]

The third travelling picture of the trio, Golden Rays, enjoyed 'good audiences' at the Public Hall throughout a successful stay in February 1908, and another from 23 March even though New Century Pictures were filling the Provident Hall with a series of fourteen short films including a version of the Oberammergau 'Life of Christ'.[86] During May 1908, Pringle's films filled the entire bill at the Circus, where one of his nine North American Touring Shows stayed until the Circus was demolished in midsummer, and the new Hippodrome built. The films shown in the last week were several - the most notable being 'Incendiary Fireman' and 'The Last Cartridge', which depicted a tale of heroism during the Indian Mutiny. Pringle returned to the town in early August 1908 and placed a special advert in the *Rochdale Observer* telling of the new films he had secured for Rushbearing.[87] He stayed at the Public Hall for twenty-two weeks, up to Christmas 1908. Before that, in November, films were being screened at the newly opened Hippodrome (with variety), the Provident Hall (New Century) and the Empire, which Pringle was in the process of taking over.

Cinemas and super-cinemas

In 1910 the Cinematograph Act became law. It required all cinemas to provide a projection room which was separate from the main body of the hall, and either asbestos-lined or built on to the main structure of the hall, before licences were granted. This action followed serious fires at Barnsley, Newmarket and Stratford between 1907 and 1908. The Empire Picture Palace and the Hippodrome continued to show their blend of variety and films in an atmosphere of increased competition, for although the travelling theatre companies' visits had ceased by 1912 - no doubt as a result of the Act - two new cinemas had opened. In 1911 the Coliseum boasted well-heated waiting rooms and prices of 1d., 2d., and 3d. for films showing twice nightly.

Owned by J.F. Moore and Monty Beaudyn,[88] the Coliseum was built next to the Palace skating rink, which they also ran. In that year a new theatre called the Palace was opened under the direction of T. Hargreaves, who had once been a part-owner of the old Circus; dramas were presented similar to the ones offered at the Theatre Royal. The following year saw the second of the new cinemas open - the Pavilion Picture House, where continuous performances were aided by a small orchestra.[89] The Public Hall started to be used permanently, on Monday, Tuesday, Wednesday and Saturday by Lee and Ratcliffe to show films to two houses. Another new cinema - the Ceylon - was opened in 1915; this showed twice nightly, plus matinees.

The content of films during this early period tended to refract life through celluloid, but quite clearly came from the semi-religious twilight days of the chapel and drew on themes for long the staple of melodrama and music hall:

Before the war the great audience was the poorer working class, and the films they apparently preferred were those of high moral value and didactic tone; the taste was a heritage of Victorian times. The films of the pre war era favoured bible stories, morality dramas and melodramas in which virtue was rewarded and vice suitably punished (with poverty and virtue, riches and vice often equated) . . . . The films stressed the importance of home life and the sanctity of marriage; they frowned on get rich quick schemes and people, or those who sought to rise above their natural station. . . . Occasionally social issues might be raised - female suffrage or white slavery perhaps - but as an historian Lewis Jacobs has shown stories involving political corruption or capital-labour issues or racism, generally adopted strictly reactionary values.[90]

The American films especially turned away from the working man and his world and towards the rich and the problems they had with their lives; but the whole framework owed less to sermonizing than it did to a growing preoccupation with entertainment. The next time social considerations or messages were to permeate a definite grouping of films was when Warner Brothers began a series of films, including 'I am a Fugitive' and 'Cabin in the Cotton', during the depression. But very few of these films were successful as social documents or as box office attractions.[91]

Very much an example of the old order, the Pavilion in the week beginning 30 March 1914 showed 'The Streets of New York' to large audiences:

An old sea captain placed most of his fortune in a bank but very quickly afterwards decided to withdraw it in consequence of rumours he heard. Whilst he was at the bank he discovered that the owner was making preparations for leaving the country, and being unable to get his money the captain died suddenly. The receipt given to him for his deposit was secretly taken from him by a clerk, and the dead body was carried into the street. As a result of the sea captain's deposit the bank flourished and the owner lived in great luxury, whilst the dead captain's family endured much misery. In the end however they got possession of the receipt which showed where the sea captain's money had been banked.[92]

In that same week Pringle's Empire Picture Palace showed 'The Price of Thoughtlessness':

The picture 'The Price of Thoughtlessness' is a picture which gives excellent lessons to young folk as to the necessity of always being careful.[93]

Again in that week the Palace Theatre was showing a live drama called 'The Sin of her Childhood!'[94] Further on into the early months of the war, 'A Man's Sacrifice', 'The Seeds of Chaos', 'Hearts Adrift', 'What Every Woman Wants' and 'Enemy in our Midst' (a spy film) were shown together with recent war newsreel by Gaumont.[95] By the end of the war films like 'Never too Late To Mend', 'Pearl of the Army' (serial), 'The Girl and the Game', 'Jack and the Beanstalk', 'Ten Tommies', 'The Pillory', and 'A Little Hero' were showing in the town.[96]

In addition to the Coliseum, Empire, Pavillion, Hippodrome, Palace (a cinema by 1918), Public Hall and Ceylon, the King's Road Cinema was added in 1922:

The cosiness of the new King's Cinema, Oldham Road, is equalled by the excellence of the programme submitted. Tonight the chief picture is 'Her Unwilling Husband', a film illustrating the complex situations that may arise from extending to a friend a standing invitation.[97]

As the 1920s progressed, cinema advertising in the local press made much of the fact that the latest films were becoming longer. The Pavillion, for example, boasted 'The Mansion of Aching Hearts' in seven reels; the Empire, 'The Happy Warrior' in seven reels; the Ceylon, 'The Great Sensation' in six reels.[98]

On 26 March 1928 the Victory Super Cinema was opened, making a total of nine commercially run cinemas within a one-mile radius of the Town Hall, each showing twice nightly or continuous programmes plus matinees.[99] Six months later the Rialto (Rialto Cinema Rochdale Ltd), with directors Madigan, Close, Lord and Hoyle, was opened with a film called 'Dawn'. Full programmes started at 2.45, 6.45 and 8.45 p.m.; prices were 1s. 3d. and 6d. Perhaps most significant was the fact that the Rialto offered a cafe and lounge plus a well-appointed cinema, with carpets and comfortable seating. The owners emphasized:

whilst famous for their industry and thrift, Rochdale people are removed from misery, and it seems a fairly pure prophecy that not a single unit of the twenty five thousand homes will resist the appeal of the stately Rialto pleasure house.[100]

During 1929 the name 'Jackson's Amusements' appeared at the head of local amusements advertisements in the press for five of the town's cinemas - Hippodrome, Empire, Ceylon, La Scala (late Public Hall) and Coliseum. The Jackson family, ex-music hall artists, had taken control of the Hippodrome shortly after its completion.[101] Also during that year the Pavillion and Victory had joined the Rialto in boasting sound-track films. By the end of 1930 the Rialto, King's Road, Empire De Luxe, Victory and Pavillion were laying great store by the fact that they were screening talkies, even though, as Keller points out, silent Chaplin and Keaton films were shown well into the 1930s (e.g. at the Victory for a week from 14 April 1930[102]).

The best American silents had not ceased to bring in crowds even by the early 1930s, and American talkies were regularly the main film at most of the town cinemas; in January 1934 the Empire was showing 'Jenny Gerhardt', the story of

a girl whose beauty of face and disposition attracts for her attention from those on high . . . whilst helping her mother to clean at a swagger hotel, she is noticed by a middle aged senator, who presses his attentions on her and who succeeds in his designs when she has to ask for his help to save a brother from prison.[103]

The King's was showing 'Haunted House Ghost' and 'Frisco Jenny'; the Victory showed 'The Rebel', a series of adventures about an Austrian outlaw in the last century. The Rialto screened 'Bitter Sweet', a film version of the famous musical by Noel Coward, and the Hippodrome, 'Life in the Raw', where 'George O'Brien appears as a wandering cowboy, clever with untrained horses and tremulous females.'[104] The Ceylon showed 'Anne', in which a girl inherits a soap factory but needs money to run it; she borrows money from a man who she agrees to marry if she becomes bankrupt, but in the end her business is successful and she marries her foreman. The Pavillion showed 'Baby Face' with Barbara Stanwyck and George Brent: the Palace showed MGM's 'Rasputin'; the Coliseum, 'Brittania of Billingsgate'. Five of the nine cinemas in Rochdale in that week[105] showed American-made or financed films.

Cinema and oligopoly

In the 1930s, when the British cinema was at its peak, it took £40 million annually. Twenty million tickets were sold in a week. Forty per cent of the population went to the cinema once a week; 25 per cent twice or more weekly.[106] A revival of the production side of the industry in Britain took place in this period too: the Korda films from 1933 onwards generally lifted standards with films like 'The Private

Life of Henry VIII', 'Catherine the Great' and 'The Scarlet Pimpernel', which were
followed in the immediate post-war years by the Ealing comedies. Films like 'The
Lavender Hill Mob and 'Whisky Galore', plus the characteristic literary adaptions
like 'Great Expectations' and 'Oliver Twist', temporarily continued the new lease
of life.[107] None the less in the 1930s a high proportion of films were American-
made, as they had been since before World War I when the American industry took
advantage of the reduction in European production. During World War I the British
cinema had suffered and almost collapsed under the strain of growing American
competition.[108] Mass production of popular films with Mary Pickford, the Key-
stone Kops or Charlie Chaplin laid the major foundations for a film industry
consisting of a few giant companies which dominated at all levels, from production
to exhibition. Films, at least in America, became big business. Adolf Zukor, head of
the powerful Paramount distribution organization, pushed for the establishment of
the longer feature films which eventually became the vogue and effectively reduced
the market for the smaller firms like Edison, Biograph, Melies and Kalem, all of
which either withdrew or collapsed.

As salaries and production costs mounted, producers sought ways of standardising
production methods, or discovering sure fire values that could be injected into their
films to guarantee success at the box office. Hence there came into being certain
characteristics of American production which were to persist for several decades: the
star system; the formula picture (the repetition ad-nauseam of a style or subject
that was successful with the public); massive use of advertising and publicity.[109]

   Mergers within the British industry began as the individually owned cinemas
and circuits started to combine in the 1930s. One of the earliest chains, the Provincial
Cinematograph Theatres founded in 1909, merged with Gaumont British (which had
connections with Fox). British Gaumont had some 300 cinemas by 1929 and also
had control of Shepherds Bush Studios. The second major group to emerge by the
end of the 1920s was the British International Picture Group with its new studios
at Elstree and connections with the First National Circuit of America as well as
Pathe News. The BIP and its exhibiting organization, Associated British Cinemas,
like the Gaumont-British organization, had developed a presence in the industry
which extended from production and distribution; but even in 1929 over 2500
cinemas were independently owned. The 1930s and 1940s saw tendencies towards
further concentrations: in 1940 Arthur Rank, son of the flour miller, bought
Gaumont-British and, in 1941, the Odeon group of 200 super-cinemas built up by
Oscar Dentsoh, a Birmingham metal-broker.[110] At the end of the war Rank owned
500 cinemas, plus the two studios at Ealing and Shepherds Bush. The second of
the two major British companies to emerge after the war was, of course, the ABC/
EMI grouping.
   Perhaps the most significant feature of the cinema was its rapid development,
in a period of forty years, from its small artisan, almost amateur, beginnings. The
early cinema had been brought to popularity first by the travelling fairs; in the case
of Rochdale, Parker's pop concerts were a good vehicle for Inman, Holt and

Woolfenden, the three local businessmen, to exhibit their wares. Later the more established itinerant picture companies - Johnson-Wood, Golden Rays and Pringle's - took over from these local men and offered entertainment on a fortnightly basis in hired halls or as part of a vaudeville programme in an established business. The 1910 Cinematograph Act probably did a lot to reduce the number of halls where films could be shown legally, and thereby gave the picture companies the choice of settling down or fading away. Technological advances offering 'no flickering pictures' and general improvements in quality seem to have acted against the early two-way Lumiere machines: as equipment became more sophisticated it became more expensive; the American competition pressed home its advantages gained by an increasing division of labour and centralization:

The new cinema demanded a new kind of director and between 1912 and 1918 there was a large recruitment of new young artists to replace the old master crafts-men of the primitive years and the film factories.

Vast new film studios built especially for the purpose began to mushroom around the undisputed centre of the world film industry, which was the first to capitalize on sound-track film from the late 1920s on. This development was instrumental in widening the rift between what were to become the super-cinemas wired for sound and the less comfortable 'flea-pits'. It is possible that the cinema mergers which took place in the late 1920s and the early 1930s were partly due to the expense of conversion to sound as well as the prevalence of the new super-cinemas which demanded high capital outlay. The radio was beginning to bite before sound was introduced and it is probable that the silent cinema fell behind in the revival.

The popularity of the early cinema had been determined by a mixture of forces. On the one hand it developed in a period when feelings concerning the Empire occupied a central place; early film both contributed and owed much of its popularity to this atmosphere. Many of the films of fictitious content had military themes, while newsreels on South Africa and World War I met with 'large and intent audiences'. The film of Queen Victoria's funeral filled the two establish-ments which had the commercial foresight to show it in March 1901. In this early phase trends were set whereby halls and cinemas would take names closely associated with the Empire: Ceylon, Pavillion, Empire, Coliseum, Victory, Palace, Wings and Regal. On the other hand the cinema met a considerable amount of abuse from those who saw it as immoral:

It was partly the gloom, as well as its comparative novelty, which made the cinema in the 1900's a focus for adult anxiety about the sexual morality of youth. There were reports published by bodies such as the National Council of Public Morals deploring what these unsupervised groups of young people might be led to think of in such conditions.[111]

But as Roberts says, 'cinema owners protested virtue'[112] and as the days drew on price differences made it more easy for those preoccupied with maintaining their social caste to keep face by claiming a more expensive seat.

With few exceptions film content in the early period tended to centre on moralistic sagas which, though not strictly coinciding, shared some ground with indirect religious considerations. When film content began to change it did so largely under the initiative of the big new film companies which started to develop with their increasingly frivolous subject matter just before World War 1. Increasingly and at the most significant commercial level, the cinema dropped its sermonizing mask and began to move in realms framed by its own reality.

Some conclusions

The first and most obvious conclusion concerns the extension of recreational provision itself. This was bound up with two central features: the overall though fluctuating trend towards an improvement in the conventional standard of living for the majority of the population and, secondly, the reduction of hours spent at work. The time and income for private consumption which was won in this way - and it was 'won', unevenly and always reversibly, in national and local struggles - must also be seen alongside the development (and then often the deconstruction) of more or less stable working-class communities. It was in these spaces and communities that the consumption of goods and services increased, a tendency first observable from the 1880s and sufficiently marked again in the 1930s to prefigure the 'affluence' of the post-war boom. The striking growth of the industries of entertainment formed a part of these general developments, which also embraced the 'revolutions' in advertising, retailing and the production of relatively cheap consumer goods. Looking across the Edwardian period, Paul Thompson concludes:

Perhaps the most fundamental change in the standard of life was that affecting leisure. Standard weekly working hours had fallen from sixty or seventy in the nineteenth century to fifty-three in 1910, not much more than the average forty-eight hours still worked, due to increasing overtime, in the 1950s . . . . There was thus more opportunity as well as more money for entertainment. For the moment the favourite choice for leisure-time activity remained either drinking or religion but their successors were already on the scene.[113]

In the years with which we have been concerned here, press, cinema, dancing, the record industry, spectator sports like football and cricket were all commercially organized forms of provision that partook of the general increase. To these we would have to add newer forms which were not commercial - the growth, for example, of municipal provision. Book issue in Rochdale's libraries grew, for instance, over the period as did the provision and use of parks and swimming baths.

More important, perhaps, were the changing *forms* of provision. The new forms seem to 'fit' with the more structured day, week and year of the fully industrialized work pattern. They involved a limited commitment and an essentially casual usage. Cinema performances and football matches began at a set time and lasted for a scheduled period. Similarly, the recreational 'event' became more specialized, geared around a particular activity or commodity. Like the original types of football, the fair, or early popular theatre, earlier forms were multi-purpose, sanctioning a more general enjoyment. Though sometimes invested with quite other purposes than watching films or dancing to music, cinemas and dance halls were, formally, altogether more bounded occasions.

A further set of differences concern the actual provenance and geographical scope of the newer and older forms. The older forms were localized and class or group based. This seems to apply to all the most important recreational occasions developed during the nineteenth century: clubs of different kinds, brass bands, chapels, Co-operative and friendly societies, unions. Though sometimes organized nationally or regionally, the heart of union or of denomination remained the local chapel or local branch. The early extension of leisure provision, pub or music hall apart perhaps, seems often to have taken the form of the cellular growth of such club-like agencies. The extent and richness of religious and secular societies in Rochdale in the early part of our period suggests this. The newer forms often started with a local base - even in the case of film production! But they soon conformed to capital's tendency to concentrate and centralize, to unify and reduce the centres of control. Thus, leisure provision was increasingly removed from any kind of popular control, a tendency hardly offset by municipalization.

It is important, without further research, not to draw simple conclusions from this fact. We need to know much more about how the newer forms of provision were (and are) used - their place within the broader culture of a class or group. From the study of post-war sub-cultural groupings, for instance, we already know how commercialized activities and commodities themselves are often re-appropriated by their 'consumers' as a sort of raw material for further cultural work.[114] One cannot 'read off' (as mass culture theorists have tended to) the use and indigenous meanings of mass-produced messages or objects. Leisure commodities or commercial events might be distinguished one from the other, indeed, by the *opportunities* they provide for particular appropriations of this kind. Even so, historically, the shift to a provision of recreational facilities through the market and through oligopolies is of great importance. Through it, and for the first time, important sections of capital itself have acquired a direct stake in (and therefore control over) a supposedly 'private' sphere.

7 Football since the war

Chas Critcher

It is the basic premise of this essay that general arguments about changes in working-class culture since the war will always remain unsatisfactory unless they are specified with reference to particular aspects of working-class culture. Here it will be argued that professional football can be taken as one index of tradition and change in working-class culture, both reflecting and affecting broader changes.

The primary focus here is socio-historical, an attempt to trace significant changes. This requires a sketch, however simplified, of football's role as an element of working-class culture in pre-war English society. It was and still is a predominantly working-class activity, the majority of both players and spectators being recruited from a distinctive social grouping and a specific cultural tradition. Pre-war football was an integral part of that corporate working-class culture rooted in the late nineteenth century. The core values of the game as a professional sport - masculinity, aggression, physical emphasis and regional identity meshed, according to one account,[1] with other elements of that (male-dominated) working-class culture, elements carried within its network of small-scale organizations and supportive mechanisms (working men's clubs, mutual insurance schemes, co-operatives, public houses, trade unions) and in a myriad of smaller leisure-time groupings (pigeon fanciers, whippet trainers, amateur footballers and the rest). It is easy to over-estimate the homogeneity of this culture. It reflected some variations and oppositions within the class, according to region and internal boundaries, notably that between the rough and the respectable. Nevertheless Hopcraft's emphasis on the centrality of football to the common working-class experience remains a valid generalization:

By the 1920s football was an established employer in a community where jobs were scarce. The clubs had grown up out of pride on athleticism, in local importance, in corporate endeavour. The stadiums were planted where the supporters lived, in among the industrial mazes of factories and hunched workers houses. The Saturday match became more than mere diversion from the daily grind, because there was often no work to be relieved. To go to the match was to escape from the dark of despondency into the light of combat. Here, by association with the home team, positive identity could be claimed by muscle and in goals. To win was personal success, to lose another clout from life. Football was not so much an opiate of the people as a flag run up against the gaffer bolting his gates and the landlord armed with his bailiffs.[2]

However, while this subordinated class culture struggled to maintain a fixed corporate identity, it would be a mistake to confuse continuity with a lack of dynamism. This applies especially to football. Some of those most evident changes in post-war football - an expanded transfer market, declining attendances and defensive football - had their counterparts in inter-war football. There were differences of scale but the presence of these factors is not new. We have to resist the temptation to construct a changeless inter-war history, against which to dramatize post-war changes.

Since here we are concerned with trends and influences rather than moments or personalities, the effort will be to identify significant long-term factors rather than to offer a detailed chronological account. Any selection of such factors is bound to be arbitrary. In his survey of football in the 1950s, for example, Geoffrey Green offers a list of major developments in football during that period: the return to FIFA, the effect of the Hungary defeat of 1953, new tactics and training methods, changed style of kit, the arrival of floodlights, entry into European competition, the players' struggle for wages and status, the mythology of Manchester United and the advent of substitutes.[3] I have chosen to structure this essay around five particular aspects of football which I take to be both essential to its own self-conception and integral to its status as a central element of working-class culture. These are the player, the supporter, the mass media, the clubs and international influences on tactics. I begin with an examination of the professional footballer as working-class hero.

The player

From 1945 to 1963 professional footballers were engaged in a continuous collective struggle to improve their economic situation. The details of that struggle have been adequately recounted elsewhere: the annual bargaining over the maximum wage ceiling, the obdurate behaviour of the Football League, the strike threats, the players' final victory with the abolition of the maximum wage in 1960; then the struggle over contracts, culminating in a High Court judgment against Newcastle United in an action brought by George Eastham in 1963. Here it may suffice to note three main implications of these events. The first is the clear roots of the struggle in working-class activity outside the game. This was neatly noted in a *Times* editorial at the moment of abolition:

They ask for two freedoms: freedom for a player to negotiate his own contract of employment, and freedom to negotiate his own wages with his employer. These are freedoms which are basic, unarguable, and the right of every working man in Britain.[4]

The second feature is the characteristic attitude adopted by the League, seeing absolute control over players as the only bulwark against the rampant greed of the players and the tyranny of the transfer market. In the event some of their worst fears were proved justified, in so far as higher wages did contribute to the ever-

widening gap between rich and poor clubs. But this was due at least as much to
a spiralling transfer market, about which the League have done precisely nothing. In
any case the massive wage differentials opened up by abolition were in part attributable to the form and intensity of League opposition, which ruled out the
possibility of negotiating some alternative form of wage control which would have
benefited the average as well as the exceptional professional footballer.

Thirdly, and less often noted, are the implications of economic developments
for the cultural situation of the player. The professional footballer was traditionally
a kind of working-class folk hero, and knew himself to be such. He came from, and
only moved marginally out of, the same economic and cultural background as
those who paid to watch him. In such a context, a dramatic change in the economic
situation of the player was bound to have severe repercussions on the cultural
significance of his role as hero. Put simply, the effect of these changes was that 'for
some of the star performers in football the "new deal" has meant an everyday life
transformed from the kind led by the previous generation'.[5]

The emphasis here must be on 'everyday life'. It was not just a question of
footballers having gained the right to more money and more bargaining power in
relation to their employing club. What became gradually clear was that the 'new
deal' had fractured the set of social and cultural relationships by which the player's
identity had previously been structured. His relationships with management were
strained by the constant demands for performance returns on the investment in
him; his attitudes towards fellow players became more neurotically competitive
and the search for a common footballing code found only an uneasy justification
of cynicism in the ethos of 'professionalism'; his relationship with the spectators,
increasingly mediated by heightened expectations of the successful and the
spectacular, came more and more to resemble that of the highly acclaimed enter-
tainer required to produce the 'goods' for public consumption.

If the economic emancipation of the professional footballer was differentiated
in distribution and impact, so were its effects on the cultural identity of the
professional footballer. A symptomatic reading of household names which span
the post-war period - Stanley Matthews, Jimmy Greaves, Bobby Charlton, George
Best, Kevin Keegan - may only reveal differences of personality, economic position
and social status. However, equally crucial for our purposes is the relationship
between the footballer's behaviour on the field and his bearing off it. Together they
form his public presence, what public relations terminology would appropriate as
his 'image' and which, following Arthur Hopcraft, we shall describe as his style:
'We are not dealing with the style of play, but also with the style and substance of
the man, as affected by the game.'[6]

The footballer as hero is culturally defined by two related sets of expectations -
of his abilities on the field and his role as a public figure. This may be understood
historically in the post-war period as a sequence of typologies of cultural identity.
Three qualifications need to be made before embarking on such a typology.
Firstly, it includes only English players on the grounds that other British players
are products of a distinctively different cultural environment. (The one exception,

for reasons which will become apparent, is George Best.) Secondly, since we are
dealing with hero figures, we take them as symptomatic, though by definition they
are not typical. Thirdly, this definition tends to exclude footballers belonging to a
more subterranean tradition of hero. Valued at times for their anti-heroic qualities,
these are the destroyers, the hard men, the villains. Nobby Stiles, Norman Hunter
and Tommy Smith are representatives of this style.

Four styles or typologies will be offered here. The first - *traditional/located* -
represents and draws on the values of a traditional respectable working-class culture
in a way which becomes increasingly difficult, though not impossible, after the
'new deal'. Those benefiting from greater economic rewards may be typified as
transitional/mobile, exploring the possibilities of their new freedom. As even more
money becomes available to the chosen few and the game as a whole becomes more
respectable, players seek and find acceptance into overtly middle-class life-styles.
Incorporated/embourgeoised, they become small-scale entrepreneurs, a world away
from their predecessors and most of their contemporary supporters. Finally, the
combination of apparently limitless remuneration and the publicity machine of
the mass media nominate a handful of players as 'superstars' raised to new levels
and kinds of public adulation and attention. The correct typification of such
players, however, is as *superstars/dislocated* from any available models of style.
For a while their behaviour on and off the field is a source of tension to themselves
and others before they develop a new identity as superstars/relocated into the
world of show-business personalities and public celebrities; taking their places,
metaphorically and sometimes literally, alongside film and television stars, members
of the *nouveau riche* and the more publicity-conscious of the politicians.

The traditional/located style is relatively easy to identify, and has been caught
in Arthur Hopcraft's perceptive analysis of Stanley Matthews:

we were always afraid for Matthews, the non-athlete; the sadly impassive face,
with its high cheekbones, pale lips and hooded eyes, had a lot of pain in it, the deep
hurt that came from prolonged effort and the certainty of more blows. It was a
worker's face, like a miner's, never really young, tight against a brutal world even
in repose . . . . The anxiety showed in Matthews too: again like the frail miner's
fear of the job which must always be done, not joyfully but in deeper satisfaction,
for self-respect . . . . In communicating this frailty and this effort Matthews went to
men's hearts, essentially to inconspicuous, mild, working men's. He was the opposite
of glamorous: a non-drinker, non-smoker, careful with his money. He had an habitual
little cough. He was a representative of his age and class, brought up among thrift and
the ever-looming threat of dole and debt. For as long as he could remember world's
fleetest movers he never had exuberance. He came from that England which had no
reason to know that the twenties were Naughty and the thirties had Style.[7]

Matthews was symptomatic but not unique. Others of his generation - Lofthouse,
Finney, Lawton - continued to dominate the football of the immediate post-war
period. Some new recruits continued the old tradition: Derek Dooley, for example,
is described by Hopcraft as the essentially local (Sheffield-born) boy - 'Thunder-

boots'. He was a Saturday hero by and of the people, his identity contained and gladly expressed in football. According to this account 'this honest industrial yeoman . . . epitomizes the footballer of the forties and fifties'.[8]

Yet change was evident. Duncan Edwards, whose career was tragically cut short by the Munich air disaster, is described by another writer as revealing 'that surging irrepressible determination for self-expression and self-reliance of the post-war teenager', yet remaining identifiably working-class.[9] In less symbolic terms money made the difference. Still drawn from and having affinities with the mainstream working class, the salaries of top players began to take them out of the most skilled worker's economic grouping. Johnny Haynes made one kind of breakthrough to become the first £100-a-week player but for various reasons - an unglamorous club, restricted media access, a reluctance to score goals — Haynes never fitted properly into the heroic mould. The central figure of the transitional style is Bobby Charlton - a working-class gentleman who could live like one:

He gets the star footballer's profusion of flattery. His name is chanted to raise the spirits of ticket queues in the rain; vivid coarse girls have to be held off by policemen when he gets into and out of the Manchester United coach; small boys write him letters of charming clumsiness and kick footballs with his autograph on them; he has been European footballer of the year and a poll of referees voted him model player. His wife is pretty, so are his two daughters, and he lives in a rich man's house in a rich man's neighbourhood. He is the classic working-class hero who has made it to glamour and Nob Hill.[10]

Charlton's long career, like that of Matthews, tends to disguise real changes. The dominance of the transitional style was over long before his World and European Cup triumphs of 1966 and 1968. It flourished in the early 1960s when the England team contained Charlton, Haynes and Jimmy Greaves, who was to bear witness to the changes in style by having lived through all four stages.

By the late 1960s the style of incorporation was becoming dominant, as star footballers became self-conscious participants in the process of their own embourgeoisement. It was this rather than the transitional style that was truly anonymous. This was partly due to the impression of conformity which the description 'incorporated' is meant to convey: the image of the small businessman is hardly laden with heroic qualities. The development of tactics, too, had made playing styles more rigid: over-collective, remorseless and functional, the new demands were for the runner, the 'worker' who could fit into a preconceived pattern. Alan Ball is a symptomatic player here: his total style is defined by the new tactics:

All the adjectives, the superlatives as well as the clichés which surround the modern game apply to Ball - the 90-minute man, genius clothed in sweat, perpetual motion, the essential team-man, hating to lose, living and breathing the game, awesome opponent and valued colleague, selfless yet still essentially a star . . . these are the terms in which one talks of Ball.[11]

A whole generation of such men played for England in the middle and late

1960s: who will remember them? Those who stand out are hybrids. Bobby Moore, for example, maintained a detachment more typical of the transitional style and was accorded, as a result, as much envy as admiration. Perhaps the real anonymity of the incorporated style fed the search for the unusual, on and off the field. If those interested in footballing skills looked in vain for some variation from the stereotyped football of such teams as Leeds, Arsenal, and England, then those with a vested interest in glamour sought celebrities to populate their portrayal of life at the Top. Their separate desires were fulfilled by the superstar.

The superstar emerged most clearly in the late 1960s and early 1970s, and the central figure has to be George Best. But there had been earlier attempts to collude in the cultural dislocation of footballing heroes. Jimmy Greaves and others who followed the lure of gold to Italy in the early 1960s helped to dislocate themselves: a process further dislocated by the press exploitation of their subsequent discontent. *The Times* made this comment on the Greaves affair as early as 1961, when Greaves was finally transferred back to Spurs:

There it stands, and may the man and the game be spared any more. Seldom in the history of British football can any man have commanded so much attention in so short a time. Not even the deeds of men like G.O. Smith, Bloomer, Meredith, Gallacher, Morton, Jackson, Matthews, Dean, Lawton and Wright across the years caught the same fierce glare of concentrated publicity.

Much of it has been unwelcome . . . . Yet the suspicion is that latterly Greaves has been as much sinned against as sinning. His every daily action caught the spotlight and much of it was magnified unduly. The whole affair has become tedious beyond words.[12]

In the same year as the Greaves affair a fifteen-year old boy from a Belfast housing estate came as an apprentice to Manchester United. Within forty-eight hours he and his travelling companion were back in Belfast. Three years later he was a regular member of Manchester United's championship side at the age of eighteen; in 1968 he was instrumental in United's European Cup victory and was voted Footballer of the Year. In 1971 he was sent off the field during an international match for throwing mud at the referee and, amidst increasing controversy over his private life and business associates, he quit the game in 1972. Returning briefly in 1973, he finally left the game, apparently for good in 1974, only to return with Fulham in 1976, then to leave finally for the USA.

That is the bare outline of the career of George Best. But much more was involved in the 'superstar' treatment he received. For seven years his every move was plotted by journalists and photographers; he was alternatively told - in newspaper columns and to his face - that he was the greatest footballer in the world and a spoilt brat; on the field he was kicked, held, punched, and admonished when he retaliated. All these were forces acting on Best, who in response lived it up with fast cars and beautiful women, while securing his future in a chain of boutiques. He lived out, part by personal choice, part by cultural compulsion, the newspapers' dream version of the superstar's life. As crisis succeeded crisis, he eventually exerted

his own will in the only way left open to him, and left the English League, con-
tracting himself out for individual appearances.

Of course it is possible to interpret this odyssey as the biography of a not-very-
bright and immature lad, who let success go to his head and listened to the wrong
people; or as the due reward for a headstrong, conceited man who wanted fame
and reward on his own terms and was not prepared to work for it. The suggestion
here is that the saga of George Best should be read in wider cultural terms, as the
biography of a dislocated footballing hero, whose talent, personality and background were insufficient to withstand the pressures, both on and off the field, to
which the new type of superstar was to be subjected. Uprooted early from his
Irish origins he had limited psychological resources - family or friends - who would
treat him other than as a superstar. He had to live through that identity as the only
one available to him.

The crisis in the identity of the superstar was short-lived, thought more widespread than a concentration on Best alone might indicate. At least one other
England international underwent treatment for a nervous breakdown. The pressures
internal to the game were also increasing and spreading down the divisions, as one
diary account demonstrates.[13] Eventually, however, the expectations of a superstar
became clearer, more rationalized both for the players and those who sought to
exploit their newsworthiness or feed off their glamour and money. Not, it should
be said, that the mix of personal idiosyncracy and the cultural definition of the
superstar wholly ceased to be instructive for particular players (Rodney Marsh,
Charlie George, Alan Hudson). Still, the negative example of Best prepared those
who were to follow. They avoided London clubs, married and 'settled down', took
proper economic advice, learnt how to handle interviews. By the mid 1970s young
men like Kevin Keegan and Trevor Francis had learnt to cope with their new
identity.

The cultural crisis of the superstar did have ramifications outside the few players
directly involved. George Best gained as much notoriety for his confrontations with
referees as ever he did for his nightlife or arguments with managers. The changing
styles of the footballer as hero were reflected on the football field especially in an
apparent increase in gamesmanship and petulance. The evidence is uneven: older
players argue that they too feigned injury, committed sly offences and argued with
the referee. Nevertheless it seems fair to state that post-war football has been characterized by an increase in, and institutionalization of, deliberate infringement of the
laws of the game. There is apparently nothing new about the content or tone of an
FA circular of 1964, but it may indicate a felt sense of crisis.

Foul play, abusive language, gamesmanship and petulance will be taken note of or
punished - dependent on the severity of the offence. Players must learn to discipline
themselves. If not, they will be disciplined. Until the present wave of disorder
ceases, they can expect severe penalties for misconduct.[14]

There is no easy explanation for these trends. The exposure to continental
tactics and the use of deliberate cheating - the professional foul - as a tactical ploy

also contributed. Here it is argued that certain specific forms of misconduct, especially forms of 'display' behaviour such as diving in the penalty area or feigning injury, can be defined negatively, as unthinkable to those traditional heroes who subscribed, however unwittingly, to a working-class version of masculinity and its sense of appropriate violence. Elsewhere I have suggested that football

offered a formalization of the informal attitudes to violence so long held by working men, that it is a normal part of life in which any individual may periodically become involved, but it is never expected to get out of hand or become a pervasive frame of mind.[15]

Similarly pain was something to be endured - historically the working class is well schooled in it - and the dramatic exaggeration now exhibited by professional footballers would have been defined as (the ultimate condemnation) effeminate. To appropriate this in terms of the footballing hero, we may quote the case of Tommy Lawton:

Lawton probably took more punishment in the way of tripping, unscrupulous tackling, hammering and bumping than any man of his period. The specialist centre forward was the natural target for it. No-one ever saw Lawton retaliate, or deliberately foul anyone. That he should lose his temper or be sent off was unthinkable. In over twenty years, he never did and never was.[16]

Lawton may have been an exception in his day, yet such conduct is now almost inconceivable. The implications are cumulative and widespread. The jeering by opposing crowds at players stretchered off is partly informed by the knowledge that pain is simulated for tactical advantage too frequently on the field for its actual occurrence to cause much grief. The players' lack of an agreed code of conduct - above and beyond the actual laws of the game - is reflected and reinforced by the attitudes and behaviour of the crowd. They too had problems coming to terms with the new trends.

The supporter

What will be described here as the disaffection of the supporter from his traditional relationship to professional football has taken three main forms: firstly, a disinclination to continue following the local team regardless of its achievement; secondly and relatedly, a preference for armchair viewing of weekly televised excerpts: thirdly, a symbolic redefinition of the role of the supporter through the activities of ritualized aggression adopted by younger fans.

The first signal of the spectators' disaffection was the fall in total annual attendance at league matches. By 1955 it was clear that the great post-war boom in attendances was over. The peak had been reached with the record total of 41,250,000 in the 1948-9 season, after which the figure decreased steadily to 34,000,000 in 1954-5. By the early 1960s the total figure had stabilized to around

28,000,000 and after a further peak in 1968 a new low was reached in 1971-2 with only 21,000,000 rather less than half of the 1948 figure. By the middle 1970s, however, a further stabilization had taken place at around 25,000,000. The clubs outside the first division have fared worst: in 1964 they accounted for 56 per cent of all attendances but ten years later they had only 48 per cent.[17] Such numbers are a barometer of success or failure. The common response to declining attendances has been to define football as in competition with other often more attractive leisure opportunities. In 1961, *The Times* noted that the changing social habits - 'H.P., the weekend family car, bingo and the rest' - meant 'mediocrity is harder to sell now'. The conclusion was that football's falling gates reflected changed class aspirations: 'Once football was the opium of the masses. No longer. There is a greater awareness of standards and comfort now. So perhaps the real answer at last is for a complete spring clean.'[18] An opinion poll commissioned by the Football League in 1962 came to similar conclusions. Noting the main factors for staying away as changed attitudes towards family and home, the lack of comfort at grounds - and, in a minor key, defensive football and players' lack of discipline - the report concluded that 'the arrest of the fall in gates can be achieved only by making football matches and their surroundings more attractive than other leisure activities.[19] The government-sponsored Chester Report of 1968 took a similar line.

This financial deterioration has taken place during a period when the general standard of play has reached a very high level. The explanation therefore lies not there but probably in the radical changes which have taken place in the social pattern and in people's attitudes and leisure activities.[20]

The message, then, was clear. Spectators were not disaffected from the game as such, but from the facilities it offered and its inability to adopt a more modern style of self-presentation. Some writers went farther, arguing that the image of the traditional supporter was outdated and being replaced by 'a new type of spectator':

Someone who can take his choice of the games he will go to and seek out of a variety of entertainment on any Saturday afternoon..... You can either choose the best First Division soccer or opt for a quiet backwater in the Second or lower division .... Apart from isolated centres and the odd ten or a dozen clubs with huge working class followings, the day of the dedicated fan has passed.[21]

There are many potential objections to such comments which are only the logical extension of the remarks previously quoted. (The last passage could, for example, have been written only by someone whose current knowledge of anywhere north of Enfield has come from looking out of the window of a first-class railway carriage.) The main point to note here is that the major response to real changes in spectators' attitudes to football has not been to examine the cultural changes in the game and its immediate context. Rather it has been to import into discussion of the spectator an image which comes not out of a cultural concern but from the heart of commercial activity: the image of the consumer. Raymond Williams has noted the historical development of three kinds of cultural relationship between an individual or social group and social institutions: member, customer and consumer.[22] The first, however illusorily, thinks of himself as a member, and may recognize an informal set of reciprocal duties and obligations between himself and the institution. The customer, more detached, is seeking satisfaction for specific wants: if they are not met over a certain period of time, he may, somewhat reluctantly, take his patronage elsewhere. But the consumer has no loyalty or habit. He is informed of the choices open to him, and when he wants something will make a rational choice about where he will get the best bargain. Such choices are continually made, and the logic of the market is that those who wish to sell their products will compete with each other for his attention.

If this model is applied to the supporter, we may see how his relationship to the main social institution of football, the club, has been changing. Ian Taylor has convincingly suggested that the traditional supporter was able to think positively about his relationship to the club.[23] He could feel that the club and its players belonged to him and his fellow supporters. The players were 'available subcultural representatives' conscious of their closeness, cultural and economic, to their supporters, who in turn fulfilled that role and provided him with cultural and economic support. Thus "the rank and file supporter could (however wrongly) see himself as being a member of a collective and democratically structured enterprise'.

With the fall in attendances, it became apparent that this illusion was no longer enough to maintain supporters' loyalty. It had to compete with other more powerful illusions. The response of those who dominated the public discussion and practical administration of football was not to look for a model of membership more culturally relevant and more firmly founded than the traditional illusion. It was rather to assume that the only possible relationship was that dominant in other more commercially minded leisure activities. If there was still much talk of the romance of being a supporter, if managers still claimed theirs were the best supporters in the country, if there was a campaign to improve the poverty of the ground facilities, these were more than counterbalanced by the image, explicit or implicit, of the supporter on which major policy decisions were based. The effects, Taylor has argued, were devastating - football was subject to a process of professionalization:

Professionalization does not consist simply of entry into the transfer market and the beginnings of large transfer fees. It is also the process whereby clubs began to accommodate themselves to their changing role in a declining entertainments industry. Developmental processes in the wider society were increasing the leisure opportunities of an increasingly differentiated working-class. Football was competing for customers over and above football subculture. In one sense, this was a technical question involving the provision of covered accommodation, increasing the number of seats, and most obviously the fitting of floodlights to enable evening matches to be played. In another sense, however, the process involved a transformation of the stereotype of the football supporter. Where once the stereotypical supporter was a working-class man, living for Saturday and inextricably involved - in his own perception - with the fortunes of the club, now he was of undefined class membership, enjoying an escape from responsibilities, the provision of a spectacle from time to time, and expecting fulfilment of these needs from a team of professional entertainers . . . . From the participatory and masculine values of the working-class supporter, and from an exclusive concern with victory, football turned its attention to the provision of spectacle, skill and efficient performance - values understood to be important to the stereotypical i.e. middle-class supporter.[24]

If this is a little overdrawn and smacks too much of class conspiracy, it is nevertheless more convincing than other analyses. It also opens the way to an explanation of the second symptom of the supporters' disaffection; ritualized and occasionally realized aggression. Into the hiatus between traditional supporter and modern consumer stepped the football hooligan.

It is almost impossible to write seriously about the problem of 'football hooliganism'. Not only is the phrase itself a label rather than a descriptive or analytical category, but there are virtually no statistics on its incidence even in terms of arrests in or around football grounds. Further, the label is used indiscriminately: are all the Stretford End 'hooligans', and if not, how do we distinguish those who are from those who are not? Finally, in terms of evidence, the media are an extremely unreliable source, involved as they are not merely in reporting but in sensationalizing and socially constructing the image of the 'football hooligan'.[25]

It needs to be said that those who commit - or at least are arrested for - criminal acts at football matches are an infinitesimal proportion of all supporters. The average number of arrests at Manchester United home games, out of gates of 50,000 to 60,000, is 3.2. In so far as it can be traced historically, the problem of 'hooliganism' seems to stem from the early and middle 1960s; at least, there is little evidence of it before that period. What is important for our present purposes is what new forms of spectator behaviour, especially amongst the young, can reveal about the attitude of football authorities to the spectator, and what the 'hooligans' own self-perceptions can reveal about their relationship to the game.

The Times response was equivocal: crowd disturbances were both 'mindless thuggery' and a 'social problem'. James Callaghan, then Home Secretary, took it upon himself to define as *non*-supporters those involved in such incidents.

I agree that wanton destruction is perpetrated by a relatively small number of people who call themselves football fans. They are nothing of the sort and the clubs will be well rid of them. The authorities who try to stamp this out have the full support not only of myself but of the overwhelming majority of the public.[26]

The press weighed in with its careful, constructive analysis of the situation - savages, animals, thugs, lunatics were included amongst the repertoire.[27] Even the more responsible journalists insisted that the phenomenon had nothing to do with football itself. John Arlott argued that such a 'drunken mob' was attracted to football by the possibility of violence and nothing else.[28] Arthur Hopcraft perceived them as 'louts with pimples and knives' and recommended a strategy of draconian measures which he admittted to have 'fascist overtones'.[29]

According to this definition, troublemakers at football matches are a mob of undisciplined psychopaths with minimal interest in football; the source of their behaviour is seen to be outside the game, as part of the social malaise of our times. This not only allows football authorities to disavow any responsibility towards such supporters, other than those of containment and control; it also denies that such behaviour has any rationale in terms of the development of post-war football.

An alternative thesis has been outlined by Ian Taylor.[30] Extending arguments we have already touched upon, he sees football 'hooliganism' as a distorted attempt to restore some meaning and commitment to the role of the supporter. All the developments we have seen to be characteristic of the 1950s and 1960s - spiralling transfer fees, the economic and cultural dislocation of the top-line players, European competition, the attempts to make the game 'respectable' for a new 'model' spectator - have contributed to the undermining of the traditional role and image of the supporter. Thus those who look to the game for the assertion of traditional values are left behind; they are a 'subcultural rump'. With no former channels available to them to express their loyalty, and informal access to club and players closed, they draw on what few resources they have left. They evolve their own songs and chants, institutionalizing long-established individual obscenity and defiance at a collective level. They try to 'help' their team by booing and jeering the opposition, and extend the violent conflict of the field to the terraces and beyond.

But more than that. In symbolically displaced ways they reassert the traditional values which are being discredited in the organization and ideology of the game. They are not selective consumers but totally committed supporters of their team alone; not individual spectators, but part of a collectively responding crowd; not politely passive in their appreciation, but actively interventionist. They are thus the 'real supporters' in the traditional definition. Their general life-experience is reproduced inside football - that of 'cultural alienation', divorced from those communal activities which previously gave those in their situation some possibilities for identification and commitment. They look to football not as an excuse for a punch-up, but for a regeneration of football's role in working-class culture:

the centrality of soccer as a form of consciousness in sections of the working-class leads these sections to locate their alienation and isolation in the soccer club itself (their club). That is, violent resistance at the point of soccer consciousness is not an arbitrary reflection of some vague frustration. Rather, the violence around soccer may be seen as a specific (if inarticulate) choice produced by the hold the game has had over generations of working-class experience.[31]

The argument is by no means completed. Taylor tends if anything to go too far in one direction. If the mainstream attitude to 'football hooliganism' has been to deny its connections with the game, it may be overreacting to locate it wholly within the game. Rather we need to understand more fully this relationship between the game and more general cultural pressures to which some sections of the working class are being subjected. The fusion of the 'skinhead' phenomenon and 'football hooliganism' may have provided a moment when some of those relationships became clear: how football appeared as an element alongside other cultural experiences like housing redevelopment and the break-up of the traditional neighbourhood, frustrated expectations in education and employment, the commercialization of leisure, the 'threat' posed by immigration.

The seminal work of Peter Marsh and others has helped to expose exactly why football should be selected as the venue for the ritualized aggression of working-class youth.[32] Contrary to the popular image, violence is not widespread, random or uncontrolled. On the contrary, the behaviour of the End is internally structured: a career from Novice to Rowdy to Town Boy, with an emergent figure not much different from the average employed, courting, early 1920s working-class youth. The culture has its own limits - the rules of disorder - and transgression is socially sanctioned. The 'nutter' though a source of some amusement, is defined as beyond the pale. His is not a model to follow.

What is happening on the terraces is similar to what is happening on the field. There is occasionally discussion of the relationship between violence among players and that amongst spectators, either as a simple causal one (punch-up on the foeld equals punch-up on the terraces) or in terms of players setting a 'bad example' for younger impressionable players to follow. The connection seems to me more subtle and more indirect. The traditional player and supporter inhabited a set of cultural definitions of themselves and each other: what I propose to call separate but related codes. Neither the laws of the game nor those of the society governing behaviour on the terraces are sufficient to guarantee order. What there has to be in addition is a set of unwritten rules - a code - as to what is acceptable behaviour. For contemporary working-class youth, such a code is not absent (the Town Boy does become like his father), but it is more fragile and tenuous. Within the specific cultural arena of football an appropriate code cannot be generated by the armchair viewer, the sophisticated TV pundit or the club chairman. Their vision of the selective passive family grouping bears little relationship to the general life experience of working-class youth, to their particular involvement behind the goal. In the absence of a code appropriate to their circumstances, the young supporters generate one. It appears to the outsider to be unrestrained in its commitment, uncontrolled in its participation, uncivilized in its demeanour. But for the young supporter, it restores adolescent male working-class identity. The football ground is the established venue for the exploration and expression of this identity. In the absence of alternatives, it is likely to remain so.

The mass media

The concern here is not with the general 'standard' of sports reporting, or with its inability to avoid cliché or bias. The crucial effects of the mass media on the game as here defined are those which seek to alter or influence the nature of public response. The argument will be that the main emphasis of the press is on the exploitation of the footballer as celebrity, while television has more far-reaching and less generally appreciated effects on the presentation of the game. The press has long brought its own demands for controversy and sensationalism to bear heavily upon its presentation of football. There are the usual arguments about what is newsworthy; the excuse trotted out is that 'it's what the public are interested in'. As long as this was confined to the context of a local team, then its effects were likely to be counterbalanced by the supporters' access to primary knowledge, e.g. about how certain players or the team as a whole were shaping up. But wherever the press is more or less the only source of information, then its own particular interests work against those of the game in general. The false opinion of 'ghosted' articles, the deliberate provocation of trivial controversy, the exaggeration of enmity within or between teams - all these are attempts to transform the genuine drama of the match into the artificially sensational image of society which the press too often conveys.

Since it is more localized than television, the press comes increasingly to stand as the main intermediary between the supporter and the club and its players, in those areas the supporter can have no knowledge of. His perception of a player's performance on the field may be coloured by the image of his life off it as portrayed by the press. The transfer request, night-club incident or family tragedy in which any player may become involved are delivered to us in a press package. We may receive it with that partial cynicism we always have towards newspaper stories, but we read it none the less and it comes to constitute part of our sub-cultural knowledge, The effects on the player can be disastrous, not only because of the strain of trying to live in the constant glare of publicity, but because his game and the attitude of crowds towards him may suffer as a result. The 'success' of the media in the case of George Best was to infuse — with no little help from Best himself - the controversial nature of his behaviour off the field into his actual playing performance, finally destroying the base of real talent on to which they had parasitically grafted their own image of the superstar. And the public, with no alternative source of information, colluded in this process.

Both the individual player and the club - its financial crises, power struggles, entries on to the transfer market — are filtered through the press. The effect is to further distance the supporter from any sense of participation and membership. At least, it may be thought, he still has his own evidence of the matches he sees to form his own attachments and ideas. This remains true for those who regularly attend matches, and football supporters do in general display a remarkable capacity to defend the authenticity of their own perceptions. But for those 'missing millions' who have ceased to attend matches, and for an altogether new public, access to football only exists through the medium of television.

The role of television in the presentation of football has been the object of rigorous semiological scrutiny by members of the British Film Institute. Here we must necessarily confine ourselves to a few brief remarks. These are, however, in accord with the specific analysis they have offered and accepts their basic premise that although football programmes claim merely to present reality, in fact this 'reality' is a construct.[33] Television never presents to us the game as we might have seen it had we been there ourselves. Commentary, camerawork and retrospective analysis by experts all contribute to a very particular structuring of the match. We do not, for example, require a running commentary at a live match; why then do we have one on television? Beyond the communication of some basic information, about team selection, for example, its role is superfluous. We have two eyes; we can see what is happening. In fact, the commentator is the first stage of interpretation. He comes between us and the event: he represents it to us. His comments go well beyond the descriptive into the interpretive. In order to take the game at all we have to encounter his continuous interpretation of it. The history of television football demonstrates the commentator's increasingly interpretive conception of his role. The descriptive style (Kenneth Wolstenholme) is superseded by that of the instant analyst (David Coleman): the shift is from describing what is happening to explaining it. We see what is happening and we are told why; our own interpretation, if it still exists, must grapple with that of the commentator.

Camerawork is also highly selective. What passes as increased efficiency - shot from different angles, better close-ups, immediate action replays - is in fact a more sophisticated restructuring of the footballing event. Focusing on a very small part of the pitch where the ball is prevents us seeing what is happening off the ball. (When forwards are described as 'coming from nowhere', what is really meant is that they were not originally in the camera shot.) Editing of ninety minutes down to thirty represents the game as a series of detailed moments rather than as a more general flow of action. Action replays may be shown while the game is still going on so that when we return live we must guess what has gone on before. Close-ups of players in moments of joy and anguish intensify the dramatic self-exposure required of a superstar.

As if all this wasn't enough, we are subjected to expert analysis afterwards; If kept at the level of simple opinion, this may be no more harmful than the cavortings of a few particularly extrovert players and managers. And there is no reason why some comments should not be made after a game has been shown. But things have got out of hand when film of a game is curtailed to get the 'experts' in; the game itself is playing second fiddle to television's idea of a show.

What is at stake here is the effect of television and the press on the footballing sub-culture: on the large-scale perception of a popular cultural activity. It has not been anything but debilitative. They have brought to the game their own definitions of newsworthiness (the sensational, the dramatic), their own ways of personalizing events ('great men under strain'), and their own self-interpretation as experts ('it is my job to tell you what all this means'). Far from understanding or defending the traditional role of the 'supporter', they have sought to educate him out of it into the world of technical sophistication and managed melodrama which they fondly believe to be an accurate and desirable presentation of the game.

The club

In 1954 a *Times* article, taking the form of a post-mortem on the double international defeat by Hungary, concluded that 'if football's place in the national culture is lost, the game will lose as a business and an entertainment as surely as it will lose as a sport and a game.' This recognizes the essential paradoxes of the professional football club while run as a business, it is generally unable (by law) or unwilling (by inclination) to pay out much interest or investment in it; while catering for a substantially working-class following, its finances and policies are controlled by capitalist entrepreneurs. Ever since the late nineteenth century when clubs began to take gate money, pay players and register as limited liability companies, these have been integral characteristics of the football club. The problem here is how these contradictions have worked themselves through in the post-war period and how such developments affect the role of the game as working-class culture.

The finances of a football club are as complex as those of any medium-size business. It is not easy to unravel them and a national picture would require pains-taking research. The main trends, however, were analysed by the Chester Report in this fashion:

The picture we have described in terms of the current financial situation and of the broader social forces at work, is complex. It is not possible to say simply that English League football is in good or bad condition, that the outlook is rosy or bleak. There are a number of quite different conditions, some apparently very rosy, some rather grey, and some very black. For the various reasons set out earlier in this chapter - the distribution and concentration of population, the abolition of the maximum wage, the inflation of transfer fees, the growth of personal affluence and private transport, the demand for highest quality amenities, the impact of television and the introduction of new European competitions which concern and reward only the top clubs - quite distinct classes have developed within the Football League. The League is only theoretically composed of ninety-two equal clubs. In practice, it has an established plutocracy, a middle class who normally just manage to keep their heads above water, and a large proletariat living in nearly permanent poverty. Admittedly the boundaries between the football middle class and the classes below may be fluid and blurred. Exceptionally good management or quirks of good fortune may also help some of the proletariat to above-average achievements. But in general the pattern of relative success is well established. All of the influences outlined above reinforce them, tending to make the rich richer and the poor poorer. What we are witnessing is a circular process in which success tends to perpetuate success, and membership of a lower division to make continued membership of a lower division more likely.[34]

This account is an uneven one. The recounting of specific costs (wages, ground, travel) is put alongside assumptions of consumer orientation. Indeed the report subsequently decides that, 'The question we must ask is - what will the customer buy?' The assumption of the dominance of a dozen or so top clubs is also question-able if extended beyond the assessment of capital assets. While the gates of some clubs do guarantee a set amount of income, this is dependent upon sustained success on the field. If one measures the extent of dominance by examining the distribution of major league prizes and status, the situation is much more open than the report implies. If one takes some indices of dominance over ten-year periods since 1919 the results are not what common sense would suggest. The number of clubs winning the league championship, finishing in the first four places or appearing in the first division has not declined in the post-war decades. Indeed, there may be an argument that the game has become more open: certainly fewer clubs are able to maintain an 'automatic' position in the first division.

So the presence of what might be described as an oligopoly of new football clubs dominating attendances, transfer fees and league success needs to be qualified. The last does not follow on from the first two and, on occasions, however temporarily, the last may be obtained without any immediate expansion of the first two. A successful team may attract resources to the club both in terms of the income from gate money and those willing to provide private capital. For any club in a city or large town, there is a reservoir of public support and private capital ready to be tapped at the first sign of success. While success is more difficult to come by without such resources, it can and does happen if a manager is particularly skilful and/or lucky.

Nevertheless the Chester Report's argument does have validity when applied to the lower divisions. Costs have risen relatively faster than in the first division, while income, especially that of gate money, has declined. A particular cost is that of travel, which leads the committee to recommend reverting to the old system of regionalizing competition in the lower divisions. Further, a very careful analysis of the operations of the transfer system in the mid 1960s demonstrated quite incontrovertibly that the transfer system worked to the disadvantage of the lower divisions all the way down the scale. First division teams paid out less to second division teams than they received and so on.

The response of the Chester Report was not, however, to seek to redress this apparently increasing inequality. Using a 'lame duck' metaphor fashionable at the time, they argued that any form of subsidy to smaller clubs would encourage inefficiency. Clubs which came to rely on such contributions for much of their income would have less incentive to balance their accounts and progressive management would not be encouraged. So other than regionalised competitions and more immunity from tax, the Chester Report only recommended that the smaller clubs should embark on programmes in conjunction with local authorities to establish their grounds as focal community resources. There is, of course, a divergent role for the bigger clubs - what the report saw as

the basic point whether it is not just improvement but a change in the nature of the football club which is under consideration - either towards great entertainment centres or towards smaller community social centres.[35]

What we have here are two very different and yet specific images of the cultural role of the football club. The bigger clubs are to provide facilities for an amorphous group of consumers and their families: squash courts, swimming pools and the rest. The smaller club is to encourage various forms of 'involvement': drinking at a club bar, listening to a 'blue' comic, selling a quota of tote tickets.

The central question omitted here is whether or how the supporter should have any control over the clubs he regards as his. The irony is that the supporter has been almost universally treated with contempt by football clubs. He has been expected to urinate in the open air, queue for ages for a stewed cup of tea, wait his turn for tickets while directors and season ticket holders (and their friends) are served first. He has been crammed into a small space with thousands of others to an extent which has literally put life and limb at risk. Now all this is to change: seats are provided, bars opened, car parks provided - all of course at a price around three times the original. He has been changed from supporter into consumer.

The motives are far from altruistic. At their simplest, these are measures to increase attendance revenue. Thus the conversion of a terrace to seating may half capacity but it will double revenue. Plush enclosed boxes may be leased - at several thousand pounds a season - to businesses who can entertain their own and other executives, whisky in hand, to a spot of instant entertainment. Meanwhile those too young, too poor, or too traditional to understand or appreciate these improvements will be huddled together behind the goals.

The new consumer then receives more status but has no more power. Further, his role, as defined by the surroundings, is essentially a passive one: no impassioned troublemaker he - no physical involvement, chanting or swearing in these new stands. The drive towards all-seated stadia, motivated by the convenient theories that they increase revenue and decrease the possibilities of hooliganism, involves a redefinition of the club's relationship to the supporter.

It remains an open question of whether professional football really is insolvent, or whether it suffers from increasing inequality. The apparent availability of private capital, money from sponsorship and advertising, revenue from pools and television, hardly seems in short supply. Each club, however, is kept in a state of constant competition for resources and no attempt is made to cushion the club against the possibility of failure. It is, in short, a paradigm of capitalism. The strategies which do exist tend to fit images of the supporter as consumer; measures to reduce inequality, such as transfer levies, are steadfastly rejected. This failure is hardly surprising since the Football League is effectively run by the votes of the directors of first and second division clubs, with the two lower divisions having a token four votes between them. A body so constituted is hardly likely to concern itself with the minions. That a typical third division crowd is, in terms of any other sport, a substantial gathering of people who are expressing, through their attendance, support for a specific cultural institution - the local football club - will find little purchase amongst those whose latest investment - a footballer - will be worth more than all of a third division side put together.

It may not matter to football long term that a few obscure small-town northern clubs drop out of the league, or that others depend on the forbearance of the bank and the generosity of a local builder. But even at the very top, financial instability matters, for it is reflected on the field. Between the directors and the players stands the manager: it is on his ability to produce a successful side that the annual accounts - and the continuity of his job - depend. The end product of financial instability is fear of failure.

The international influence and tactics

In 1953 a new queen was crowned, an Englishman was one of the first to climb Everest, and Stanley Matthews at last won the Cup Winners' medal which had so long eluded him. All seemed right with the world. But in the same year England were soundly thrashed 6-3 by Hungary at Wembley, the first national side from the continent to beat England on their home ground. To prove it was no fluke they handed out an even more severe beating, 7-1, in the return some months later in Belgrade. This provoked a bout of self-criticism throughout the game. *The Times* was strident in its analysis:

British footballers have a four-point programme to master if they are to survive. They must become athletes, 100 per cent fit; they must become gymnasts; they must make the ball a slave, answering every command, and they must start thinking intelligently ahead of the pass . . . . We must reshape our whole outlook. The w/m formation against a team such as these Hungarians with its new ideas, is as outdated as a horsedrawn bus . . . . The basic trouble, of course, quite apart from the difference in fundamental styles, was our tactical inefficiency.[36]

As Percy Young has observed, this defeat reproduced within the game of football a more general crisis of British imperial philosophy - 'more often felt subconsciously than consciously and born of the realisation that Britain does not stand where she did'.[37]

There was little in the form of the English side in the 1950s and early 1960s to reawaken confidence. Only two of the next nine internationals after Hungary were won. England performed indifferently in the 1958 World Cup and were beaten 1-0 by Russia in a group play-off. A disastrous tour of South America in 1959 included a 1-2 defeat by Mexico and was followed by a second Wembley defeat, this time Sweden being the 3-2 victors. Despite the concession of some power and status to team manager Walter Winterbottom, the string of poor results continued and the 1962 World Cup was an action replay of 1958, the only consolation being that England's quarter-final conquerors, Brazil, went on to win the competition. Winterbottom resigned, his assistant Jimmy Adamson declined to replace him, and Alf Ramsey was appointed manager with complete responsibility at last for team selection and preparation. A new phase had begun.

If the Football Association were slow to grasp the absolute need for efficient administration, serious preparation and extensive experience to have any success at all in international competition, one or two league clubs were more open to experimentation. Manchester United led the way with a series of friendlies against major European club sides. Thus when the Football League was finally prevailed upon to discontinue its embargo on English clubs participating in European competitions, United were more prepared than most. The first English side to enter the European Cup in the 1956-7 season, they reached the semi-finals before going down to the all-conquering Réal Madrid. In the next year, they again qualified for the semi-finals but the tragedy of the Munich air disaster cut short the progress of a young team, whose members might have introduced a whole new style to English football at both international and club level. They were succeeded in the next two season's competitions by Wolverhampton Wanderers, then by Burnley, neither of whom were able to cope with the sophistication of continental sides. It was left to another exceptional team, Tottenham Hotspurs, to emulate United in the 1961-2 season, going down by the odd goal in seven to Benfica in a two-legged semi-final.

In 1963, Spurs won the European Cup Winners' Cup, beating Athlético Madrid 5-1 in Rotterdam, and West Ham emulated them more narrowly - and on the home ground of Wembley - in 1965. But a year earlier, a run of eight games without defeat by the English national side had resulted in another defeat at home, this time by Austria.

It had become obvious that English football was tactically and organizationally anachronistic in international terms. There had been little innovation since the w/m formation produced by the change in the offside law of 1925. It involved three at the back - two full-backs and a defensive centre-half - two wing halves, who were primarily fetchers and carriers, and five forwards, all of whom were expected to attack, but the two inside forwards had special distributive responsibilities. This formation dominated English football from its institution by Herbert Chapman in the 1920s to the innovation of Alf Ramsey in the early 1960s.

The response to the challenge of the continent - and eventually that of South America - was less to alter the basic orientation to the game than to capitalize on the 'English virtues': discipline, organization and stamina. The first move was to withdraw one of the wing halves into the rear line of the defence and one inside forward into the middle position. This was the 4-2-4 system. It became evident, however, that the midfield was the crucial arena: here the opposition must be cramped for space, the ball won and distributed. This was too much for two men so another forward was withdrawn, generally a winger, regarded in the new system as a luxury since he depended on others for the ball. This gave us 4-3-3. The pattern of innovation was abruptly terminated because a 'system' was perceived to have won the World Cup for England in 1966. Ramsey experimented throughout the tournament but the lesson learnt from his success was that exceptional work-rate, team understanding and defensive impenetrability could overcome more skilful but less effective foreign sides. Without Ramsey's successful institutionalization, the subsequent tactical system of English football might not have become quite so rigid or have been so slavishly reproduced throughout the league. The essential was the attitude that (in Arthur Hopcraft's words) 'success was overridingly important, that positive method, was indispensable, that attractiveness was incidental'.[38]

In 1968 Manchester United won the European Cup - though again home advantage was crucial. Theirs was not an example to follow: a team of uniquely skilful players, dependent on Celtic flair - Crerand, Law, Best - not without tactical organization but reliant on a kind of individual talent to which few ordinary league clubs could aspire. In the World Cup of 1970 England were eliminated in late and dramatic fashion by West Germany in the quarter final. The method, it was apparent, had its limitation, though there were those who defended Ramsey's record, pointing to the narrow 0-1 defeat by Brazil as possibly the best game of the tournament.

By the early 1970s the necessity to compete seriously at international level had established a new objective and incontrovertible way of testing the health of English football: the performance of the English national side in international competitions, especially the World Cup. It was to be the elimination of England by Poland in the qualifying competition of the 1974 World Cup which was to cause Ramsey's downfall, just as the failure to score sufficient goals against Luxemburg and Finland was the end of his successor, Don Revie.

The immediate impact of these developments on the domestic game is measurable - the number of goals scored annually in the first division dropped from around 1600 in the early 1960s through 1400 in the middle of the decade to less than 1100 by 1971. Though a slight increase was evident in the middle and late 1970s the average was no more than 1200, a loss of one in four goals over twenty years. Amongst its other legacies, systems football had given us the 0-0 draw. Essentially its emphasis was defensive: if you couldn't score, you made sure the other team didn't. The perilous economic situation of some clubs reinforced the tactics of fear, while the defensive emphasis helped further to drive potential supporters away. The player too was affected by the new tightness of the game; ball players were a luxury, work-rate the norm, one small error could cost a game. In such an atmosphere it was hardly surprising that brutality could become incorporated as a tactic. The professional foul was born.

Its conception was at the international level. A loose framework of laws appropriated by different cultural traditions was bound to bring out differences of emphasis. Even so there seemed to be a virtual incompatibility between English versions of acceptable physical contact and those of south European and South American sides.

There are now two types of football in the world - the British style and the Continental, Latin-American counterpart. When brought face to face - as in Milan recently - they tend on occasions to provide an unhappy marriage. The foreigner, nourished on a game of infiltration and sly intervention, with the minimum of physical contact, regards the British attitude of hard tackling as quite brutal.

However fair and within the laws, this is considered overseas as ugly, coarse and ruthless. The foreigner, for his part, employs subtle body-checking, shielding of the ball and other tricks that rile the Briton. So the bonfire is ready for burning, unhindered by crowds and referees who penalize the British method because it is against their natures and upbringing.[39]

As English football had to face up to the international unacceptability of its essential roughness, so it tacitly agreed to drop some of the more extreme features, especially shoulder-barging and challenges on the goalkeeper. But the essential toughness remained, and the best that could be achieved was an uneasy form of truce which is still in force. In conjunction with the players' removal from the context of traditional working-class attitudes towards violence, the continental influence encouraged the development of premeditated forms of violence. The worst elements of the traditional English game and the new continental game were merged into a pattern of violence which was at once deliberate and uncontrolled.

The one modern English team to successfully master continental styles has been Liverpool. In their current phase (1976-8) they are undisputed club champions of Europe. This has been achieved frequently with only two specialist forwards, but with a midfield of such flexibility that there are always men up in support. Yet still a question remains about the attractiveness of this form of football. It is an effective and efficient combination of pace and skill, determination and virtuosity - but few can hope to emulate it. Such football is essentially cerebral; the comparison frequently made is with chess. The ball is moved sideways and backwards, carefully retained until an opening becomes apparent. Nothing is attempted which may lose possession and the overall effect is frequently claustrophobic. It depends crucially on some exceptional individual skill - first Keegan, then Dalgleish, supplemented by Heighway - and on a managerial ability to convert average players into exceptional ones. Ray Kennedy can never produce his Liverpool form for England.

Perhaps the English national side under the open-ended philosophic approach of a significantly unsuccessful club manager, Ron Greenwood, may prove in the long run a more liberated approach than that of club sides. The structure of league football has (not to mention that Celtic influence) always been geared to club strength. Where clubs have to be prevailed on to release players between Saturday league games for a couple of days before a midweek international, success at a national level will always be hard to come by.

In any case it may be unreasonable to expect a national side to do anything but reflect the weaknesses and strengths of the league game. While the ability to create or score the unusual goal is prized more than ever, the system of coaching, of tactics, of defensiveness, ensures that such tendencies will be quickly eliminated amongst younger players. If there is a source of cultural innovation it may be ethnic. Anderson of Nottingham Forest, Regis and Cunningham of Albion, Hazell of Wolves may provide a confidence and freedom of expression lacking in the indigenous game. Orient's fielding of five black players at the beginning of 1978-9 may be a sign of things to come. It remains to be seen whether such influences make any headway against the influences which have dominated the tactics of post-war football; the need to succeed internationally, the financial penalties of failure, the sheer negative and defensive response of tactical thought.

Conclusion

The argument here has been that in the post-war period there have been significant qualitative shifts in the game of football, as it is played on the pitch, relayed by television, organized through clubs, understood by the spectators, and experienced

by the professional footballer. It would be too easy to summarize these developments as a conversion of a pure traditional working-class activity into some form of
mass-produced and mass-consumed culture. Ian Taylor argues that the outcome is
that

we are presented with a soccer that is dominated by contractual relationships
between clubs and player and between player and supporter, a soccer in which
clubs are increasingly concerned to provide a passive form of spectacle, and a soccer
that is dominated by financial rather than by sub-cultural relationships.[42]

We may not have a language to describe adequately the continuing transformation
of football. If there is a concept which can help to distill the dominant tendencies
it may be that of the spectacle. The spectacle is an item produced for consumption.
The essential relationship is that between producer and consumer. To this end the
event itself - in this case the ninety-minute match - is situated within specific
'demands' universally held by the consumer for adequate car parks, pre-match
entertainment, organized response, and fed information. The consumer is provided
for; his main activity is to decide whether to come, but beyond that he is expected
to exert himself little. As has been argued above, the provision of minimal comfort
is long overdue, and the loyalties of the existent footballing sub-culture are not
easily turned into the vagaries of consumerism. No Aston Villa supporter goes to
Birmingham City except to support the away team.

There is an example of a situation where the idea of the spectacle has dominated
football, and that is in the United States of America. Adequate information is hard
to come by since the English press has alternated between condescension and
sycophancy in its reporting of American football.[43] A few characteristics still
emerge: the ownership of whole clubs by corporations, the franchise system
enabling clubs to be moved from city to city at will; the pre-match car-park
barbecues, organized cheerleading, continuous commentary, scoreboards which
light up when a foul is committed with the slogan 'Did You See That'. The game
itself has also been altered: offside restricted to part of the pitch, the abolition of
the draw replaced by 'sudden death' playoffs of beating the goalkeeper on the run;
even extending the size of the goals has been mooted. The objection is not to any
of these individually. The laws, for example, are subject to continuous reinterpreta-
tion and change and there may be a good case for experimenting with the offside
law. The question is what kinds of consideration govern innovation. In the American
example the direction is consistently towards the spectacularization of football.
The event has been surrounded and penetrated by the need to provide instant
entertainment to keep the consumer interested.

It is unlikely that English league football will ever approximate to this kind of
cultural aberration (though Queens Park Rangers, among others, have installed a
declamatory scoreboard). But what has been happening in the post-war years has
been that football has lost its partial autonomy as a form of popular culture from
the economic and cultural forces dominant in the rest of society. This is not to
suggest that football has ever been in any sense oppositional. It was rather a symbolic

displacement, produced, transmitted and recognized by working-class men as expressive of their situation. It could be argued that changes in the relative economic situation of the post-war working class has rendered irrelevant traditional forms of cultural expression, of which football was one. The redefinition of football has not, however, primarily been by the supporters. An unholy and unwitting alliance of the Professional Footballers Association, the Football League and Football Association, the pundits of press and television, underwritten by objective financial considerations (actually of their own making), have begun the long process of making football respectable, malleable to the needs of the mass media, aesthetic rather than exciting, aimed at an audience of consumers rather than a body of supporters.

There may be some measures which could divert football from its likely fate as one of a number of uniformly packaged spectacles presented by capitalist business. These might include: a change in the points system, to encourage attacking play; severer penalties, including reductions in points, for clubs guilty of persistent foul play; an abolition of the transfer system to stabilize the game's finances; nationalization of the pools, and a subsidy to smaller clubs. But in the prevailing climate such proposals are likely to seem too radical a break for those in charge of the game's fortunes, whose sense of tradition is actually a habit of authority. Ultimately the problem is that in football, as in many of its corporate cultural activities, the power to control the institution does not rest with those on whose behalf it has been created. The susceptibility of football to the financial dictates, consumer ideologies and cultural definition of advanced monopoly capitalism may be revelatory of weaknesses inherent in the traditional corporate working-class culture. The need, in football as elsewhere, may be to take control.

8 Shop floor culture, masculinity and the wage form

Paul Willis

The noise on our line is what drives you almost mad. You can never really get used to it, and I have been there ten years (and in another factory ten years before that). It would drive you mad, if you let it. Imagine nine men beating hammers and mallets on steel. If there were some sort of rhythm to it, it wouldn't be so bad.

Bryan Slater, a line worker[1]

Excruciating noise is probably the most unpleasant sensual concomitant of industrial work. Its invocation serves to remind, even those who pride themselves of their penetration of the consumer-egalitarian-liberal mythology, that not only are commodities produced under specific and determinate social conditions, but also that they are produced under specific and determinate *experiential* conditions. What is the human meaning and actual experience that lies behind our easy use of cars, cosmetics, clothes and buildings? What degree of frenzy, activity, boredom and suffering has been objectified into the thousand articles on glamorous display in the department store? Is the meaning and pleasure of these things as they are consumed any more important than the meaning of the drudge of their production? It is often forgotten that the main reality for most of the people, for most of the time, is work and the sound of work - the grind of production, not the purr of consumption, is the commonest mark of our industrial culture.

In what sense can we link factory sounds with culture? In what sense can we link *work* with culture? It is one of the fundamental paradoxes of our social life that when we are at our most natural, our most *everyday*, we are also at our most cultural; that when we are in roles that look the most obvious and given, we are actually in roles that are constructed, learned and far from inevitable. Whenever we are under pressure, late, worried; whenever there is little time for self-reflection, pretence; whenever we are pushed and thankful for any role, any role, to get us through time and the hour: then it seems we act in the obvious single way, the way dictated by 'reality'. So too with work - for many, *dead* time, human time sold for the possibility of a real life later: it seems the most obvious and self-evident category of human experience, the area where manners, culture and artifice intervene least into our daily existence.

This view is wrong not because it mistakes the nature of work, but because it mistakes the nature of *culture*. Culture is not artifice and manners, the preserve of Sunday best, rainy afternoons and concert halls. It is the very material of our daily lives, the bricks and mortar of our most commonplace understandings, feelings and responses. We rely on cultural patterns and symbols for the minute, and unconscious, social reflexes that make us social and collective beings: we are therefore most *deeply* embedded in our culture when we are at our most natural and spontaneous: if you like at our most work-a-day. As soon as we think, as soon as we see life as parts in a play, we are in a very important sense, already, one step away from our real and living culture.

Clearly this is a special use of the concept of culture. In part it can be thought of as an anthropological use of the term, where not only the special, *heightened,* and separate forms of experience, but *all* experiences, and especially as they lie around central life struggles and activities, are taken as the proper focus of a cultural analysis.

Given this perspective, it should be clear that not only can work be analysed from a cultural point of view, but that it must occupy a *central* place in any full sense of culture. Most people spend their prime waking hours at work, base their identity on work activities and are defined by others essentially through their relation to work.

This is partially allowed in our common-sense knowledge of men and their gender definition, but consider the stereotypical cultural role of women in our society. A central and defining feature of womanhood in our society is still a very definite set of expectations about her in relation to 'work'. She is supposed to take a 'light' job, with relatively low status and rewards, and be prepared to give it up without complaint in order to take on the 'more important' job of having children. So complete is the denial of 'real' work to women, that even exceptionally and manifestly demanding domestic taks are not allowed as serious work. The woman at home is simply a 'housewife', complementing presumably, in the unspoken couplet, the 'work-husband'. Her role is to provide the *emotional* home for the family, and to wipe the brow of the 'bread winner': this is seen not as work but as a service, or a state of being.

In speaking of work and culture, then, in the same breath I am not positing some esoteric link between Shakespeare and employment statistics, but a simple proposition that work, and the massive experience of it, is right at the centre of our living culture. Work is a living and active area of human involvement - it makes, and is made, by us. It affects the general social nature of our lives in the most profound ways.

There is then no question, for me, of counterposing the 'cultural' with the 'productive' or the 'real' as if the former had no actual constitutive role in the basic social relations which govern the form of our society. I am arguing against a *trivialization* of the notion of culture, of working-class culture and especially of its central domain: cultural relations/struggles/forms at the point of production. Culture is not simply a *response* to imposition which blinds or blunts a 'proper' understanding, nor is it merely a compensation, an adjustment to defeat - these are essentially mechanized, reactive, models. Cultural forms occupy precisely those same spaces and human potentialities which are fought over by capital to continue valorization and capital accumulation. There are different logics possible in the direct experience of production than are posed in the capital relation itself, for itself. Merely because capital would like to treat workers as robots does not mean they are robots. The direct experiences of production are worked through and over in the praxis of different cultural discourses. To be sure, these discourses do not arise purely on the basis of production, and many of their important contents and inner relationships arise from or in articulation with external forces and institutions: the family, state, labour organizations, etc. It is also clear that in this society, for the moment, the material consequences of these cultural forms are for continued production in the capitalist mode. But none of this should blind us to the complexities, struggles and tensions on the shop floor even if they do not always call their name in a way which we can recognize. There are forms of praxis arising from definite human agency at the site of production which, in the very same moment, provide the conditions for capitalist relations and also partially penetrate and variably challenge those relationships.

It is also specifically working-class cultural forces from the place of production which help to mould the whole of the class culture. Production is not simply the engine house of the social totality producing, somehow, its 'effects' elsewhere on the social plane. Production, and its relations, is social and cultural to its very roots, to its very surface. It is the privileged site and generator of working-class culture both because of its massive presence and also because the struggle there *fixes*, organizes in a particular combination, those discourses and external influences which play over the place of work - helping to develop them in a particular way, clinching certain features, even when appearing manifestly outside of production. Work is where the demands of capital must be met but from the resources not simply of potential *abstract* labour but from concrete, cultural forms of labour power. Whatever 'free' play there is in cultural forms articulates always around this most central point of reference. Non-work supplies many of the categories and meanings for work but it can only be understood in relation to work and is finally shaped by it. The following data, unless noted to the contrary, was collected in a town which is part of a large Midland's conurbation in the course of an SSRC-supported research project of 'The transition from school to work' between 1973 and 1975.[2] This article refers to male cultures of work.

The first thing to say about the working-class culture of the work-place is that it exists in hard conditions set by others. It is also worth remembering that for all the talk of 'massive' wage settlements in the face of union 'blackmail' since the war, the income of wage earners, as a proportion of GNP, has not changed in the last fifty years.

The system of capitalism still means essentially, despite its contemporary 'human face', that labour is bought, detached from the individual, and directed towards the production of commodities for the profit of others. Labour is dispossessed from its owners. This labour is directed, emphatically, not for the satisfaction of its providers, but for the profit of its new owners. If this requires work in inhuman and meaningless circumstances, then, there is nothing in the logic of capitalism to prevent this.

Writing in a completely different context, and addressing a completely different problem, G. C. Mathew,[3] claims that fully 79 per cent of the ESN (educationally sub-normal) could be placed in *normal* employment, since such employment requires only a mental and emotional age of twelve. Now while one may welcome this news on behalf of the ESN, what are its implications for the other 95 per cent - the regular incumbents of these jobs? It must be that they are doing work which twelve-year-olds could do.

The main effect of this dispossession is most obvious in the case of boring, repetitive, mindless jobs - a numbing sense of boredom and meaninglessness: sheer unhappiness, if you like. This is most dramatically shown up by the many working-class accounts of how *time* drags at work. Time and the task to be done become utterly divorced. A job is undertaken not out of interest, but merely because one's *bought* labour is directed there. Without an intrinsic interest in the job, then, the full focus of the detached consciousness is thrown on to the passing of time. This focus *itself*, to say nothing of the actual drudgery of the job, slows time down to a painful existential drag. Here's a young lad who has just left school and started to work in a car component factory:

I knew I'd be working eight to five [. . .]* but I thought, you know, go to school 'that's nothing', it's only an hour before I normally go to school, and an hour after, like I did at school', but it's a lot longer, seems to drag [. . .] like now [. . .] me and Les, we're always looking at that clock, thinking to ourselves, 'so many hours before we leave', something like this [. . .]. The worst part of the day is about quarter to nine in the morning, and it's really rotten, you think of the time you've still got to the end of the day, especially if that three quarters of an hour has dragged [. . .] when I first start like I don't usually look up at the clock and see what time it is [. . .] I start working, then about half past nine, that's the time it really gets you, 'God blimey, it's dragging, the time, I wish I warn't here, I wish I could be at home in bed, sort of thing.'

Although distinctions must be made for region and occupation, the absolutely central thing about the working-class culture of the shop floor is, however, that, despite the dispossession, despite the bad conditions, despite the external directions, despite the subjective ravages, people do look for meaning, they do impose frameworks, they do seek enjoyment in activity, they do exercise their abilities. They repossess, symbolically and really, aspects of their experience and capacities. They do, paradoxically, thread through the dead experience of work a living culture which isn't simply a reflex of defeat. This culture is not the human remains of a mechanical depredation, but a positive transformation of experience and a celebration of shared values in symbols, artefacts and objects. It allows people to recognize and even to develop themselves. For this working-class culture of work is not simply a foam padding, a rubber layer between humans and unpleasantness. It is an appropriation in its own right, an exercise of skill, a motion, an activity

* In the transcriptions, time passing is indicated by . . . and material edited out is denoted by [. . .].

applied towards an end. It has this specifically human characteristic, even in conditions of hardship and oppression.

What are the elements of this culture? In the first place there is the sheer mental and physical bravery of surviving in hostile conditions, and doing difficult work on intractable materials. It is easy to romanticize this element, of course, and in one way it is simply charting the degree of brutality a heavy work situation can inflict. But in another way it is the first and specifically human response - the holding of an apparently endless and threatening set of demands by sheer strength and brute skill. Already in this there is a stature and self-respect, a human stake on the table against the relentless pressure of work to be done. This is the vital precondition of more developed cultural forms and accomplishes the basic and primitive humanization of a situation: it marks a kind of limit of dispossession. It halts the rout of human meaning and takes a kind of control so that more specifically creative acts can follow. This primitivist base of work experience is also the material for a crude pride and, as will be developed much more fully later, for the mythology of *masculine* reputation - to be strong and to be known for it. Here is a retired steelman describing the furnaces in a steel-making area of the west of Scotland as they were before World War II:

They were the cold, metal, hand-charging sort and they catered for strong men, only very strong men. About one steel worker in every ten could stand up to them successfully, which was one reason why the furnacemen were looked up to in the world of heavy industry. That they got the biggest pay packets was another reason. They also had the biggest thirsts and that too was a prideful possession in that part of the world [. . .] a legend grew up about the steel smelters. [. . .] The whole district and for miles beyond it was a hotbed of steel works, iron puddling works and coal mines. It was a place given over to the worship of strength and durability. Indeed it needed strength to look at it, and durability to live in it.[4]

In a much less articulate way, but for that perhaps more convincing, the following extract shows the same elemental self-esteem in the doing of a hard job well. It also shows that in some respects the hard environment can become the most natural environment. There is also the grudging recognition of the profound charge this kind of acclimatization can make on a normal social life, *even at the same time* that it is one of the major ways in which the hostile work environment is made habitable. This is a foundry man talking at home about his work:

I work in a foundry. . . . you know, drop forging . . . do you know anything about it . . . no . . . well you have the factory know the factory down down in Rolfe Street, with the noise . . . you can hear it in the street . . . I work there on the big hammer . . . it's a six-tonner. I've worked there twenty-four years now. It's bloody noisy but I've got used to it now . . . and its hot . . . I don't get bored . . . there's always new lines coming and you have to work out the best way of doing it . . . . You have to keep going . . . and it's heavy work, the managers couldn't do it, there's not many strong enough to keep lifting the metal . . . I earn eighty, ninety pounds a week, and that's not bad is it? . . . it ain't easy like . . . you can definitely say that I earn every penny of it . . . you have to keep it up you know. And the managing director, I'd say 'hello' to him you know, and the progress manager . . . they'll come around and I'll go . . . 'all right' [thumbs up] . . . and they know you, you know . . . a group standing there watching you . . . working . . . I like that . . . there's something there . . . watching you like . . . working . . . like that . . . you have to keep going to get enough out . . . that place depends on what you produce [. . .]. You get used to the noise, they say I'm deaf and ignorant here, but it's not that I'm deaf like . . . it's that you can hold a conversation better, talk, hear what people say better at work . . . I can always hear what they say there, I can talk easy, it's easier . . . yet in the house here, you've got to make . . . pronunciations is it? yeah, you've got to like, say the word, say it clearly, and that's hard sometimes . . . sometimes I can't hear straight away . . . they say, 'you silly deaf old codger' . . . it's not that . . . it's just . . . well it's just getting used to the noise, I can hear perfectly well in the factory . . . . If I see two managers at the end of the shop, I know, like I know just about what they're saying to each other.

It may be objected that the pattern of industrial work has changed: there are no rough jobs today. Besides, it can certainly be argued that there is nothing heroic about the elemental qualities of strength and pride. They are not only made anachronistic by today's technology, but are insulting, oppressive and right at the poisonous heart of male chauvinism and archaic machismo.

Be that as it may be, two things are clear. Rough, unpleasant, demanding jobs *do* still exist in considerable numbers. A whole range of jobs from building work, to furnace work to deep-sea fishing still involve a primitive confrontation with exacting physical tasks. Secondly, the basic attitudes and values developed in such jobs are still very important in the general working-class culture, and particularly the culture of the shop floor; this importance is vastly out of proportion to the number of people actually involved in such heavy work. Even in so-called light industries, or in highly mechanized factories with perhaps mixed sex work-forces, where the awkwardness of the physical task has long since been reduced, the metaphoric figures of strength and bravery *worked through* masculinity and reputation still move beneath the more varied, visible forms of work-place culture.

Let us go on from this general minimum proposition to look at some of the more specific and developed human patterns of the work-place. One of the marks of the lived and contemporary culture of the shop floor is a development of this half-mythical primitive confrontation with *the task*. It is a familiarity and experiential sense of control of technology, or at least a sharing of its power. At the most positive and extreme this can be not merely a meeting of demands, but a strange kind of celebration. Here is a description from a toolmaker of his first day at work.[5] It inverts the usual middle-class account of the dark satanic mill:

On every piece of open ground lay metal shapes; some mere bars and sheets straight from the steelworks: others gigantic welded constructs covered in a deep brown rust . . . Then I entered the great main workshops. Each chamber, or aisle as they were called, was about 150 feet across and anything between 500 and 700 hundred yards long. Several of these great vulcan halls lay parallel to each other [. . .] Overhead rolled the girded cranes capable of carrying weights of more than two hundred tons [. . .] one passed over my head. [. . .] My startled attitude to the crane's passage amused the men at work [. . .] a series of catcalls followed my passage down the aisle. Mostly the shouts were good-natured advice to get out of the plant while I had the youth to do so. Such advice never even penetrated my outer consciousness, for how could anyone abhor this great masculine domain with its endless overtones of power and violence?

Of course this is a special case of a skilled, elitist view of work. Changes in the labour process are no doubt squeezing out the space for such views.[6] But we should not underestimate the surviving degree to which mechanical, sensuous and concrete *familiarity* with the tools of production (despite the dispossession of labour) mediates the demands of the labour process, allowing, for instance, the possibility of an easy and confident mobility which at least brings alleviating changes in the *form* of particular work experience if not in its deep structures.

Even, or perhaps especially, among the formally 'un/semi/skilled' there is a process of obtaining skills as if by osmosis from the technical environment. There is a profound air of competence in the culture of the shop floor, a competence which always exists prior to the particular situation. It is not always based on strict ability, but mixed in with cheek and confidence; it is enough to pull a worker through any number of jobs and problems. Here is a man talking about his industrial career. He gives us a glimpse of the real paths beaten between different jobs and occupations: the paths, incidentally, which make it sensible to speak of the working class not only as an abstract group of those who share similar interests, but as at least something of a self-experienced organic whole with real and used inner connections:

Well, I've got four trades really, you know I've only been in this job seven weeks. I'm in a foundry now [. . .] on the track you know [. . .]. I was a metal polisher before. It's a dirty job, but it pays good money, and a skilled job, you know metal polishing. [. . .] Yes and I was a fitter down at drop forgings, as well, well I mean in the situation today, you've got to go where the money is. Polishing is the best money, but it's up and down, there was four or five months run of work and then it 'ud go dead [. . .] I got out of it didn't I [. . .] Friend o' mine got me a job down at the MMC [. . .] I've worked in a garage, er . . . I worked for the council paperhanging and decorating, I worked for a fella . . . chimney sweeping in the winter, decorating and painting in the summer and all this but I've always took an interest in what I've been doing you know, I mean, I'm pretty adaptable, put it that way you know [. . .] I've always had a motor of my own, and I've always done me own repairs, whenever I've broken me motor, only through experience doing it meself [. . .] Paper hanging, decorating, I've got an in-law ain't I, that's a decorator, give me a lot ot tips you know [. . .] I bluffed me way in to decorating. I said I was a decorator you know, went to work for the council. Actually I subcontracted for the council, and they give an house to do, an empty house, and I done it see. Course the inspector come round from the Council and they was satisfied with the work, you know, so you know if the inspector's satisfied, you're all right see. It's only common sense really.

In one sense this can be seen as a way of regaining *some* control over one's labour power and its disposition. This leads us to another important element in shop-floor culture: the massive attempt to gain informal control of the work process. Limitation of output or 'systematic soldiering' and 'gold bricking' have been observed from the particular perspective of management from Taylor onwards, but there is evidence now of a more concerted - though still informal - attempt to gain control. In many plants the men, themselves, to all intents and purposes actually control at least manning and the speed of production. Of course the downward limit for this possibility is set by the production of the costs of subsistence of the worker. If control is exerted on production it is indeed a control of minima as well as of maxima. Nevertheless the exertion towards *control* should not be minimized. Here is a man on track production of car engines:

Actually the foreman, the gaffer, don't run the place, the men run the place. See, I mean you get one of the chaps says, 'Allright, you'm on so and so today. You can't argue with him. The gaffer don't give you the job, the men on the track give you the job, they swop each other about, tek it in turns. Ah, but I mean the job's done. If the gaffer had gi'd you the job you would . . . They tried to do it one morning, gi'd a chap a job you know, but he'd been on it, you know, I think he'd been on all week, and they just downed tools [. . .]. There's four hard jobs on the track and there's dozens that's, . . . you know, a child of five could do it, quite honestly, but everybody has their turn. That's organized by the men.

This tendency rests on the social force most basically of the informal group. It is the zone where strategies for wresting control of symbolic and real space from official authority are generated and disseminated. It is the massive presence of this informal organization which most decisively marks off shop-floor culture from middle-class cultures of work.

Amongst workers it is also the basis for extensive bartering, 'arranging foreigners' and 'fiddling'. 'Winning' materials is widespread on the shop floor and is endorsed by implicit informal criteria. Ostracism is the punishment for not maintaining the integrity of this world against the persistent intrusions of the formal.

A foreman is like, you know what I mean, they're trying to get on, they're trying to get up. They'd cut everybody's throat to get there. You get people like this in the factory. Course these people cop it in the neck off the workers, they do all the tricks under the sun. You know what I mean, they don't like to see anyone crawlin' [. . .] Course instead of taking one pair of glasses from the stores Jim had two, you see, and a couple of masks and about six pairs o' gloves. Course this Martin was watching and actually two days after we found out that he'd told the foreman see. Had 'im, Jim, in the office about it, the foreman did, and, [. . .] well I mean, his life hasn't been worth living has it? Eh, nobody speaks to him, they won't give him a light, nobody'll give him a light for his fag or nothin' . . . . Well, he won't do it again, he won't do it again. I mean he puts his kettle on, on the stove of a morning, so they knock it off, don't they, you know, tek all his water out, put sand in, all this kind of thing [. . .] if he cum to the gaffer, 'Somebody's knocked me water over' or, er, 'They put sand in me cup', and all this business, 'Who is it then?' 'I don't know who it is.' He'll never find out who it is.

Another clear aspect of shop-floor culture is the distinctive form of language use and a highly developed form of intimidatory humour. Many verbal exchanges on the shop floor are not serious or about work activities. They are jokes, or 'piss-takes', or 'kiddings' or 'windups'. There is a real skill in being able to use this language with fluency: to identify the points on which you are being 'kidded' and to have appropriate responses ready in order to avoid further baiting.

This badinage is necessarily difficult to record on tape or to re-present, but the highly distinctive ambience it gives to shop-floor exchanges is widely recognized by those involved, and to some extent recreated in their accounts of it. Here is a foundry worker:

Oh, there's all sorts, millions of them [jokes]. 'Want to hear what he said about you', and he never said a thing, you know. Course you know the language at the work like. 'What you been saying about me?' 'I said nothing' 'Oh you're a bloody liar', and all this.

Associated with this concrete and expressive verbal humour is a well-developed physical humour: essentially the practical joke. These jokes are vigorous, sharp, sometimes cruel, and often hinge around prime tenets of the culture such as disruption of production or subversion of the boss's authority and status. Here is the track worker again;

They play jokes on you, blokes knocking the clamps off the boxes, they put paste on the bottom of the hammer you know, soft little thing, puts his hammer down, picks it up, gets a handful of paste, you know, all this. So he comes up and gets a syringe and throws it in the big bucket of paste, and it's about that deep, and it goes right to the bottom, you have to put your hand in and get it out . . . This is a filthy trick, but they do it [. . .] They asked, the gaffers asked Charlie to make the tea. Well it's fifteen yours he's been there and they say 'go and make the tea'. He goes up the toilet, he wets in the tea pot, then makes the tea. I mean, you know, this is the truth this is you know. He says, you know, 'I'll piss in it if I mek it, if they've asked me to mek it' [. . .] so he goes up, wees in the pot, then he puts the tea bag, then he puts the hot water in. [. . .] He was bad the next morning, one of the gaffers, 'My stomach isn't half upset this morning.' He told them after and they called him for everything, 'You ain't makin' our tea no more.' He says 'I know I ain't not now.'

Many of the jokes circle around the concept of authority itself and around its informal complement, 'grassing'. The same man:

He [Johnny] says, 'Get a couple of pieces of bread pudding Tony [a new worker] we'll have them with our tea this afternoon see.' The woman gi'd him some in a bag he says, 'Now put them in your pocket, you won't have to pay for them when you go past, you know, the till' [. . .] Tony put 'em in his pocket didn't he and walked past with his dinner [. . .] When we come back out the canteen, Johnny was telling everbody that he'd [i.e. Tony] pinched two pieces of bread pudding [. . .] he told Fred, one of the foremen see, 'cos Fred knows, I mean . . . Johnny says, I've got to tell you Fred,' he says, 'Tony pinched two pieces of bread pudding' I mean serious, the way they look you know [. . .]. He called Johnny for everything, young Tony did. Fred said, 'I want to see you in my office in twenty minutes', straightfaced you know, serious. Oh, I mean, Johnny, he nearly cried.[. . .] We said, 'It's serious like, you're in trouble, you'll get the sack', you know and all this. [. . .] they never laugh. He says, 'What do you think's gonna happen?' 'Well, what can happen, you'll probably get your cards.' [. . .] 'Oh what am I gonna do, bleeding Smith up there, he's really done me, I'll do him.' I says, 'Blimey, Tony', I says, 'it ain't right, if other people can't get away with it, why should you 'a' to get away with it.' 'Ooh.' Anyway Fred knocked the window and he says, 'Tell Johnny I want him.' He says, 'You've got the sack now, Johnny', you know. 'Hope I haven't', he says, 'I dunno what I'm gonna do.' [. . .] After they cum out, laughing, I said, 'What did he say to you, Johnny?' He says, 'He asked me if I pinched two pieces of bread pudding, so I couldn't deny it, I said I had. He says, "All I want to know is why you didn't bring me two pieces an' all.' "

Another important element of this culture is the massive feeling on the shop floor, and in the working class generally, that practice is more important than theory. As a big handwritten sign, borrowed from the back of a matchbox and put up by one of the workers, announces on one shop floor: 'An ounce of keenness is worth a whole library of certificates'. The shop floor abounds with apocryphal stories about the idiocy of purely theoretical knowledge. Practical ability always come first and is a *condition* of other kinds of knowledge. Whereas in middle-class culture knowledge and qualifications are seen as a way of shifting upwards the whole mode of practical alternatives open to an individual, in working-class eyes theory is riveted to particular productive practices. If it cannot earn its keep there, it is to be rejected. Here is a man currently working as a metal polisher:

In Toll End Road, there's a garage, and I used to work part time there and . . . there's an elderly fellow there, been a mechanic all his life, and he must have been seventy years of age then. He was an old Indconsville professional, been a professional boxer once, an elderly chap and he was a practical man, he was practical, right? . . . and he told me this. [. . .] I was talking to him, was talking about something like this, he says [. . .]. 'This chap was all theory and he sends away for books about everything', and he says, 'Do you know', he says, 'He sent away for a book once and it came in a wooden box, and it's still in that box 'cos he can't open it.' Now that in't true, is it? But the point is true. That i'nt true, that didn't happen, but his point is right. He can't get at that book 'cos he don't know how to open the box! Now what's the good of that?

This can be seen as a clear and usually unremarked class function of knowledge. The working-class view would be the rational one, were it not located in class society, i.e. that theory is only useful in so far as it really does help to do things, to accomplish practical tasks and change nature. Theory is asked to be in a close dialectic with the material world. For the middle class, more aware of its position in a class society, however, theory is seen partly in its social guise of qualifications as the power to move up on the social scale. In this sense theory is well worth having even if it is never applied to nature. It serves its purpose in society as a ticket to travel. Paradoxically, the working class distrust and rejection of theory comes partly from a kind of recognition, even in the moment that it oppresses, of the hollowness of theory in its social guise.

The wage and the Thursday afternoon wage packet are an essential element of shop-floor culture. Weekly wages, not yearly salaries, mark the giving of labour. The quantity of the wage packet is the quantitive passage of time. Its diminution is loss of measured time, its increase 'overtime'. Such an orientation makes it that much easier to overlook the real, continuous, sensuous and variable quality of labour power and to miss the sense in which its full giving over time opens up enormous human energies which are actually unmeasurable. What amounts to a fetishism of the wage packet - nurtured with tight-gummed compact brown envelope - breaks up the weeks, quantifies effort, and presents to consciousness the massive effort and potential of human labour power as a simple concrete weekly equivalent to the crisp 'fair' wage. In the elemental weekly exchange, it seems, labour power must be spent in order to obtain every week the cash necessary to live. The loss of the wage packet is the loss of a week. That is why this loss is so feared and mythologized on the shop floor. This loss posits concretely the atomization of labour power and its quantitative equivalence with the wage. More effectively than a monthly cheque paid unseen into a bank account, the weekly wage prevents a realization of the disjunction between the variability of long-term vital effort and a fixed wage return.

Of course, part of the case here is that shop-floor relations operate at a *cultural* level in a number of ways to resist intensification and to exert *some* control on production. There is, so to speak, a *partial* recognition of the special nature of labour power as a commodity 'like no other', of its essentially *variable* nature. There are 'cultural instincts' to limit its use and further exploitation. These processes should be understood, though, not as finally and formally successful, but as in permanent tension with counteracting ideological tendencies. Perhaps they are most held in check by the classic version of the wage form considered here. Experiential forms of the awareness of time, for instance, can centre decisively around the wage packet and what it offers. Though even here a resistance is registered, at least negatively and individually in the strange time warp around the inherently meaningless weekly work cycle and its illusory wage form. The young lad in a car components factory:

You know, at work, say stapling sort of thing, you come 'Cor blimey, what am I doing here?' sort of thing you know. I just imagine me in say ten years time, I'll still be doing the same thing I expect, and I just don't you know . . . It'd send me mad I think, just keep doing it, a lifetime, I want something better out of life. [. . .] The nice part of the week is Friday dinner time when I get me wages . . . they bring it on a tray, the wages. It's funny though, all week I'm thinking, 'Roll on Friday, and we can go down town Saturday,' and you look forward to it. When you get to town Saturday, you think, 'What was I looking forward to?' But I still look forward to it every week, just the same.

Perhaps the most prosaic but actually startling element of shop-floor culture is the articulation of manual labour power - as it is concretely practised - with assertive male gender definitions. There is an infusion of assertive masculine style and meaning into the primitive, mythologized elements of confrontation with 'the task'. It is also a masculine *expressivity* which often delivers or makes possible some of the *concrete* revelatory or oppositional cultural practices we have considered: resistance to authority; control through the group; humour and language; distrust of theory. There are profound implications here for the *internal* (to production) disorganization of a proper recognition of the nature and capitalist use of labour power and for *external* gender definitions and forms of family life. The conjunction of elements of manual labour power with certain kinds of masculine gender definitions in the culture of the shop floor is one of the truly essential features of the social organization of the shop floor. Yet it is usually un- or mis-recognized.[7] The sexist attitudes of the male shop floor, the inevitable nubile pin-up over well-worked machinery, heavy sexual references and jokes in language are simply accepted as the *natural* form of shop floor life. One of our central tasks must be to critically understand this relationship.

Manual labour is suffused with masculine qualities and given certain sensual overtones. The toughness and awkwardness of physical work and effort - for itself and in the division of labour, and for its strictly capitalist logic quite without intrinsic heroism or grandeur - takes on masculine lights and depths and assumes a significance beyond itself. Whatever the specific problems of the difficult task, they are always essentially masculine problems, requiring masculine capacities to deal with them. We may say that where the principle of general abstract labour has emptied work of significance from the inside, a transformed patriarchy has filled it with significance from the outside. Discontent with work is turned away from a political discontent and confused in its logic by a huge detour into the symbolic sexual realm.

The brutality of the working situation is partially reinterpreted into a heroic exercise of manly confrontation with 'the task'. Difficult, uncomfortable or dangerous conditions are seen, not for themselves, but for their appropriateness to a masculine readiness and hardness. They are understood more through the toughness required to survive them, than through the nature of the imposition which asks them to be faced in the first place.

Though it is difficult to obtain stature in work itself, both what work provides and the very sacrifice and strength required to do it provides the materials for an elemental self-esteem. This self-esteem derives from the achievement of a purpose which not all - particularly women - are held capable of achieving. The wage packet is the provider of freedom and independence: the particular prize of masculinity in work. This is the complement of, and what makes it possible, the fetishism of the wage packet. A trade is judged not for itself, nor even for its general financial return, but for its ability to provide the central, domestic, role for its incumbent. Clearly money is part of this - but as a measure, not the essence: 'You can raise a family off polishing.' The male wage packet is held to be central, not simply because of its size, but because it is won in a masculine mode in confrontation with the 'real' world which is too tough for the woman. Thus the man in the domestic household is held to be the bread-winner, 'the worker', while the wife works for the extras. Very often, of course, the material importance of her wage may be much greater than this suggests, and certainly her domestic labour is the lynchpin of the whole household economy. The wage packet as a kind of symbol of machismo dictates the domestic culture and economy and tyrannizes both men and women.

In the machismo of manual work the will to finish a job, the will to really work - is posited as a masculine logic, and not as the logic of exploitation. 'It's a man's want to be finished when he starts a job.' The very teleology of the process of work upon nature, and the material power involved in that, becomes, through the conflation of masculinity and manual work, a property of masculinity and not of production. Masculinity is power in its own right, and if its immediate expression is in the completion of work for another, then what of it? It has to be expressed somewhere because it is a quality of being. That is the destiny which a certain kind of self-esteem and dignity seems naturally to bring. Where the intransigence and hardness of a task might bring weakness, or collective opposition or questioning, an override of masculinity - a transferred teleology of production - can cut in to push back fatigue and rational assessment of purpose.

And if the nature of masculinity in work becomes a style of teleology, completion and production, femininity is associated with a fixed state. Its labour power is considered as an ontological state of being, not a teleological process of becoming. Housework is not completion. It is rather maintenance of status. Cooking, washing and cleaning reproduce what was there before. Female domestic work is simply subsumed under *being* 'mum' or 'housewife'. Mum will always do it, and should always be expected to do it. It is part of the definition of what she *is*, as the wage packet and the productive world of work is of what dad is.

Though this is speculation only, I pose the following concluding remarks just to explore the breaking open of the constructedness of cultural forms. The public and visible struggle of the labour movement too often renders invisible the ocean of what it moves through: shop floor culture. This is not to minimize the historic importance of the trade unions but it might be suggested that the type of masculine expression and identity we have considered influence *the form* of trade union struggle in the most profound ways. It has certainly been remarked that the acceptance of the wage form - and of the struggle delimited by that - has profoundly influenced British trade unionism. Can we add that both conscious and unconscious masculine structures have confirmed this and also helped to develop a characteristic trade union consciousness? And on both accounts we should not ignore the reverse shaping force of trade unions on cultural forms - or at least the significance of their *failure* to formally develop nascent forms not only of opposition but of repossession in shop-floor culture.

Certainly the union official or shop steward uses particular shop-floor cultural forms to mobilize 'the lads' - the spectacle or bluff, or strong and combative language which are suffused with masculine feelings. This establishes a real expression of anger and opposition which may be very effective in the short term, and is certainly a force to be reckoned with. This is, however, a *selective* working up and use of cultural forms, one which ominously corresponds with certain profound features of the wage form. It may be that longer-term objectives - which are at least partially expressed in other cultural forms - simply cannot be conceptualized in this way and are, to a certain extent, made inoperative by default at the face-to-face and grass-roots level. The masculine style of confrontation demands an appropriate and honourable resolution: visible and immediate concessions. If this is its price, however, it can be bought off in the most 'concrete' of all forms: 'hard cash'. But the visibility of the concessions won in this way - the *larger*, masculine, fetishized, brown wage packet - may actually conceal longer-term defeats over the less visible issues of control and ownership. It is possible to satisfy violent and possibly even frightening demands by short-term, visible and dramatic concessions without changing any of those basic arrangements which the violence might appear to threaten.

It may be the unholy interlocked grip of masculinity and the wage form which holds in check the other possibilities of shop-floor culture and settles, for the moment, the nature of its influence on other social regions.

Part 3
Theories

9 Three problematics: elements of a theory of working-class culture

Richard Johnson

We return now to the more general problems posed at the end of the first part of this book. Do we need new ways of thinking about working-class culture and what should these be? We proceed by identifying three main approaches. We suggest that each is, in some way, inadequate. We end by suggesting pointers to a better practice.

The three main approaches are rooted in the larger tendencies which we discussed in Chapter 2. Each employs its own key terms. Within orthodox Marxism the key terms have been 'class' and 'class consciousness'. In the work of Williams, Thompson, Hoggart and others, 'culture' replaced 'consciousness' or forced a reworking of its meaning. 'Culture' and 'consciousness', however, remained closely coupled to 'class'. The term 'working-class culture' lies firmly within this problematic. Finally, in 'structuralist' approaches the consciousness/class couplet altogether disappears. As two not-dissimilar terms in Althusser's work we might choose 'ideology' and 'mode of production' or 'ideology' and 'social formation'. But the truth is that there are no real *equivalents* across these traditions. Each semantic shift represents a major theoretical and political movement.

The notion of 'problematic' and the procedure of 'symptomatic reading' are absolutely indispensable tools of analysis and critique. They inform this essay throughout. 'Problematic' may be defined as a 'definite theoretical structure', a field of concepts, which organizes a particular science or individual text by making it possible to ask some kinds of questions and by suppressing others. In 'symptomatic reading' a text is read as much for its 'absences' or 'silences' as for what it more directly 'says'.[1] The problematic(s) of a particular text may be more or less explicit. In works of history the organizing ideas and presuppositions may lie very deep. They none the less exist. One aspect of critique, then, is to render explicit what is implicit, and to consider the underlying propositions. For Althusser, concerned with historical materialism as the 'science of the history of social formations', intellectual productions in the human sciences are organized around a conception of the relation of 'thought' and other practices (an epistemology) and a conception of the general nature of societies (a sociology). His repertoire of critical terms - 'humanist', 'historicist', 'empiricist', etc. - designate particular faults in either aspect or in both.

The Althusserian 'reading' is inadequate is so far as it stops short at the analysis of 'problematic'. For the appearance of finality in the method is quite illusory. Symptomatic reading provides us with a *description* of a work, or of its main internal structures. The dismissal, at this stage, of a text as 'historicist', 'empiricist', etc., can only rest upon a very formal idea of 'science', in Althusser's case, of 'Marx's immense theoretical revolution'. To stop at this stage is merely to say, 'This is not a Marxist text according to the way I have defined Marxism.'

It is not possible to accept, just like that, Althusser's own definition of Marx's uniqueness and scientific superiority, or his own taking of sides within Marxism as a tradition. Structuralism has certainly recovered *a* Marx: one might be pardoned for doubting whether it recovered *the* Marx. *Reading Capital's* conception of 'Marxism-as-science' and all else including Marxist heresies as 'ideology' tends to a closure, prematurely cutting off that open exploration which Althusser himself has defined as the key to science. Answers to the question 'What is Marxism' remain far too difficult to be a valid way of closing debates of substance.

Allied to this difficulty is the strongly reductive character of some forms of symptomatic reading. The whole of an account is reduced to its problematic. This is particularly gross when applied to works of great empirical density, to most histories for example. Presuppositions once identified, it is necessary to return to the surface of the text and to show the effects of theoretical structures on the detailed treatment of events, the construction of narrative, the portrayal of relations, on the actual texture of the historical account. And there are arguments to be conducted on this level too: 'within *this* problematic it is not possible to account for this or that phenomenon which other research reveals'; 'the incoherences of that part of the account is related to the failure fully to theorize *these* sets of relations'; 'theoretical rigidity has produced this or that a priorism with no corresponding research'. In other words, the adequacy of a particular problematic can only be assessed at the author's preferred level of analysis. In such a critique, the proposition that 'historicism' (or any other -ism) is, in general, flawed, is itself on test.

The third main difficulty is the absence of historical critique.[2] This is allied to the high 'theoreticism' of *Reading Capital*, its stress on *general* epistemological or philosophical questions, its 'speculative' or 'rationalist' character. This old and correct criticism of 'structuralism' has been endorsed by Althusser himself in his *Essays in Self-Criticism*. The corrective is simple: to recognize that every problematic has a history or, as Althusser puts it, 'material', social, political, ideological and philosophical conditions'.[3] The adequacy of a theory cannot be judged outside these conditions by purely internal criteria.

Finally, in some usages, 'problematic' has a tendency to simplify or homogenize texts or theories.[4] There is a temptation to look for the 'essence' of a text. As essential unities, then, texts or theories may be discarded wholesale. The method adopted here rests on different assumptions. The struggle over definitions depends precisely on the fact that the concepts that constitute a given problematic are not 'all of a piece'. As elements, reorganized, they may constitute the basis for more adequate accounts. Elements taken from different existing problematics may, in a new order and constituting a new field, yield us greater explanatory power and political purchase.[5]

In what follows we try to learn from this settling of accounts with our erstwhile Althusserianism. No full history of our three problematics can be attempted; but the historical nature of the ideas we use is fully recognized.

Class and class-consciousness in 'Manifesto Marxism'

This view of class had its origins in the collaborative work of the young Marx and Engels. It was an attempt to understand their political experiences in the early communist movement and the novel features of English social life, especially of the English 'proletariat'. The key texts are Marx's *Poverty of Philosophy* (1847), the jointly authored *German Ideology* (1845-6), and *The Communist Manifesto* (1848) and Engels's own *The Condition of the Working Class in England* (1844); the last two works are especially important. The political and intellectual moment represented by Engel's *Condition* was as important as the departure from philosophical communism represented in the classical work of 'the break', *The German Ideology*. Engels's encounters with English working-class movements and English radical theory, together with his strategic location in Manchester, the 'shock city' of the Industrial Revolution, supplied 'the changing questions which provoked the new theory'.[6] Many of the themes of *The Communist Manifesto* are demonstrably present in Engels's *Condition*; the second text is, in many ways, a working up of Engels's primary insights.

Certain key elements of the classic Marxist view of the proletariat were formed, therefore, *before* the emergence of a modern working class. They also preceded Marx's mature understandings of the capitalist mode of production and the character and constitution of classes within this mode. *The Communist Manifesto* view of classes remains somewhat 'philosophical', based upon a generalized view of proletarian destinies (the 'negation' of bourgeois society) rather than a full grasp of capitalism's internal dynamics.[7] The political features of Britain and Europe before 1848 are no less significant. The character of the writing - the feeling of wide-eyed discovery in Engels's *Condition* ('Of the vehemence of this agitation no-one in Germany has any idea'), the assured sweep of *The Communist Manifesto*, the intoxicated polemic against Proudhon's idealism - all testify to the expectancy out of which historical materialism was born. Yet theories generated from the intellectual consumption of very specific events do not always serve well as more generalized truths 140 years later.

The class and class-consciousness problematic rests on a distinction made explicit in *The Poverty of Philosophy* between two aspects of the proletariat as a class. The proletariat is a class in its relations with ('as against') capital: under capital's domination 'this mass' acquired 'a common situation, common interests'.[8] At the heart of this definition of class is the figure of 'the worker' or 'the labourer': 'a class of labourers, who live only so long as they find work, and who find work only so long as their labour increases capital'.[9] In this first guise the proletariat is understood, passively, as a creation of capital, thrown hither and thither by its movements; only in a second moment does it become active, a collective agency or force 'for itself'.

Proletarians acquire the capacity to struggle and to conceive of their place within capitalism and history.

Some such distinction (between economic classes and political forces) is, analytically, indispensable. But these two forms of analysis are also bound, in the original formulation, into a necessary and causative unity: they are stages in one necessary historical process. The grand design of proletarian politics is already present in the economic position of the labourer. The position of proletarians in their relation to capital produces the proletariat as a revolutionary class. Capital produces its own negation, its own 'grave-digger'. In the early texts this doctrine permits of no contingencies. As Stuart Hall has noted, of *The Manifesto*: 'what is so fatally seductive about this text is its simplifying revolutionary sweep . . . above all, its unmodified sense of historical inevitability'.[10]

There are, perhaps, two possible readings of how this argument is actually secured in the early texts. Priority could be given to the stress on class struggle. Though antagonisms are founded in the direct relations of capitalist production, outcomes are not. The proletariat as a political force is 'made' in protracted and repeated struggles; major difficulties, especially capital's tendency to place labourers in competition, must be overcome. One might call this the 'activist' reading of the early texts: it points to the priority of politics developed in later Marx-Engels texts and in Lenin's theory and practice.

But this reading cannot be sustained textually. The various forms of class struggle always appear in the guise of 'phases' or 'stages', a 'growing revolt': individual acts of crime, followed by trade union combinations, followed by Chartism as a political party, followed by a communist-led proletarian movement.[11] The stages themselves are very little explored, even in *The Condition*. There is no consideration of the ways in which these working-class practices (forms of class struggle within capitalism) may actually modify capitalism's structure or affect bourgeois strategies, including strategies of accumulation. Engels in *The Condition*, indeed, found trade unionism an index of the English 'social war' and a stage along the road to the abolition of 'competition' but doubted its practical effects in other ways.[12] The whole discussion of 'stages' is organized teleologically, not in terms of particular effects. Attention is drawn forward to the revolutionary future, with little pause for study on the way.

That future, moreover, is given in the character of capitalism itself. The proletariat is the agent of revolution, but its revolt is not merely 'growing', it is also obligatory. E.J. Hobsbawm's summary of the main lines of argument in *The Condition* is quite faithful to Engels's text but reveals a whole theoretical legacy.

Socially Engels sees the transformations brought about by the Industrial Revolution as a gigantic process of concentration and polarization, whose tendency is to create a growing proletariat. . . . The rise of capitalist industrialism destroys the petty commodity producers, peasantry and petty-bourgeoisie, and the decline of these intermediate strata, depriving the worker of the possibility of becoming a small master, confines him to the ranks of the proletariat which thus becomes 'a definite class in the population, whereas it had only been a transitional stage towards

entering into the middle-classes'. The workers therefore develop class consciousness
. . . and a labour movement. Here is another of Engels' major achievements. In
Lenin's words 'he was among the first to say that the proletariat is *not only* a class
that suffers; that it is precisely its shameful economic situation which irresistibly
drives it forward, and obliges it to struggle for its final emancipation'.[13]

The problems are concentrated in the breath-taking sentence: 'the workers
therefore develop class consciousness'! But this 'therefore' is plainly present in the
texts themselves. It is present in the oft-repeated argument about the massification
and concentration of working-class thought.[14] But the most important generator of
class consciousness is the sheer force of economic relations. The proletariat is
driven to revolt. If the bourgeoisie simplifies society, it simplifies the proletarian
too. It strips him of all incidentals. He is reduced to economic simplicity itself: to
naked necessity and need, pure lack, 'bare existence'. He has 'nothing to lose but
his chains'. He is stripped of all illusions, including those of nationality. No mean
English bourgeois he, but full of 'passions as strong and mighty as those of the
foreigner'.[15] Moreover the relations in which he stands, the cause of his suffering,
become more and more visible. In the end the modern labourer has no choice but
to revolt while capitalism opens itself to him, as a book. It cannot even guarantee
the means of his existence:

In order to oppress a class, certain conditions must be assured to it under which it
can, at least, continue its slavish existence . . . . The modern labourer . . . instead
of rising with the progress of industry, sinks deeper and deeper below the conditions
of existence of his own class . . . . And here it becomes evident, that the bourgeoisie
is unfit any longer to be the ruling class in society, and to impose its conditions of
existence upon society as an over-riding law. It is unfit to rule because it is incompetent to assure an existence to its slave . . . because it cannot help letting him sink
into such a state. . . . Society can no longer live under this bourgeoisie, in other
words, its existence is no longer compatible with society.[16]

The historical content of this passage is clear through the 'philosophical' forms.
The feeling that capitalist society provided no lodgement for the worker, that the
position of proletarian was simply not habitable, is a dominant tone of early
working-class radicalism. It was based certainly on extreme privations but, as
Edward Thompson has stressed, also on a widespread sense of loss. This was the
experience of the small-producer-becoming-proletarian, not yet, one must insist,
the characteristic experience of the proletarian as such. Of course, the modern
working-class was to be made and remade and made again in struggles against
capital, but the content of these later struggles was to be more the taming of
capital than its abolition. Based upon observation of a particular phase, 'Manifesto
Marxism' extrapolated its features into a law of capitalism as such.

It is possible to add more theoretical criticisms, based, that is, in a knowledge
of subsequent events and of contemporary needs. These points are relevantly made
since 'Manifesto Marxism' remains a mid-twentieth-century presence. This form of

Marxism does not grasp specifically cultural or ideological conditions of oppositional working-class politics. Though Marx and Engels continually argued against
early European socialisms, they remained incurious about popular cultural legacies.
Engels's portrayal of pre-Chartist popular culture, for instance, is self-confessed
guesswork that achieves a high comic character:

They could rarely read and far more rarely write; went regularly to church, never
talked politics, never conspired, never thought, delighted in physical exercises,
listened with inherited reverence when the Bible was read, and were, in their
unquestioning humility, exceedingly well-disposed towards the 'superior' classes.
But, intellectually, they were dead . . . .[17]

His accounts of Chartist culture are, by contrast, full of excitement and particu-
larity. But it is precisely the less overtly 'political' elements of a culture that most
need study, since their role in politics is most obscure.

Other criticisms concern the neglect of complexity.[18] Within this problematic
internal complexities of the class ('in itself') cannot be grasped. Yet historically the
labourer's dependence on capital has taken varied forms. Divisions within the class
have been exceedingly complex. 'Simplification' seems always to produce further
internal structurations. Similarly, the simple class/party relation gives us little purchase on the complexities of working-class politics and representation. These
points will recur later in the argument.

Several commentators have noted important subsequent shifts in Marx's theory
of classes. These amount to a profound practical self-criticism of *The Manifesto*,
which was necessary to preserve some organic relation between Marxist theory and
the train of events in Britain and Europe after 1848. There were, perhaps, two main
moments of revision: the first, identified precisely by Gwyn Williams, was the
immediate aftermath of the counter-revolutions in the late 1840s. Revision followed
the disappointment of the expectations of *The Manifesto* and the subsequent
political isolation of the communists. The most important text of this moment is
The Eighteenth Brumaire of Louis Bonaparte. In this essay, as Hall argues, the faults
of *The Manifesto* are transformed, through attempts to understand the complexity
of the relations between economic classes and political parties.[19] Fernbach makes a
similar point when he argues that in *Class Struggles in France*

Marx began, for the first time, to develop a systematic set of concepts for coming
to grips with the phenomena of a politics which is certainly that of class struggle
. . . but which is nevertheless *politics*, practised in the field of ideology and coercion
that gives it its specific character.[20]

The second moment of revision, a longer period but still an attempt intellectually
to recoup political defeats, is the moment of *Capital* and its preparatory works, the
rendering of the historical and philosophical generalities of *The Manifesto* into a
much more precise account of the economic position of 'the labourer' under
capital. Nicolaus argues that the 'Hegelian choreography' of *The Manifesto* - the

'negation' of bourgeois society by the proletariat - was replaced by categories that allow us to understand the rise of intermediate classes and the complication (rather than the simplification) of the structure of capitalist society.[21]

These revisions certainly provide the *means* for a full recasting of the older problematic. Yet they resemble the more familiar tussles with 'old Hegel' himself in that they were never completed. The earlier simplicities were not replaced by the new complexities - rather the two co-exist, often in the same texts. There are, in Hall's phrase, 'echoes' of *The Manifesto* in *Capital*. The prospect of proletarian revolution, no less inevitable, merely delayed till capital's maturity, remains one organizing assumption even of *The Eighteenth Brumaire*.[22] Later commentators have sometimes underestimated their own roles in teasing out the implications of later formulations for earlier ones. It is not clear that Marx was always so perceptive. For today, it is more important to recover the 'best' Marx, than to continue to chastise the elements of 'economism', 'teleology' or 'class reductionism' in Marx at his worst. But the *historical* significance of the absence of a developed Marxist theory of classes has been immense. Since *The Manifesto* remained the most widely used agitational text of the communist movement, since *Capital* itself gave warrant to the earlier problematic, and since Engels's interpretative work tended to disguise rather than highlight the revisions of the 1850s and 1860s, the theoretical resources of working-class movements in the period from the Great Depression to the rise of fascism were severely weakened.

Lenin and Gramsci

It has become a somewhat routine procedure to identify a whole middle period of Marxist theory ('Second International') with various species of 'economism'. Much less understood are the historical conditions of this 'deviation'. No such history is attempted here, but it is important to say that while the problematic of *The Manifesto* made its argument less relevant in Britain after 1850, it acquired relevance again in late-nineteenth-century Europe, whenever large masses of peasants, small producers or semi-proletarians were caught up in industrial transformations similar to those of early nineteenth-century Britain, whenever the subordination of labour to capital was conspicuously deepened and in the times of 'syndicalist' excitement which often accompanied these transformations. Deep and rapid economic change seems often to produce a neglect of political and ideological conditions even in theorists whose thought generally is opposed to this tendency. One thinks of the young Gramsci, of the 'Red City' of Turin and the Factory Councils.[23]

It is to Lenin, however, that we should turn for the further development of the *Manifesto* problematic. Lenin developed that side of 'Manifesto Marxism' that emphasized the importance of political struggles in determining outcomes. At the same time he stressed the historic role of the proletariat 'as the builder of socialist society'. This was, indeed, 'the chief thing in the doctrine of Marx'.[24] In effect, then, Lenin grafted a Marxist political theory on to the basics of the *Manifesto* scheme. His analysis moves constantly between the 'objective' or 'economic' aspects of immediate tactical situations and the 'subjective' features, matters of organization and consciousness. The economic/political duo is the key structure of his thought. Yet the main themes of Lenin's writing - science and ideology; spontaneity and political consciousness; masses and party - are handled in a way that suppresses the cultural or ideological content or object of politics and obscures questions about popular attitudes and feelings.

This follows, in part, from Lenin's version of the science/ideology divide. Marxism may not be a completed science but it is a science of a very developed order. For most situations it is important to recapitulate the findings of Marx and Engels - Lenin's characteristic polemical mode is precisely to recapitulate thus, confronting 'revisionism' with the findings. Marxism is a 'strikingly integral and harmonious scientific theory' which needs to be applied to new situations, and to be completed, but is not in need of revision.[25] This creates the distinction between science and ideology in its most closed form: true knowledge/the bumbling mistakes of revisionism; proletarian knowledge/petty bourgeois conceptions; consciousness of class/'deceptions' or 'self-deceptions'. The content of ideology, in a sense, matters little; it may swiftly be reduced to its class character;

People always have been the foolish victims of deception and self-deception in politics, and they always will be until they have learnt to seek out the *interests* of some class or other behind all moral, religious, political and social phrases, declarations and promises.[26]

In this conception of ideology, not inappropriate certainly for analysing a state with few ideological resources, the main absence is the force of belief or conviction. The models continuously evoked in Lenin's language are those of delusion or corruption. The contents or logic of opposed positions are lost in the pejorative labels: 'revisionism', 'opportunism', 'petty-bourgeois mentality'. It is not, after all, beliefs that move people, but 'interests'.

Much the same could be said of Lenin's understanding of bourgeois strategies, especially in the West. Out of a largely pre-war and then Russian experience, Lenin understood the state mainly in its repressive moment.[27] Where this was not adequate, he used notions of manipulation or top-downward, one-dimensional control, the language of 'bribery and corruption'. As he said of 'labour aristocracy', 'they are bribing them in a thousand different ways, direct and indirect, over and covert'.[28]

A similar structure is to be found in the spontaneity/politics couplet. The masses learn, to be sure, from their practical activity, and leaders may fall behind as well as lead, but the source of conceptions is a pre-given theory which is developed outside the class and communicated to it.[29] There are 'spontaneous' and 'conscious' elements, a distinction which threatens to become that of thinking head and political muscle.[30] Even 'propaganda' (hardly a nuanced way of thinking how popular conceptions may be changed) is given a heavily organizational emphasis. Lenin's writing on 'party literature' or the need for 'an all-Russia political newspaper' understands such projects as foci for unities, but is silent about the relations to be sought, ideologically, between such productions and their readers.[31]

The obvious comparison is with Gramsci. While the very notion of 'spontaneity' disguises the fact that the masses already have conceptions of the world beyond mere 'force of habit', Gramsci insisted that 'all men are philosophers', and share in some conception of the world.[32] 'Pure spontaneity' does not exist in history since it would amount to 'pure mechanicity'. It exists only in the fact that conscious leadership is diffused rather than concentrated, or has beliefs that do not transcend 'traditional conceptions of the world'. It follows that there is a need 'to study and develop the elements of popular psychology, historically and sociologically, actively (i.e. in order to transform them by educating them into a modern mentality)'.[33] Much of *The Prison Notebooks* are an elaboration of this point. This project Gramsci found to be 'implicit' in Lenin - 'perhaps even explicitly stated'. Yet despite many similarities and later development in Lenin's own position, their emphases *do* seem dissimilar and lead to different analyses of the relation of party to class. Gramsci was the first major Marxist theorist to take the culture of the popular masses as the direct and privileged object of study and of political practice.

These deficiencies were the reverse side of Lenin's political virtues: his stress on 'concrete' analysis, intervention in immediate political contingencies and impatience, in situations demanding heroic activity, of 'mere words'. These features, aspects of the tightest of theory-practice relations, may distinguish Leninism from its subsequent corruptions in Stalinism where a mechanical notion of Marxism as pre-given 'science' is allied to a rigidly organizational and authoritarian conception of party.[34] But Lenin's legacy had a tendency to relieve Marxism from the concrete study of working-class culture, and to narrow the range of what was considered relevant to political practice.

Later orthodoxies: two examples

Two further expressions of this problematic are especially revealing. These are rather dissimilar examples, but share a historical dilemma and a structure of argument: first, the theory of 'labour aristocracy', casually present in the later Engels, developed in Lenin's writing on imperialism and reformism, reintroduced into English Marxist historiography by Eric Hobsbawm and currently the subject of much historical debate;[35] second, the early work of Georg Lukacs, whose book *History and Class Consciousness*, is the fullest development of the class/class-consciousness position.[36]

The dilemma is that posed in the contradiction between the theoretical destiny of the proletariat and the actual course of Western working-class politics. Marxist theory has worried around the problem of the revolutionary class *manqué*, not only in the classic debates around 'reformism' or 'labourism' but also in much of the thinking around culture-ideology-consciousness. To speak rather rashly, there have been two responses to this situation: to abandon recognizably Marxist analysis or to construct a second level of theory or special explanations, to show why a 'normal' or long-term historical development had somehow been blocked, or delayed. These

have been commoner responses than attempting to reconstruct the original problematic.

The commonest form of second-order theory has been the recovery of elements
absent in the original problematic though often present, in a different, less accented
form in the historical experience which it expressed. These new elements, not
theorized as part of the central dynamics of the capitalist mode of production, are
then understood as historically contingent factors, features of a particular phase.
They are fetters or inhibitions on more organic processes, a belief in the simpler
forms of which are thereby preserved. Features central to the constitution of the
working-class appear in a displaced or reduced role.

The 'theory' of labour aristocracy is an excellent example. It has been used to
explain the 'liberalization' of mid-nineteenth-century Britain, labour 'reformism'
and the failure of early-twentieth-century working-classes to develop a counter-
hegemonic strategy. Two kinds of argument are embraced in the same term: the
first centres on labour organization and its partial incorporation within the agencies
of the state; the second posits some larger social-structural division within the class
itself, commonly between 'skilled' and 'unskilled' sectors.[37] Both arguments
correspond to observable tendencies in the post-1850 history of the working class,
but also limit the effects of such observations on the fundamental inadequacies of
an older orthodoxy. Theories of the incorporation, 'corruption' or detachment of
'leadership' have actually hindered a more fundamental reconceptualization of the
relationship between economic classes and political parties, or a more adequate
analysis of the dispositions of the 'rank and file'.[38] Similarly, 'the mid Victorian
aristocracy of labour' may not be a very helpful construction. For it was not just
a unique historical phenomenon: but rather a particular *form* of a more general
tendency. As Marx discovered in his deeper analyses, the expansion and the movements of capital do not simply unify and massify labour, even in the direct relations
of production. Rather, the working class is continuously recomposed around major
internal structurations. These internal divisions - within factories, within industries,
between occupations, between the sexes and between the employed and the reserve
armies - ought to be an object of any primary theory of the working class. We need
to start, indeed, politically and theoretically, not from the assumption of simplification and unity but from that of complexity and division.[39] These divisions are
based on hierarchies of labour modified by the effects of gender relations which
are reproduced mainly within the family. These forms of division are, however, also
the object of ideological and political practices. A whole politics may be wrought on
top of them. Socialist strategies are not at all aided by the rooted belief that such
divisions must somehow pass away, or be easily transcended in the name of some
essential unity.

Lukacs's *History and Class Consciousness*, essays written or revised in the heat
of struggles within the Hungarian Communist Party in 1922, share the general
features of labour aristocracy theory. For his early project was an attempt to graft
a more developed theory of consciousness on to the classical root. The result is a
similar hybrid. Lukacs was a forerunner of the extreme abstractness of 'Western

Marxism' and his borrowings were colossally heterogeneous: a classical Marxist root, a recovery of Hegel and the pre-*Manifesto* Marx, a debt to Weber and Simmel and a reading of part 1 of volume 1 of *Capital*.[40]

His starting point was Marx's distinction between the class 'as against capital' and the class 'for itself'. The first characteristic move was to render 'class consciouness' a 'sacred' category.[41] Despite its 'profane' origin in Chartism and Owenism, it now acquired a wholly theoretical status. It became 'the thoughts and feelings men would have in a particular situation if they were *able* to assess both it and the interest arising from it', or 'rational reactions "imputed" to a particular typical position in the process of production'.[42] How then to explain the distance between such a consciousness and the contents of proletarian heads, this side of revolution?

'False consciousness' has fundamental forms, differently inhabited by the two main classes. (Lukacs accentuated the schematism of *The Manifesto* by denying to other classes an effective historical role.)[43] These forms had been described by Marx in *Capital* as the mechanism of 'fetishism'. Relations between people acquire, under capitalism, a 'phantom objectivity', appearing as things. By a series of daring homologies, the features of a fetishized consciousness were discerned throughout capitalist society: in its bureaucracy, its sexual relations, its economic ideologies, its jurisprudence and, especially, its philosophy and epistemology.[44]

The bourgeoisie inhabits this world with a necessarily partial vision, having knowledge of practical management but not of the totality of processes nor of those elements that point to future transformations, the tendency to recurrent crises, for instance. Faced with the instability of its domination, its objective interests force it to deceive itself. The proletariat has no such interest, but in its immediate perspective, it has its own 'bourgeois' (i.e. 'false') consciousness within which it is held by 'opportunist' politics. But a knowledge of the totality is both possible and necessary - 'a matter of life and death'. Crises force the proletariat to self-realization. In this moment the duality of class 'as against capital' and class 'for itself', transformed in Luacks's thought into the Hegelian dialectic of subject and object, is resolved. The proletariat becomes the identical subject - object of history.[45]

So questions inadequately treated in earlier accounts return to the tradition with a vengeance. Lukacs remains important for his concentration on consciousness, for his criticisms of an unreflexive epistemology, and for the attempt to theorize the relation between capital's economic forms and the *general* features of bourgeois thought. But he is also a classical instance of two recurrent tendencies commoner in sociological traditions: the tendency to see class cultures as straightforwardly and wholly conditioned by social postion (for this is the argument, ultimately, about class consciousness); and the tendency to ascribe to whole societies one 'central' or 'essential' modality of thought which enters the consciousness of all classes (for this is the argument about 'false consciousness'). The major fatality, as always in the class/class consciousness problematic, is any concrete, complex account of lived cultures, how they are formed and how they may be transformed.

Origins of the culture problematic

The complicated origins of 'culture' belong to the same history as early Marxist theory. The cultural paradigm was formed in the Industrial Revolution, was re-defined in the 1880s and 1890s and was recovered as a 'tradition' in the 1950s. Some elements were then worked into a theory of cultural -ideological processes.

Yet the social origin of these two traditions differs very much. Early Marxism was a rendering into theory of the experience of the small-producer-becoming-proletarian. The problematic of culture expressed the dilemmas of some English intellectuals sufficiently removed from industrial capital, in situation or sympathies, to distance themselves from its morality and purposes. Except for three main moments - the 1790s (fleetingly), the 1880s and 1890s and the 1950s and 1960s - these intellectuals were distanced from popular movements and almost uniformly dismissive of popular moralities. Their 'autonomy' can be seen in the very structure of their thought: 'the emergence of *culture* as an abstraction and as an absolute', as a separate set of moral and intellectual activities, and as 'a court of human appeal', even as 'a mitigating and rallying alternative'.[46] Williams's description of this 'structure of feeling' seems also to spell out the increasingly differentiated functions of intellectual labour (whether of poet, novelist, artist, critic or academic) and the desire to find in specialized pursuits some cannon of judgement and behaviour relevant to the whole society. Since this tradition was an overwhelmingly 'literary' one, the debate was evaluative rather than analytic. It concerned appropriate social moralities or what Edward Thompson has called 'the education of desire'.[47]

This long line of 'literary sociology' has been much discussed. We will mainly concentrate on the post-war advocates of culture, and especially upon Raymond Williams and Edward Thompson. Yet these writers seems to have found themselves in some account of predecessors: Williams in a long detour in search of 'a general theory of culture', Thompson in his twenty-year espousal of the ideas of William Morris.[48] Why did they choose to write about their deepest political convictions through the presentation of significant persons, mostly long dead?

Williams's *Culture and Society* constructs a 'tradition' around the history of a word - 'culture' - and a succession of writers who contributed to its sum of meanings. Perhaps the most obvious conclusion of a return to the book is the great variety of this 'tradition'. Yet Williams's sharpest critics have constructed a still more homogeneous entity - 'the literary intelligentsia' - and attacked his 'social tradition' as one of 'almost uniform political reaction'.[49] There has even been a tendency to take the *'Culture and Society'* intellectuals as typical of English intellec-tuals as a whole, thereby excluding a whole middle-class radical and liberal tradition from the historical record.[50] Edward Thompson's critique is much more perceptive: there was not one *Culture and Society* tradition, but several.[51]

A more discriminating history would have to make some distinctions. Though all these writers were distanced from the ruling interests and ideas of their time, their evaluations were more or less interesting or useful to different social classes or groups. Often they were taken up (and thereby changed) by particular parties or movements. On such a basis three main strands might be distinguished among those discussed in *Culture and Society*. The first strand is a Conservative tradition, the ideological *alter ego* of Liberalism: Burke, Southey, Disraeli, Newman, Mallock and Eliot are central here. One distinctive feature is a deep distrust of democracy. If capitalism is opposed, it is because it is a 'leveller'. The social bases of this conservative organicism were the Anglican Church, the Conservative Party and the social order and institutions of an agrarian capitalism. 'Culture' was understood as the repository of traditional social values, whose most important practical function was to distinguish between leaders and led and to defend attendant privileges. Since 1945 it has become difficult, except as an eccentricity, to avow fully hierarchical philosophies; under the pressure of the ideological assumption of 'equality' the Conservative Party has changed its repertoire to a more liberal variant.

Edward Thompson has written the history of the second strand a radical Romanticism.[52] The succession runs from the early Romantics (especially Blake, Keats and Shelley) through Carlyle and Ruskin, to William Morris, in whom Romanticism and Marxism are conjoined. There are two points of junction with popular movements: between plebian radicalism and the utopian intellectuals of the 1790s and with Morris's crossing of 'the river of fire', to take the standpoint of the working class in the 1880s.[53] Later projections of the tradition are not altogether clear: it should include, perhaps, 'Marxisante independents' like G.D.H. Cole and 'ethical socialists' like Tawney or Orwell. It should include perhaps the radical populism of the 1930s and 1940s, without the 'Stalinist pieties'. But the most important test of the organicity of Morris and of the earlier tradition is their reception into working-class traditions of independent socialist education and the continuance of utopian and ethical elements in the British labour movement.[54]

Thirdly, we might distinguish writers whose very lack of an organic connection is their defining feature. They explore the dilemmas of people like themselves, express the viewpoint, for instance, of those Oxbridge-civil-service-literary circles in which Mathew Arnold moved. This thought remains, in Gramsci's word, 'intellectualistic'. One might include here Arnold, the various artistic Bohemias (e.g. the pre-Raphaelites) and Leavis and the Leavisites, whose dilemmas are very much those of the academic layer in a modern education system. Elements of the thought of such traditional intellectuals may, of course, influence more organic thinkers, as Arnoldian formulations influenced Tawney's thought on education, for instance.

It would require a proper history of these traditions to show the force of these categories and to refine them. But it should be clear that wholesale acceptance or rejection of the 'culture' tradition is perilous. It will hardly do to dismiss the whole sequence as one of unmitigated reaction, or to see the idea of culture as contaminated at root. At the very least one must ask, *whose* idea of culture? In the end, though, such questions cannot be answered by historical pedigrees, only by modern relevances.

Yet why should it have been so important for certain intellectuals of the left to discover themselves in 'traditions' at all? Some answers have already been given in contextualizing the sociologies. The 1950s were a period of crisis for those who based their politics on a criticism of capitalism and a faith in the mass of the people. The conditions of this decade were particularly testing for the characteristic politics of the English left: strong in popular sympathies and moral sensitivity, weak in the concrete analysis of capitalism and its twentieth-century adaptations. The 'radical populism' of the 1930s and 1940s depended on the crisis-ridden state of the inter-war economy, the immediacies of the fight against fascism, and opposition to the most overt forms of social inequality and class rule. When these conditions seemed to evaporate, underlying weaknesses were clearly displayed. A generally leftist climate among intellectuals was rapidly dispersed, leaving only a harder contingent. But it could offer, from inherited theoretical resources, no adequate explanation of capitalism's success to place beside the gospels of growth and affluence. So confident were right-wing intellectuals in this period that they even began a reappraisal of the less 'acceptable' moments in the history of British capitalism, rehabilitating the Industrial Revolution as a moment of 'growth'.[55] A reviving leftism took up the weaker points of this analysis - overwhelmingly, the analysis of culture. One consequence was the reproduction of a persistent dichotomy within English ideologies: between a liberal, utilitarian and 'economist' pole, where the progressive side of capitalism was well but one-sidedly understood; and a romantic, literary and 'qualitative' pole with popular political sympathies but a romantic and equally one-sided view of capitalism's evils.

This pressure was accompanied by major internal stresses. Intellectuals in the Labour Party were affected through the party's loss of confidence and the bitter debates about 'revisionism'. Intellectuals to the left of this, in the Communist Party or with a firmer alignment to Marxism, were even more beset, their party paralysed, then split, by the half-revelations of the Twentieth Congress and the Soviet invasion of Hungary.[56] To judge from the force of the explosion to which they gave rise, the pressures must have been intense. The moment of culture can be understood as an attempt to vindicate critical social thought (from Marxism to Left Leavism) in an exceptionally hostile climate and in circumstances where even 'the people' seemed content. Every single national resource was important in such an effort. What could English culture offer to stem the tide of 'Progress'? Answer: The Tradition. Answer: William Morris. Answer: The English working class in a more heroic phase.

Culture, experience and theory

The culture paradigm is distinguished by an overriding concern with describing the actual forms of popular practices and beliefs. The manner of this commitment, the sharpness of an accompanying politics, even the key term of definition, differ very much. The term 'culture', for instance, remains central in Williams's cultural theory whether thought of as 'a whole way of life' or in its latest more difficult formulation as 'a constitutive social process, creating specific and different ways of life'.[57] Thompson's concern with culture, values, ideas and moral evaluations is no less marked; and he defines this as the crucial absence in Marxism.[58] But his solution was less a long meditation on culture and more, in his early work, a reworking of familiar Marxist categories, especially of 'class consciousness'. The engagement with culture or lived experience is secured by insisting that class consciousness is the way in which experiences are 'handled in cultural terms: embodied in traditions, value systems, ideas and institutional forms'. It has a definite history: it is neither an abstraction nor a hopeful projection. It is a category to be made 'profane' again. Any idealist or normative version - of class consciousness 'not as it is, but as it ought to be' - is rejected.[59]

'Experience' defines both the object and the method of inquiry. It is a method in which the author himself, *his* experience, is very intrusive: there is much self-revelation in Hoggart's portrayal of his childhood, in Williams's pursuit of 'the implications of personal experience to the point where they have organically emerged as methods, concepts, strategies'.[60] and in Thompson's style of polemical address. The method rejects sociologies in which lived relations are marginalized or over-borne by theory. Part of the criticism of elite cultural theory and of the restrictions of creativity to the artist is that it provided a flattened stereotypical view of the life of the 'masses': 'there are in fact no masses; there are only ways of seeing people as masses'.[61] Thompson attacks a whole range of otherwise very dissimilar positions on the same grounds: economistic Marxism, 'ideological' economic history, a 'Platonist' Leninism, structural functionalism, the construction of abstract typologies in anthropology or sociology and, latterly, a Marxist structuralism.[62] These all have the same moral and epistemological features: 'violent abstraction', the 'imposition' of *a priori* schema on a living history, the forcing of historical materials into the mould of the theorist's own preoccupations, speculative or dogmatic. Advocated instead is an explicitly anti-rationalist epistemology in which theory is restricted to critique and hypothesis, and the key moment is likened to listening:

If you want a generalization I would have to say that the historian has got to be listening all the time. He should not set up a book or a research project with a totally clear sense of exactly what he is going to be able to do. The material itself has got to speak through him. And I think this happens.[63]

Williams argues a very similar position, defining, with great accuracy, common tendencies in both older (base and superstructure) and modern (structuralist) Marxisms:

The analytical categories, as so often in idealist thought, have, almost unnoticed, become substantive descriptions, which then take habitual priority over the whole social process to which, as analytic categories, they are attempting to speak.[64]

There are immense strengths in this position. Culturalism conducts a profound critique of theory-as-dogma, of a rationalism or a conceptual *a priorism*, in the first place in the name of 'experience', in the second in the name of 'materialism'. This response was first formed against economistic Marxism; but it has an equal force against many forms of the explosion of 'theory' in the 1970s. If, like Marx, one regards various forms of idealism as the occupational vice of 'the philosopher' (for which read intellectual or academic), the culturalist argument remains immensely important.

But it also has considerable weaknesses. The stress on the privilege of 'experience' leads to an underdeveloped theoretical enterprise and a tendency to avoid abstract or generalizing discourse in itself. There are several aspects of this: the tendency of rejecting analytical distinctions as a matter of principle, the tendency to disguised or unselfconscious theoretical borrowings and the failure fully to theorize the results of concrete studies. We might take some examples of each of these. Thompson's *Making of the English Working Class*, for example, an historical master-piece, remains a work whose findings are seriously under-exploited by the author himself. It is full of profound insights about the relations between the lived, cultural level and the transformative ideological practices, whether those of Methodist preachers or of radical journalists. For such insights to become fully available they would have to be stated more abstractly, or generally. They would have to be abstracted from the particular patterns of 'lived' historical complexity in which they occurred. Their relation to a more general debate about, say, culture and ideology, would have to be explored and a specifically theoretical contribution developed from them. Such abstractions do not have to be thought of as completely general or trans-historical in scope - the historian's nightmare of 'theory'. A proper use of concepts involves arguments about their historical scope of reference. Still, if such abstractions are not made, findings remain locked up in accounts of specific historical contingencies: they cannot be consumed theoretically, cannot generate parallel questions for other instances, cannot contribute to the development of conceptual tools. In one sense, *The Making* is a very theoretical book: it is organized, very consciously, around a particular problematic and conducts an extended historical critique of other positions. This case, these big bold truths, are mightily made page after page. Yet, as many readers find, there are great rich-nesses in the book (and in the history it describes) which are difficult to grasp for want of a more explicit theoretical labour. A work of this stature ought to *produce theory*.

The concluding sections of *Whigs and Hunters*, Thompson's latest major text, illustrate a rather different problem. Here Thompson does generalize from his findings on the subject of class and the law. He conducts an argument against notions of the law as the simple expression of the interests of a dominant class, stressing those features of law as a practice which may limit its use as a class instrument. Yet this very convincing argument is presented as a polemic against 'modern structural Marxists' who, in fact, adopt a very similar view of the juridical as that pressed by Thompson![65]

This is simply a case of inattention to the arguments of theoretical works, an inattention that would hardly be tolerated for the usual order of historical 'sources'. Williams's *Marxism and Literature*, by comparison, represents a very advanced position within the culturalist problematic since it is explicitly a long and challenging theoretical statement based upon more concrete work. In general, however, culturalist premises tend to interrupt the full movements from the concrete to the abstract(and back again) that distinguished Marx's method and which would make possible a continuous revision and development of a theoretical legacy from the products of new research.

The point about analytic distinction is best illustrated through particular questions: how does culturalism understand the relation of culture to not-culture and, in particular, how is this distinction handled in relation to class? These questions are central to our subject, 'working-class culture'.

Classical Marxism handled these problems through the base-superstructure metaphor and the class/class consciousness distinction. Both Williams and Thompson have consistently, in all their work, argued against the base-superstructure formulation. Williams has traced a kind of pathology of the notion from Marx's ambiguous statements to later rigidities, has stressed the tendency to empty the 'superstructure' of any really material force and to compartmentalize areas of social life rather than examine their 'constitutive processes'.[66] Thompson has argued, similarly, that the initial separation out of the 'economic', on which the metaphor is based, was a product of the traditions which Marx contested and that real historical problems are not thinkable in this way:

There is no way in which I find it possible to describe Puritan or Methodist work discipline as an element of the 'superstructure' and then put work itself in a 'basis' somewhere else.[67]

Both Thompson and Williams attempt to find better ways of thinking about these things. Their solutions differ, however, and have to be treated separately.

Williams and culturalism

Williams has, characteristically, refused to make rigorous or systematic distinctions between cultural and other processes. The following formulations, one from the early works and one from the late, are quite typical:

The truth about a society, it would seem, is to be found in the actual relations, always exceptionally complicated, between the system of decision, the system of communication and learning, the system of maintenance and the system of generation and nurture. It is not a question of looking for some absolute formula, by which the structure of these relations can be invariably determined. The formula that matters is that which, first makes the essential connections between what are never really separable systems, and second, shows the historical variability of each of these systems, and therefore the real organisations within which they operate and are lived.[68]

Orthodox analysts began to think of 'the base' and 'the superstructure' as if they were separable concrete entities. In doing so they lost sight of the very processes - not abstract relations but constitutive processes - which it should have been the special function of historical materialism to emphasize . . . . It is not 'the base' and 'the superstructure' that need to be studied, but the specific and indissoluble real processes . . . .[69]

The procedure of both these passages is to identify certain distinctions, to insist
that there can be no adequate general formulation of relations between different
spheres, and, finally, to insist on the importance of totalities or 'constitutive social
processes' that lie behind the distinctions anyway. In practice this procedure
amounts to the collapse of distinctions, since the weight of the argument is always
about their essential artificiality. 'Experience', it seems, can always grasp a process
that is beyond or beneath analytical distinctions and which they may (perhaps
must?) obscure. Collapses of this kind can be seen all the way through *Marxism
and Literature*. The distinction between economic production and other practices
disappears in the expansion of production as an undifferentiated concept akin to
'creativity'. The term 'material' is applied to all aspects of a social and political order
in a parallel expansion.[70]

There are several difficulties in this solution. First, there is the difficulty of
arriving at any precise view at all of the characteristics of culture. Such questions
are referred back, all the time to total social process, 'real men' and classes in
specific situations. Yet at no moment in the whole Williams *ouevre* does a clear
definition or boundary of culture emerge. Thus 'way of life', as Edward Thompson
suggested in 1961, tends to become everyone's shopping list of elements of thought,
action, organization, work or leisure.[71] 'Cultural studies' tends to inherit and to
develop the extreme descriptive heterogeneity of this object. It follows that it is
not possible to speak coherently about the relation between culture and other
(kinds of?) practices, except continually to insist that all is part of one totality.
A persistent fuzziness must result. But more serious consequences may follow,
for a second set of problems concern what relations actually are, in practice,
dominant in Williams's accounts of the world: how the failure to specify is actually
supplied more pragmatically. As literary critic and cultural theorist, Williams does
stress certain kinds of practices, all of them broadly cultural and, within that,
mainly literary. Other practices tend to be marginalized or defined away. There is
no check on this from theoretical controls. Thus the early works are particularly
inattentive to political processes, a tendency which Williams himself has
acknowledged.[72] The tensionless 'expansion' of culture replaces struggle over
values and definitions. Though some of this is repaired in later work, there is a
persistent neglect of the particular character and force of economic relations and
therefore of economic definitions in relation to class. This 'culturalism' is
described by Anthony Barnett, the most careful of Williams's critics, as a kind of
inversion of economism, a reduction 'upwards'.[73] This is the characteristic tendency
of 1950s' and 1960s' texts in both history and 'literary sociology'. It is very
characteristic of Hoggart's *Uses of Literacy*, for example, from which both
economic production and politics are literally absent. Even Thompson's work
is not altogether exempt from it.

The nature of Williams's culturalism can best be seen in his treatment of class.
As others have noted, the category 'class' is hardly present as an active shaping idea
in Williams's early work: it tends to emerge in conclusions, especially in the famous
passages at the end of *Culture and Society*. But here we encounter a further set

of problems. Since culture is an expansive or inclusive term (potentially including everything), the only way to give a coherent account of a particular lived culture is to reduce it to its organizing *principles*. It is not the elements of a culture that are important, but the principles or values which, overall, it expresses. If no categories (distinctions) of a systematic kind exist with which we can grasp complexities, there is no option but to simplify. One way to simplify is to seek 'essences' or 'principles' and this is very much how, in a classic form of idealist reduction, Williams approaches class cultures. We are offered a simple typology of cultures: bourgeois culture is individualistic but is modified by the idea of service; working-class culture, by contrast, revolves around collectivity and solidarity. It then becomes possible to examine the strengths and weaknesses of such principles in a Mathew Arnold-like search for the elements of a 'common culture'. The procedure produces results that are very close to other idealist accounts of class elements in English culture, including those of several historians.[74] But it also produces stereotypes as misleading as 'mass culture' or 'false consciousness'. Is solidarity a *general* feature of working-class culture? Does it apply to *all* the social sites and internal relations of a culture: to relations between men and women and men and children, for instance? How powerful have solidarities been outside the culture of the work-place? Such compressed descriptions-*cum*-judgements can hardly hope to capture the complexity of a lived culture, let alone the forces, material and ideological, which form it.

Thompson and socialist-humanist history

Thompson's position often resembles Williams's, with a similar tendency to refuse certain distinctions. Relations of production are not only economic but also 'human' relationships. Production *involves* culture. Every mode of production carries with it corresponding modes of culture. 'Economics' and 'culture' are 'two sides of the same coin', or are in a dialectic of interaction. Certain values are 'consonant' with certain modes of production and therefore an inextricable part of them. Relations of production are simultaneously expressed in all areas of social life.[75] More commonly, Thompson has worked with a minimum distinction, taken from Marx, between 'social consciousness' and 'social being'. Social being is understood as the mode of production of material life and the 'human relationships' to which it gives rise. These human relationships include exploitation, but also relations of domination and of 'acquisitiveness', knowledge of which we owe not only to Marx but also to Weber, Tawney and Veblen. Thompson has employed this distinction very much as the young Marx did, to attack positions which are seen as idealist. Thompson insists against the early Williams (as Marx did against Hegel or Proudhon) that social being determines social consciousness. This often co-exists with an insistence on the 'dialectical interrelationship' of being and consciousness, a formulation which appears inconsistent with the notion of determination. Partly, no doubt, because of these inconsistencies, Thompson's latest position seems to be different again: it is not possible, even for capitalist societies, to maintain the social being/social consciousness distinction as a general guide or control. In studying the folklore or common sense of particular groups within the subordinated classes 'we cannot conceive of social being apart from social consciousness or norms' and it is therefore 'meaningless' to ascribe priority of one over the other.[76]

These shifts indicate difficulties in a position that gives overwhelmingly priority to the portrayal of 'experience'. Faithfulness to experience, an impulse with moral and literary roots, comes into conflict, at a certain point, with what we can only call 'scientific' intentions, using the term in its broader continental senses rather than its narrower English ones. Systematic knowledge and the search for more adequate *explanations* of social processes require developed analytical procedures. Within Marxism as a science, abstraction plays a part occupied in other systems by ideal types, model-building or the testing of hypotheses. Abstraction precisely depends upon a necessary simplification of 'real history', a presentation of elements in it in a quite formal way. Most of *Capital* as a work is 'abstract' in this sense: theory is derived from the study of the concrete and is used to illuminate particular instances, but in its form and presentation, most of *Capital* does not at all resemble real history. Abstraction is both a condition for thinking clearly about the world and for learning from concrete instances in such a way as to be able to transfer insights or consider them in relation to another case. If we refuse analytical distinctions of the most elementary kind (e.g. culture/not culture) we will not be able to examine that real history whose integrity we aim to preserve. Distinctions like base/superstructure or economic/political/ideological practices, properly used, are no more than the means with which to grasp 'total social process'. To reject these tools and supply no others is to return us, scientifically, to a radical historical relativism and the denial of any generalizing or accumulative intellectual procedures.

Attempts at a proper theoretical enterprise must always, within this problematic, be 'guilty' or inhibited, so we ought to turn to Thompson's portrayals of the relation of culture and class in his actual histories. How can we describe the characteristic object of Thompson's history?

All the histories from *The Making of the English Working Class* to *Whigs and Hunters* have shared a common theme: the conflict between two cultural modes.[77] The first mode is rooted in the characteristic relations and values of a society of small producers, artisans and semi-proletarians which existed within cultural and political horizons set by agrarian capital - the first English form of a bourgeois ruling class - and were policed, centrally, by law. The second mode includes the cultural world of industrial work discipline, of Protestant or Puritan notations of time, of the psychic disciplines of Methodism, of political economy, utilitarianism and the 'Gradgrind school' and of the cultural aggressions associated with the requirements of commercial and especially industrial capital. The conflict of these modes involves a long co-existence that corresponds to Maurice Dobbs's long transition in relations of economic production. It is, indeed, the political-cultural expression or aspect of these very same changes: the long transition in culture and politics and in forms of struggle between classes. Thompson's earlier work, especially *The Making*, looks at the later points of the transition: the English working class is formed, politically and culturally, out of the collapse of the older moral framework ('paternalism' and 'the moral economy') and through popular opposition to the imposition of the new. If, as was argued earlier, *The Making* recounts the end of a story rather than the beginning of a new one, we can understand why Thompson's trajectory is back into the eighteenth century rather than forward once again to the nineteenth or later. He has developed, once more, the territory opened up by the initial explorations of Dobb and Torr, planning a historical rendezvous, perhaps, with the work of Christopher Hill. This later work has concentrated on the forms of gentry hegemony and of popular self-assertion, but has never lost sight of the transition in cultural - economic modes. *Whigs and Hunters*, for instance, deals not only with the importance of juridical relations in the eighteenth century, but also with the enforcement of capitalist property rights over the customary use rights of the foresters.

Before we look more closely at the treatment of class, it is important to note one general weakness of these histories. They rest on a reduction not dissimilar to Williams's 'culturalism'. It is not that economic relations and changes in ways of producing are absent from these histories: their presence is *assumed* all the time. But the changes in economic relations are understood *through* their experiential or political effects, not, for the most part, in themselves. Thus, in *The Making* the transformative character of the Industrial Revolution is grasped largely through the experiences of artisans, weavers and others: the character of this shift in economic social relations is never full described and is only passively present in the story. The characteristic move is to *assume* the force of economic changes, to insist upon the force of cultural and political processes too, but only to describe the latter in any detailed or active way.[78]

It is very easy to see how this tendency occurred. The problem with existing historiographies, especially of older Marxisms and its assailants in the shape of the economic historians, was the absence of any proper consideration of 'values'. *The Making* conducts a powerful critique of both these traditions, rehearsing much of Romanticism's objection to utilitarianism and political economy. The working class is not just made by the Industrial Revolution ('steam power plus the factory equals the working class') but also through political counter-revolution, and a reworking, in the light of new experiences, of inherited cultural traditions. It made much sense, then, to occupy the ground of experience from which to criticize the orthodoxies. All of Thompson's own 'traditions' - Romanticism, the concern with moralities, the literary mode, the historiography of the Hammonds and of Tawney and the Morris-inspired reading of Marx - pushed hard in the same direction. But it is now possible to see that the stress on culture involved vacating the ground of economic relations, leaving the heart of opposing positions untouched and threatening an impoverishment of analysis.

Class, class struggle and class-as-relationship are central categories of Thompson's history. Historical outcomes are the product of class struggles. Even the apparently assured control of the eighteenth-century gentry is secured and 'lived' through conflicts: the challenge of crime or riot; the response of magistracy or law. *The Making* commences with a major redefinition of class which then forms the central argument of the book. This is the emphasis that marks Thompson's history as 'Marxist' and distinguishes it from, say, the early Williams or the passivity of Hoggart's account.

Yet, as we have suggested, 'class consciousness' is reworked in the light of 'culture'. Retained from the older problematic are all the activist elements: classes as agents, present at their own making, forged in struggles: the stresses of Marx's 'class for itself'. Suppressed or rendered peripheral are the more 'objective' or passive elements in the classic concept: 'class as against capital' in the earlier formulations, developed, in *Capital*, into a profound analysis of the labourer's subordination within capitalist economic relations. Economic class relations are not entirely absent from *The Making*. Some of their force is carried in an extended and much looser notion of 'relationship': classes are groups of people in historical forms of human relationship. A more developed notion of relations of production sometimes seems about to emerge. But, generally, it is the *quality* of human relation*ships* rather than the *structuring* of these through *relations* that is the key concern. One symptom of this is the massive overloading of the term 'experience'. It is made to carry the full weight of objective determinations but also expresses the relay or relation between economics and culture. Two quotations with rather different emphases illustrate this:

The class *experience* is largely determined by the productive relations into which men are born - or enter involuntarily. Class-consciousness is the way in which these *experiences* are handled in cultural terms: embodied in traditions, value-systems, ideas, and institutional forms.[79]

In Part Two I move from subjective to objective influences - the *experiences* of groups of workers during the Industrial Revolution which seem to me to be of especial significance.[80]

In the first case 'experience' is seen as a relation *between* productive relations and culture; in the second it is *identified with* 'objective influences'. In either case, since 'objective influences' are little described, 'experience' is made to carry all their weight. It indicates, at once, the way in which individuals or groups are subject to external or uncontrollable pressures and the most located or immediate of their understandings. In it are contained, in the most compressed form, the unwillingness to distinguish culture and not-culture and many of the difficulties that arise.

Against this it is important to argue for certain minimum distinctions. In the analysis of the major classes of capitalist social formations the distinction 'class as against capital'/'class for itself' should be retained. The latter term reminds us that people stand in relations that are independent of their wills and of which they are more or less conscious. These relations do stamp a social character on people, but should not be *reduced* to relationships between people (of a nicer or nastier kind). The proletarian is not faced, merely, by greedy or exploitative middlemen or mill-owners, nor, just, by the 'inhuman' doctrines of political economy. Rather, by virtue of occupancy of a particular economic class position, the proletarian is forced to expend life energies under the control and command of capital in order to

acquire the means of subsistence, in order to live. Underneath the cultural handling
of this relation (in its particular historical forms) the figure of the 'naked' labourer
still moves, according to the fundamental disciplines of the capital relation. It
matters, certainly, whether labourers work willingly, or with murder or even
socialism in their hearts: but go to work they must or they and their children must
starve or sink into still deeper forms of dependency. Since the early nineteenth
century, the force of this economic relation has certainly been modified through
the active political interventions of the class of labourers themselves. But it is still
present and the arrangements which mitigate its severity may always be removed
or rendered more oppressive or conditional. This is why it remains possible, in
1979, to speak meaningfully of a working class in Britain, irrespective of the strength
or weakness of labour organization. At one (indispensable) moment of analysis, the
class is composed of those who partake in a proletarian relation to capital, are a
class 'as against' it. The complexities of this form of class analysis, and the need for
research as well as categories, should not lead us to abandon it.

This is of the utmost importance for the general problems raised in this book.
Any analysis of 'working-class culture' must be able to grasp the relation between
economic classes and the forms in which they do (or do not) become active in
conscious politics. If the two aspects of class analysis are conflated, this is not
possible. If class is understood only as a cultural and political formation, a whole
theoretical legacy is impoverished and materialist accounts are indistinguishable
from a form of idealism. It may indeed be that the relation between what culturalism calls 'experience' and the marshalling of political forces, or, more correctly,
between economic classes and political organizations, is never or rarely as simple
as 'transitive' or 'expressive' models imply. Economic classes rarely appear as
political forces. Most of Thompson's work, for instances, has concerned periods in
which the political representation of popular interests has, apparently, been secured
with a relative faithfulness. In the period 1790 to 1840, the class character of
political and cultural forms is relatively easy to see. Either that, or, as in the work
on the eighteenth century, the absence of economic class categories has permitted
the presentation of political forces *as* classes. Thompson's 'patricians' and 'plebians'
are a case in point. But whatever happened to small producers, semi-peasants and
semi-proletarians? And why must eighteenth-century classes borrow the garbs of
antiquity? As soon as we enter a period when formal political arrangements for the
representation of working people become more complex and acquire firm institutional continuities, these problems become inescapable. Do the British Labour
Party or British trade unions simply or expressively 'represent' working
people? At the very least they define or structure what passes for politics as such,
so preventing the representation of some elements and promoting others. These
questions cannot even be properly *posed* within the culturalist problematic.

There is one final set of temptations that lies along the route of 'culture'. The
one-sided stress on class as a cultural and political formation commits analysis to
discover such forms in every place or period. Such searches will never be altogether
in vain since the class organization of society will always find expression of *some*

kind. But the temptation is to present such findings as always analogous to a developed and politically conscious opposition. The 'class' is 'struggling' after all. Such a search slips easily into a Romantic abasement before every manifestation of 'resistance', however exotic, peripheral, displaced or contained. Edward Thompson retains, perhaps, too conventional a view of what counts as class organization to fall into this trap: a stress on party, unions and socialist intellectual traditions may, indeed, disguise the elements of 'primitive rebellion' in a *modern* working class. Yet some tendencies in modern sociology, focusing especially on the symbolic oppositions of groups of young working-class men do parallel Thompson's own stress on crowd actions, rituals of protest and moments of exceptional popular excitement and communal mobilization. The point is that we can only reach a proper assessment of the character of such moments - then and now - by placing them within a wider analysis of economic and social structures. This requires conceptual tools for a properly historicized analysis of capitalism's continued economic transformations and of the position of groups of men and women in relation to it and each other.

'Structuralism' and 'humanism'

It is neither possible nor necessary to discuss structuralist emphases as fully as the previous problematics. This is partly for pragmatic reasons: the range of structuralist writing on matters that might be judged relevant is immense. An adequate account would have to include work as different as the two quite distinct moments in Althusser's project (the 'theoreticist' phase as well as subsequent self-criticisms), elements in French structuralist anthropology, those (diverse) tendencies summed up in the term 'semiology' (the science of signs or of signification), the historical analysis of discursive practices in the work of Michel Foucault and, perhaps, on an outer 'structuralist' limit, French historical traditions, especially the treatment of popular *mentalité* by the *Annales* historians. The solution adopted here is to concentrate on Althusser's central and symptomatic contribution. In general, however, structuralist contributions are more important for their critical edge than for what they produce as alternative accounts. They have already informed our critique of other positions. In any very direct sense, structuralism has little to contribute to an account of working-class culture. This is not an object recognizable within this problematic. Structuralist theories push into the background the association between culture (or particular ideologies) and class and focus instead on the relation between ideology, as a general feature of historical societies, and mode of production as their determining base. In general, this tendency opposes what is termed a 'class-reductionist' view of culture-ideology. The main purposes of this section are, then, to recapitulate, briefly, some of the elements we take from a structuralist critique of other positions, and to identify the points where structuralism actually falls behind earlier achievements.

Althusser's project was formed under general conditions similar to those which faced the English New Left, but in a society that offered very different intellectual

and political materials.[81] It, too, was a response to the crisis of the social democratic and communist left in Western Europe in the 1950s and early 1960s. The
writing of *For Marx* and *Reading Capital* was exactly contemporaneous with the
'culturalist break'. The search for solutions was also conducted within a national
tradition in which Marxism was a weak presence, weaker, perhaps, than in
England. The elements that were drawn on in the construction of structuralist
theory were, likewise, diverse. The chief antagonists were, once more, the Cold
War critics: the task of vindicating Marxism, this time as a 'science', against contemporary calumnators and past corruptions. The chief targets within the tradition
were, again, 'economism' and 'Stalinism'. Similar situations beget similar solutions.
Both the English New Left and the Althusserians took non-economic questions as
their central concerns, supplying 'absences' in an existing Marxism: the stress on
'culture' was paralleled by the absorption in questions of 'science' and 'ideology',
initially with a strongly epistemological emphasis, latterly with a more general
concern with the formation of subjectivities. Similar solutions also begat similar
problems: notably in the whole area of the relation between ideology and non-
ideological relations.

In polemics between the two traditions these similarities are often forgotten.
The differences, however, are also very marked. We might best grasp them by
noting one founding divergence: while the English New Left took dominant post-
1956 developments in Marxist theory as a source of inspiration, Althusserianism
was formed in resolute hostility to them. In the early 1960s, when writing his
critique of Williams, Edward Thompson was mulling over 'alienation' and 'the
subject-object antithesis', reading early Marx, especially the *1844 Manuscripts*,
searching *Capital* for its most 'humanist' moments and eagerly awaiting the publication of works by George Lichtheim and C. Wright Mills.[82] The new history was
helped on its way by the discovery of a Marx whose problematic predated that of
The Manifesto and the encounter with the English working class. Althusser's
Marxism was formed *against* these very tendencies. Perhaps this reflected the greater
pull of the communist political presence in France compared with the situation
of the English 'rebels' and the American Marxists; but it also grew from the desire
to establish Marxism as a science, Althusser's most powerful lesson learned from
the emasculation of the intellectuals in the struggles of the day. So Althusser and
his colleagues, hostile to 'humanism' and the Hegelian 'taint', returned to Marx in
his most 'scientific' mood, in the 'mature' works, especially *Capital*. They constructed from Marx's greatest work a thorough-going critique of the Marxisms of the
moment. So it happened that the Althusserian critique was formed in a double
movement; opposition to economism and Stalinism but also to the commoner
forms of the 'liberation' of the intellectuals. Indeed, a common intellectual anatomy
was discerned in these two opponents: economism and humanism were both
understood as forms of existentialism; Stalinism was understood as a combination
of economism and humanism.[83]

Many of the strengths of the position derive from this double movement. We
might quote two passages that sum up, respectively, the critiques of humanism and

economism, and illustrate some basic emphases. Both are taken from *Essays in Self-Criticism*, a summation of the position without, it may be thought, many of its earlier difficulties.

Against humanism:

Marx shows that what in the first instance determines a social formation . . . is not any chimerical human essence, or human nature, nor man, nor even 'men', but a *relation* the production relation, which is inseparable from the Base, the infrastructure. And, in opposition to all humanist idealism, Marx shows that this relation is not a relation between men, a relation between persons, nor an intersubjective or psychological or anthropological relation, but a double relation: a relation between groups of men concerning the relation between groups of men and things, the means of production . . . . Naturally human individuals are parties to this relation, therefore active, but first of all in so far as they are held within it . . . . If you do not submit the individual concrete determinations of proletarians and capitalists, their 'liberty' or their personality to a theoretical 'reduction' [i.e. an abstraction], then you will understand nothing of the terrible practical 'reduction' to which the capitalist production relation submits individuals, which treats them only as bearers of economic functions and nothing else.[84]

Against economism:

The capitalist social formation, indeed, cannot be reduced to the capitalist production relation alone, therefore to its infrastructure. Class exploitation cannot continue . . . without the aid of the superstructure, without the legal - political and ideological relations, which in the last instance are determined by the production relation . . . . These relations too treat concrete human individuals as 'bearers' of relations, as 'supports' of functions, to which men are only parties because they are held within them . . . . But all these relations . . . determine and brand men in their flesh and blood just as the production relation does.[85]

Many of the emphases which have informed our critique so far are stated more generally in these passages: the stress on 'relations' and the abstraction of certain kinds of relations from the social formation as a whole producing the Althusserian 'instances' - economic, political - juridical, ideological. Each of these kinds of relation are held to have their own effects on historical outcomes, though the economic - the capitalist 'production relation' - retains an over-arching determination on the forms of struggles between classes. Though the base - superstructure metaphor is retained, the irreducibility, 'effectivity', even 'materiality' of ideology is repeatedly emphasized: no *mere* superstructure.[86] Ideology is so far from being dispensable that it is the medium in which people, in all societies, live their conditions of existence, experience their world. If certain conditions of this kind are not met, on this 'level', societies, including capitalist societies, will cease to reproduce themselves.[87] It follows (it *should* follow - unfortunately it does not always in Althusser's texts) that ideology is an important and necessary site of political struggles; that there is, indeed, a class struggle in ideology.

There is much to say about weaknesses in this way of thinking, but it is important first to stress the advances. As a 'theoretical' intervention, as a criticism of other tendencies at a high level of generality, these protocols retain an enormous force. Paradoxically, in view of the degree of abstraction and the fundamental epistemological difficulties, they represent an advance for concrete historical analysis, chiefly by removing earlier obstructions. It becomes possible to think about a materialist history which is not organized around some unfolding 'essence', whether this is the progress of productive forces, the deepening of alienation or even a simplified view of the class struggle as a predetermined battle between two composite historical agents, to the force of which every institution or element of culture must equally and synchronically bend. In other words, 'social formations' (historical societies) can be thought of with a complexity that approximates to that of the historian's sources and of the practices they reveal. It is this step, from essential to complex unity, which contributes most to historical practice.

More pragmatically, the Althusserian protocols (we had better say 'reminders') warn against tendencies we should strive to avoid. They lead us to ask, clearly, whether we are slipping back into a neglect of the cultural-ideological, or are so obsessed with literature, artistic production or human creativity in general that we forget the material conditions from which such creativity is never free. They help us to avoid the conflations of the culture problematic and the reductionism of 'consciousness'.

No supercession: problems with 'structuralism'

The relation between structuralism and earlier problematics is not, however, one of supercession. The sharpest way to demonstrate this is to focus on features that debar it as a basis of alternative accounts. There are three important aspects here: the inhibitions to concrete analysis created by structuralism's major absence - a developed epistemology of historical research; a tendency to functionalist portrayals of the operation of ideological social relations; an alternative tendency to produce accounts of ideology, 'discourse' or 'representation' in which what began as a rational abstraction becomes a complete autonomy. We might call this tendency the 'autono-mization of instances'.

Out of a particular French philosophical tradition, Althusser and his co-workers derived a view of Marx's contribution to knowledge. This 'philosophical' reading was not limited to the discussion of intellectual procedures - indeed, the character-istically philosophical contribution was pursued rather incompletely. *Reading Capital* pronounced too on the character and substance of *historical* materialism. It presented a philosophy with decidedly unphilosophical ambitions - no mere help-meet to 'science', but a fully fledged theoretical sociology in philosophical disguise, inheritor not of Literature nor yet of History but of Philosophy as the Great Tradition!

This philosopher's reading was, in fact, very selective.[88] It effected a radical simplification of Marx's results and a truncation of his procedures. Simplification is best seen in Balibar's part 3 of *Reading Capital*. Here Marx's extended three-volume definition of the capitalist mode of production is reduced to some formularies about the invariant elements of modes of production in general, their variant modes of combination, and an account of 'transition' (best compared with the richness of Maurice Dobbs's) in terms of the formal principle of non-correspondence.[89] There is no serious consideration here of Marx's 'laws' of accumulation, the existence of countervailing tendencies, the possibilities of capitalist 'solutions' to crises and to the declining rate of profit, and the forms of the reproductive circuits — all of which constitute the substance of the description of the capitalist mode. This inattention to the detail of Marx's economic analysis parallels the culturalist absence and has, as we shall see, not dissimilar results.

Marx's procedures are similarly treated: Marxist science, the opening of 'the continent of history' is held to have occurred through a practice which had as its object previous problematics, especially that of political economy. It follows that development within Marxism may occur through critical commentary upon Marx's own categories: the raising of these to full theoretical status, the supplying of silences, the making explicit or uniform implicit new problematics. The value of this theoretical labour has already been acknowledged, along with the need to take Marx's own texts and the work of other historians as its object. But this theoretical enterprise by no means exhausts the whole circuit of knowledge. It by no means describes the whole of Marx's best practice. It says nothing of research, of the stages in inquiry which Marx described as 'appropriating the material in detail' and analysing its forms of development and their inner connection.[90] It deals in part with the character of abstractions, but hypostasizes the 'concept' as finished knowledge. In particular Marx's own concern with the rush and muddle of observable phenomena is lost in the objections to 'empiricism':

I should under no circumstances have published the second volume before the present English industrial crisis had reached its climax. The phenomena are at this time singular, in many respects different from what they were in the past . . . . It is therefore necessary to watch the present course of things until their maturity before you can 'consume' them 'productively', I mean *'theoretically'*.[91]

Althusser is right to argue for a non-empiricist mode of working and his texts pose important questions. Yet *Reading Capital* is singularly devoid of solutions. The problems at the end of part 1, are simply left in suspension.[92]

Yet this absence - the connection between the investigation of specific situations (the 'English crisis' of 1879) and the development of more general categories (the theoretical consumption) - is the really damaging feature of the Althusserian epistemology. Around this lack, a whole history of post-Althusserian epistemological agonies could be written.[93] In the absence of a model of research, a 'vulgar Althusserianism' becomes a mirror image of the empiricism of the historians. Althusserianism renders the 'appropriation of the real in thought' peculiarly difficult by stressing only one side of Marx's epistemology - the 'rationalist' side, the emphasis on the distinctiveness of thought. Culturalist epistemologies stress only the other side - the 'materialist premise' which insists that these categories always express social relations.

social relations. *It* 'forgets' that thought does indeed have its own rules, that it proceeds by abstraction. Each represents aspects of Marx's best practice, whose organic relation in *Capital* and elsewhere we are only beginning to understand. At its worst, then, Althusserianism of the theoreticist period does become an 'idealism', the characteristic ideology of the intellectuals. It is easy to see its origin in the protest against the over-politicization of knowledge in an earlier communist politics.[94]

One consequence of the particular form of abstractness which is a feature of Althusserian philosophy is the failure to realize a theoretical promise in the production of specific histories. For this requires categories - fresh abstractions - at a lower level of generality than those of the abstract social formation. We cannot hope to grasp actual societies only in terms of the dominant mode of production and its ideological and political conditions. We encounter immediately the problem of 'survivals', of unthought relations that can only be grasped by historical research.[95] And if we attempt to bridge this gulf by simple extensions of Althusser's insights, we risk further failings: especially the use of simplified functionalist models and a neglect of the specificities of economic relations. It is to these failings we may now turn.

Althusser's essay on 'Ideological state apparatuses' is the classic site of these difficulties. The essay is a series of notes on the part played by ideology and the state in the reproduction of capitalist relations of production. Potentially, this essay is of great value not least to our object, working-class culture. We might expect it to deliver an account of the forms of class struggle in ideology: the way in which capital and the agencies of the capitalist state seek to secure the reproduction of a working class in a form appropriate to the requirements of accumulation and the ways in which, on the basis of their own economic conditions of existence, proletarians struggle against this process. We might expect Althusser to have built upon Marx's own account of reproduction, adding a characteristic emphasis on cultural-ideological forms.[96] For in historical reality the working class is never simply reproduced as a 'naked' proletariat, pure bearers of the capital relation. Labour is always reproduced with historically specific habits and 'needs' and within a social and cultural world whose character is never exhausted by the functional requirements of capital.

This essay has been exhaustively criticized and none of the points made here is new.[97] We can, therefore, be very brief, recapitulating criticisms germane to our purpose. The essay represents 'reproduction' which, in Marx, is a necessarily contradictory and antagonistic process, as the functional necessity of a system. Rather than being a process in which the state intervenes in the primary contradictions of economic relations, reproduction is a function performed *by* ideology *for* capital *through* the state. The whole sphere of the ideological - the very processes by which consciousness and subjectivities are formed - is subsumed within this function. Ideology-in-general - the natural culture-bound state of man - is conflated with ideology in another of its meanings, the specific conditions of a cultural kind that prepare labourers and others for the places in the hierarchical division of labour.

What is correctly understood as a condition or a contingency becomes, in the course of the argument, a continuously achieved outcome. Dominant ideology, organized especially through apparatuses like schools, works with all the certainty usually ascribed to natural or biological processes. We are returned to a very familiar model of one-dimensional control in which all sense of struggle or contradiction is lost. Althusser's account resembles nothing more than those (unrealized) bourgeois visions of the perfect worker which reoccur across the capitalist epoch, whether images of the sober and prudent aristocrat of labour or those soon-to-be employed young men and women, complete with aptitudes, 'employability' and 'social and life skills' who are the object of the Manpower Services Commission. And all this is achieved, apparently, by and through ideology: no hint of the force of economic relations themselves which in Marx's own account (and an unemployed future) provide the main disciplines. In general, the overriding concern with outcomes - reproduction - suppresses the fact that these conditions have continually to be won - or lost - in particular conflicts and struggles. Some of these dimensions are supplied by Althusser in a later postscript, but this self-criticism is of a very radical kind, which actually demands a recasting of the argument. The sense in which this falls behind existing accounts might be seen in a comparison with Edward Thompson's 'Time, work-discipline and industrial capitalism', a history of the construction of some of the conditions which Althusser's essay takes for granted - and eternalizes.[98]

Conclusions: elements of a theory of working-class culture

We end by presenting three main arguments. These are offered, not as a finished theory of working-class culture, but as indications of how to work towards more adequate accounts. Any fully developed theory, a reconstruction of Marx's original problematic for instance, could not rest on theoretical clarification alone, but only on research and fresh abstractions.[99]

First, we want to argue a case about the nature and rationality of culture-ideology as an abstraction. This involves a distancing from several positions discussed in this essay (and several more not discussed): from the refusal to abstract at all (Williams); from the tendency to regard culture-ideology or the ideological 'instance' as a concrete set of institutions or apparatuses (some readings of the ISA essay); and from all partial or trivializing conceptions of culture (e.g. its identification with 'leisure pursuits').

Second, we suggest that there is a need to differentiate moments or aspects of cultural-ideological processes. The complexity of this instance cannot be grasped through one term of analysis only, whether culture or ideology. One sympton of this is the way each term becomes overburdened with meanings, as if a massive terrain could be encompassed by a tiny word. One useful move here is to differentiate the two major terms in use - culture and ideology - and to attempt to define what is specific to each and how cultural-ideological processes might be seen as a unity.

Third, we shall return to the issue of working-class culture primarily as an example of how the relation, culture to class, may be rethought in the light of earlier discussions.

It is clear from the earlier discussion that the character of the cultural-ideological as such remains persistently difficult to grasp. Culture expands infinitely, a slide indexed by 'whole way of life' or 'constitutive social process'. But there are also problems with 'ideology', whose meanings accumulate through successive usages: ideology as false or inadequate knowledge and as opposed to science; ideology as an instance - a set of practices which occurs in all social formations; ideology as a site of conditions which must be met if capitalism as a system is to continue; ideology as a trans-historical, ever-present concomitant of human existence, the medium in which men and women live their conditions of existence - 'the representation of the imaginary relationship of individuals to their real conditions of existence'. Althusser's insistence that 'ideology has a material existence' parallels the slide of 'whole way of life'.[100] In the ISA essay ideology as an instance in the social formation seems to be identified with particular institutions or sites, with ideological state apparatuses, especially the family and the school. These different uses are, at the least, very confusing.

One solution is to distinguish very much more sharply between the notion of 'level' or 'instance' and the notion of 'apparatus', 'institution', 'site' or 'sphere' of social relations. The two ideas are different forms of abstraction: the abstraction of instances focuses on practices of a similar kind that occur throughout the whole society and in different concrete locations; the notion of 'site' or 'apparatus' tries to grasp what is specific to a particular sphere or set of institutions - schools, family, the factory, To conflate these two forms of analysis, and especially to understand 'instance' in terms of a set of concrete institutions, is a serious vulgarization. It is vulnerable to Williams's strictures on the idealist tendency to make analytic distinctions into things.[101]

We understand the notion of 'ideology' to be an abstraction of the first rather than of the second kind. It does *not* denote specific institutional sites but practices or moments in social processes *that have a distinctive character.* It involves particular kinds of relations and movements. Social formations or processes may be looked at *from this aspect,* with this most closely in focus.

What then is specific to the ideological-cultural aspect? It is important to insist, in a thoroughly 'orthodox' way, on the specifically mental (as opposed to 'material') character of these relations - their equivalence to Marx's general category of 'consciousness' (not the consciousness of class but consciousness-in-general as used by Marx in *The German Ideology*). Consciousness, in this sense, is a necessary but 'simple' abstraction, a feature of human beings as such, evident in all history. Just as men and women have always won a living from nature and sustained their material existence, so also they 'possess consciousness'.[102] This, indeed, is a specific feature of human labour, 'an exclusively human characteristic'. It distinguishes architect and bee:

At the end of every labour process, a result emerges that had already been conceived by the worker at the beginning, hence already existed ideally. Man not only affects a change of forms in the materials of nature; he also realises his own purpose in these materials.[103]

The characteristic feature of the ideological-cultural instance, then, is the production of forms of consciousness - ideas, feelings, desires, moral preferences, forms of subjectivity. This is fully recognized in Thompson's stress on 'values' and in the Althusserian usage, 'imaginary'. It is not so much a question that schools or families *are* ideology, more that they are *sites* where ideologies are produced in the form of subjectivities.

All this is to say, of course, that there is no separate institutional area of social life in which forms of consciousness arise: mentalities and subjectivities are formed and expressed in every sphere of existence. Subjectivities are very powerfully formed, as Paul Willis argues, in processes of economic production. Economic practices - production and consumption - have a cultural aspect and rest on cultural conditions. Concrete political processes similarly always involve an ideological moment. As Foucault puts it, writing of punishment:

We should admit rather that power produces knowledge . . . ; that power and knowledge directly imply one another; that there is no power relation without the correlative constitution of a field of knowledge, nor any knowledge that does not presuppose and constitute at the same time power relations.[104]

Beliefs and preferences are formed and expressed in practices which are not commonly understood as involving signification or representation. Perhaps they operate more powerfully there than in practices evidently organized for the production of consciousness: schools, media, art. Yet even these cases show the dangers of collapsing institutions and instances, for a proper concrete analysis of schools or media would involve examination of economic and political conditions as well as ideological effects. The notion of 'instance' in other words, is *theoretical* in the strongest possible sense: it is a *means* for analysing concrete situations, not a description of a chunk of concrete experience itself. Just as Marx abstracted from a living historical whole those relations most directly implicated in the production of material life (i.e. economic social relations) and left aside concrete human persons in favour of 'personifications of economic categories',[105] so a similar abstraction can be made of those relations most implicated in the production of specific forms of consciousness. Relations having been understood in this way, we may then return to actual history, 'but this time not as a chaotic notion of an integral whole, but as a rich aggregate of many determinations and relations'.[106]

The distance between this conception of culture-ideology and trivializing ones will by now be clear. Such a conception has nothing in common with 'culture' as a residuum when other practices - work and politics - have been subtracted, that is with culture-as-leisure. Nor is it in any way similar to 'culture' as limited to certain specialized activities - writing, reading, consuming films or playing football.

There is an underdeveloped tendency in both structuralist and culturalist accounts
to make some distinction between levels or moments in the cultural-ideological.[107]
Althusser has distinguished between 'theoretical' and 'non-theoretical' ideologies,
or 'theoretical' annd 'practical' ideologies.[108] More interestingly, there is the
distinction, implicit in the description of ideology-in-general, between a lived
relation to real relations (what culturalism would call 'experience') and the
representation of that lived relation. This distinction implies the need to understand
both the 'lived relation' itself and the representation of it in ideology. There are not
dissimilar distinctions in the culturalist tradition. In Thompson's history, for
example, several terms other than culture and consciousness are in play, especially
'values' or 'value systems' and 'ideology'. 'Value system' seems to describe cultural
or ideological elements in their most organic relation to a mode of production;
ideology, by contrast, has classic *German Ideology* connotations of ideas and
idealism.[109] In practice, however, these distinctions are not rigorously used and
there is a tendency in the histories for theoretical problems to be solved by a mixture of moral evaluation and political choice: utilitarianism, Methodism, political
economy, Evangelicalism (each of which may be 'lived' by middle-class people) are
'ideology'; working-class radicalism is 'culture' or 'consciousness'.[110]

The most developed distinctions of these kinds are, however, to be found in
Gramsci's *Prison Notebooks*. Gramsci employs three key terms of analysis where
culturalism and structuralism mainly employ one. 'Common sense' refers to the
lived culture of a particular class or social group, understood as a complex, located
whole. It is the 'philosopher' in everyone, carried in language, 'good sense' or 'folklore'. It has many of the connotations of culture in the English usage.[111] 'Philosophy' (occasionally 'ideology'), on the other hand, refers to some organized set of
conceptions produced by intellectuals (those with the *function* of philosophers)
and having a more or less organic relation to social classes and 'the necessities of
production'. Ideologies, if 'organic', are understood as essentially active and transformative, transformative, especially, of 'common sense'.[112] 'Hegemony', Gramsci's
third major term, indicates the state of play, as it were, between the whole
complex of class-based 'educative' agencies and ideologies on the one hand, and the
common sense or lived culture of the masses on the other. It concerns the extent
and the modes by which common sense is made to conform to 'the necessities of
production' and to the construction of 'consent' and a political order. Gramsci
builds on Marx's realization of the importance of the cultural conditions of capitalist
production - all the moral and subjective aspects of labour power for example[113] -
by examining the way in which such conditions are organized and fought over
politically. 'Hegemony' is, in effect, Althusser's 'reproduction', but a reproduction
without the functionalism. It incorporates, indeed, a view of the relation between
structure and superstructure that is distinctive and, perhaps, unique. The normal
state of the relation is far from a meeting of functional requirements: it is a state of
massive disjunctions and unevenness. Gramsci described, in other words, the normality of 'survivals', concrete features of a society that cannot be grasped as the
dominant mode of production and its conditions of existence.[114] Hegemony

describes the processes by which some greater conformity is sought. 'Reproduction' is, then, a hard and constantly resisted labour on very obstinate materials indeed.

These ideas are in a 'practical state' in Gramsci's writing. It was indeed the connection with concrete analysis that produced the theorizations in the first place. They are peculiarly pertinent for today. In what follows we indicate some key moments in the study of culture/ideology drawing heavily on Gramsci's categories.

The importance of 'culture'

It is important to retain 'culture' as a category of analysis. By culture is understood the common sense or way of life of a particular class, group or social category, the complex of ideologies that are actually *adopted* as moral preferences or principles of life. To insist on this usage is to insist on the complex recreation of ideological *effects* as a moment of the analysis of consciousness. The effects of a particular ideological work or aspect of hegemony can only be understood in relation to attitudes and beliefs that are already lived. Ideologies never address ('interpellate') a 'naked' subject.[115] Concrete social individuals are always already constructed as culturally classed and sexed agents, already have a complexly formed subjectivity. Outside some structuralist texts, the 'lonely hour' of the unitary, primary, primordial and cultureless interpellation 'never comes'. Ideologies always work upon a *ground*: that ground is *culture*. To insist on this is also to insist on 'history' and to enter a protest against large parts of the Marxist tradition for its neglect of the ground of *its own* political practice too.

The retention of elements of a cultural analysis is also important for checking tendencies to functionalism. It is genuinely difficult to disengage the notion of ideology from a mode-of-production analysis in which all ideologies are seen as functionally related to the conditions of production. There *are* ideological conditions for a given mode; but these by no means exhaust the whole sphere of the cultural - ideological in any concrete society. There are cultural elements to which capitalism is *relatively* indifferent and many which it has great difficulty in changing and which remain massively and residually present. Similarly it is not easy to think the forms of cultural resistance to capitalism and to its particular restructuring of patriarchy within this frame of reference. Cultural analysis, especially in the form adopted by Edward Thompson, may attach cultural struggles too closely to class, but guarantees thereby that struggles within culture will not be ignored.

The second major check to functionalism is the culturalist insistence, derived from the heart of the culture tradition, on the production of self or self-making. We have already noted the dangers of a theoretical humanism that ignores the conditions under which choices are made, moral preferences formed. But to neglect the *moment* of self-creation, of the *affirmation* of belief or of the *giving* of consent would, once more, return us to 'pure mechanicity'. It is clear that one specific feature of processes within consciousness is exactly this cultural moment. *It is what distinguishes the force of ideological social relations from relations of political coercion or economic necessity.* Outcomes of ideology or consciousness are not determined *in the same kind of way* as in economic or political relations.

The heterogeneity of cultures

It is an error, certainly in modern capitalist conditions, to view working-class culture as 'all of a piece'. The degree of homogeneity (and of distinctiveness) is undoubtedly historically variable. It is probable that working-class culture from the 1880s to the 1930s was more homogeneous and distinct than in any period before or after. Yet, all notions of culture as coherent value systems tend to mislead; Gramsci's stress of the radical heterogeneity of (even) peasant culture is a better general guide.[116] We have already noted many of the forms of internal difference: those organized around geographical unevenness and the social and sexual divisions of labour, and the divisions into sites or spheres of existence, products of ideological work, economic development, and legally enforced institutional separations. We have noted, too, specific forms of hierarchization (e.g. 'aristocracy of labour'; the depoliticization of the role of women) which are secured on top of these divisions. If there are features in the position of the 'labourer' that are common to a whole working class, there are a myriad features that are not. These may always become objects of political practices seeking greater division or a unity. It follows that there can be no simple or 'expressive' relation between economic classes and cultural forms, and that we should start any such analysis by looking for contradictions, taboos, displacements in a culture, as well as unities. This is one way of breaking from the bad 'romantic' side of cultural studies. Another very important way is to recognize the gender-specific elements in any class culture and the ways in which the subordination of girls and women is reproduced, in part, within the culture itself.

The place of the analysis of ideologies

More generally, heterogeneity of a lived culture is an index of the effects of hegemony. Once classic form of heterogeneity is that described by Gramsci thus:

The active man-in-the-mass has a practical activity, but has no clear theoretical consciousness of his practical activity, which nonetheless involves understanding the world in so far as it transforms it. His theoretical consciousness can indeed be historically in opposition to his activity. One might almost say that he has two theoretical consciousnesses (or one contradictory consciousness); one which is implicit in his activity and which in reality unites him with all his fellow workers in the practical transformation of the real world; and one, superficially explicit or verbal which he has inherited from the past and uncritically absorbed.[117]

Gramsci goes on to argue that such 'verbal' conceptions have their consequences, especially in inducing passivity by contradicting a more 'lived' impulse. The political problem, for Gramsci, is to develop critical forms of theoretical consciousness that actually engage with practical activity, develop it and give it a sense of its own historicity, and its ability to change the world.

Cultural contradictions of this kind are the product in part of ideological work. Against the humanist view of 'self-making' it is important to stress that what is affirmed or assented to, or rejected or transformed, has its own particular origin and history. The model of culture as a working up on 'experience' lacks one vital element - the instruments of labour themselves, in this case the conceptions, categories and preferences already present. As we have seen 'experience as a term conflates the raw materials (the way, especially, in which capitalist economic relations impinge on human beings) with the mental means of their representation (the existing cultural repertoire). It is by supplying conceptions where none exist (or merely aiding in the reproduction of old) that ideology operates on culture to hold it below the level of 'critical', 'historical' or 'hegemonic' understanding.

There is an important role, then, for the analysis of ideologies in a developed cultural studies. This may take an altogether more abstracted form than the study of a class culture. In the case of culture the most 'lived' conceptions are closely tied into practical activity; it is necessary to describe the physicality of labour in order to grasp its cultural significance. It is possible on the other hand to examine ideologies in terms of 'fields' and 'discourses' which, in their own internal structures, position or address (ideal) 'subjects'. This, perhaps, is the predominant form of ideology - analysis within the structuralist tradition, resembling, more than anything, a literary model of investigation that treats ideologies as 'a text'.[118] This form of analysis has an important part to play in discerning the logics and internally generated pressures of particular ideologies or ideological fields; but we will still need to know the effects of such discourses on actual already-acculturated subjects. Ideology-analysis of this kind, in other words, does not replace, though it should certainly supplement, a more 'historical' analysis of lived cultures. Without this the origins and effects of ideologies, in the common sense of classes and the labour of intellectuals, will remain obscure.

Culture and class

We have noted the structuralist tendency to detach the analysis of ideologies from classes and class struggle, and the value of this as a critique of expressive and economistic formulations. The relation between the economic conditions of existence of a particular class and its culture *is* a problematic one. Yet it is absurd to believe that there is *no* relation between ideological and political forms and economic classes.

There are two main ways of understanding this connection for working-class culture. The first concerns the material conditions of the class itself and the sense that is made of these. The second concerns the particular relation to capital and capital's need continuously to transform the cultural conditions of labour.

Particular economic relations have a particular salience for particular classes. The economic form of the wage is, for example, a salient relation for the proletarian, just as the rate of profit has a special importance for the capitalist. Such relations become a focus for more symbolic processes; they are the raw material of culture. The sense that is made of, say, dependence on capital, the probability of unemployment or relative poverty depends, of course, on the conceptions that are available or may be worked up from existing class practices. There is nothing in these relations themselves that produces a particular form of understanding of them, no automatic relay between class and class consciousness. Yet to have any purchase on the culture of a class, new ideologies must address relations of this kind. It is only in that way that ideologies, including socialism, can become principles of life. The conditions of existence of classes profoundly shape class cultures, less by specifying 'interests', more by supplying a kind of agenda with which the culture must deal. It is a matter of historical record that working-class culture has been built around the task of making fundamentally punishing conditions more inhabitable.

We must end, however, by looking at this process from the viewpoint of capital. Though this is stressed, by Althusser, to functional excess, capital *does* have certain requirements in relation to the reproduction of labour power.[119] Though working-class culture cannot be seen as having a simple functional relation to capital's needs, capital certainly has a *stake* in the forms of working-class culture. Minimally, it is a stake in labour's availability, willingness to labour under conditions rational for the production of surplus, and a suitable level of skill and aptitude. More particular conditions require historical specification, but from this viewpoint 'working-class' culture is *the form in which labour is reproduced*. In this respect capitalism is far from being a self-policing system; far from labour continually being reproduced in appropriate forms, these processes require continual management. Moreover, capital's requirements are frequently themselves undergoing transformation. This process of reproduction, then, is always a *contested transformation*. Working-class culture is formed in the struggle between capital's demand for particular forms of labour power and the search for a secure location within this relation of dependency. The outcome of such necessary struggles depends on what ideological and political forces are in play, and, ultimately, upon the existence of socialist organization with an integral relation to proletarian conditions and working-class cultural forms.

10   Capital and culture: the post-war working class revisited

John Clarke

We have sought, so far, to explore working-class culture through some general
problems of interpretation and some very specific cases in the more or less distant
past. Important as theoretical clarification may be (as a *means*), the most significant test is its usefulness in the work of historical and conjunctural analysis.
In this last section, then, we want to return to some of the questions raised at the
beginning of the book - the questions about the disappearance, reappearance and
character of working-class culture that concerned the sociologists of the 1950s
and 1960s. There is no intention here to write a full history of the post-war working
class, though perhaps that should be the next project. Our aim is to provide some
pointers towards such a history, an indication of the dimensions that would have
to be grasped. At the same time we want to illustrate, more concretely, some of
the theoretical issues that have emerged throughout the book.

The 'affluence' debate raised issues that are important but largely unrecognized
and unresolved. They are not issues that can be answered by a 'lazy' Marxism: by
a ritualistic defence of the category of class itself, by the demonstration of the
continued polarity of labour and capital, or by insisting that we still stand within
the epochal structure of the capitalist mode of production. The answers lie at a
lower level of abstraction: they concern, for the most part, more specific, short-run
historical movements which cannot be grasped fully at that level of generality.

Our starting point, then, is that 'affluence' theory, like some kinds of Marxism,
misrecognized post-war changes which, in themselves, were real enough. It tended
to exaggerate them or understand them one-sidedly and to present them as permanent shifts (out of a class society altogether) rather than as conjunctural moments.
It would be more accurate to say that the working class was transformed in these
years - restructured and recomposed. This was not just a question of some sectoral
changes - on 'standard of living', education, housing, etc. - but of a deep and
thorough reorganization of working-class life. The class did not, of course, disappear,
but its forms and conditions of existence were certainly transformed.

We have argued, in general, that working-class culture can be seen as the ground
of transformations wrought by capitalist development itself but supported by
ideological and political work with a definite relation to the 'necessities of production'. Our approach to the post-war working class follows this way of thinking about
culture. We look at the movements of capital in the post-war period and at capital's

requirements for new forms of labour power. We chart some of the transformative work of state agencies in this period, arguing that these are connected (more or less tightly) with changes in capital's requirements. We look at some key working-class cultural forms and the ways in which they have been transformed in this period. Finally we note the importance for understanding working-class culture itself of looking at the ways in which it is represented to working people by more general political and ideological processes. We should add that these later questions - of culture and ideology - are not marginal to class structure and class struggle. They involve the forms in which these struggles are fought out.

We may begin by detailing some trends in capitalist development in Britain since the war, those with most pertinence for working-class life. None of these tendencies were new in the period; they are often long-term trends in capital accumulation that have been intensified, proceeding at a greater pace or with a deeper impact on social relations. Among these trends we would want to point to the growing tendency to the concentration and centralization of capitals; the expansion of labour processes that are based on production-line technologies and forms of control; the continuing decline of 'heavy industry' and the movement of capital into modern 'lighter' forms of production, most notably the production of consumer durables; and major shifts in the composition of labour power - the secular tendency to 'de-skilling', the separation of 'conception' and 'execution' and the creation of new technical or control skills, the shift of labour out of direct production and into circulation and distribution, and the expansion of labour within the state.[1]

Concentration and centralization as well as the policies of large-scale companies often involve shifts in the geographical distribution of capital - shifts which must be understood in an international as well as a regional and national framework. Localities that suffer the sudden withdrawal of capital also suffer major disruptions in their patterns of social and cultural life.[2] Cultural forms that have developed, for instance, in a close connection with the original division of labour, may lose their very rationale. From the point of view of capital, its mobility requires the mobility of labour. It therefore also requires the continual fractioning of the local and more fixed patterns of reproduction: it specifically requires the destruction of locality as a major form through which working people experience their social life. The resistance of locally bound labour to capital's migration has, in turn, produced state policies that seek a greater conformity - here in the form of industrial grants to tempt capital to move to pools of labour, there in the form of mobility and redundancy payments to encourage labourers to pursue capital.[3]

The stripping of capital from an area and less dramatic forms of 'industrial reorganization' always have effects upon local forms of culture, the forms in which labour is actually reproduced. Thus Cohen shows how, in the East End, the rationalization of the docks has had profound consequences for forms of family life based upon neighbourhood patterns and upon inter-generational recruitment to the dominant male occupations.[4] Similarly, the mobility of capital, has in many instances, deepened the division between home and work-place, between the social relationships of the world of production and those of family. This division has also been increased by forms of local state planning in which the industrial and residential zones of urban areas are sharply separated.

One way of understanding these changes has been in terms of the undermining of 'working-class community'. Some reservations have to be stated against this view. We must not take 'the working-class community' as the archetypal 'traditional' moment of the English working class as a whole, as a de-historicized sociology sometimes does. The working class has not produced such cultural forms every-where, nor has it produced them continuously in the period up to the 1950s. Gareth Stedman Jones points, for example, to the growing physical distance between the man's place of labour and the domestic sphere as one of the changes underlying the cultural adaptions of skilled workers in late-nineteenth-century London.[5] We would argue that the particular cultural form - 'working-class commun-ity' - rests especially on a close, dovetailed relationship between work and non-work and a geographical concentration of intra-class social relationships of all kinds. Hoggart's Hunslet or Hessle Road did seem to rest on the continuity of work and home. Yet if the patterns in Hunslet (or Ashton) were particular, localism in a looser sense has been a pervasive mode of working-class culture. A class culture has often been identified with specifically local experiences, relationships and practices; it has been articulated around specifically local points of reference, contact and conflict. To some extent, then, in the 1950s and 1960s, the structures of localism and even, for some sections, of 'community' have been undercut by the combined effects of changes in production and the effects of political and social policies. This has affected the primary forms of identification and antagonism - Hoggart's 'us' and 'them'. It may involve a greater sense of dislocation from 'them' in the form of local agencies of control and regulation: contacts and conflicts with police or schools or local councils may indeed be systematically deparochialized.[6]

Though, at one level, these tendencies are functional for capital accumulation, they also produce new problems in the cultural and political domains which them-selves require new forms of state intervention. For example, both Cockburn and Corrigan have shown the decline of working-class involvement in local forms of political representation and a reduction in the legitimacy attributed to them.[7] Schools have complained of the decline of parental involvement in the education of children; the police have spoken of a loss of public confidence and a decline of community commitment to the control and reporting of crime. Housing authori-ties have complained about the reluctance of tenants to identify with their area and 'take pride' in its maintenance.[8] A common response to these forms of dis-engagement has been to attempt to reconstitute local identification and commit-ment - hence community work, community schools, community liason, community development and so on.

This partial and uneven reconstruction of British capital also involved other changes, especially those associated with the demand for an expended application of scientific knowledge to the labour process and more sophisticated methods of control of labour. We may doubt if the expansion of the education system since 1944 can wholly or even mainly be explained in terms of capital's requirements: the tendency to a more egalitarian provision owed as much to the need to win the consent of different classes of parents and to retain an alliance with the teachers.[9] But the reorganization of education, which included the coming of universal state secondary education and some expansion of the tertiary sector, undoubtedly had effects upon established patterns of working-class culture. For example, it restructured the age relations which shape both the internal social relationships of the family and the family economy itself. Most obviously, these changes defer, for different lengths of time, the entry of children of the family to full-time waged labour, thus necessitating new economic adjustments within the family patterns of reproduction. In addition, this reorganization of the educational apparatus produced a new range of possible 'career' patterns for working-class youth, affecting in different ways their relations to their located cultural patterns of street, neighbourhood and friendship groupings, and to the passage through the educational apparatus to waged labour. It also provided some of the symbolic indices of differentiation which mark out these different trajectories (e.g. the secondary modern boy, technical college boy or grammar school girl).

This reorganization of education also raises other central questions for our concerns here, for it is not simply a case of an administrative recording of an agency which is in some sense external to the working class. It involves the political and ideological interpellation of the class into the processes of politics and education. Crucial here are the symbolic figures of 'equality' and 'achievement' as expressions of working-class demands articulated through the complex mechanisims of social-democratic politics.[10] This political representation of a working class presence is no simple ideological mystification through which the working classes are bemused, but a representation that must be taken seriously as exerting definite force, what Poulantzas calls 'pertinent effects', on both lived experience *and* the material forms of reconstructed institutions. Even where institutions meet a logic required by capital, their form and direction are never the outcome of a simple unidirectional imposition by capital. They involve a complex political work of concession and compromise, if only to secure the legitimacy of the state in popular opinion. Thus, for example, while parts of the welfare state may be attributed to capital's need for a healthy and stable work force, these needs in no sense prescribe a solution which takes the form of a universal and free National Health Service (as we are now learning by example).

The area of youth is one in which the changed conditions of existence of the working class and the destruction of existing cultural forms have had their most visible consequences in the construction of new cultural forms and practices. As Cohen and Hall *et al.* have shown, the emergence of particular youth sub-cultures in post-war Britain is made possible by the changing material conditions of the working class (the reorganization of education, changes in the composition of labour power, and the reconstruction of local economies).[11] These processes had specific effects on the local forms of class reproduction and cultural representations -

the material and cultural elements of communities. But they also had specific consequences for the structure of age relations within the working class and for the ideological representation of 'youth'. The expansion of youth employment laid the basis for the greater financial autonomy of working-class youth within the family economy, and underpinned the creation of the 'youth market'. But this greater financial autonomy (especially in the form of rising disposable incomes) also allowed the construction of new forms of youthful *cultural* autonomy - a separation from existing milieux and modes of informal regulation of adolescence.

But, as Hall *et al.* have argued, this autonomy of working-class youth cannot in any sense be taken as a severing of youth from class; rather, youth sub-cultural formations are elaborated on the terrain of class cultures but through the mechanisms of 'generational specifity'. The stylistic and symbolic repertoires of sub-cultures such as the Teds, Mods and Skinheads are cultural representations of the class's conditions of existence, and the changes taking place in them, but these representations are articulated through the position of youth within the class. For example, the style of the Mods involves the symbolic representation of affluence (and especially of affluent youth) through styles of conspicuous and highly developed consumption. From this standpoint the Mods appear to be the ideal representation of the affluence thesis, but the sub-cultural relations and practices which support this consumption also produce it in a form which is alien to that of the supposedly privatized and passive consumer of commodities. In the Mods, the commodities are transformed collectively into new uses and new cultural representations of the conditions of that particular fraction of working-class youth. These collective sub-cultural practices subvert the supposed role of the consumer, and transform the cultural meanings attached to the commodity - for example in the transofmation of the motor scooter from a cheap and highly functional means of transport into an object of collective display.

The points raised here about youth have wider ramifications in relation to the affluence debate. There the dormant tendency was to assume that possession of similar objects or commodities by different groups necessarily indicated similar life-styles and outlooks. The possession of a car, fridge or television necessarily indicated a convergence of life-style with those who had previously been the privileged possessors of these commodities. As the example of the Mods shows, this conception suppresses the possibility of the same object or practice being located within different sets of relations and being endowed with different sets of cultural valuations. In this sense, the object or commodity is not unidimensional, but involves some (however limited) possibilities of being appropriated as a different sort of use value in a different class-cultural context. This is not to argue that the changes in commodities possessed by the working class (or sections of it) during the post-war period has had no consequences. These cannot, however, be reduced to an equalizing or convergence of cultural practices.

We have pointed to some of the tendencies undercutting locality, but it is equally important to note how other tendencies have registered on the family - another site of reproduction. Central among these has been a tension between capital and the state hinging around women's double position as the source of domestic labour and as a section of the reserve labour.[12] In the expansion and restructuring of post-war English capitalism, capital stood to benefit from women's role as waged labourers in two main ways: first, in the expanding unskilled labour sector of the new light production industries, and secondly, in the rapid expansion of the service and distributive sectors. In both, of course, the key to the desirability of women's labour is its relative cheapness.[13] However, this requirement for cheap labour to intensify the profitability of such development conflicts with other demands bearing on the sexual division of labour. In part, it conflicts with wartime guarantees won by the trade unions about the priority to be given to employing men in the post-war period. More significantly, it conflicts with the state's concern to regulate and control the privatized reproduction of labour power. From the standpoint of the state, then, women's other function, as domestic labour, is of paramount importance, and a series of wartime investigations and studies raised the spectre of a maladjusted, badly nourished and potentially incompetent future generation of bearers of labour power.[14] The central theme of these studies, and of subsequent state initiatives, was the centrality of the family and of the woman's position as wife and mother. From the state's standpoint, then, the employment of married women, at least, threatened to interrupt the necessary mechanism of generational reproduction, and thus required action by the state to secure those processes.[15]

Thus, for example, the establishment of the Children's Departments in local authorities at the end of the war must in part be seen as an attempt to construct a mechanism through which the state could monitor, and intervene, the 'private' processes of reproduction, and, where necessary, supplant the family (the incompetent, negligent or dangerous family, that is) with institutional alternatives.[16] In a different way, the state's control over the provision of alternative child care facilities such as nurseries provided a mechanism through which the state could intervene to change the balance between women's two functions.[17] In the post-war period the state's removal and reduction of institutional child care indicates its predominant commitment to returning women to the tasks of reproduction. This stress on reproduction in the activities of the state is also visible in Beveridge's conception of the 1946 National Insurance Act:

The attitude of the housewife to gainful employment outside the home is not and should not be the same as that of the single woman . . . . In the next thirty years housewives as Mothers have vital work to do in ensuring the adequate continuance of the British race and British ideals in the world.[18]

These tensions act upon attempts to establish viable family economies among the working class, often dependent upon the need for two wages to maintain standards of living, in many cases producing the adaptation of part-time work by married women.[19] In addition, in this period women were increasingly ideologically interpellated into yet another role, that of the consumer of the new durables and domestic goods by a capitalism striving to accomplish a mass domestic market for its products, producing new images and conceptions of motherhood, housewifery and femininity.[20] We are in no position to be able to assess the consequences of these changes in any systematic way, but in broad terms these conditions, together with the hidden substratum of changes in contraceptive availability and practice, have substantially unhinged the established practices and conceptions of the sexual division of labour and its ideological, political and emotional concomitants in all classes (though differently and unevenly, it is true).

The disruption of family and friendship patterns surrounding and supporting domestic labour and especially child care through the processes of rehousing and social reconstruction in the post-war period have, of course, been the focus of much conventional sociological inquiry, but there are elements and aspects of these processes which have been less remarked upon. For example, Cohen has pointed out how the processes of rehousing not only involved the disruption of established patterns of family relationships through enforced geographical mobility, but involved their curtailment in the very material forms which such relocation took.[21] He suggests that the patterns and models of house-building in the post-war period were shaped by an invisible ideological norm of the nuclear family which excluded other variants of family relationships by determining the physical and spatial arrangement of housing. Thus, the 'ideal form' of reproduction is enshrined in the very bricks and mortar within which reproduction takes place.

We would also want to indicate something of the way in which these reconstructions of housing in the hands of the local state have acted, together with larger economic forces, to undercut other established practices of reproduction within the working class. We have in mind here the activity of shopping as one vital (though extremely hidden) element of domestic labour. The old estates and housing areas with their variety of very local shopping facilities (the corner shop) produced certain rhythms and relationships which organized shopping as a social activity. New council and private housing estates have involved the replacement of local shops with more centralized shopping areas. This process has gone on alongside the tendency to concentration among distributive capital, with its steady supplanting of the traditional petit-bourgeoise. This centralization of shopping changes the rhythms of shopping, creating pressures for adaptations and adjustments within working-class culture. Thus the apparent supplanting of Saturday afternoon spectator sports by Saturday afternoon family shopping in the 1950s is in no sense the 'free choice' of a rational and free-floating consumer, but is in part determined by the changing social conditions of shopping which require more systematic, large-scale expeditions (and thus more 'rational' reproduction . . .). From this standpoint the 'disappearing corner shop' is not a folk-tale derived from excessive viewing of 'Coronation Street', but a direct consequence of the long-term tendencies of capital accumulation and concentration, and a critical reorganization of the conditions of existence of working-class culture. To grasp working-class culture as an empirical problem it is necessary to hold on to both ends of this chain - on the one hand, the broad movements of capital and, on the other, its specific, local consequences for the patterns of class reproduction.

Another related example of the consequences of the broad movements of capital for specific and local forms of class reproduction can be found in the position of the pub.[22] The pub has held a central position in the local articulation of working-class culture as a sort of 'colonized' institution which, though not formally owned by the class, has been internally moulded by the class's custom. Here certain customary rights and expectations could be enforced through what Foster in another context has called 'exclusive dealing',[23] and users of the pub stood in a relationship to publicans which might be described as 'membership'. In working-class culture, then, the pub has historically been a 'local' - a term signifying its patronage by an established local clientele who shaped the internal dynamics, relationships and patterns of drinking. In the post-war period the development of an oligopolistic brewing industry has led to critical economic and social changes in the public houses. First, it has led to a tendency for owners or tenants to be replaced by brewery-controlled managers, thus interrupting the relations of patronage between the clientele and the publican, and producing industrial rather than local domination of the internal dynamics and patterns of the pub. Second, the breweries have tended to rationalize (i.e. close) or 'improve' their pubs, with design changes having important consequences for the patterns and experience of drinking (e.g. the substitution of large lounges for a series of snugs, public bars and tap rooms). Much of this has been done in accordance with an image of a changing clientele identified by the breweries. The new consumer differs from the old in terms of age (s/he is young), class (s/he is classless) and taste (Campari not beer). The effect of this attempt to address the new consumer is to fundamentally change the social and economic conditions under which drinking takes place, that is, to change the determinants of a particular historically developed form of reproduction. We may borrow from Althusser to suggest that these changes in material conditions and signifying practices (and the commercial ideologies which guide them) function to interpellate a new identity for the drinker - that of the 'consumer' rather than the 'member'. This newly forged interpellation dissolves previous patterns and habits of 'how to drink' and substitutes for them new 'preferred' styles of drinking:

It is high time that Andy Capp was given a new suit and a car and took his wife out to one of the many popular North East pubs where he can still enjoy his pint of beer and Florrie can have a glass of sauterne with her scampi and chips.[24]

(In the light of our earlier comment about how women were addressed as the new consumers, it is interesting that here it is Florrie who is to change her consumption patterns.)

This quotation serves to illustrate something of the complexity of the forms which the reorganization of capital takes at the point of consumption. It is not a matter of a neutral technical or financial process. It is a process born and conducted in ideological conceptions about 'the market' and the 'consumer' which are the professionalized variants of contemporary ideological and political discourses. Marketing ideologies about the consumer echo political ideologies about the disappearance of traditional class differences and the rise of an affluent, middle-class Britain. In a sense, these marketing ideologies and practices attempt to 'complete the circle' by producing precisely that affluent middle-class consumer they claim to have already recognized. Subsequently, of course, political ideologies register these changes as the changed conditions of political practice and debate.

Working-class cultural forms have also been disrupted by processes of class recomposition stemming in large part from the economic/productive formation of the class. The changing occupational structure, together with the deskilling and reskilling of labour, play a part in this, changing both the relations supporting occupational and trade union solidarities, and also the symbolic indices of internal differentiation within the class (craft skills, differentials, etc.). The most significant disruption of established class solidarities and differentiations, however, has been the importation of immigrant labour to meet both capital and the state's need for low waged labour.[25] Ethnic, national and racial divisions are not new to the structure and culture of the British working class, of course; for example, nationalist divisions between the indigenous working class and Irish immigrant labour, and the effects of imperial competition between the national and colonial work-forces have played an important role in the making and remaking of the English working class economically, politically and ideologically.[26]

What is new, however, is the internalization of racial differences within the national working class in visible and distinctive forms. For the sociologists, working-class culture has seemed always to refer nostalgically to some all-white golden age. It does not register the presence of the temples, Asian films and corner shops, reggae and rastafarianism; these are relegated to a different part of the sociological empire, the sociology of ethnic minorities or race relations. Yet these, too, are the forms in and through which labour is reproduced; they are also the cultural experiences, the material, from which new ideological and political forces address the class, or, more precisely, aim to divide it.

However, we must also not make the error of assuming that such divisions and the material for them is a recent consequence of the racial structuring of labour - the image of a working-class culture has always hidden a complexly stratified and divided class in which particular cultural forms have provided the symbols and signals of division. Regionalism and localism carried and reproduced in accent, vocabulary, dress and the varieties of local and civic pride have been a persistent source of suspicion, mistrust and hostility, while one of the most fertile grounds of intra-class differentiation has been the whole repertoire of 'respectability'.[27] Though drawing on work experience (and especially the distinction between employed and unemployed), the forms and practices of reproduction have acted as central symbolic formations in this repertoire. The rough-respectable division has been firmly lodges in the visible signs of the home, street, neighbourhood and patterns of consumption. As Robert Roberts has shown, it was the scrubbed and painted or polished front steps, the front room, the types of food, sobriety, orientation to schools, children's clothes, the best suit or coat - the very stuff of reproduction - which provided the material of intra-class division.[28] These repertoires have also been drawn on, added to and solidified by particular forms of ideological and political addresses to the class - the respectable trade unionists or labour politicians, the conservative appeal to freedom and the family life of Britain, the stigma of the visit from the welfare, school board man or social worker, the rough neighbourhood's reputation, the 'scroungers' and so on.[29] All of these have at different times provided mechanisms for the division of the class and the insertion of its 'respectable' elements into bourgeois political discourse and action.

In the processes of social reconstruction in post-war Britain some of these conditions and forms of the reproduction of the working class as a complexly stratified, divided and contradictory unity have been dissolved or put to one side. Blocks of flats and relative anonymity undermine the significance (or possibility) of the polished step; the mobility of labour tends against localism and the establishment of 'reputation'. But in their dissolution, new forms of division, new repertoires of signifying differentiation have been constructed and developed. The interruption and dissolution of established class practices of reproduction produced in their wake new tensions, divisions and contradictions requiring new cultural solutions, new forms of living the relation to the relation of production, new habits, forms of common sense and so on.

What we have said so far has been an attempt to point to the variety of processes of class struggle (in economic, political and ideological forms) which have transformed the conditions of existence of the working class in post-war Britain - processes which have acted to reorganize the sphere of production and the sphere of reproduction. In the transformation of those conditions of existence (and the dominant political and ideological representation of them), the basis of the cultural forms within which the working class represent those conditions, or live their experience of them, has been undermined. The change in those material conditions require the elaboration of new cultural practices and repertoires which are capable of producing (however partial and contradictory) new cultural frameworks in which to live the experiences of being working class.

We cannot detail the whole process of the transformation and reconstitution of working-class culture between 1945 and 1978, but we can offer some elements that seem to us to be involved in that process. Central to this is an awareness that what we are discussing is in no simple sense the overthrow of one working-class culture and its replacement by a new one. What we can be certain of is that the period with which we are dealing involves a process of cultural transition - a transition which begins not from some homogenous entity called working-class culture, but from a complex, uneven and contradictory ensemble, made up of internal contradictions, a range or repertoire of different 'cultural solutions' - trade unionism, religion, respectability, crime, domesticity, socialist politics, etc.[30] The process of transition involves both continuities and breaks; some elements continue unmodified, others are sustained in new forms and other disappear and are replaced by new cultural forms.

We may begin here with the central continuity - the persistence of the cultural

forms and practices of solidarity based within production - the informal cultures of
the shop floor discussed in Chapter 8 - the collective definitions of work, the
cultural forms expressing resistance to work, and the transformation of those
resistances into valued social identities (identities based in 'skills', 'masculinity'
and 'being the bread-winner').[31] Here, in the process of socialized labour, workers
have continued to forge positive, though partial, cultural responses based on
collective solidarity, which transfers the necessities and degradations of waged
labour into some form of valued cultural identification. That this is a culture of
subordination which, in the process of resistance (of sabotage, of doing the bosses
down, of absenteeism), continues to reproduce its own subordination (and the
oppression of others - for example, women through the particular cultural valuations
of masculinity) is beyond doubt. But it does form a persistent, though often
hidden, element which provides core elements of working-class culture: work and
the cultural strategies developed around it persist *underneath* the more apparent
and visible changes in the patterns of working-class consumption which dominated
the conceptions of affluence. The discipline of the wage relation persists throughout
this supposed abolition of the working class.

But even here, some of the cultural forms are changed. Some of the conditions
which are culturally represented within shop-floor cultures are modified. Skills are
eroded and removed by managerial initiatives, dissolving established cultural patterns
of location, hierarchy and identity, and removing resources for working-class
resistance and struggle within production.[32] New, and often equally jealously
guarded, hierarchies and forms of distinction are constructed within the process of
production, but also new broader solidarities and identities are constructed out of
the process of deskilling, involving cultural recognition of the forms in which labour
becomes generalized and more interdependent.[33] New cultural foci and points of
resistance become articulated around the changes which capital produces within
the labour process. No longer the foreman as the personalized bearer of control,
but the domination exercised by the pace of the production line itself.[34] No
longer the patronizing self-assurances of the bosses, but an attack on the abstract
intellectuals - the management scientists with their university training, who erode
skills and pour scorn on the world of 'experience'.[35] In addition, the tendencies to
both economic and political concentration in the period have produced new informal
cultural resistances and responses. The greater distance from capital itself in this
period, and the greater involvement of trade union organizations in national forms
of economic planning and bargaining with industry and the state, creates the ground
for the creation of new informal responses (or, more correctly, the elaboration of
subterranean traditions of shop-floor resistance to a greater position of significance).
The period of centralization of bargaining and planning from the 1950s is also the
period of the growth of informal shop-floor action - unofficial disputes, the growth
of shop steward power in representing shop-floor interests, the tendency of 'wage
drift' through local control of output and bonus schemes, as well as the more
'individual' strategies of sabotage, absenteeism and high labour turnover.[36] All
these developments had come to haunt political and managerial planning by the

mid 1960s: they produced, among other things, the Donovan Commission, the Labour Party's 'In Place of Strife' and the Industrial Relations Act, as well as the neo-human-relations strategies of management (such as Volvo's semi-autonomous work groups, job rotation and job enrichment schemes), profit-sharing schemes and plans for worker directors.[37]

What we are faced with here is not the simple unfolding of some unidirectional historical logic, guided by the unerring hand of capital, but of new iniatives by capital changing the conditions and forms of resistance from within labour, requiring new 'solutions' from capital and the state and so on. It is a permanently contradictory process of class struggle, which may not always take the traditionally recognized correct or 'modern' forms but involves a variety of hidden and informal dimensions which may more closely resemble, in fact, the protests of Hobsbawm's 'primitive rebels'.

We want now to turn to the sphere of reproduction and the changes there, but before doing so it is important to enter a word of warning. Though these are *theoretically* distinct elements of capitalism, involving clear analytic divisions, they are in no sense 'lived' as such. We cannot assume that they are experienced as two distinct and separate areas, in which the cultural formations developed around work have no bearing on the cultural formations which deal with the 'private' world of home and leisure. That is, we must not mistake the cultural formations which distinguish the relationship between 'home' and 'work' for the analytic or theoretical distinction between production and reproduction. The forms in which people register culturally the gap between home and work may be based on the conditioning of the relation between production and reproduction in a particular stage of capitalism but they cannot be reduced to those distinctions. Thus the male worker who returns at night to feed his tropical fish, and expects his wife to feed him, experiences a different cultural representation of the relation between home and work from that of a woman worker who returns to the home and is faced with feeding husband and children and doing the rest of the housework before returning to work the next day, even though both of these are based on the same structural arrangement of production and reproduction.

Here, too, we can begin by considering not the extent of change but the persistence of certain key elements of working-class culture. Central here is the persistence of the sexual division of labour as the mechanism through which production and reproduction are articulated, and the persistence of cultural definitions of sexual identify within the working class. These two elements - the sexual division of labour and cultural representations of sexual identity - have played a major role in the historical development and creation of working-class culture. The archetypal community is founded upon this (largely hidden) structure. It depends upon the home (and therefore the wife/mother) as the focus around which the other elements hang; it depends on the pride 'in the home' (as Hoggart's accounts show), on female friendship and kinship networks to carry out domestic labour and so on. But the cultural valuation of sexual identities plays an equally central role in both the forms of working-class culture and working-class politics.

Historically, the organized labour movement has drawn a firm and clear line between 'men's work' and 'women's work' - from the early Factory Acts where women's work was restricted, through negotiations in both world wars to ensure that jobs temporarily filled by women would be returned to their 'rightful owners' (men) at the end of war.[38] This line has only recently begun to be eroded (and often grudgingly) in the face of women's increased involvement in production in the post-war period and largely as a consequence of women themselves struggling to gain trade union support and recognition.

In terms of working-class cultural repertoires, sexual identity has also played a key role. 'Respectability' within the working class historically has been demonstrated by the ability of the man to keep his wife at home, away from the world of work.[39] In a different way, the shop-floor culture, which we mentioned earlier, has always been contradictorily constituted in that many of its elements of resistance have been articulated through specific conceptions of toughness and masculinity about being 'one of the boys', being able to 'take it', and so on.[40] A culture of resistance is here based in a crucial sense on a more hidden culture of oppression. In non-work cultural forms, this sexual structure also organizes the pattern of many elements - for instance, the worlds of football and drinking have within them these valorizations of masculinity and of the 'boys'.

These sexual and cultural structures have persisted as the organizing elements of working-class life in the post-war period, though, again, not without some modifications. Thus, for example, the commercialization of football, involving the creation of some overlap with the world of pop music also created a space (with a very particular sexual structure), through the production of male superstars, for a certain amount of female involvement in football,[41] although the responses (from obstruction to 'humour') to women attempting to play football themselves indicates how marginal those changes have been. Similarly, the vast commercialization of other leisure areas by 'cultural capital' (discos, cinemas, skating rinks, pubs, etc.) has altered the local and sexual structure of cultural activities to a certain extent. Certainly the local structure of leisure has been massively undercut by the tendency to concentration of leisure facilities within city centres, but those changes (as the quotation about Andy Capp earlier indicates) also have attempted to address women specifically as the consumers of their facilities. This does not imply any 'equalization', but it does begin to create new cultural forms within which women have a place. That place is, of course, heavily circumscribed by a particular sexual construction of women as consumers - as, for example, in the practice of free admission for women to discos as a way of attracting more male customers.[43]

This is only one element of a series of massive (and often contradictory) attempts to reconstruct 'femininity' during this period - initiatives which address women - (occasionally) as workers, but more often as mothers and as consumers (the gateway to the establishment of new needs), using 'femininity' as the symbolic mechanism through which to stimulate consumption. These changes have opened up certain limited and carefully prescribed new areas and forms of 'being a woman'.[43]

The expansion of consumption and the stimulation of new needs through women has had particular consequences for the nature of women's roles in domestic labour. The woman is not only the ideological figure through which those needs have been stimulated - she is also the *means* through which those new needs are often realized. The 'quality of life' may be found in the tins and packets on the supermarket shelves, but they require domestic labour to turn them into a reality. There is a hidden history in this period of the changes in the content and form of housework: changes induced partly by the commercial stimulation of new needs (the 'moral and historical element' in the determination of the value of labour power, often, in fact, financed by women's waged work), but also by changes in political and ideological demands about the 'quality' of reproduction (demands about how to care for children, what to provide for adolescents, how to look after your husband, etc.). These changes also take place within a shift in the social connections which historically supported at least some working-class families, and which have moved them towards a more privatized existence. Cohen's commentary on this process is worth quoting;

the isolated family unit could no longer call on the resources of wider kinship networks, or of the neighbourhood, and the family itself became the sole focus of solidarity. This meant that any problems were bottled up within the immediate personal context which produced them; and at the same time family relationships were invested with a new intensity, to compensate for the diversity of relationships previously generated through neighbours and wider kin.[44]

Though, as Cohen recognizes, this may overestimate the extent to which solidary relationships have been dissolved, there is no doubt that it does register a trend in the changing position of the working-class family which has had specific consequences for women. Given the invisibility of women in most sociological research, it is impossible to conclude whether these processes have produced new sets of cultural responses and resistances,[45] although it is possible to see some of their consequences in rising rates of mental illness and neurosis among working-class women, and the increased medical regulation of and tranquilization for 'women's problems'.

At this point, we wish to return to the importance of 'locality' as an element of working-class culture. We have tried to indicate earlier some of the processes which effectively undercut local economic and cultural patterns, but 'localism' continues to have cultural importance in a number of forms. Locality continues to act as a focus for some working-class cultural identifications, often among those who are in some senses marginal to production and to the collective solidarities generated there. Locality continues to act as a basis for collective activity among working-class adolescents, both in the sense of providing cultural identities (most obviously developed around football and during the period of the Skinheads, but also for many otherwise 'unnamed' youth groupings), and of constituting their 'social space' - the streets, alleyways, etc., which are public and less tightly regulated than other areas (the home, the school, the youth club, etc.).[46] Sometimes the importance of locality also appears here as what Gramsci would call a 'trace' of an earlier cultural configuration - an oral tradition about the old days of working-class communities. Thus, for example, the significance of local identities to Skinhead groups can in part be seen as a 'magical' or 'imaginary' reconstitution of community.[47]

Locality also seems to play a particular role within the cultural representations of older members of the working class - those who have been 'retired' from the front line of production, and are without collective defences against either their dependence on the state or their subjugation to market forces. Here locality appears to be one of the central cultural configurations around which their responses are articulated; the area and what has happened to it becomes a key form or cultural metaphor in which processes of economic, political and ideological change are represented and evaluated.[48]

Finally, it is important to note that new localized cultural forms are being created. There are processes of ethnic 'colonization' of particular areas, in part as a consequence of defensive aggregation, but also in order to provide supportive cultural patterns and networks. In the construction of these cultural forms, racial groups have also been forced to develop their own infrastructure of institutions to carry and maintain those cultural patterns: shops, restaurants, clubs, temples and so on.[49] Here, too, these processes of cultural colonization are not the simple provision of a monolithic cultural formation, but involve a cultural dynamics of resistance, response and transformation. This is perhaps most clear in the forms in which second-generation black youth in Britain have rejected many of the cultural options developed by their 'parent culture' and have produced new cultural strategies based on more positive valuations of being black, especially centring around the use of reggae and rastafarianism.[50]

In all of this it is important not to proceed as if working-class cultural forms were made and remade within a vacuum, to take them as solely expressing, in some transparent way, the material conditions of the class. In the production of these 'imaginary relations', other representations and ideological ensembles make themselves felt and are drawn on. We have tried to indicate some of the ways in which new ideological initiatives have had specific consequences for the forms of working-class culture (in the production of new needs, in the creation of new sexual identities, etc.), but these are only some of the processes in which dominant ideological repertoires have penetrated and reshaped aspects of working-class culture.

The working class and its changing conditions of existence have been 'spoken to' in a variety of voices from within dominant ideologies, in attempts to provide favourable or harmonizing representations of these changing conditions.[51] These have included, for example, addressing the working class as the national interest in a variety of guises - from Macmillan's national interest of self-interests, to Wilson's 'progressive nation' forged in the 'white heat of the technological revolution' (not to mention the subsequent return to the Dunkirk spirit). More recently the Thatcherite strategy has called for the reconstitution of 'old' England, interpellating the working class as an aggregation of free and independent men and women.

welded together through the values of the family but enmeshed and frustrated by the bureaucracies of creeping socialism. They have been addressed both by the state and by capital as 'consumers', a common identity aimed at overriding the 'sectional interests' of production. They have also been addressed as the 'English' whose way of life has been destroyed by the influx of black criminals and scroungers, whose streets are no longer safe to walk in, and who have been betrayed by 'liberal' politicans and intellectuals.

These attempts to organize or orchestrate cultural definitions work by addressing some aspect of changed conditions and offering relatively coherent ideological structures within which they can be 'realistically' represented (and also be removed from the deeper organizing structures of class relations and class struggle). These forms of address are not uni-vocal. They involve different fragments, or what Poulantzas terms 'sub-ensembles', of the dominant ideological repertoire.[52] Nor must we be led to assume any simple outcome from these ideological practices. They may, indeed, come to provide organizing themes for 'common sense', but they may also be rejected for their inability to render experience coherent and meaningful, or they may be subsumed as sub-themes within other cultural formations.

We have been trying to demonstrate that the question of working-class culture remains an important one for Marxist analysis when the position, conditions and supporting relations of this terrain are adequately identified. Central to this must be a refusal to collapse 'working-class culture' into some simple, expressive, homogeneous entity. We have tried to indicate that working-class culture does not exist (nor has ever existed as a simple unity). We have pointed to how working-class culture is produced as a complex, uneven and contradictory ensemble, involving a variety or repertoire of strategies, resistances, subordinations and solutions, and how these cultural forms are permanently being remade and transformed. These forms are materialized and embedded in sets of practices, rituals, relationships and institutions which go to make up the terrain of 'civil society' in capitalism. We have also tried to show how both the economic and the politico-ideological initiatives of capital constantly require and produce the necessity for these cultural forms and supporting practices to be transformed. The 'problem' of working-class culture is not that posed by the mythologies of affluence or kinship networks, but must be located in the problems of understanding the complex and contradictory forms within which the working class lives its subordination in capitalist societies.

Notes and references

1 Sociology, cultural studies and the post-war working class

1   M. Young and P. Wilmott, *Family and Kinship in East London* (Penguin, 1962), pp. 198-9.
2   J.H. Goldthorpe and D. Lockwood, *The Affluent Worker* (3 vols., Cambridge University Press, 1968-9), vol. 3, p.21.
3   Speech to the Labour Party Conference, 1959, quoted in S. Hall *et al.*, *Policing the Crisis* (Macmillan, 1978), p. 230.
4   Gordon-Walker, quoted in *ibid*.
5   C.A.R. Crosland, *The Conservative Enemy* (Cape, 1962), p. 92.
6   Richard Hoggart, *The Uses of Literacy* (Penguin, 1958), p. 323.
7   *ibid*., p. 13.
8   *ibid*., p. 24.
9   e.g. B. Rosenberg and D.M. White, *Mass Culture: the Popular Arts in America* New York: Glencoe Free Press, 1957).
10 For the classic statements see T.S. Eliot, *Notes Towards a Definition of Culture* (Faber, 1948); F.R. Leavis and Denys Thompson, *Culture and Environment* (Chatto & Windus, 1933).
11 Hoggart, *Uses*, pp. 18-22.
12 Colin Sparks, 'The abuses of literacy', in CCCS, *Working Papers in Cultural Studies*, No. 6 (Birmingham University, 1974).
13 Hoggart, *Uses*, p. 17.
14 *ibid*., pp. 104-5.
15 *ibid*., p. 248.
16 N. Dennis, F. Henriques and C. Slaughter, *Coal is Our Life* (Tavistock, 1969), p. 76.
17 *ibid*., p. 35.
18 *ibid*., p. 138.
19 *ibid*., pp. 228-9.
20 K. Coates and R. Silburn, *Poverty: The Forgotten Englishmen* (Penguin, 1970), p. 13.
21 *ibid*., p. 21.
22 *ibid*., p. 26.
23 *ibid*., p. 50.
24 *ibid*., p. 34.

25   *ibid.*, pp. 26, 111.
26   *ibid.*, p. 142.
27   Goldthorpe and Lockwood, *Affluent Worker*, vol. 3, p. 195.
28   *ibid.*, vol. 2. p. 75; vol. 3, p. 119.
29   *ibid.*, vol. 3, pp. 50-1.
30   *ibid.*, vol. 1, p. 36.
31   *ibid.*, vol. 1, p. 146.
32   For an elaboration of the separation of conception and execution in modern
     forms of the labour process see H. Braverman, *Labour and Monopoly Capital*
     (Monthly Review Press, 1974). See also Paul Willis, p. 185 above.
33   See, for instance, Goldthorpe and Lockwood, *Affluent Worker*, vol. 1,
     p. 149.
34   *ibid.*, vol. 1, p. 180.
35   *ibid.*, vol. 1, p. 36.
36   *ibid.*, vol. 3, p. 181.
37   *ibid.*, vol. 3, pp. 162-3.
38   Stuart Hall, 'A sense of classlessness', *Universities and New Left Review*, no. 3,
     (1958), p. 27.
39   John Eaton, New Left Review, *Towards Socialism* (New Left Review, 1965),
     p. 109.
40   *ibid.*, p. 105.
41   *ibid.*, pp. 107-8.
42   Raymond Williams, *Culture and Society, 1780-1950* (Penguin, 1961), p. 312.
43   *ibid.*, pp. 313-4.
44   See especially pages 217-22.
45   *Towards Socialism*, p. 12.
46   *ibid.*, p. 39.
47   For critical comments on Anderson's appropriation of 'hegemony' and on
     much else see Edward Thompson, 'Peculiarities of the English', *Socialist
     Register* (1965). For an assessment of the debate as a whole see Richard
     Johnson, 'Barrington Moore, Perry Anderson and English social development',
     Working Papers in Cultural Studies, no. 9 (University of Birmingham, 1976).
48   *Towards Socialism*, p. 34.
49   *ibid.*, p. 160.
50   *ibid.*, p. 201.

2   Culture and the historians

I would like to thank successive MA groups in CCCS who have provided a forum
for the discussion of many of the issues raised in this paper.

1   Perry Anderson's exploration of this 'absence' does not mention the Marxism
     of the historians. See P. Anderson, 'Components of the national culture', in
     A. Cockburn and R. Blackburn, *Student Power* (Penguin, 1969).

2   J. Gould, 'The attack on higher education', Institute for the Study of Conflict (September 1977).

3   Among the most useful items of these various kinds are: N.B. Harte (ed.), *The Study of Economic History: Collected Inaugural Lectures 1893-1970* (Frank Cass, 1971); E.J. Hobsbawm, 'From social history to the history of society', in M.W. Flinn and C. Flinn (eds.), *Essays in Social History* (Oxford University Press, 1974); G. Stedman Jones, 'History: the povery of empiricism', in R. Blackburn (ed.), *Ideology in Social Science* (Fontana, 1972). E.J. Hobsbawm, 'Karl Marx's contribution to historiography', in the same volume, and N.S.B. Gras, 'The rise and development of economic history', *Economic History Review*, vol. 1 (1927) are all the more interesting for not fitting any of the above categories. See also the essays on the history of the discipline in *Economic History Review*, 2nd series, vol. 30, (1977).

4   See especially L. Althusser, *For Marx* (Penguin, 1969); L. Althusser and E. Balibar, *Reading Capital* (New Left Books, 1970); L. Althusser, *Lenin and Philosophy and Other Essays* (New Left Books, 1971); L. Althusser, *Essays in Self-Criticism* (New Left Books, 1976).

5   See especially Quintin Hoare and Geoffrey Nowell-Smith (eds.) *Selections from the Prison Notebooks of Antonio Gramsci* (Lawrence & Wishart, 1971).

6   Hoare and Nowell-Smith, *Prison Notebooks*, p. 276.

7   The best discussion of the general context of the 1880s debates remains Helen Lynd, *England in the 1880s* (1945; reprint ed., Frank Cass, 1968). For some criticisms of Lynd's account see E.P. Hennock, 'Poverty and social theory in England', *Social History*, vol. 1 (January 1976). For an excellent and more detailed account of the late nineteenth-century debates see John Mason, 'Anti-socialist thought in late-Victorian England' (Unpublished PhD thesis, Birmingham Univeristy, 1974).

8   For this especially N.S.B. Gras, 'The rise and development of economic history', *Economic History Review*, vol. 1 (1927).

9   Clapham, 'The study of economic history', in Harte, *The Study of Economic History*, p. 67; see also the similar argument in W.J. Ashley, 'The place of economic history in university studies', *Economic History Review*, vol. 1 (1927).

10   See, for example, the inaugural lectures of Clapham, Tawney, Eileen Power in Harte, *Study of Economic History*.

11   e.g. Amy Harrison, one of their research assistants, and co-author with B.L. Hutchins of *A History of Factory Legislation*, 1903. Beatrice Webb, *Our Partnership* (1948), pp. 153-4, note 1.

12   *ibid.*, p. 45.

13   *ibid.*, p. 151.

14   *ibid.*, pp. 152-3.

15   S. and B. Webb, *History of Trade Unionsim*, preface to 2nd ed. (1894; reprint ed., Longmans,1950), p. viii.

16   For the whole argument see *ibid.*, ch. 1.

17 For sober trade unionists see below, for prudent administrators see *English Poor Law History*, Part 2, *The Last Hundred Years*, vol. 1 (Longmans, 1929), ch. 2, 'Poor Law Commissioners'.

18 S. and B. Webb, *History of Trade Unionism*, pp. 239-40.

19 B. Webb, *Our Partnership*, pp. 33, 160, 172; Margaret Cole, *Life of G.D.H. Cole*, (Macmillian, 1971), p. 173.

20 See especially G. Orwell, *The Road to Wigan Pier* (Penguin, 1970).

21 Ivy Pinchbeck, *Women Workers and the Industrial Revolution* (Routledge & Kegan Paul, 1930), esp. pp. 310-11.

22 *ibid.*, p. 307.

23 There is no adequate biography, but see Gilbert Murray in *Dictionary of National Biography*. The most important of their historical works for this essay are *The Village Labourer* (1911; reprint ed., Longmans, 1966); *The Skilled Labourer, 1760-1832* (1919; reprint ed., Longmans, 1920); *The Town Labourer, 1760-1832* (1917; reprint ed., Longmans, 1966).

24 Hammond & Hammond, *Town Labourer*, p. 289.

25 J.F.C. Harrison, *Robert Owen and Owenites in England and America* (Routledge & Kegan Paul, 1969).

26 *Bulletin of the Society for the Study of Labour History*, no. 9 (August 1964), pp. 4, 7.

27 *ibid.* (spring 1966), p. 4.

28 See the reported judgements of K. Knowles and E.P. Thompson quoted in Cole, *Cole* (pp. 206, 274; and the tributes to Cole in Asa Briggs and John Saville (eds.), *Essays in Labour History* (Macmillan, 1960).

29 *Life of William Cobbett* (1924); *Robert Owen* (1925); *Chartist Portraits* (1951); and the beginnings of what has become the *Dictionary of Labour Biography*.

30 *A Short History of the British Working Class Movement 1789-1925*, (3 vols., Allen & Unwin, 1925-6).

31 *British Working Class Politics 1832-1914* (1946); *A History of the Labour Party from 1914* (1948); *A Century of Co-operation* (1944)

32 *History of Socialist Thought*, vols. 1-5 (Macmillan, 1953-60).

33 Cole, *Cole*, pp. 17-19. Since Postgate seems mainly to have been responsible I have excluded the work from full consideration as part of Cole's *oeuvre*.

34 G.D.H. Cole, *The Meaning of Marxism* (Gollancz, 1948), p. 12. Other relevant works here are *What Marx Really Meant* (Gollancz, 1934) and the introduction to Marx's *Capital*, vol. 1 (Everyman, 1957), pp. v-xxv.

35 Cole, *Meaning of Marxism*, p. 80.

36 *ibid.*, p. 82.

37 *ibid.*, p. 49.

38 *ibid.*, pp. 42-3.

39 *ibid.*, p. 39.

40 *ibid.*, p. 25.

41 See especially F. Braudel, 'History and the social sciences', in P. Burke (ed.),

Economy and Society in Early Modern Europe (Routledge & Kegan Paul, 1958), and Althusser and Balibar, *Reading Capital*, chs. 4 and 5.

42   This is Postgate's description of the objects of the book (Cole, *Cole*, p. 217).

43   L.P. Carpenter, *G.D.H. Cole: An Intellectual Biography* (Cambridge University Press, 1973), p. 13.

44   cf. *ibid.*, p. 227. See also J.M. Winter, *Socialism and The Challenge of War: Ideas and Politics in Britain 1912-18,* (Routledge & Kegan Paul, 1974), ch. 4, which examines Cole's 'Marxist learnings'. For a caustic assessment of Cole's politics see J. Hinton, 'G.D.H. Cole in the stage army of the good', *Bulletin for the Society for the Study of Labour History*, no. 28 (spring 1974), pp. 76-83.

45   Dona Torr, *Tom Mann and His Times,* vol. 1, *1856-90* (Lawrence & Wishart, 1956), p. 144. This chapter was written by A.L. Morton.

46   Cole, *British Working Class Politics*, p. 6; Cole, *Short History of the British Working Class*, vol. 2, p.v.

47   See several of the essays in Flinn and Smout (ed.), *Essays in Social History.*

48   e.g. *British Working Class Politics*, p. 254.

49   Cole, *Meaning of Marxism*, p. 49.

50   Cole, *Chartist Portraits*, pp. 3, 20.

51   See especially the essay on Lovett.

52   *ibid.*, pp. 22-3.

53   Cole, *British Working Class Movement*, vol. 2, ch. 7, especially p. 137.

54   Cole, *British Working Class Politics*, pp. 7-8.

55   cf. Clapham's treatment of Chartism in *Economic History of Modern Britain: The Early Railway Age 1820-1850* (Cambridge University Press, 1926), esp. p. 584.

56   e.g. E.P. Thompson, 'The moral economy of the English crowd in the eighteenth century', *Past and Present*, no. 50 (February 1971), pp. 76-9.

57   Hobsbawn, 'Karl Marx's contribution to historiography', p. 270.

58   *Bulletin of the Society for the Study of Labour History*, no. 7, (autumn 1963) reporting the declining interest in history in WEA and extra-mural classes.

59   The first board included Maurice Dobb, R.H. Hilton and C. Hill, with E.J. Hobsbawm as assistant editor.

60   The first committee of the society consisted of Asa Briggs, E.J. Hobsbawm J.F.C. Harrison, F. Bealey, R. Harrison and S. Pollard. Henry Collins, John Saville, E.P. Thompson and Dorothy Thompson have also been involved.

61   See especially Dobb, *Studies*, ch. 1. But each chapter has its own definitional section, usually at the beginning. The account of *Studies* given here owes much to Bill Schwarz's study in Richard Johnson, Gregor McLennan and Bill Schwarz, 'Economy, culture and concept', CCCS stencilled occasional paper, no. 50 (1978).

62   John Saville (ed.), *Democracy and the Labour Movement: Essays in Honour of Dona Torr* (Lawrence & Wishart, 1954).

63   *ibid.*, p. 270.

64   Dobb, *Studies*, p. 277.

65   Johnson, McLennan and Schwarz, 'Economy, culture and concept', p. 12.
66   Especially for explaining the different histories of feudalism in Western and
      Eastern Europe. Dobb, *Studies*, p. 51.
67   Dobb, *Studies*, pp. 161-76; Hill, *The English Revolution* (Lawrence & Wishart,
      1940), p. 12.
68   This theme is considered again in chapter 9.
69   Saville, *Democracy and the Labour Movement*, p. 9.
70   Hobsbawm, *Labouring Men* (1964; Weidenfeld, 1968), p. vii. There are some
      important differences in this collection between essays that were written in
      the late 1940s or early to mid 1950s and those of a somewhat later origin.
71   Hence 'the standard of living controversy'.
72   See especially essay 8 in *Labouring Men* in which 'explosions' of labour
      militancy are traced mainly to economic variables plus 'the part played by
      bodies of agitators, propagandists and organisers' (p. 146).
73   'The labour aristocracy in nineteenth century Britain' and 'Trends in the
      British labour movement', again in *Labouring Men*.
74   Henry Pelling's work is paradigmatic for this side of 'labour history'.
75   E.P. Thompson, 'Homage to Tom Macguire', in Briggs and Saville (eds.),
      Essays in Labour History, vol 1, pp. 276-7.
76   It is especially to be hoped that those who were actually involved in the work
      here described will offer their own interpretations.
77   R. Williams, *The Long Revolution* (Penguin, 1965), p. 63.
78   My own personal encounter with *The Uses of Literacy* may serve as an
      example of one kind of youthful middle-class reaction, though it was perhaps
      an hilariously exaggerated response. I read the *Uses* in my last year at a private
      boarding school for boys (known for an emphasis on the natural sciences and
      its attractiveness to northern businessmen) and straight away dashed off to
      Hunslet in a fit, first, of philanthropic excess and in a context resembling that
      of a late-nineteenth-century 'settlement'. Pub talk, experience of early rock
      and roll and the 'feeling' of the working-class youth sub-cultures of the time
      shifted this mode of relationship into a more fashionable one: we returned,
      about a year later, to make a film of Hunslet life in the mode of Lindsay
      Anderson. The experience was close enough to home, actually and meta-
      morphically, to have profound reverberations, for we lived in Hull where, it
      seemed to me, my father fought a running battle with 'the dockers'. It may
      be that the book 'spoke' especially to working-class scholarboys; but it
      certainly spoke to others too.
79   The development of oral history may be traced in the journal *Oral History*
      (1970-   ). See also Paul Thompson, *The Edwardians* (Weidenfeld & Nicholson,
      1975), a first product of a large-scale project of this kind.
80   John Foster, *Class Struggle and the Industrial Revolution* (Weidenfeld &
      Nicholson, 1974). See also 'British imperialism and the labour aristocracy', in
      J. Skelley (ed.), *The General Strike* (Lawrence & Wishart, 1976). For a route
      of Hobsbawm's and Foster's Leninism, see R.Q. Gray, *The Labour Aristocracy*

in Victorian Edinburgh (Oxford University Press, 1976) and Gray's critique of Foster in *Marxism Today* (December 1977), pp. 367-71.

81   It is not possible to list all the later, 1970s texts. Some of the most significant have been Helen Mellor, *Leisure and the Changing City* (Routledge & Kegan Paul, 1976); Stephen Yeo, *Religion and Voluntary Organisations in Crisis* (Croom Helm, 1976); Hugh Macleod, *Class and Religion in the Late Victorian City* (Croom Helm, 1974); R. Price, *An Imperial War and the British Working Class* (Routledge & Kegan Paul, 1972); several of the essays in J. Mitchell and A. Oakley (eds.), *The Rights and Wrongs of Women* (Penguin, 1976), and in the Women's History issue of *Oral History*, vol. 5, no. 2 (autumn 1977). Perhaps the most interesting attempt to bring the new concerns into some connection with the staple fare of the older labour history is to be found in the work of Gareth Stedman Jones; see especially his 'Working-class culture and working-class politics in London, 1870-1900: notes on the re-making of a working class', *Journal of Social History* (summer 1974), pp. 460-508. For a 'limit case' of labour history, and one of the best books of the whole genre, see James Hinton, *The First Shop Steward's Movement* (Allen & Unwin, 1973).

82   E.J. Hobsbawm, *Primitive Rebels: Studies in Archaic Forms of Social Movement in the Nineteenth and Twentieth Centuries* (Manchester University Press, 1959), p. 2.

83   I have in mind such cases as the Nairn-Anderson view of the English working class as enduringly, essentially 'corporate', or, in the more 'optimistic' variant, Raymond Williams's argument that working-class culture is 'the basic collective' or, indeed, where it assumes a prospective or teleological form, the notion of an enduringly democratic popular tradition in Britain. Such essences cannot be relied on. For a development of our own formulations see pages 230-7

84   For reviews of Marxist-feminist and other work on these problems see CCCS Women's Studies Group, *Women Take Issue* (Hutchinson, 1977). Highly speculative and very interesting on the forms of this division is Eli Zaretsky, *Capitalism, the Family and Personal Life* (Pluto, 1976).

85   These formulations owe much to Simon Frith and Paul Corrigan, 'The politics of education', in Michael Young and Geoffrey Whitty, *Society, State and Schooling* (Falmar Press, 1977). See also the similar argument on page 95 also in the context of education and social democracy.

86   Hobsbawm, *Primitive Rebels,* p. 175.

87   E.P. Thompson, *The Making of the English Working Class* (Gollancz, 1963), pp. 12-13.

88   C. Hill, *The World Turned Upside Down* (Penguin, 1975), pp. 363-4.

89. Eugene D. Genovese, *Roll Jordan Roll* (Pantheon, New York, 1974), p. xvi.

90   *History Workshop Journal,* no. 1, pp. 1-8.

91   These arguments were established in the Nairn-Anderson *œuvre* on British history mainly written in the 1960s. The most important items are P.A. Anderson, 'Origins of the present crisis', *New Left Review,* no. 23; T. Nairn,

'Anatomy of the Labour Party'. *New Left Review*, nos..27, 28; E.P. Thompson 'Peculiarities of the English', *Socialist Register* (1965); N. Poulantzas, 'Marxist political theory in Great Britain, *New Left Review*, no. 43; and the latest reiteration of the original themes: Tom Nairn, 'The decline of the British State', *New Left Review*, nos. 101-2. For my own view of the debate see Richard Johnson, 'Perry Anderson, Barrington Moore and English social development', *Working Papers in Cultural Studies*, no. 9. There is a need to return to these themes again.

92 For the argument about the intellectuals more specifically see P. Anderson, 'Components of the national culture', in Blackburn and Cockburn, *Student Power*.

93 This argument is developed on pages 233-4.

94. viz. the work of the groups around *Theoretical Practice* (1971-3), especially that of Paul Hirst and Barry Hindess; and around *Screen* magazine.

95. For symptoms of this see the introduction to Mitchell and Oakley (eds.), *The Rights and Wrongs of Women*, and Sheila Rowbotham's review of *Women Take Issue* in *New Society* (4 May 1978).

96 This is how G.M. Young described the object of *Victorian England: Portrait of An Age* (Oxford University Press, 1953), founding text for a whole school of Victorian studies within a literary and strongly 'anti-sociological' mould. See, for example, Geoffrey Best, *Mid Victorian Britain* (Weidenfeld & Nicolson, 1971). Best succeeds in breaking with the high political - cultural emphasis but his accounts of popular culture remain interestingly descriptive. He refuses, for instance, the most elementary definitions - of class for example (pp. xv-xvi).

97 e.g. Terry Eagleton v. Raymond Williams, *New Left Review*, no. 95; Hindess and Hirst v. some historians, *Pre-Capitalist Modes of Production* (Routledge & Kegan Paul, 1975); Rosalind Coward v. Stuart Hall *et al.*, *Screen* (spring 1977).

98 Interview with *Radical History Review*, vol. 3, no. 4 (fall 1976), pp. 18-26. This article was written before the publication of Thompson's major critique of Althusser, *The Poverty of Theory and Other Essays* (Merlin Press, 1978).

99 e.g. *Whigs and Hunters* (Allen Lane, 1975), pp. 258-69.

3. 'Really useful knowledge'

Notes

This is a much shortened version of a chapter originally intended for a book on early ninteenth-century educational ideologies. A still shorter version was discussed at the Ruskin History Workshop, May 1976, and was published in *Radical Education*, nos. 7 and 8 (winter 1976 and spring 1977).

1 e.g. A.E. Dobbs, *Education and Social Movements, 1700-1850* (Longman, 1919).

2 Brian Simon, *Studies in the History of Education, 1780-1870* (Lawrence & Wishart, 1960); J.F.C. Harrison, *Learning and Living 1790-1960* (Routledge &

Kegan Paul, 1961); Harold Silver, *The Concept of Popular Education* (MacGibbon & Kee, 1965); E.P. Thompson, *The Making of the English Working Class* (Gollancz, 1963), especially pp. 711-45. Also important for first opening up many questions was R.K. Webb, *The British Working Class Reader, 1790-1848* (Allen & Unwin, 1955).

3   Especially Patricia Hollis, *The Pauper Press* (Oxford University Press, 1970); Joel H. Wiener, *The War of the Unstamped* (Cornell University Press, 1969); Dorothy Thompson, *The Early Chartists* (Macmillan, 1971); J.A. Epstein, 'Feargus O'Connor and the *Northern Star*', *International Review of Social History*, vol. 21 (1976), part 1, pp. 51-97; Eileen Yeo, 'Robert Owen and radical culture', in S. Pollard and T. Salt (eds.), *Robert Owen: Prophet of the Poor* (Macmillan, 1971); J.F.C. Harrison, *Robert Owen and Owenites in England and America* (Routledge & Kegan Paul, 1969).

4   The importance of private schooling before 1870 has been stressed by those who now favour a return to market principles in education. See especially E.G. West, 'Resource allocation and growth in early nineteenth-century British education', *Economic History Review*, vol. 13, no. 1 (April 1970). For an example of the kind of careful local study that we badly need see John Field, 'Private schools in Portsmouth and Southampton 1950-1870', *Journal of Educational History and Administration*, vol. 2 (1978), pp. 8-14.

5   The major study of Sunday schools - T.W. Laqueur, *Religion and Respectability: Sunday Schools and English Working Class Culture* (Yale University Press, 1976) - argues that Sunday schools as such were working-class institutions, democratically controlled. For an interesting example of a local study which shows the variety of practices under the term 'Sunday school' see Michael Frost, 'Working-class education in Brimingham 1780-1850' (Unpublished M Litt thesis, University of Birmingham, 1978).

6   For the first of these faults see Simon, *Studies*, p.275; the latter simplification are commoner in conservative historiography.

7   For Cobbett see page 88. But Wooller, Carlile, O'Brien and O'Connor among others used this description of themselves or others.

8   *Poor Man's Guardian*, 26 February 1831. The *Guardian* was the longest-lived and intellectually most impressive of the unstamped weeklies in the 1830-6 phase of the radical press.

9   Tom Paine, *The Rights of Man*, ed. Henry Collins (Penguin, 1969), especially p. 163.

10   William Cobbett, *Advice to Young Men* (London, 1906), p. 261.

11   e.g. *Black Dwarf*, 4 March 1818; Cobbett's or Hone's version of the catechism or Cobbett's 'Sunday school hymn'; *Black Dwarf*, 6 October 1819; *Political Register*, 7 December 1833, p. 603.

12   For infants schools see *New Moral World*, 8 July 1837; and *Northern Star*, 7 January 1843. But for a more favourable view see the *Midlands Counties Illuminator* (Thomas Cooper's paper), 20 March 1841.

13   Even the most favourable assessments of the popularity of the mechanics

institutes are open to the interpretation that the institutes were used for their 'really useful' content, e.g. the late acquisition of skills of literacy. See for example Edward Royle, 'Mechanics institutes and the working classes 1840-1860', *Historical Journal*, vol. 14 (1971), where it is shown that elementary classes teaching the three Rs were the most popular aspect.

14 *English Chartist Circular*, no. 37, p. 145.

15 *Poor Man's Guardian*, 18 May 1833.

16 *ibid*., 22 June 1833.

17 *ibid*., 24 September 1831.

18 Listed in Joel H. Wiener, *A Descriptive Finding List of Unstamped British Periodicals 1830-6* (Bibliographical Society, London, 1970).

19 'Heddekashun' was defined in Cobbett, *Cottage Economy* (London, 1850), p. 1.

20 For a similar argument see Yeo, 'Robert Owen and radical culture', in Pollard and Salt, *Robert Owen: Prophet of the Poor*, p. 108, note 2.

21 G.J. Holyoake, *Sixty Years of an Agitator's Life* (London 1892), vol 1, p. 4.

22 [Thomas Wright], *The Great Unwashed by a Journeyman Engineer* (1868; reprinted Cass, 1970), p. 7.

23 Samuel Bamford, *Early Days*, 2nd ed. (Manchester, 1859), p. 41.

24 *ibid*., pp. 2, 43-4, 92.

25 William Lovett, *Life and Struggles in Pursuit of Bread, Knowledge and Freedom*, Fitzroy ed., ed. R.H. Tawney (MacGibbon & Kee, 1967), pp. 1-6.

26 Joseph Gutteridge, *Lights and Shadows in the Life of an Artisan* (Coventry, 1893), pp. 7-9.

27 Gwyn A. Williams, *Rowland Detroisier: A Working Class Infidel, 1800-1834* (St Anthony's Press, York, 1965), pp. 5-6, 8.

28 John Wood, *Autobiography* (Bradford, 1881), p. 5.

29 Joseph McCabe, *Life and Letters of George Jacob Holyoake* (London, 1908), vol. 1, pp. 8-10.

30 J. Passmore Edwards, *A Few Footprints* (London, 1905), p. 5.

31 A.R. Schoyen, *The Chartist Challenge: Portrait of Julian Harney* (Heinemann, 1958), p. 3.

32 Gutteridge, *Lights and Shadows*, pp. 6-7, 14-15.

33 Lovett, *Life and Struggles*, pp. 3-6.

34 For this distrust see Richard Johnson, 'Educational policy and social control in early-Victorian England', *Past and Present*, no. 49 (1970), p. 114.

35 See for example, David Jones, *Chartism and the Chartists* (Allen Lane, 1975), pp. 30, 25.

36 Mary Smith, *The Autoboigraphy of Mary Smith, Schoolmistress and Nonconformist* (Carlisle, 1892), pp. 15, 39-40.

37 Asked by a friend whom they should invite as a speaker she replied, 'Send for Henry Vincent. He will please you all.' *ibid*., p. 148.

38 *ibid*., pp. 260, 271-2.

39 Roger Langdon, *The Life of Roger Langdon told by Himself* (London, n.d.),

pp. 28-41.

40   *ibid*., p. 68.

41   For example Gutteridge's desire for *Culpepper* - a standard work of botanical reference; or Cobbett's encounter with *A Tale of a Tub*.

42   F.M. Leventhall, *Respectable Radical: George Howell and Victorian Working Class Politics* (Weidenfeld & Nicolson, 1971), pp. 6-9.

43   Thompson, *Making of the English Working Class*, p. 674.

44   For the best account of the unstamped as, itself, a political force see Wiener, *The War of the Unstamped*; for the best account of radical ideology in this phase see Hollis, *Pauper Press*.

45   Epstein, 'Feargus O'Connor and the *Northern Star*', p. 95.

46   For Cobbett see Thompson, *Making*, especially p. 749; for O'Connot see Epstein, 'Feargus O'Connor and the *Northern Star*', p. 84.

47   *ibid*., p. 79.

48   For lectures see *Northern Star*, 5 May 1838, 2 June 1838, 28 July 1839; for schoolmasters see 25 August 1838; for Dickens see 1838, *passim*.

49   e.g. *Northern Star* 6 and 13 January, 10 and 31 March, 21 and 28 April 1838.

50   *ibid*., 9 June 1838.

51   *ibid*., 13 and 20 April 1844, 14 December 1844.

52   For this argument in full see Epstein, 'Feargus O'Connor and the *Northern Star*', *passim*.

53   R.C. Gammage, *History of the Chartist Movement, 1937-1854* (Merlin Press, London, 1969), p. 197.

54   *Co-operator*, 1 January 1830; *Pioneer*, 31 May 1834; *Political Register*, 21 September 1833, p. 731; *Poor Man's Guardian*, 25 October 1834 and 14 April 1834 ('Letter from a 'labourer' in Poplar').

55   For a typical attack on this score see *Le Bonnett Rouge* (journal of the neo-Jacobin, Lorymer), 16 February 1833.

56   *Pioneer*, 25 January 1834.

57   *Poor Man's Guardian*, 14 June 1834.

58   *Crisis*, 1 June 1833.

59   e.g. Hollis, *Pauper Press*, p. 219.

60   e.g. *Poor Man's Guardian*, 26 March 1831, leader on the reform bill, and for a more developed version the leader on 14 June 1834.

61   *ibid*., 26 May 1832.

62   *ibid*., 30 November 1833.

63   *ibid*., 14 April 1832.

64   The most 'authoritative' source for Owenite theory was the *New Moral World*, the 'official' journal of the movement. But see Harrison, *Owen and Owenites*, and Thompson, *Making*, pp. 779-807, for the two most interesting contemporary interpretations.

65   *Crisis*, 19 May 1832.

66   *Pioneer*, 16 November 1833.

67   For a fuller account see E. Halevy, *Thomas Hodgskin 1787-1869* (London,

1903); R. Pankhurst, *William Thompson* (1877-1833): *Britain's Pioneer Socialist, Feminist and Co-operator* (Watts, 1954). For their influence on working-class theory see Hollis, *Pauper Press* and Thompson, *Making*.

68 Hollis, *Pauper Press*, p. 225.
69 On Owenite educational ideas see especially Silver, *The Concept of Popular Education*, and Harrison, *Owen and Owenites*.
70 He was not at all the Tory obscurantist that his vote against the education measures of 1833 has sometimes suggested to educational historians.
71 *Political Register*, 10 April 1830.
72 Cobbett, *Cottage Economy*, pp. 9-10.
73 *Political Register*, 7 December 1833, p. 581.
74 e.g. Cobbett, *Cottage Economy*, pp. 10-14. In this way, and with a typical inconsistency, he managed to blame philanthropy both for destroying an old order and trying to maintain it!
75 Cobbett, *Advice to Young Men*, p. 40.
76 For a typical but intelligent argument of the Tory kind see [John Weyland], *Letter to A Country Gentleman on the Education of the Lower Orders* (London, 1808).
77 Cobbett, *Advice to Young Men*, p. 40.
78 Quoted in William Reitzel (ed.), *The Autobiography of William Cobbett* (Faber, 1967), p. 194.
79 Cobbett, *Advice to Young Men*, p. 48.
80 *ibid.*, p. 41.
81 His own history book was *History of the Protestant Reformation*, of which Cobbett boasted: 'unquestionably the book of greatest circulation in the whole world, the Bible only excepted'.
82 Thompson, *Making*, pp. 755 and 759.
83 *Political Register*, 21 September 1833, p. 735; Reitzel, *Autobiography*, pp. 123-5; Cobbett, *Rural Rides* (Penguin, 1967), p. 41.
84 Cobbett, *Advice to Young Men*, pp. 247-55.
85 *Poor Man's Guardian*, 14 September 1833.
86 e.g. Shepherd Smith's lecture on Education, *Crisis*, 31 August 1833.
87 What follows is drawn mainly from *An Inquiry into the Principles and Distribution of Wealth*, but see the similar argument in *Crisis*, 21 April 1832.
88 *Birmingham Co-operative Herald*, 1 June 1829. This is a part-quote from William Thompson, *Labour Defended*.
89 *Co-operator*, 1 January 1830.
90 Jones, *Chartism and the Chartists*, p. 170.
91 *Poor Man's Guardian*, 23 February 1833.
92 *English Chartist Circular*, nos. 22 and 27.
93 *Poor Man's Guardian*, 11 January 1834.
94 Epstein, 'Feargus O'Connor and the *Northern Star*', p. 69, for a discussion of various estimates.
95 e.g. at Benjamin Heywood's Miles Platting or at Crewe. See W.H. Challoner,

The Social and Economic Development of Crewe 1780-1923 (Manchester University Press, 1950), pp. 233-4; Edith and Thomas Kelly (eds.), *A Schoolmaster's Notebook* (Manchester University Press, 1957), pp. 31-2.

96   See the maps of branches of the National Charter Association and the Land Plan in Jones, *Chartism and the Chartists*, for example.

97   For Gramsci's discussion of parties based on the inter-war Italian experience see Quintin Hoare and Geoffrey Nowell-Smith (eds. and trans.), *Selections from the Prison Notebooks of Antonio Gramsci* (Lawrence & Wishart, 1971), *passim*. The distinction between 'organic' and 'traditional' intellectuals is central to Gramsci's discussion of party and working-class culture.

98   Thompson, *Making*, p. 789.

99   On Fielden see Paul Richards, 'The state and the working class 1833-1841' (Unpublished PhD thesis, University of Birmingham, 1975); on O'Connor see Epstein, 'Feargus O'Connor and the *Northern Star*', and 'Feargus O'Connor and the English working-class movement' (Unpublished PhD thesis, University of Birmingham, 1977).

100   Hoare and Nowell-Smith, *Prison Notebooks*, p. 330.

101   This mutation is examined in Dan Finn, Neil Grant and Richard Johnson, 'Social democracy and the education crisis', in CCCS, *On Ideology* (Hutchinson, 1978).

102   *Black Dwarf*, 6 May 1818.

103   *Pioneer*, 21 June 1834 (Senex was Shepherd Smith. See John Saville, 'J.E. Smith and the Owenite Movement', in Pollard and Salt, *Robert Owen: Prophet of the Poor*).

104   Lovett often put the case against state education; O'Brien the case for.

105   See also Thompson, *Making*, especially the discussion of Carlile and 'rationalism'.

106   *The Poor Man's Guardian* compared Cobbett's impracticalities with the enthusiasm with which the Co-operative Congress 'spoke of the formation of schools' (*Guardian*, 14 September 1833).

107   *Pioneer*, 7 and 21 December 1833.

108   *New Moral World*, 16 November 1838.

109   e.g. *Northern Star*, 22 June 1838 and 26 December 1840.

110   *Pioneer*, 16 November 1833.

111   Harrison, *Owen and Owenites*, p. 139. For the distinction between 'education', 'institutions' and 'writing and discourses' see William Thompson, *Inquiry*.

112   *Poor Man's Guardian*, 14 January 1832.

113   Pankhurst, *Thompson,* p. 140; *Pioneer*, 31 May 1834; *Crisis*, 19 April 1834.

114   Silver, *The Concept of Popular Education*, p. 176.

115   *Birmingham Co-operative Herald*, 1 August and 1 September 1830.

116   *Crisis*, 1 and 8 June 1833.

117   *Crisis*, 28 September 1833.

118   *New Moral World*, 1 August 1835.

119   *ibid.*, 10 March and 14 April 1838.

120 *ibid.*, 24 August 1838.
121 Most accounts of this episode are heavily biased in favour of Lovett and the 'new movers'. See M. Howell, *The Chartist Movement* (Manchester University Press, 1966), pp. 230-6. For criticisms of the 'physical force' - 'moral force' polarity on which such accounts were based see D. Thompson, *The Early Chartists*, pp. 16-27 and Asa Briggs, 'National Bearings' in Briggs (ed.), *Chartist Studies* (Macmillan, 1965).
122 J. Collins and William Lovett, *Chartism, A New Organisation of the People* (reprinted·Leicester University Press, 1969). There is a useful collection of cuttings and other materials on the scheme in the Lovett Collection, City of Birmingham Reference Library.
123 Lovett, *Life and Struggles*, p. 301.
124 For Ellis see W.A.C. Stewart and W.P. McCann, *The Educational Innovators 1750-1880* (Macmillan, 1967), pp. 327-39.
125 Most recently in John Foster, *Class Struggle and the Industrial Revolution* (Methuen, 1977) and R.Q. Gray, *The Labour Aristocracy in Victorian Edinburgh* (Oxford University Press, 1976).
126 A tendency shared, for example, by two very different books - Foster, *Class Struggle*, and T. Tholfsen, *Working-Class Radicalism in Mid-Victorian England* (Croom Helm, 1976). I think this criticism also applies, in the end, to Thompson, *Making*, for reasons to do with the author's conception of class.
127 It is one of the weaknesses of the *Making* that though it deals with just this transition as experienced by 'the artisan', it tends to understand it in terms of 'loss of status' and perhaps 'independence' without an adequate analysis of changing modes of exploitation or subordination. For an interesting opening out of some of these questions see Gareth Stedman Jones, 'England's first proletariat', *New Left Review*, no. 90 (March - April 1975). The categories, 'real' and 'formal' subsumption of labour, however, may not be adequately complex, as they stand, to describe the early nineteenth-century transitions. I am grateful to Bill Schwartz for suggesting this argument.
128 These suggestions are based, of course, on economic and other histories and are not entirely theoretical speculations. There is much in the following sources especially which point to these conclusions: Thompson, *Making;* N.J. Smelser, *Social Change in the Industrial Revolution* (Routledge & Kegan Paul, 1959); Michael Sanderson, 'Literacy and social mobility in the industrial revolution in England', *Past and Present*, no. 56 (August 1972).
129 This is not to deny the recurrent revivals of independent working-class education especially in the 1880s to 1920s. Nor is it to argue that there is nothing to be learnt from the radical experience. It could be said, indeed, that it is precisely the stress on education as an aspect of socialist politics that needs to be revived today. The inhibitions that remain are less material (though to be sure some exist) than ideological and political'. They include, centrally, the obsession of British socialists with education of the most formal kind conducted through a system articulated through state or local state

agencies. The exhaustion of this social democratic repertoire is very evident today.

4.   Imperialism, nationalism and organized youth

1   Coster-monger culture, which included 'dressing up flash' and wearing the hair 'Newgate-knocker style' is described in Henry Mayhew, *London Labour and the London Poor* (4 vols., New York: Dover, 1968), vol. 1, especially pp. 33-46.

2   What follows draws heavily on J.R. Gillis, 'The evolution of juvenile delinquency in England 1890-1913', *Past and Present*, no. 67 (May 1975), and J.R. Gillis, *Youth and History* (New York, 1974).

3   This essay is based on Chapter 14 of my thesis. See M.D. Blanch, 'Nation, Empire and the Birmingham working class, 1899-1914' (Unpublished PhD thesis, University of Birmingham, 1975). I am grateful to the editors of this volume for suggestions for revisions.

4   For 'belt' see Sam Shaw, *Guttersnipe* (Samson Lord, 1946), p. 20. Out of 605 children brought before Birmingham Juvenile Court in 1911 for non-indictable offences, 132 were charged with playing ball in the streets (M.G. Barnett, *Young Delinquents: A Study of Reformatory and Industrial Schools* [Methuen, 1913], p. 12). Manchester youth workers had to object that even 'respectable boys' were being prosecuted for loitering (Hugh Oldham Lads' Club, *Annual Report* [Manchester, 1902], p. 4).

5   Quoted in W. Collinson, *Apostle of Free Labour* (London, 1913), p. 3.

6   W. Goldman, *East End My Cradle* (Faber, 1940), p. 18.

7   Anti-police epithets were common, it seems, even in the villages. See Flora Thompson, *Lark Rise to Candleford* (Penguin, 1973), p. 485. The police rarely appeared in 'Penny Dreadfuls' as heroes - 'they are constantly shown as stupid, cowardly, or ill-looking' complained the *Quarterly Review*, vol. 171 (July 1890), p. 150.

8   e.g. James Spenser, *Limey Breaks In* (Longmans, 1934), p. 3; F. Willis, *Peace and Dripping Toast* (Phoenix House, 1950), p. 59.

9   The first two were Birmingham terms, the last from Manchester.

10   Gillis, *Youth and History* p. 122; the Rev. T.J. Bass, *Every Day in Blackest Birmingham: Facts not Fiction* (Birmingham, 1898), p. 8.

11   V.W. Garratt, *Man in the Street* (Dent, 1939), p. 66, see also *Birmingham Daily Mail* (hereafter *BDM*), 7 October 1905.

12   e.g. Goldman, *East End My Cradle*, pp. 81-5; Garratt, *Man in the Street*, p. 89.

13   F.P. Gibbon, *A History of the Heyrod Street Lads Club and of the Fifth Manchester Company of the Boys Brigade, 1899-1910* (Manchester, 1911), pp. 7, 17.

14   This is fully documented in Blanch, 'Nation, empire and the Birmingham working class; ch. 2 on 'Drill, discipline and moral education'.

15   I have drawn here on modern writing on sub-cultural formations. I have found

Phil Cohen, 'Sub-cultural conflict and working-class community', *Working Papers in Cultural Studies* no. 2 (1972), especially useful.

16 M. Anderson, *Family Structure in Nineteenth-Century Lancashire* (Cambridge, 1971), pp. 112-13, 119-24. Among sources which note continuing familiar support in skilled-worker families are C. Stella Davies, *North Country Bred* (London, 1963), p. 35; L. Halward, *Let Me Tell You* (London, 1938), pp. 56-7; A. Freeman, *Boy Life and Labour* (London, 1914), pp. 13-21; and P. le Rousiers, *Labour Question in Britain* (London, 1896), pp. 1, 20.

17 These roles could often be combined. One Manchester teacher was also a member of the First Volunteer Battalion, Manchester Regiment. His room in Lower Mosley Street School 'has a military appearance', twenty to thirty boys being caned there regularly each day at 4 p.m. *Manchester City News*, 31 January 1914.

18 These differed from area to area. For a militaristic example, complete with bayonet exercises, see Jewish Lads Brigade, Manchester Battalion, *Annual Reports 1899-1903* (Manchester, 1903), pp. 22-3.

19 i.e. Market Hall, St Mary's, St. Bartholomew's, St. Paul's, St. Martin's and Deritend as listed in *Handbook for Workers Among Boys in Birmingham* (Birmingham, 1913). These wards all had relatively high death rates and low-standard housing. All figures quoted below for these areas are from this source, cited as *Birmingham Handbook*, unless otherwise stated.

20 These do not cover the whole central working-class area; they exclude Ancoats for example. See, for most figures, Manchester Juvenile Organisations Committee, *Handbook of Juvenile Organisations in Manchester* (Manchester, 1918). Cited as *Manchester Handbook*.

21 *Handsworth Herald*, 25 July 1903. Lt Rev. Selwyn was also assistant chaplain to the Handworth Volunteers. The Boys' Brigade was founded in Glasgow in 1884; by 1913 it claimed 100,000 members.

22 *BDM*, 28 April 1909; *Birmingham Handbook*, p. 9. This was about 2 per cent of males aged 12 to 17 years.

23 Or 5.7 per cent of males aged 12 to 17 years. *Manchester Handbook*, pp. 8 and 16.

24 *Birmingham Handbook*, p. 9.

25 *Boys' Brigade, Tenth Birmingham Company 1908-29; a Souvenir Booklet* (Birmingham, 1929).

26 Gibbon, *Heyrod Street Lads' Club*, p. 27.

27 *Fifth Monthly Chronicle of the Heyrod Street Lads' Club* . . . , 8 May 1905.

28 Birmingham = *c*.200; Manchester = *c*.300; total boys 12 to 17 = *c*.9000.

29 *Nelson St Adult School Magazine* (April, June, October 1902); and Supt. Robert Best in the issue for May 1902.

30 *Brigade*, vol. 1, no. 1 (October 1894).

31 *Boys' Brigade Gazette*, 1 January 1911; 87 per cent against, 13 per cent for.

32 *Birmingham Handbook*, p. 9.

33 *BDM*, 30 July 1909; Reveille 0530, drill, church parade; every morning eight

hours of exercises, drills and parades - 'instilling of a healthy, manly sense of religion'.

34   *Birmingham Handbook*, p. 9; Bass, *Blackest Birmingham*; Bass, *Hope in Shadow Land* (Birmingham, 1903).

35   *Scout Message*, September 1911. Scout Law No. 2 of the *ICSP*.

36   *BDM*, 6 May 1908; First Cadet Battalion, Manchester Regiment, *Annual Report* (1890), p. 10.

37   *Royal Commission on Militia and Volunteers* (Cd. 2061-4; 1904): Col. Ledward, First Cadet Battalion, qq. 23906-4006 (hereafter cited as *Norfolk Commission*).

38   Fifty per cent join the Volunteers and a 'great many' the Regulars. See also *Norfolk Commission*, qq. 24033 and 24072 for evidence from two London Cadet Battalions.

39   First Cadet Battalion, Manchester Regiment, *Annual Report* (1890): Object 1 - 'interest and attractive occupations for lads of the poorest class'.

40   *Norfolk Commission*, qq. 24072-150.

41   *ibid.*, qq. 23966-8 and 23981, evidence of Col. Ledward.

42   *ibid.*, q. 23990.

43   *BDM*, 21 January 1909.

44   School Management Committee, *Minutes* (MSS, Birmingham Education Offices), Minute 2797, 11 February 1886; amended by Minute 5605, 7 April 1892; *Mr Boscombe's Reports* (MSS, Birmingham Education Offices), 2 March and 8 September 1896.

45   By 1911 one in every eleven males aged 17 to 25 was a member of the TF in Manchester (Blanch, 'Nation, empire and the Birmingham working class', ch. 12 and p. 384).

46   *BDM*, 21, 28 January 1909 - growing to 130 boys by August. *ibid.*, 25 August 1909.

47   *BDM*, 29 November 1909.

48   *BDM*, 4 December 1909.

49   *BDM*, 6 December 1909.

50   Birmingham: total all organizations = 700; male population aged 12 to 17 = *c*.6850; Manchester: total all organizations = 450; male population aged 12 to 17 = *c*.3500. These figures assume full strength companies and no 'commuter' cadets, and may, therefore, overestimate membership.

51   The Boys Life Brigade was founded in 1899 in Nottingham by the Rev. Patton to combat 'jingoistic' organizations. National membership in 1906 was 8000.

52   There is no information available for the GLB in Birmingham. The size of Manchester companies was thirty-five to forty girls each.

53   J. Springhall, 'Youth and empire: a study of the propagation of imperialism to the young in Edwardian Britain' (DPhil thesis, University of Sussex, 1968; subsequently published as *Youth, Empire and Society*, Croom Helm, 1977).

54   *BDM*, 20 January 1908.

55 Springhall, Thesis, p. 217.
56 Birmingham District Association of Boy Scouts, *Yearbooks* (1910-15); National Service League, Birmingham Branch, *Report*, (1907-10).
57 *BDM*, 19 February 1909. Report of NSL meeting.
58 Birmingham District Association of Boy Scouts, *Yearbook* (1910) p. 19.
59 *ibid*., (1913), p. 41.
60 R.S. Baden-Powell, *Scouting for Boys* (London, 1910), pp. 334, 339.
61 Birmingham District Association of Boy Scouts, *Yearbook* (1910) p. 9; *ibid*. (1913), p. 41.
62 *ibid*., 1914.
63 *BDM*, 7 July 1914 (advertisement).
64 4300 Scouts, 2300 Cubs, 2500 Guides, plus 1000 Catholic Scouts; the population aged 10 to 18 years was 128,770. *Manchester Handbook*, pp. 8, 17, and *Census* (1911).
65 Based on mean size of Manchester boys' troops the number of Scouts in 1917 = 70 and Guides = 38; sixteen boys' troops and eight girls' troops; population 10 to 18 = 10,700.
66 Mean size of Birmingham troops was less (86 troops = 3200).
67 *Birmingham Handbook*, 1913.
68 Birmingham District Association of Boy Scouts, *Yearbook* (1914).
69 Digbeth Institute, *Reports* (1908), vol. 1, p. 16.
70 *ibid*. (1910), p. 15.
71 *ibid*. (1908), p. 15.
72 *BDM*, 17 March 1909.
73 *BDM*, 22 March 1909.
74 *BDM*, 19 March 1909.
75 *BDM*, 25 March 1909.
76 *ibid*.
77 Springhall, Thesis, pp. 228 ff.
78 Birmingham: paramilitary 700; semi-military 850; or 22.6 per cent of males 12 to 17. Manchester with 450 paramilitary and 650 semi-military, involved 21.0 per cent of males 10 to *18* (sic).
79 The Rev. H.S. Pelham, *The Training of the Working Boy* (Macmillan, 1914), p. 9; *ibid*., p. 120.
80 *ibid*., pp. 55 ff; *Cost of Living of the Working Classes: Report of an Inquiry by the Board of Trade* (Cd. 3864, 1908) p. 82.
81 J.H. Muirhead, 'Social work in Birmingham', in *Handbook for Birmingham* (British Association, 1913), p. 279.
82 *Reports of the Birmingham Street Children's Union* (1906-14); *hereafter BSChU. Birmingham Street Children's Union A Souvenir* (1913).
83 *Birmingham Handbook*, p. 9. Characteristically this source does not mention girls' clubs.
84 High Oldham Lads' Club, *Annual Reports* (1914), p. 3.
85 Hulme Lads' Club, *Annual Report* (1899); Ancoat's Lads' Club, *Annual*

Report (1902).
86   Not all clubs worked with 'problem children'. The Hugh Oldham Club was
     not for 'really vicious children . . . criminals . . . really bad boys . . . and the
     absolutely destitute . . . . we aim to provide for the respectable working lad'.
     Annual Report (1898), p. 5.
87   Pelham, *The Training of the Working Boy,* p. 31. The author was a senior
     Birmingham Street Children's Union organizer.
88   *BSChU, Souvenir* (1913), p. 2.
89   *BSChU* Edwardian Branch, *Report of Annual Meeting* (1907).
90   Hugh Oldhams Lads' Club, *Annual Report* (1898), p. 5.
91   Hulme Lads' Club, *Annual Reports* (1907, 1909).
92   *Report of the National Service League,* Birmingham Branch (1908-9), p. 6;
     Report of the BSChU, Nos. 2-4, (1906-8).
93   *Report of the National Service League, Birmingham Branch* (1907); *Chamber
     of Commerce Journal*; *Birmingham Red Book* (1908); *Kelly's Directory:
     Cornishes' Directory of Birmingham*
94   *BSChU Report* (1910-11), p. 7; *ibid.*, pp. 49-51.
95   Pelham, *Training of the Working Boy*, pp. 49-51.
96   Freeman, *Boy Life and Labour*, p. 130.
97   R.H. Bray, 'The boy and the family', in *Studies of Boy Life in Our Great
     Cities* (London, 1908); p. 100; W.B. Carnegie, *Problem of the Street Child*
     (Birmingham, 1910).
98   Freeman, *Boy Life and Labour*, pp. 21, 52, 71.
99   Sources: *Birmingham Handbook* (1913); *Manchester Handbook* (1918);
     Census (1911), taking account of the extended area of Birmingham in 1913
     and the additional areas covered by the *Manchester Handbook.*
100 Estimate: Street Children's Union (SChU), 670; Scouts, 270; Boys' Life Brigade
     (BLB), 70; Church Lads' Brigade (ChLB), 175; Boys' Brigade (BB), 100.
101 Even broad comparisons between pre-war Birmingham and wartime Manches-
     ter are open to the objection that numbers in the two cities had been radically
     different. This is unlikely. The two cities show similar numbers in para-
     military adult organizations. Some differences between particular youth
     organizations (e.g. a strong Boys' Brigade in Manchester) are balanced out
     overall, and youth club membership suggests parallel membership totals in
     1913.
102 *BSChU, Annual Report* (1908), p. 9.
103 The whole theme of women as mothers and imperialist ideology is explored
     in Anna Davin, 'Imperialism and motherhood', *History Workshop Journal*,
     no. 5 (May 1978).
104 *BSChU Annual Report* (1913-14), p. 7.
105 Harold Johnson, *Moral Instruction in Elementary Schools: A Return from
     Official Documents* (1908), pp. xi, xii. Birmingham began moral lessons,
     twice weekly, in 1879. One of the most popular teacher's books on how to
     teach 'moral education' was written by a Birmingham headmaster:

F.W. Hackwood, *Notes for Lessons on Moral Subjects: A Handbook for Teachers in Elementary Schools* (1888, 1906). See also F.H. Hilliard, 'Moral Instruction League 1897-1919', in *Durham Research Review*, vol. 3, no. 12 (September 1961).

106 V.E. Chancellor, *History for Their Masters* (Adams & Dart, 1970); see also LCC Education Committee Reports on conferences on teaching history and geography (1911).

107 Warwickshire County Council, *The Prefect System in Elementary Schools*, Education Essays no. 8 (1913), p. 18.

108 *The Times*, 24 May 1921.

109 *Norfolk Commission*, q. 9151.

110 *ibid.*, qq. 5185-91, evidence from Galloways of Manchester; e.g. in 1909 in Birmingham; Ansells, BSA Gun Factory, Corporation Gas Works, Metropolitan Carriage Works, etc.

111 Our conclusions differ therefore from those of Richard Price, *An Imperial War and the British Working Class* (Routledge & Kegan Paul, 1972).

112 e.g. Aston Municipal Elections Poster (November 1905), Birmingham Reference Library Collection, f. 319.

113 e.g. Chamberlain in *Straightforward*, no. 1 (May 1914), reporting a speech of 5 June 1906.

114 e.g. *BDM*, 30 November 1910, in which home rule is presented as an American plot.

115 e.g. *Midland Express*, 24 November 1901; see also J.A. Garrard, *The English and Immigration, 1880-1910* (Oxford University Press, 1971).

116 This is argued in Blanch, 'Nation, empire and the Birmingham working class', especially p. 200.

117 *ibid.*, p. 242.

118 *ibid.*, p. 266.

119 *ibid.*, p. 231.

120 *ibid.*, p. 346.

121 Hugh Oldham Lads' Club, *Annual Report* (1915). Out of 217 lads, 169 joined the army in the first eight months.

122 Hulme Lads' Club, *Annual Report* (1914), p. 7.

5 Daughters and mothers - maids and mistresses

I am grateful to Richard Johnson for suggesting revisions to an earlier draft. This essay is based in part on my MA thesis completed at CCCS in 1978. I thank my personal respondents for permission to use extracts from their accounts.

1 e.g. John Burnett, *Useful Toil* (Allen Lane, 1974), pp. 135-42; Pamela Horn, *The Rise and Fall of the Victorian Servant* (Gill & Macmillan, 1975), p. 171, Robert Roberts, *The Classic Slum* (Penguin, 1973), p. 222.

2 For the full argument see J.P. Taylor, 'Women domestic servants, 1919-1939:

the final phase' (Unpublished MA thesis, University of Birmingham, 1978).

3   *Census* (1921, 1931).

4   This estimate is based on the following considerations: 60 per cent of those in private households (see the sample survey quoted in 1931 *Census*) plus 80 per cent of those in institutions. For the full working through see Taylor, 'Domestic servants', p. 48.

5   A. Chapman and R. Knight, *Wages and Salaries in the U.K., 1920-1938* (Cambridge, 1957), p. 218. See also N. Branson and M. Heineman, *Britain in the 1930s* (Weidenfeld & Nicolson, 1973), p. 175.

6   Just as the position of married women in the home seemed natural until challenged by the women's movement.

7   Published autobiographies are cited below in the usual form. Oral evidence collected specially for this study is cited as 'p.o.e.' (personal oral evidence); written accounts produced specially for this study are cited as 'p.w.e.' (personal written evidence). In all, ten published autobiographies were used, and oral evidence was collected, directly, from twenty-four ex-servants. Though the sample remains small no less than 120 actual job situations are covered by this material.

8   For the full argument see Taylor, 'Domestic servants', pp. 18-26.

9   Rowntree in C.L. Mowat, *Britain Between the Wars* (Methuen, 1968), p. 503. For the inter-war economy in general see R.S. Sayers, *A History of Economic Change in Britain 1880-1939* (Oxford UP, 1967); especially useful on sectoral differences and shifts is S. Pollard, *The Development of the British Economy 1914-1970* (Edward Arnold, 1962).

10   Winifred Foley, *Child in the Forest* (London, 1974), p. 19.

11   Flora Thompson, *Lark Rise to Candleford* (Penguin, 1973), p. 155.

12   Foley, *Child in the Forest* (Unpublished MS), quoted in J. Burnett, *Useful Toil*, p. 227.

13   For fuller evidence see Taylor, 'Domestic servants', pp. 15-26. The evidence includes heavy rates of migration from depressed areas in this period, evidence of personal accounts especially of Welsh girls who moved to London or Birmingham, and the very high concentrations of domestic servants in particular parts of the country.

14   For the figures of different kinds of areas see Taylor, 'Domestic servants', pp. 47-56.

15   J.A. Banks, *Prosperity and Parenthood* (Routledge, 1954).

16   Leonore Davidoff, 'Mastered for life', *Journal of Social History*, vol. 7, no. 4 (summer 1974).

17   This is based partly upon personal experience of family life in the 1920s and 1930s but also on autobiographical accounts.

18   G. Tyack and WEA class, 'Service on the Clivedon estate between the wars', *Oral History*, vol. 5, no. 1 (1977).

19   Harold Macmillan, *Winds of Change 1914-39* (Macmillan, 1966), p. 195.

20   e.g. the account in Jean Rennie, *Every Other Sunday* (Coronet, 1975), p. 54.

21. This is based partly on personal experience and on servants' own accounts of the work they had to perform. See also Florence Jack and Philippa Preston (eds.), *The Women's Book*, (London, n.d. [1931]).
22 Anne Oakley, *The Sociology of Housework* (London, 1974), especially p. 111.
23 Anonymous recollections from *Within Living Memory*, a collection produced by the Norfolk Federation of Women's Institutes (Norfolk, 1972), p. 80.
24 Horn, *Rise and Fall*, p. 173.
25 For an expansion of this point with special reference to fiction see Taylor, 'Domestic servants', pp. 161-86.
26 Uniform, for example, on such questions as hours off, rates of pay, the exclusion of boyfriends, the purchase of uniform by the servant herself, etc. There appears to have been a high degree of customary consensus on these matters among the employing classes as late as the 1930s.
27 Margaret Powell, *Below Stairs* (P. Davies, 1968), pp. 4-5;
28 *ibid.*, p. 36
29 Dolly Scannell, *Mother Knew Best* (Macmillan, 1974), p. 89.
30 Thea Vigne, Open University programme transcript.
31 Oral evidence quoted in G.E. Evans, *From Mouths of Men* (Faber, 1976), p. 73.
32 Rennie, *Every Other Sunday*, p. 112.
33 Maud Walton, p.o.e.
34 Daisy Noakes, *A Town Beehive* (Brighton, 1975), p. 29.
35 Mrs E. Ellis, p.w.e.
36 Noakes, *Town Beehive*, p. 31.
37 By 1921, minimum rates had been set for adult women in thirty-five trades. R.S. Sayer, *A History of Economic Changes in England 1880-1939* (Oxford UP, 1967), p. 137.
38 A government committee of 1923 recommended more generous time off for servants. See Ministry of Labour, *Report on the Committee appointed to enquire into the present conditions as to the supply of female domestic servants* (1923).
39 Mrs Jennie Owen, p.o.e.
40 The moment of transition is also remembered vividly by the women themselves, colouring and emphasizing the abrupt break between familiar home and the new home which was also work-place.
41 Minnie Cowley in *Spare Rib* (March 1976).
42 Foley, *Child in the Forest*, p. 160.
43 *ibid.*, p. 166.
44 Noakes, *Town Beehive*, p. 46.
45 *ibid.*, p. 48.
46 Mrs Jennie Owen, p.o.e.
47 John Burnett, *Useful Toil*, p. 173.
48 North West Archives of Oral History, Manchester Polytechnic.
49 Thea Vigne, Open University programme.

50 Ministry of Labour and National Service, *Report on the Post War organisation of private domestic service.* Cmd. 6650 (1944).

51 Roberts, *Classic Slum,* p. 37.

52 Powell, *Below Stairs,* p. 54.

53 Jack and Preston (eds.), *The Woman's Book,* p. 37.

54 Mrs Florence Follet, p.o.e.

55 Mrs Lilian Cross, p.o.e.

56 Rennie, *Every Other Sunday, passim.*

57 Foley, *Child in the Forest,* p. 229.

58 Powell, *Below Stairs,* p. 146.

59 Mrs Gladys Evans, p.o.e.

60 'Mrs A', Oral History Broadsheet, West Oxfordshire WEA, p. 20.

61 Powell, *Below Stairs,* p. 113.

62 Mrs Gladys Evans, p.o.e.

63 Mrs Jennie Owen, p.o.e.

6 Recreation in Rochdale, 1900-40

This essay is a revised and shortened version of an MA dissertation written at CCCS in 1976. I am grateful to the editors of this volume for suggestions about the more general themes that frame the case study.

1 Some of the most significant contributions have been within the more general framework of the study of working-class culture as a whole. The work of Edward Thompson, in particular, transformed the study of popular culture of the eighteenth and early nineteenth centuries. Important studies of popular recreation more narrowly defined or covering the period dealt with in this essay include Hugh McLeod, *Class and Religion in the Late Victorian City* (Croom Helm, 1974): Paul Thompson, *The Edwardians* (Weidenfeld & Nicolson, 1975); Stephen Yeo, *Religion and Voluntary Organisations in Crisis* (Croom Helm, 1976); Helen Meller, *Leisure and the Changing City, 1870-1914* (Routledge & Kegan Paul, 1976).

2 At the turn of the century most of Rochdale's occupied population worked in the textile or engineering mills of John Bright, Kelsall and Kemp, Tweedale and Smalley and numerous smaller concerns. The town was very much more compact than now: it centred around Kelsall's mill, the Wellington Hotel and the Town Hall square. The two main shopping streets, filled with mainly local family firms, stretched north and south from the centre. In a roughly circular area, about a mile wide, the majority of the population lived and worked.

3 *St Mary's Bazaar Handbook* (1908, 1912).

4 C.E. Warrington, *The History of a Parish* (1968), p. 48. A football club was formed to replace the cricket and rugby clubs, but was disbanded between the wars.

5 *Rochdale Observer,* 7 February 1934, p. 5.

6   *Rochdale Wesleyan Mission Nineteenth Anniversary Handbook* (1924), p.5.
7   A. W. Whithead *The Baptist Church in Rochdale* (1973), p. 45.
8   *ibid.*, p. 48.
9   Warrington, *The History of a Parish*.
10 *Dearnley Methodist Church 1868-1968.* Centenary Souvenir Brochure, p. 6.
11 An article in the *Rochdale Observer*, 4 April 1934, p. 5, by the Vicar of St Luke's pointed to the remaining popularity and importance of these 'special days' against the more regular events of the churches and chapels in the town.
12 See p. 151 ff.
13 Warrington, *The History of a Parish*, p. 66.
14 W. H. Brown, *The Rochdale Pioneers: A Century of Co-operation in Rochdale* (Rochdale: REPS, 1944).
15 Lowerfold Methodist Church, *Sunday School Centenary Souvenir 1835-1935*.
16 *History of Holland Street Chapel and Sunday School Since its Formation* (1942), p. 20.
17 *Rochdale Observer*, 6 September 1922, p. 7.
18 *Rochdale Observer*, 3 January 1914, p. 1.
19 Rochdale County Borough, *Accounts and Reports* (1900-50). The baths had 50,000 bathers in 1900: by 1931 this had risen to 71,000. Similarly the number of library issues quadrupled over the same period to 450,000.
20 See especially Thompson, *The Edwardians*, p. 213, where he talks of a shift from about 1910 in the locus of influence away from the church and towards the mass media, as well as more emphasis on the home as centre for leisure.
21 Robert Roberts, *The Classic Slum* (Manchester University Press, 1971), p. 140.
22 *Rochdale Observer*, 4 July 1900, p. 1.
23 *ibid.*, 14 March 1914, p. 5.
24 Brown, *The Rochdale Pioneers*.
25 P.F. Clarke, *Lancashire and the New Liberalism* (Cambridge University Press, 1971).
26 'Temperance work in Rochdale', *Rochdale Observer;* the article was written in 1909 to celebrate the society's past.
27 For a typical report see 'Cycling news', *Rochdale Observer*, 25 July 1900, p. 2.
28 *ibid.*, 24 November 1900, p. 5.
29 The first official Clarion Cycling Club was formed in March 1894 by seven Birmingham men in what was formerly a Wesleyan Chapel. By 1898 membership had reached 7000. See *National Clarion Cycling Club 1894-1944 Jubilee Souvenir*.
30 *ibid.*
31 see Chapter 7.
32 Rushbearing or Rushbearing Week had taken its name from a traditional festival which dated back to before the Reformation in many north-western towns. Initially the festival had centred on a day which was given to the cutting of rushes to be placed on the clay floors in churches in preparation for winter. Events centred on a cart which had a highly decorated pyramid

of rushes on it, and a team of young men, who were to pull the vehicle firstly
to the local inns and later to neighbouring mansions where the ladies traditionally gave garlands and money. But the original point of the festival, i.e.
the Rushbearing procession, became more and more peripheral to the associated fairs and festivities as the nineteenth century progressed, until by 1900
only the name remained to refer to an increasingly commercial week of
fairs, railway excursions and holidays. As early as the censorious 1830s a
local contemporary described the festival as a "mere rustic saturnalia . . .";
see John Harland and T. Wilkinson, *Lancashire Legends* (Heywood, 1872),
pp. 112-13. See also John Ashworth, *Jimmy the Rushcart Driver*, Butterworth
Union of Sunday School Teachers Tract; L. Nuttal, *Rushcarts* (both written
c. 1870 and in Rochdale Reference Library); and Alex Helm, 'Rushcarts of
the north west of England', *Folk Life*, vol. 8 (1970).

33   *Rochdale Observer*, 28 July 1900, p. 1.
34   *ibid.*, 4 July 1900, p. 1.
35   *ibid.*, 14 July 1900, p. 1.
36   *ibid.*
37   *ibid.*, 21 August 1901, p. 2: 'Holiday Report'.
38   'The history of Kelsall and Kemp Ltd.', *Rochdale Literary and Scientific
     Society Transactions*, vol. 24, p. 37. Holidays were nearly always
     without pay; in the pre-war period only 1.5 million workers were entitled
     to an annual paid holidat in Britain. See Charles Lock Mowat, *Britain Between
     the Wars*,(Methuen, 1955).
39   'Rushbearing', *Rochdale Observer*, 20 August 1902, p. 5.
40   *ibid.*, 21 August 1901, p. 2.
41   *ibid.*
42   *ibid.*, 14 July 1900, p. 1.
43   *ibid.*
44   *ibid.*, 24 August 1910, p. 5.
45   *Castlemere Methodist Church Sunday School Centenary Book 1839-1939*.
46   *Rochdale Observer*, 30 August 1922, p. 7.
47   *ibid.*
48   *ibid.*, 14 August 1926, p. 1, col. 1.
49   *ibid.*, 11 August 1928, p. 6.
50   *ibid.*, 26 August 1930, p. 7, col. 1
51   *ibid.*, 28 August 1934, p. 9: 'Holiday Report'.
52   Interview with manager of Co-operative Travel, Balloon St., Manchester 1976.
53   J.A.R. Pimlott, *Recreations* (Studio Vista, 1968), plate 157.
54   C.L. Mowat, *Britain Between the Wars*, p. 502.
55   *ibid.*, p. 453.
56   G.P. Jones and A.G. Pool, *Britain in Recovery* (Methuen, 1938), p. 37.
57   See E.J. Hobsbawm, *Industry and Empire* (Weidenfeld & Nicolson, 1968),
     p. 267, where he talks of the Holidays with Pay Act of 1938.
58   *Rochdale Observer*, 14 August 1926, p. 1.

59 *loc. cit.*
60 *loc. cit.*
61 *loc. cit.*
62 *ibid.,* 16 August 1930, p. 1.
63 *ibid.,* 5 November 1938, p. 20.
64 Robert Roberts, *The Classic Slum,* p. 188
65 *Rochdale Observer,* 18 January 1928, p. 2 (advertisement).
66 *ibid.,* 29 September 1934, p. 1.
67 *ibid.,* 5 November 1938, p. 20.
68 Dunlop had opened a social club in July 1934 which offered two lounges, a billiard room and games room, but no bar for its 2500 members (see *Rochdale Observer,* 8 July 1934, p. 11). Dances were held on a monthly basis at Dunlop and, like their contemporaries, Turner Brothers Asbestos, a yearly sports day was held for employees. Turners also provided a social club and encouraged the formation of a choir in the inter-war years. These two large companies seem to be alone in this kind of provision in Rochdale at this time.
69 *Rochdale Observer,* 5 November 1938, p. 20, col. 1.
70 Most of what follows is based on David Robinson, *World Cinema* (Eyre Methuen, 1973), pp. 15-17.
71 G.J. Mellor, *Picture Pioneers* (Newcastle on Tyne: Graham, 1971), p. 11.
72 Robinson, *World Cinema,* p. 26.
73 G.J. Mellor, *Picture Pioneers,* p. 38.
74 *Rochdale Observer,* 3 January 1900, p. 1.
75 *ibid.,* 14 November 1900, p. 2.
76 *ibid.,* 6 January 1901, p. 1.
77 *ibid.,* 15 September 1900, p. 1.
78 *Rochdale Observer,* 27 March 1901, p. 1.
79 *ibid.,* 6 February 1901, p. 2.
80 *ibid.,* 11 December 1901, p. 5.
81 *ibid.,* 17 September 1902, p. 5.
82 *ibid.,* 24 September 1902, p. 5.
83 G.J. Mellor, *Picture Pioneers,* p. 23.
84 *Rochdale Observer,* all January, 1906.
85 *ibid.,* 29 January 1908, p. 5.
86 *ibid.,* 25 March 1908, p. 5: 'Local News'.
87 *ibid.,* all December, 1911.
88 According to G.J. Mellor, *Picture Pioneers,* p. 48, Moore and Beaudyn owned sixteen halls in and around Manchester in 1914.
89 *Rochdale Observer,* 3 January 1914, p. 1.
90 David Robinson, *World Cinema,* p. 73.
91 Andrew Bergman, *We're in the Money: The Depression and its Films* (New York University Press, 1971). See especially ch. 8, 'Warner Brothers presents social consciousness!'
92 *Rochdale Observer,* 1 April 1914, p. 50.

93 *ibid.*
94 *ibid.*
95 *ibid.*, August and November 1914.
96 *ibid.*, 2 January 1914, p. 2.
97 *ibid.*, 6 September 1922, p. 7, col. 4.
98 *ibid.*, 10 July 1926, p. 1.
99 The Victory was part of H.D. Moorhouse's circuit of fifty cinemas which were mostly in Lancashire (*Picture Pioneers*, p. 75).
100 *Rochdale Observer*, 29 August 19   , p. 1.
101 *ibid.*, 3 January 1914, p. 9.
102 *ibid.*, 14 April 1930, p. 1.
103 *ibid.*, 17 January 1934, p. 2.
104 *ibid.*
105 *ibid.*
106 Mowat, *Britain Between the Wars*, p. 250.
107 Robinson, *World Cinema*, pp. 255-8.
108 Mowat, *Britain Between the Wars*, p. 246.
109 See Robinson, *World Cinema*, p. 72.
110 Mellor, *Picture Pioneers*, ch. 6.
111 Thompson, *The Edwardians*, p. 69.
112. Roberts, *The Classic Slum*.
113 Thompson, *The Edwardians*, p. 296.
114 See, for example, the discussions of 'style' in S. Hall and T. Jefferson (eds.), *Resistance Through Rituals* (Hutchinson, 1977).

7 Football since the war

1   Ian Taylor, 'Soccer consciousness and soccer hooliganism', in Stan Cohen (ed.), *Images of Deviance* (Penguin, 1971).
2   Arthur Hopcraft, *The Football Man*, rev. ed. (Penguin, 1971), p. 24
3   Geoffrey Green, *Soccer in the Fifties* (Ian Allan, 1974).
4   *The Times*, 14 December 1961.
5   Hopcraft, *The Football Man*, p. 43.
6   *ibid.*
7   *ibid.*, p. 30
8   *ibid.*, p. 51.
9   Arthur Walmsley, 'Duncan Edwards', in John Arlott (ed.), *Soccer: The Great Ones* (Pelham, 1968).
10 Hopcraft, *The Football Man*, p. 75.
11 David Miller, 'Alan Ball', in Reg Hayter (ed.), *Soccer Stars of Today* (Pelham, 1970).
12 *The Times*, 20 November 1961.
13 Eamon Dunphy, *Only A Game?* (Penguin, 1977).
14 *The Times*, 8 December 1964.

15 Chas Critcher, 'Football and cultural values', in *Working Papers in Cultural Studies,* no. 1 (University of Birmingham, 1972).
16 Tony Pawson, 'John Charles', in Arlott, *Soccer.*
17 *Rothman's Football Yearbook 1977-78.*
18 *The Times,* 11 November 1961.
19 *The Times,* 12 April 1962.
20 Chester Committee, *Report of the Committee on Football* (HMSO, 1968).
21 Peter Douglas, *The Football Industry* (Allen & Unwin, 1973).
22 Raymond Williams, *The Long Revolution* (Pelican, 1961).
23 Taylor, 'Soccer consciousness'; also Taylor, 'Football Mad', in Eric Dunning (ed.), *The Sociology of Sport* (Frank Cass, 1971).
24 Taylor, 'Soccer consciousness', p. 363.
25 Stuart Hall, 'The treatment of football hooliganism in the press', in Roger Ingham (ed.), *Football Hooliganism* (Inter-Action, 1978).
26 *The Times,* 28 March 1969.
27 Hall, 'Treatment of football hooliganism'.
28 John Arlott, 'Like running dogs through Arab villages', *Guardian,* 5 January 1973.
29 Hopcraft, *The Football Man,* p. 160.
30 Taylor, 'Soccer consciousness', and 'Football mad'.
31 Taylor, 'Soccer consciousness', p. 131.
32 Peter Marsh, Elizabeth Rouser, Ron Harre, *The Rules of Disorder* (Routledge & Kegan Paul, 1978).
33 Edward Buscombe (ed.), *Football on Television* (BFI monograph, 1975).
34 *Report of the Committee on Football.*
35 *ibid.*
36 *The Times,* 21 November 1953.
37 Percy Young, *A History of British Football* (Stanley Paul, 1968).
38 Hopcraft, p. 116.
39 *The Times,* 19 May 1955.
40 *Football League Review,* no. 515 (1969).
41 Conrad Lozdiak, *Understanding Soccer Tactics* (Faber & Faber, 1966), p. 52.
42. Taylor, 'Soccer consciousness', p. 150.
43 'Football in America', *Guardian,* 4-17 September 1978.

8 Shop-floor culture, masculinity and the wage form

I am grateful to the editors of this volume for suggesting revisions to earlier drafts and also to members of the CCCS Work Group for discussion of many of these issues.

1 R. Fraser (ed.), *Work* (Penguin, 1969), p. 63.
2 Now written up as a book which includes an ethnography of working-class forms of counter-school culture and their intrinsic connection with cultural forms of the work-place, plus a theoretical analysis of this reproduction. P.E. Willis, *Learning to Labour* (Saxon House, 1977).

3   G.C. Matthews, 'Post-school adaption of educationally sub-normal boys' (Unpublished MEd thesis, University of Manchester, 1963).
4   R. Fraser (ed.) *Work 2* (Penguin, 1969), pp. 56-7.
5   *ibid.*, pp. 22-3.
6   See, for instance, the deskilling thesis outlined in H. Braverman, *Labor and Monopoly Capital* (Monthly Review Press, 1974).
7   For a further explanation of these connections see Willis, *Learning to Labour.*

9   Three problematics

This essay is based in part on a paper given at the British Sociological Conference on Culture, 1978, but has benefited since from criticism from Edward Thompson, Keith McClelland, Philip Corrigan and Stuart Hall and from discussion in the CCCS History Group. I have also been greatly helped by discussions with John Clarke, author of the companion piece which ends this volume.

1   L. Althusser and Balibar, *Reading Capital* (New Left Books, 1970), especially pp. 13-30.
2   I am especially grateful to Keith McClelland for arguing this point with great force.
3   Althusser, *Essays in Self-Criticism* (New Left Books, 1976), p. 124.
4   See, for example, Rosalind Coward, 'Class, culture and the social formation', and the response from Ian Chambers *et al.*, in *Screen* (spring 1977 and winter 1977-8).
5   For a more rigorous exposition of a similar view see Ernesto Laclau, *Politics and Ideology in Marxist Theory* (New Left Books, 1977), especially pp. 1-13.
6   Gareth Stedman Jones, 'Engels and the genesis of Marxism', *New Left Review,* no. 106, p. 103.
7   Martin Nicolaus, 'Hegelian choreography and the capitalist dialectic: proletariat and middle-class in Marx', in *Studies on the Left,* vol. 7 (1976), pp. 22-49.
8   *The Poverty of Philosophy,* in Marx and Engels, *Collected Works* (Lawrence & Wishart, 1976), vol. 6, p. 211.
9   *Manifesto of the Communist Party,* in *Collected Works,* vol. 6, p. 490.
10   Stuart Hall, 'The "political" and the "economic" in Marx's theory of classes', in Alan Hunt (ed.), *Class and Class Structure* (Lawrence & Wishart, 1977), p. 20.
11   Similar sequences are portrayed in Engels, *The Condition of the Working Class in England* (Panther, 1969), pp. 240 ff., in *The Manifesto* and in *The Poverty of Philosophy.*
12   Engels, *Condition,* pp. 243-54.
13   *ibid.*, editor's introduction, p. 10.
14   e.g. *ibid.*, p. 152.
15   *ibid.*, p. 239.
16   Marx, *Manifesto of the Communist Party,* pp. 495-6.

17 Engels, *Condition*, p. 39.
18 For an elaboration of these points see Hall, 'The "political" and the "economic" '.
19 *ibid.*, pp. 39-50. See also Gwynn Williams, 'France 1848-1851', Open University A 321, units 5-8 (1976).
20 Marx, *Surveys from Exile* (Penguin, 1973), editor's introduction, p. 9.
21 Nicolaus, 'Hegelian choreography'.
22 Most strikingly in the 'old Mole' passage in Marx, *Surveys from Exile*, pp. 236-7. I am grateful to Greg McLennan for discussions about these elements in *The Eighteenth Brumaire* and other conjunctural texts.
23 For an interesting discussion of Gramsci's early economism see Bob Lumley, 'Gramsci's writing on the state and hegemony, 1916-35: a critical analysis', CCCS stencilled paper no. 51 (1978). For a fuller contextualization see G. Williams, *Proletarian Order* (Pluto Press, 1975).
24 V.I. Lenin, 'The historical destiny of the doctrine of Karl Marx', *Selected Works* (Lawrence & Wishart, 1971), p. 17.
25 'The three sources and three component parts of Marxism', *Selected Works*, p. 21. For characteristic attacks on revisionism see 'The state and revolution', *ibid.*, pp. 264-351.
26 Lenin, 'The three sources', *Selected Works*, p. 24.
27 See for example the stress on 'special bodies of armed men', 'the rapacious state power', the state as 'a special organization of force', etc., in 'The state and revolution', and other Lenin texts. There is nothing surprising in this emphasis given the historical circumstances of 1911 to 1919! For interesting comparisons with Gramsci see Perry Anderson, 'The antimonies of Antonio Gramsci', *New Left Review*, no. 100 (1977), especially pp. 49-55.
28 Lenin, 'Imperialism: the highest stage of capitalism', *Selected Works*, p. 175.
29 This is a basic argument of *What is to be Done?;* see also 'A talk with the defenders of economism', *Selected Works*, pp. 44-9.
30 *ibid.*, p. 47.
31 Lenin, 'Party organization and party literature', *Selected Works*, pp. 148-53.
32 Q. Hoare and G. Nowell-Smith, *Selections from the Prison Notebooks of Antonio Gramsci* (Lawrence & Wishart, 1971), p. 323.
33 *ibid.*, pp. 196-7.
34 See, for example, Stalin's essay on 'The foundations of Leninism'.
35 For a summary and critique of the debate see H.F. Moorhouse, 'The Marxist theory of the labour aristocracy', *Social History*, vol. 3, no. 1 (January 1978).
36 Georg Lukacs, *History and Class Consciousness: Studies in Marxist Dialectics* (Merlin Press, 1971).
37 Examples of the first form of argument include John Foster, 'Imperialism and the labour aristocracy', in J. Skelley (ed.), *The General Strike* (Lawrence & Wishart, 1976); examples of the second include John Foster, *Class Struggle and the Industrial Revolution* (Methuen, 1977), especially ch. 7, and

R.Q. Gray, *The Labour Aristocracy in Victorian Edinburgh* (Oxford University Press, 1976).

38 See the interesting criticism of common-sense views of the corruption of leadership or bureaucracies in Tony Lane, *The Union Makes Us Strong* (Arrow, 1976).

39 Some of these points are made in relation to *Capital* in Hall, 'The "political" and the "economic" '.

40 For the character of Lukacs' early thought see Gareth Stedman Jones, 'The Marxism of the early Lukacs', *New Left Review*, no. 70, (November-December 1971).

41 Paradoxically Marx's distinction between 'sacred' (i.e. idealist) and 'profane' (i.e. materialist) categories and histories is made in the course of his dispute with Proudhon, the source too of Lukacs' founding definitions of class. See especially Marx to P.V. Annenkov, 28 December 1846, in Marx and Engels, *Selected Letters*, (Progress Publishers, 1975), especially p. 31.

42 Lukacs, *History and Class Consciousness*, p. 51.

43 'We cannot really speak of class consciousness in the case of these classes [petty bourgeoisie and peasantry] . . . for a full consciousness of their situation would reveal to them the hopelessness of their particularist strivings in the fact of the inevitable course of events.' *ibid.*, p. 61.

44 Most of the essay, 'Reification and the consciousness of the proletariat' is concerned to establish these homologies.

45 *ibid.*, especially pp. 197-8.

46 Raymond Williams, *Culture and Society 1780-1950* (Penguin, 1961), p. 17.

47 E.P. Thompson, *William Morris: Romantic to Revolutionary* (Merlin Press, 1977), p. 791.

48. *ibid.*, p. 810.

49 See especially Perry Anderson 'Components of the national culture' in A. Cockburn and R. Blackburn (eds.), *Student Power: Problems, Diagnosis, Action* (Penguin, 1968), pp. 214-84, and Terry Eagleton, 'Criticism and politics: the work of Raymond Williams', *New Left Review*, no. 95 (January-February 1976), especially p. 9.

50 For a development of this point see Richard Johnson, 'Barrington Moore, Perry Anderson and English social development', *Working Papers in Cultural Studies*, no. 9 (1976), especially pp. 25-6.

51 E.P. Thompson, 'Review of *The Long Revolution*', *New Left Review* (May-June and July-August 1961).

52 *ibid.*, but see also Thompson, *Morris*, chs. 1 and 2, and part 4.

53 For the second see *ibid.*, ch. 7; for the first see *The Making*, especially pp. 50-2, 162, 415.

54 For these indications see, mainly, E.P. Thompson, 'The peculiarities of the English', *Socialist Register* (1965).

55 The classic polemical text of this tendency was the volume edited by F.A. Hayek, as *Capitalism and the Historians* (Routledge & Kegan Paul, 1954). But

see also the works of T.S. Ashton, W.W. Rostow and R.M. Hartwell. Latterly this enterprise has been extended to other periods, notably the 1930s.

56 For accounts of this period see the essays in *Socialist Register* (1976); Thompson, 'Review of *The Long Revolution*', and Raymond Williams, *Marxism and Literature* (Oxford University Press, 1977), pp. 1-4.

57 Williams, *The Long Revolution,* especially ch. 2; Williams, *Marxism and Literature,* ch. 1; R. Williams, *Keywords: A Vocabulary of Culture and Society* (Fontana, 1976), pp. 76-82.

58 e.g. 'Interview with Edward Thompson', *Radical History Review,* vol. 3, no. 4 (1976), p. 23.

59 The fullest statement, from which these quotations are drawn, is the preface to *The Making of the English Working Class.*

60 Eagleton, 'Criticism and politics', p. 9.

61 Williams, *Culture and Society*, p. 289.

62 *Making,* especially pp. 195, 120, 10-11; 'Interview with Edward Thompson' pp. 4-5; 'Anthropology and the discipline of historical context', *Midland History* vol. 1, no. 3 (spring 1972), pp. 41-55; 'Measuring class consciousness', *Times Higher Education Supplement* (8 March 1974): review of John Foster, *Class Struggle and the Industrial Revolution.*

63 'Interview with Edward Thompson', p. 15.

64 Williams, *Marxism and Literature,* pp. 80-1.

65 Thompson, *Whigs and Hunters* (Allen Lane, 1975), pp. 258-69.

66 Williams, *Marxism and Literature,* chapter on 'Base and superstructure'.

67 E.P. Thompson, 'Folklore, anthropology and social history', *Indian Historical Review,* vol. 3, no. 2 (January 1978), p. 262. I am grateful to Edward Thompson for drawing my attention to this article.

68 Williams, *The Long Revolution,* p. 136.

69 Williams, *Marxism and Literature,* pp. 81-2.

70 *ibid.,* chapter on 'Productive Forces'.

71 Thompson, 'Review of *The Long Revolution*'.

72 'There is no alternative, from any socialist position, to recognition and emphasis of the massive historical and immediate experience of class domination and subordination, in all their different forms.' This option is stressed against 'the alternative language of co-operative shaping'. Williams, *Marxism and Literature,* p. 112.

73 Anthony Barnett, 'Raymond Williams and Marxism: a rejoinder to Terry Eagleton', *New Left Review,* no. 99 (September-October 1976), p. 56. Barnett's criticism of Williams closely parallels my own comments on Thompson in Johnson, McLennan and Schwarz, 'Economy, culture and concept', CCCS stencilled occasional paper no. 50 (1978). Actually they apply most accurately to Williams, I now favour the more careful formulations about Thompson that follow later in the chapter.

74 Williams, *Culture and Society,* pp. 307-24; cf. the treatment of class 'ideals' in H. Perkin, *Origins of Modern English Society* (Routledge & Kegan Paul, 1972).

75   For these formulations see 'Interview with Edward Thompson'; Thompson, 'Review of *The Long Revolution*' and 'Folklore, anthropology and social history'.

76   *ibid.*, p. 265. This particular article contains many of the most interesting formulations on these questions, suggesting considerable movements in Thompson's position which are paralleled by the practice of *Whigs and Hunters*.

77   The following typifications are based on a reading of all of Thompson's published historical work - it is difficult to cite particular sources.

78   This point is argued at greater length for particular chapters of *The Making* in Johnson, McLennan and Schwarz, 'Economy, culture and concept'.

79   *The Making*, p. 10.

80   *ibid.*, p. 12.

81   For Althusser's own account of the context of his project see 'To my English readers' and 'Introduction: today' in *For Marx* (Penguin, 1969).

82   All this can be seen in 'Review of *The Long Revolution*'.

83   Althusser, *Essays in Self-Criticism*, editor's introduction, especially p. 32.

84   *ibid.*, pp. 201-2.

85   *ibid.*, pp. 203-4.

86   For these formulations see especially 'Contradiction and over-determination' in Althusser, *For Marx*.

87   See especially 'Ideology and ideological state apparatuses' in Althusser, *Lenin and Philosophy and Other Essays* (New Left Books, 1971).

88   For the general character of the 'reading' see Althusser and Balibar, *Reading Capital*, pp. 1-30.

89   See especially the reductions involved in the very formal account of 'Elements of the structure', especially p. 225.

90   Postface to the 2nd ed., *Capital*, vol. 1 (Penguin, 1976), p. 102.

91   Marx to Danielson, 10 April 1879, *Selected Letters*, p. 296.

92   Althusser and Balibar, *Reading Capital*, p. 69.

93   One post-Althusserian path can be traced through B. Hindess and P. Hirst, *Pre-Capitalist Modes of Production* (Routledge & Kegan Paul, 1975), and the same authors' auto-critique, *Mode of Production and Social Formation* (Macmillan, 1977).

94   It is not possible to pursue these issues of method further here since this would take us even further away from 'working-class culture'. The comments here and in the section on 'culturalism' will, however, be developed in later CCCS publications.

95   This point is developed more fully in 'Histories of culture: theories of ideology', in the BSA 1978 Conference volume.

96   The most important discussions of 'reproduction' in *Capital* include vol 1, ch. 23, 'Simple Reproduction', and appendix to vol 1 (Penguin), especially pp. 1060-5. For a brief reading of these and other aspects of Marx's treatment of reproduction see Johnson, McLennan and Schwarz, 'Economy, culture and concept', pp. 40-1.

97 Criticisms of the essay include: P.Q. Hirst, 'Althusser and the theory of ideology', *Economy and Society*, vol. 5, no. 4 (1976); M. Erben and D. Gleeson, 'Education as reproduction', in Young and Whitty (eds.), *Society, State and Schooling* (Palmer Press, 1977); *Ideology and Consciousness*, no. 1 (1977).

98 E.P. Thompson, 'Time, work-discipline and industrial capitalism', *Past and Present*, no. 38 (1967).

99 The main theoretical resource in what follows is Gramsci's *Prison Notebooks* and a return to those parts of *Capital* where Marx deals with the cultural conditions of production and with the problem of the relation between the 'phenomenal forms' of capitalist relations and the character of bourgeois ideologies. But there has already been, in this essay, quite enough of the exposition of positions, so the form of what follows is prescriptive or argumentative rather than expository. For the sources of many of these arguments see, however, the notes that follows.

100 Both quotations above are from the essay, 'Ideological state apparatus'.

101 Williams, *Marxism and Literature*, pp. 80-1.

102 Marx and Engels, *The German Ideology Part One*, ed. C.J. Arthur, (Lawrence & Wishart, 1970), p. 50.

103 *Capital*, vol. 1, pp. 283-4.

104 Michel Foucault, *Discipline and Punish: the Birth of the Prison* (Allen Lane, 1977), p. 27.

105 *Capital*, vol. 1, p. 92. For an extremely telling elaboration of this point see Victor Molina, 'Notes on Marx and the problem of individuality', in CCCS, *On Ideology* (Hutchinson, 1977).

106 David McLellan, *Marx's Grundrisse* (Paladin, 1971), p. 45 (from the 1857 Introduction).

107 This is in addition to any (useful) tendency to distinguish 'regions' or 'sub-ensembles' of ideologies, a contribution especially of Nicos Poulantzas.

108 e.g. Althusser, *Essays in Self-Criticism*, p. 37, note 3.

109 See especially Thompson, 'Review of *The Long Revolution*' and 'Folklore, anthropology and social history'.

110 'Folklore, anthropology and social history' marks an advance on this, but I think that in most of Thompson's work this is the characteristic solution.

111 See especially Hoare and Nowell-Smith, *Prison Notebooks*, pp. 323-43, 418-24.

112 See especially *ibid.*, pp. 330-5, 375-7, 390-3, 404-5, 407-8, and the essay on 'The intellectuals', It is important to remember that Gramsci understood Marxism, 'the philosophy of praxis', also as a transformative *ideology*.

113 e.g. *Capital*, vol. 1, especially pp. 275, 719-23, 615-17, 620-1. The meat of Gramsci's view of hegemony is to be found on the notes on 'The modern prince' and 'State and civil society'.

114 This is especially plain in the notes on 'Americanism and Fordism'.

115 'Interpellate' is taken from the ISA essay. For an interesting and historically

usable development see Laclau, *Politics and Ideology in Marxist Theory.*

116   Hoare and Nowell-Smith, *Prison Notebooks,* especially pp. 326, 333, 419.

117   *ibid.,* p. 333.

118   The classic case is the analysis of film in *Screen,* but there are elements on the 'reading of ideologies as a text' in Foucault's approach to discursive practices and in Laclau's treatment of specific ideologies. There is a problem in these approaches of remaining locked into the ideological forms themselves and *inferring* effects.

119   A fuller account should also consider capital's requirements in relation to consumption and the reproduction of the relations within which generational reproduction takes place. But for particular examples of these see the essay that follows.

10   Capital and culture: the post-war working class revisited

1   See, *inter alia,* H. Braverman, *Labor and Monopoly Capital* (New York: Monthly Review Press, 1974).

2   Community Development Projects, *The Costs of Industrial Growth (HMSO, 1976) and C. Cockburn,* The Local State (Pluto Press, 1977).

3   P. Corrigan and P. Corrigan, 'The reconstruction of the state' (Seminar paper at CCCS, University of Birmingham, June 1977).

4   P. Cohen, 'Subcultural conflict and working class community', *Working Papers in Cultural Studies,* no. 2 (1972).

5   G. Stedman Jones, 'Notes on the remaking of the English working class', *Journal of Social History* (1975).

6   See, for example, M. Cain, *Society and the Policeman's Role* (Routledge & Kegan Paul, 1973); and S. Hall, 'Education and the crisis of the urban school', in Open University, *Issues in Urban Education* (Open University Press, 1974).

7   Cockburn, *The Local State*; and P. Corrigan, 'The community strategy, the state and class struggle, 1966-76' (Paper presented to European Conference on Deviancy and Social Control, Vienna, September, 1976).

8   Cockburn, *The Local State,* ch. 4.

9   See Finn, Grant and Johnson, 'Social democracy, education and the crisis', *Working Papers in Cultural Studies,* no. 10 (1976).

10   Finn, Grant and Johnson, 'Social democracy, education and the crisis'.

11   Cohen, 'Subcultural conflict and working class community'; and S. Hall and T. Jefferson (eds.), *Resistance through Rituals* (Hutchinson, 1976).

12   See, *inter alia,* Conference of Socialist Economists, *On the Political Economy of Women* (London: Stage One, 1976); J. Smith, 'Women, work and the family', *International Socialism,* nos. 100-1.

13   See Smith, 'Women, work and the family'.

14   For example, the Women's Study Group on Welfare, *The Neglected Child and His Family* (Oxford University Press, 1947).

15   See, for example, L. Bland *et al.,* 'Women and the reproduction of labour

power', CCCS stencilled paper (University of Birmingham, 1978).

16 J. Packman, The Child's Generation (Blackwell & Robertson, 1976).

17 CSE, *On the Political Economy of Women*. Smith, 'Women, work and the family'.

18 L. Wilson, *Women and the Welfare State* (Tavistock, 1977), pp. 151-2.

19 CSE, *On the Political Economy of Women*.

20 S. Hall, 'Reformism and the legislation of consent', in National Deviancy Conference, *Permissiveness and Control* (Macmillan, forthcoming).

21 Cohen, 'Subcultural conflict and working class community'.

22 C. Hutt, *The Decline of the English Pub* (Arrow, 1976); B. Newman and D. Young, 'The pub as a leisure context' (Unpublished MS, Dept of Sociology North-East London Polytechnic); and A. Whitehead, 'Sexual antagonisms in Hertfordshire', in Barker and Allen (eds.), *Dependence and Exploitation in Work and Marriage* (Longman, 1977).

23 J. Foster, *Class Struggle in the Industrial Revolution* (Weidenfeld & Nicolson, 1974), p. 53.

24 Hutt, *The Decline of the English Pub*, p. 128.

25 See S. Castles and G. Kosack, *The Immigrant Worker and the Class Structure* (Oxford University Press, 1973); and A. Sivanandan, *Race, Class and the State* (London: Institute of Race Relations, 1976).

26 See, for example, V.I. Lenin, *British Labour and British Imperialism* (Lawrence & Wishart, 1969); P. Hartman and C. Husband, *Racism and the Mass Media* (Davis-Poynter, 1974), chs. 1 and 2; and G. Pearson, 'Paki-bashing in Lancashire', in G. Mungham and G. Pearson (eds.), *Working Class Youth Culture* (Routledge & Kegan Paul, 1976).

27 See Stedman Jones, 'Notes on the remaking of the English working class'; S. Hall *et al.*, *Policing the Crisis* (Macmillan, 1978), ch. 6; and S. Damer, 'Wine Alley: the sociology of a dreadful enclosure', in P. Wiles (ed.), *The Sociology of Crime and Delinquency in Britain* (Martin Robertson, 1977).

28 R. Roberts, *The Classic Slum* (Penguin, 1971).

29 Hall *et al.*, *Policing the Crisis*, ch. 6; and Duff and Marsden, *Workless* (Penguin, 1977).

30 See Hall *et al.*, 'Subcultures, cultures and class', in Hall and Jefferson (eds.) *Resistance through Rituals*.

31 See also P. Willis, *Learning to Labour* (Farnborough: Saxon House, 1977).

32 See H. Beynon and T. Nichols, *Living with Capitalism* (Routledge & Kegan Paul, 1977); and T. Nichols and P. Armstrong, *Workers Divided* (Fontana, 1976).

33 See Willis, *Learning to Labour*.

34 See H. Beynon, *Working for Ford* (Penguin, 1975).

35 See Hall *et al.*, *Policing the Crisis*, ch. 6.

36 See Beynon, *Working for Ford*.

37 For a discussion of one example of neo-human-relations management, see T. Nichols, 'The "Socialism" of management', *Sociological Review*, vol. 23.

no. 2 (May 1975).

38   See, *inter alia*, CSE, *On the Political Economy of Women*, and Wilson, *Women and the Welfare State*.

39   Stedman Jones, 'Notes on the remaking of the English working class'.

40   See Willis, *Learning to Labour*; and J. Clarke, 'The Skinheads and the magical recovery of community', in Hall and Jefferson (eds.), *Resistance through Rituals*

41   I. Taylor and D. Wall, 'The decline of the Skinheads', in Mungham and Pearson (eds.) *Working Class Youth Culture*.

42   See, for example, I. Taylor, 'Spectator violence around football: the rise and fall of the working class weekend', *Research Papers in Physical Education*, vol. 3, no. 2 (1976).

43   See Hall, 'Reformism and the legislation of consent'.

44   Cohen, 'Subcultural conflict and working class community', p. 17.

45   But see D. Hobson, 'Housewives: isolation as oppression', in CCCS Women's Studies Group, *Women Take Issue* (Hutchinson, 1978).

46   See P. Corrigan, *Schooling the Smash Street Kids* (Macmillan, forthcoming); and H. Parker, *View From the Boys* (David & Charles, 1974).

47   See Clarke, 'The Skinheads and the magical recovery of community'.

48   See Hall *et al.*, *Policing the Crisis*, ch. 6.

49   See *ibid.*, part 4.

50   T. Jefferson and J. Clarke, 'Down these mean streets; the meaning of mugging', *Howard Journal* (1974); and D. Hebdige, 'Reggae, rastas and rudies', in Hall and Jefferson (eds.), *Resistance Through Rituals*.

51   See Hall *et al.*, *Policing the Crisis*, ch. 6, for an analysis of some elements of an 'English Ideology'.

52   N. Poulantzas, *Political Power and Social Classes* (New Left Books, 1973), p. 210.

Index

Centre for Contemporary Cultural Studies – stencilled occasional papers as at October 1978

This list will be added to from time to time, and a copy included in the annual Centre Reports.

Payment with orders is now requested. Please make cheques payable to CCCS, and not only the University of Birmingham. Postage is charged on overseas orders, which will be sent by surface mail unless air mail is specifically asked for.

* = New titles

Media Series

SP No.			
	4	Stuart Hall: External Influences on Broadcasting	35p
	5	Stuart Hall: The 'Structured Communication' of Events	35p
	7	Stuart Hall: Encoding and Decoding in the TV Discourse	35p
	8	Dave Morley: Industrial Conflict and the Mass Media	25p
	9	Dave Morley: Reconceptualising the Media Audience	30p
	10	Marina Heck: The Ideological Dimension of Media Messages	25p
	11	Stuart Hall: Deviancy, Politics and the Media	35p
	34	Stuart Hall: TV as a Medium and its Relation to Culture	35p
	48	Roy Peters: Sport in TV – 1976 Olympics	25p

Sub-and-Popular Culture Series

SP No.			
	12	Bryn Jones: The Politics of Popular Culture	25p
	13	Paul Willis: Symbolism & Practice: The Social Meaning of Pop Music	35p
	14	Clarke and Jefferson: Politics of Popular Culture: Culture and Subcultures	30p
	16	Stuart Hall: The Hippies – an American 'Moment'	35p
	17	Jefferson & Clarke: "Down These Mean Streets" – the Meaning of Mugging	30p
	18	Clarke & Jefferson: Working Class Youth Cultures	30p
	20	Dick Hebdige: The Style of the Mods	30p
	21	Dick Hebdige: The Kray Twins: Study of a System of Closure	35p
	22	Tony Jefferson: The Teds: a Political Resurrection	30p
	23	John Clarke: The Skinheads and the Study of Youth Culture	30p
	24	Dick Hebdige: Reggae, Rastas & Rudies: Style and the Subversion of Form	35p
	25	Dick Hebdige: Sub-cultural Conflict & Criminal Performance in Fulham	35p
	28	Brian Roberts: Parent and Youth Cultures	30p
	29	C. Critcher: Football since the War: Study in Social Change & Popular Culture	35p
	35	Jefferson *et al*: Mugging and Law 'n' Order	55p
	37	Clarke, Critcher *et al*: Newsmaking and Crime (paper at NACRO conference)	35p